Calculated Kindness

Calculated Kindness

Refugees and America's Half-Open Door,
1945 to the Present

Gil Loescher
John A. Scanlan

THE FREE PRESS
A Division of Macmillan, Inc.
NEW YORK

Collier Macmillan Publishers
LONDON

The Free Press
A Division of Macmillan, Inc.
866 Third Avenue, New York, N. Y. 10022

Collier Macmillan Canada, Inc.

Printed in the United States of America

printing number
1 2 3 4 5 6 7 8 9 10

Library of Congress Cataloging-in-Publication Data

Loescher, Gil.
  Calculated kindness.

  Bibliography: p.
  Includes index.
    1. Refugees—Government policy—United States—
History—20th century.   2. Refugees—United States.
3. United States—Emigration and immigration.
I. Scanlan, John A.   II. Title.
JV6601.R4L63   1986   325'.21'0973   86–12079
ISBN 0-02-927340-4

Portions of the text have been published, in a somewhat different form, in the following articles and occasional papers:

"Human Rights, U.S. Foreign Policy, and Haitian Refugees," *Journal of InterAmerican Studies and World Affairs*, Vol. 26, No. 3 (August, 1984), pp. 313–356.

"U.S. Foreign Policy, 1959–1980: Impact on the Refugee Flow From Cuba," *Annals of the American Academy of Political and Social Science*, Vol. 467 (May, 1983), pp. 116–137.

"Mass Asylum and U.S. Policy in the Caribbean," *The World Today* (October, 1981), pp. 387–395.

"U.S. Foreign Policy and Its Impact on Refugee Flow From Haiti," Center for Latin American and Caribbean Studies, New York University, Occasional Paper No. 42 (April, 1984).

"Human Rights, Power Politics, and the International Refugee Regime: the Case of U.S. Treatment of Caribbean Basin Refugees," Center of International Studies, Princeton University, World Order Studies Occasional Paper No. 14 (1985).

For Ann, Margaret, and Claire Loescher
and
Margaret, Christopher, Patrick, and Andrew Scanlan

Contents

Acknowledgments

The idea to write a book on U.S. refugee policy originated when we both served as consultants to the Select Commission on Immigration and Refugee Policy in 1980. While doing research for the Select Commission, we discovered that no full-scale study of U.S. refugee policy had been written since the early 1950s, despite the fact that over 2 million refugees had entered the United States since World War II. In fact, there exists very little research on refugee policy making in general. Most of the work in this field has been legally oriented or concerned with problems of integration and resettlement. With a grant from the Ford Foundation nearly five years ago, we embarked on a book-length study of U.S. refugee admissions policy from 1945 to the present.

The research and writing of this book has been a very rewarding experience. It has enabled both of us to travel widely and to delve deeply into both foreign and domestic policy. Our account of the early history of refugee policy relies to a significant extent on Congressional and archival materials found at the National Archives in Washington, D.C., and at the Truman and Eisenhower Presidential Libraries. Our account of the more recent history of refugee policy depends to a much larger degree on personal interviews with many of the principal policy makers. Thus our research has taken us not only to Washington, D.C., and New York but also to heavily impacted communities in Dade County, Florida, and Orange County, California, to refugee camps in

Southeast Asia and Hong Kong, and to the Geneva headquarters of the office of the United Nations High Commissioner for Refugees and many of the principal voluntary agencies working in the refugee field. We have interviewed hundreds of international, national, and local officials, and have talked to many of them several times. It is impossible to single them out and so most of their names are included in a list in the bibliography at the back of the book.

We owe a debt of gratitude to a number of generous individuals who provided invaluable assistance or materials during the past five years. The Center for Civil and Human Rights and the Department of Government and International Studies at the University of Notre Dame granted us leave and supplemented our Ford Foundation grant. We spent a profitable year as visiting fellows at the Center for International Studies at Princeton University. Our special thanks go to Cyril Black, the Director of the Center for International Studies, and Lee Gordenker, Professor of Politics at Princeton. In Washington, D.C., we were provided with working space at the Refugee Policy Group. Dennis Gallagher, the Director of RPG and Bob Frankel, the librarian there, assisted us in numerous ways. Many people opened up archives or their files for us to study or peruse. These individuals include Robert De Vecchi at the International Rescue Committee, Michael Hooper and Mark Murphy at the Emergency Coalition for Haitian Refugees, Mark Braham at the International Refugee Integration Resource Centre in Geneva, Norman and Naomi Zucker of the University of Rhode Island, Barry Stein of Michigan State University, Beverly Hunter-Curtis, Refugee Coordinator for Orange County, California, Michael Posner of the Lawyers Committee for International Human Rights, Josh De Wind at Columbia University, and Victor Palmieri, who shared the introduction to his unpublished manuscript on refugee policy during his tenure as U.S. Coordinator for Refugee Affairs. A number of people also helped to arrange interviews and to make our research trips proceed more easily. They include Mary Jo Grotenrath and Ron Scheinman of the Select Commission for Immigration and Refugee Policy, Michael Muller, Robert Burrows, and Nick Van Praag at UNCHR, John Crowley, JVA Coordinator in Bangkok, Dan Larson, JVA Coordinator in Hong Kong, Robert De Vecchi at the International Rescue Committee, and Beverly Hunter-Curtis, Refugee Coordinator for Orange County, California.

We have presented portions of our work or our principal findings at a number of places during the last several years. These include Princeton University, Notre Dame University, New York University Center for Latin American and Caribbean Studies, Smith College, University of Southern California, University of Miami Law School, Fordham University, York University at Toronto, Queen Elizabeth House at Oxford, the University of Stockholm, Sweden, and the International Studies Association meeting in Washington,

D.C., in 1984 and the American Historical Association meeting in New York in 1985. These occasions have provided opportunities for discussion and helpful criticism of our work.

One of our biggest debts of gratitude goes to our research assistants at Notre Dame and at Princeton. The graduate and law students we would particularly like to mention are Susan Roberts and Joan Doverspike of the Department of Government and International Studies at Notre Dame; Ken Petrini, Tom Crowley, Michael Rowe, and Kirk Flagg of the Law School at Notre Dame; and Mark Steiner and Adam Sloane of the Center for International Studies and the Politics Department at Princeton. Finally, the manuscript, in each of its several drafts, was typed by the steno pool secretaries at the University of Notre Dame, and the secretarial staff at the Indiana University Law School. We are very grateful for the fine work they did, particularly since they worked under a great deal of pressure to complete the manuscript in the shortest time possible. Warm thanks are also due to our fine editor, Joyce Seltzer, who patiently prodded us to organize our materials and write as clearly as possible.

Gil Loescher
John Scanlan

Introduction
Refugees, Politics, and Humanity

REFUGEES ARE AMONG the world's most desperate people. They are people who have been pushed out of their own countries by forces entirely beyond their control: massive natural disasters, the indiscriminate violence of war, or acts of purposeful persecution. No one knows exactly how many refugees there are in the world, but famine and war in Africa and conflict and persecution in Southeast Asia, Central America, Afghanistan, the Middle East, and Eastern Europe have created a refugee population today ranging between 10 and 15 million.[1] That population, scattered in temporary camps throughout the world, lives in a condition of total dependency. Its needs for food, shelter, medicine, and clothing—and above all, for some safe haven where normal life will again be possible—far exceed the capacity of any nation to grant relief.

Yet refugees are an old phenomenon,[2] and their suffering has long prompted men and women of good will to respond with particular generosity. For most of its history this nation has reacted to their plight with a special rhetoric of welcome. In 1783, George Washington proclaimed America a land whose "bosom is open to receive the persecuted and oppressed of all nations."[3] A century later, Emma Lazarus put words in the Statue of Liberty's mouth, enabling her to welcome, indiscriminately, the "huddled masses yearning to breathe free."[4]

Despite this rhetoric and the humanitarian tradition it embodies, the United

States, like virtually every other nation in the world, grew progressively more restrictionist in the first decades of this century, shutting its gates to most newcomers. Among those almost totally excluded were refugees of every description. Efforts to save even those most patently fearful of persecution failed. In 1939, for example, President Roosevelt implicitly acknowledging the strength of popular anti-Semitism,[5] provided no support for a bill introduced in Congress which would have provided special immigration opportunities for up to 20,000 German refugee children.[6] Despite the efforts of American Jews to sway Congressional opinion, the bill failed. Thus America's response to refugees was defined by those opposed to any liberalization of immigration policy, either because such liberalization would make the United States "the dumping ground of the persecuted minorities of Europe" and encourage the influx of an "army of people who speak foreign languages, and insult the American flag,"[7] or because it would "add to our national immigration at . . . a time when at least 10,500,000 of our own people are out of employment."[8]

World War II marked the end of an epoch. Since 1945 the United States has revived its traditional rhetoric of welcome—and has matched its words with action. More than 2 million refugees have been specially selected by the American government and permitted to enter the United States outside the ordinary immigration stream.[9] Additional thousands who entered the United States as ordinary migrants have been granted political asylum and permitted to remain until the threat of mistreatment abroad vanishes. From 1975 to 1980, the United States accepted as many refugees as the rest of the world did.[10] In recent years, the rate of acceptance has diminished significantly,[11] perhaps heralding a return to some of the more restrictive attitudes of the Depression era. Yet thousands of refugees are still admitted each year, and afforded resettlement benefits which ordinary immigrants are denied. As importantly, significant segments of the American public remain committed to the rhetoric of welcome, as do the leaders of both major political parties.[12] That commitment, although shallower and more selective than it was in the late 1970s, thus appears sufficient to guarantee that some victims from some lands will continue to find refuge in the United States.

There is no way of predicting with complete accuracy which refugees will be welcomed in the future, and in what numbers. Yet only by examining the politics which shaped the American response to refugees over the past forty years can we begin to understand the forces shaping American policies today and standing a good chance of influencing them in the decades to come. This book is about those politics. It tells a story which is in large measure about kindness: the selfless efforts of American ethnics working to rescue friends and relatives trapped in refugee camps overseas, the generosity of church people, public interest lawyers, and voluntary agency personnel, the surprising commitment of "objective" newsmen and "pragmatic" bureaucrats to the relief of suffering. But it is also a story about difficult choices made by a government responsive to its constituents and its own institutional and ideological priorities. Focusing on the selection of refugees made by the executive since 1945—and on the related legislative activities of Congress—it chronicles an ongoing struggle for supremacy among three groups, each with its own distinct agenda.

The first group, which was dominant prior to World War II and remained a powerful force in the Congress until the middle 1960s, has reemerged as a significant political force in the wake of the 1979 recession and the massive refugee movements to the United States from Indochina and the Caribbean during the late 1970s and early 1980s. It considers the circumstances which drive people out of their homelands less important than the problems which they create when admitted as immigrants. Avowedly restrictionist, its principal objective is to limit overall immigration to the United States.[13] During its earlier, dominant period, it had a special animus against refugees because so many were Jewish or belonged to some other "inferior" people of Southern or Eastern Europe. Rep. Albert Johnson, the principal author of the quota acts which imposed special limits on the immigration of such peoples, also voiced another concern. Refugees are bad for the nation, he argued, because they lack the tradition of freedom:

> Today, instead of a well-knit homogeneous citizenry, we have a body politic made up of all and every diverse element. Today, instead of a nation descended from generations of freemen bred to a knowledge of the principles and practices of self-government, of liberty under law, we have a heterogeneous population no small proportion of which is sprung from races that, throughout the centuries, have known no liberty at all, and no law save the decrees of overlords and princes. In other words, our capacity to maintain our cherished institutions stands diluted by a stream of alien blood with all its inherited misconceptions respecting the relationships of the governing power to the governed.[14]

Although the recent resurgence of restrictionism is undoubtedly tied to anti-Cuban, anti-Haitian sentiments which periodically surface in public opinion polls and newspaper accounts,[15] its more reputable modern spokesmen eschew racial and ethnic prejudice and avoid statements about the general character of refugees and its effect on American freedoms. Yet many of the arguments they do make apply with special force to many refugees. Thus, if admitting voluntary migrants is bad because it deprives American workers of jobs, admitting refugees from countries like Laos and Cambodia is worse because those who enter are so "foreign" and so badly educated that most will never find work and will spend decades on welfare.[16]

Opposed to the restrictionists is a second group which regards extreme misfortune—particularly if identifiable as political persecution—as a valid reason for carving out exceptions to the nation's restrictive immigration laws. Some members of this group, who for ethical or religious reasons believe that America is obligated to welcome every stranger, advocate an "open door." Others, who believe that America cannot take every refugee who expresses a desire to come here, nevertheless insist that America cannot afford morally to turn asylum seekers who have already reached the United States back to places where imprisonment, torture, or death is probable. The most politically astute—and most powerful—members of this second, "humanitarian" group traditionally have been ethnic Americans who have employed all of the devices of interest group politics to secure the admission of people still in the "old country" facing extreme hardship or persecution, or still in transit in some land of "first asylum."

Important things can be learned about American refugee politics by examining the shifting membership of these groups, their lobbying and public relation activities, and their vulnerability to social and economic change. Governmental decisions about the admission of refugees, like other immigration decisions, impinge on the interests of many segments of the population, including taxpayers, farmers, unionized workers, industrialists, and other employers. Domestic politics have always played some role in determining how many refugees will be accommodated, and in what locations. Those politics have been, and will inevitably be, influenced by the general state of the nation's social and economic health. Thus in the 1930s it was difficult to be generous to unfortunate aliens when unemployment hovered near 20 percent,[17] soup kitchens and make-work projects abounded, and deep antagonisms between the haves and have-nots surfaced. It was considerably easier to be selfless after the war when an acute labor shortage emerged,[18] and making space for the victims of persecution helped fill jobs[19] at a minimal cost to native Americans.[20] The stagnation of the economy in the late 1970s and early 1980s has undoubtedly strengthened the hands of the restrictionists, and weakened the hands of those promoting more admissions.

But if refugee politics can be likened to a game of cards, that game is almost certainly more like bridge than poker. Thus its outcome is affected not only by the cards that are dealt but also by the partnerships that are formed and the skill the partners display when they play their hands. Since World War II, refugee advocates have generally been more effective in forming coalitions than their opponents, more successful in attracting the uncommitted and the influential to their cause. Their success, in large part, has been due to organization and effort. In 1946, American Jewish groups concerned about holocaust survivors launched a massive public relations campaign designed to tell the entire nation about the hardships of the displaced persons in Europe. By writing and distributing news stories, commercials, and appeals which emphasized the sufferings of non-Jewish as well as Jewish victims[21] and by forming local committees at the grass-roots level which included Protestant and Catholic businessmen, labor leaders, educators, and churchmen,[22] they were able to generate broad-based popular and editorial support for a more liberal admissions policy. Since the 1940s, similar campaigns have been initiated for other groups of refugees—most notably, the Indochinese. Depending heavily on press coverage sympathetic to refugees—which, since the Cuban influx of 1980, is no longer automatically available—the coalitions formed during these campaigns have exerted strong pressures on Congress to liberalize American immigration law, or on the President to apply the existing law liberally on behalf of refugees. Frequently their efforts have met with notable success. The campaign which began in 1946 resulted in displaced persons legislation. Since 1952, similar lobbying has helped effect fundamental changes in American immigration law governing refugees[23] and has played a significant role in bringing thousands of Cubans, Indochinese, and Soviet Jews to the United States.

Yet the story of America's evolving response to refugees is far broader than any account of domestic political struggles can suggest. Humanitarians clearly played a role in bringing thousands of refugees to the United States, restrictionists a role in keeping thousands of others out. But over the last four decades, it has become increasingly clear that foreign policy choices ordinarily have played the key role in determining which refugees will be permitted to enter the United States. Thus the Hungarians in 1956, the Cubans who entered between 1960 and 1966, and the Indochinese transported from Saigon in 1975 were the beneficiaries of little lobbying and no legislation,[24] yet were admitted into the United States by the tens of thousands by the Eisenhower, Kennedy, Johnson, and Ford administrations. In each instance, their entry was favored by the Department of State and regarded as an obligation or an opportunity created by the cold war. Conversely, over the last two decades, the United States has closed its borders to virtually every refugee fleeing persecution at the hands of authoritarian regimes.[25] The customary detention, denial of asylum, and deportation of thousands of Salvadorans and Haitians has been widely covered in the press, has generated considerable sympathy from a wide segment of the American population,[26] and has even induced the Congress to formally request President Reagan to liberalize his policies.[27] However, like most similar requests made without regard to the prevailing cold war ideology, it failed.

Thus the third—and most powerful—group which influences refugee admission consists of those inside government who believe that refugees are not merely immigrants and not merely victims, but are also valuable "assets" in an ongoing struggle with Communism. Members of this group sit in the White

House, the State Department, and the CIA. Since 1945, well over 90 percent of those admitted to the United States have fled Communist countries.[28] Their admission to this country has not been achieved by balancing their suffering against the suffering of other victims. It has not been achieved by quantifying hardship or persecution. Nor—in the great majority of cases—has it been achieved by internal or external pressures on Congress to take special action. Instead, after a brief period during the late 1940s and early 1950s when ideology interacted closely with traditional interest group politics, it has been achieved primarily through executive action. Guided for a generation by the view that "each refugee from the Soviet orbit represents a failure of the Communist system,"[29] successive administrations have sought to induce more defections and have consistently sought to transform each new arrival into a symbolic or literal "freedom fighter."

In so doing, they have not been indifferent to external voices. Often, over the last four decades, they have responded generously to humanitarian appeals, but the appeals they have heeded have almost always been consistent with, and have furthered, American foreign policy objectives. Today, in a markedly more restrictive era, the Reagan administration has responded to more restrictive voices. It has begun to limit the opportunities for refugee migration. At the same time it has continued to maintain—and indeed, has strengthened—the double standard which began emerging in the immediate aftermath of World War II. Thus, like all of its predecessors, it has extended special welcome to the victims of the "evil empire"—those facing persecution from Communist regimes. More openly and absolutely than its predecessors, however, it has chosen to ignore the claims of other refugees and to define suffering in rigid ideological terms. That choice reveals how calculating America's response to refugees has become, how far it has strayed from Emma Lazarus' vision and the first efforts, made soon after World War II, to resettle the survivors of the holocaust.

Chapter 1

Jews, Displaced Persons, and the First Refugee Act

I~N THE SPRING~ and summer of 1945, as the Allied armies swept across Germany and Austria, millions of desperate people moved with them across a devastated landscape. A report prepared by the State Department in that year described the situation in the last months of the war as "[one] of the greatest population movements of history taking place before our eyes. As the German retreat has rolled westward before the oncoming Soviet troops and as the Allies have pushed eastward on the western front, millions of people have been uprooted and are fleeing toward the center of Germany."[1] The report estimated that this flow, not counting some "20 to 30 million of the people of Europe already torn from their moorings by the terrific impact of war,"[2] included "some 9½ million displaced Germans returning from outside the Reich, and 4 million and probably more war fugitives who fled before the oncoming Soviet and Allied troops."[3] Among those fleeing were several million forced laborers who had been sent to Germany from Poland, the Ukraine, and almost every other Axis-occupied country; several thousand Jews who had gone into hiding during the Nazi persecution; Russian prisoners of war, as well as other Russians who had served with the German army on the eastern front; perhaps 500,000 Lithuanians, Latvians, and Estonians who had fled into "friendly" Germany in advance of the Soviet army; and Germans who either had been born in Eastern Europe (*Volksdeutsche*) or had settled there before or

1

during the war (*Reichsdeutsche*). As the concentration camps in the eastern Reich were liberated, these first migrants were joined by some 60,000 additional Jewish survivors, many in the terminal stages of starvation.[4]

Many of those uprooted in 1945 quickly reached the British, French, and American zones of military occupation. Yet the dislocation wrought by war and by the political changes in Eastern Europe which followed was massive. Millions of ethnic Germans expelled from the east under the terms of the Potsdam agreement reached the western zones in 1946 and 1947,[5] as did more than 200,000 additional Jewish refugees who had survived the war in hiding.[6] New arrivals, neither Jewish nor German, also began trickling into countries which had fallen under Soviet domination.

The entry of so many desperate people into an area where most of the housing, industry, and transportation network had been destroyed, and where the fields lay fallow, put immense strains on Western Germany and on the American military authorities responsible for administering the greater portion of it. The most significant strains involved foreigners in Germany. More than a million uprooted people huddled in the midst of a defeated and largely hostile population. Some were Soviet nationals who had fought against Hitler's army. Others were Jews who had been subjected to persecution by the German people a few months earlier and were fearful of being persecuted again. Most had no homes they were willing to return to, no place that would afford them permanent safe haven. Unassimilable and afraid, they required more than relief. In the short term they required protection; in the long term, a program that would permit them to leave Germany and reestablish their lives in some safer and more hospitable abode.

Between 1945 and 1950 the United States, working actively with other members of the western alliance, designed and began to implement such a program. Despite an immigration system designed to keep Eastern Europeans out of the U.S.,[7] a system which imposed special burdens on the poor and the dispossessed,[8] it extended a special welcome to nearly 350,000 displaced persons.[9] It did so primarily for humanitarian reasons, yet from the beginning, humanitarianism was linked with pragmatism. And almost from the beginning, it was linked with ideology. Thus a program which had as its first objective the resettlement of Jewish survivors of the holocaust changed shape as it emerged. Dependent on the passage of specific legislation and on the support of the Truman administration, it was subject to all the vagaries of American immigration politics, and grew progressively more concerned with the fate of those resisting repatriation to Communist-dominated countries. A politics of belated rescue, driven primarily by the efforts of a substantial segment of the American Jewish community, was transformed subtly into a politics which, due primarily to efforts of strong anti-Communists inside and outside the Truman administration, began equating humanity with the political objectives of the West.

Initially, however, the response of the American government to the refugee problem in Europe was pragmatic and local. America remained a highly restrictionist and intolerant nation in 1945. War's end promised a return of millions of servicemen but no certainty that all would have jobs. Two bills were introduced in the 79th Congress to end all immigration.[10] Public opinion polls taken after news of the holocaust emerged revealed no significant support for admitting Jewish refugees.[11] The "temporary" admission in 1944 of 982 predominately Jewish refugees rescued from Eastern Europe generated strong Congressional opposition and angry editorials in the conservative press.[12] Consular offices remained closed in the European war zones, and no immediate plans for opening them were proposed. Virtually no thought was given to resettling any displaced persons—or DPs, as they were commonly designated—in the United States.[13] Instead, the immediate objective of the United States—which it shared with its British, French, and Soviet allies—was to stabilize the chaotic situation by providing the DPs with emergency food, clothing, and shelter and by returning as many people as possible to their countries of origin.

Two years before the war in Europe ended, the Allied nations had drafted contingency plans for dealing with reconstruction after the Axis was defeated. At that time, an intergovernmental body, the United Nations Relief and Rehabilitation Agency (UNRRA), was created. It was entrusted with the responsibility of dealing with the displaced persons and refugees the war produced, but it was given a very limited mandate. Thus it was authorized to offer relief assistance, provided the beneficiaries were not hostile and the relief was temporary.[14] And it was authorized to take active steps to promote the repatriation of citizens of the Allied nations but was given no power to arrange their resettlement in any third country.[15] In the war's waning days, UNRRA was activated. Working directly under the Allied military command, and with the initial cooperation of U.S. civilian and military authorities, it devoted a substantial percentage of its effort to identifying DPs, putting them into trucks or boxcars, and shipping them back to the countries from which they had originally come. Hundreds of thousands of Allied soldiers from Western Europe and North America who had been held as German prisoners benefited from UNRRA's actions. However, more than 7 million Soviets and Eastern Europeans,[16] many with serious reservations about returning home which were later to prove well founded,[17] were immediately repatriated. Nearly 3 million of those returned were taken from zones under western occupation.[18] By dint of these actions, UNRRA was able to reduce the DP population to a more manageable size. Those who were considered not immediately "repatriable"—

3

including Baltic and Polish nationals whose territory had been annexed by the Soviet Union, Ukranians who convinced the American authorities that they faced virtually certain political persecution if returned,[19] and virtually all of the Jewish DPs[20]—were maintained by UNRRA. Many were housed in hastily assembled "camps" while decisions were reached about how to deal with them.

The history of refugees in modern times is replete with stories of migrants who ten, twenty, or thirty years after being uprooted had still found no permanent home.[21] Such a fate might well have befallen the majority of the DPs remaining in Germany and Austria late in 1945 if substantial segments of the American Jewish community had not become alarmed at the condition of Jewish survivors in DP camps and, despairing of any other satisfactory solution, begun lobbying for a new program of admission to the United States. Their efforts were decisive in creating a new American attitude toward refugees, and a new legislative modality which would permit the entry of many as special immigrants.

The campaign to bring Jewish survivors to the United States was deeply rooted in prewar efforts to secure visas for Jewish refugee children from Germany and other Jewish migrants who were barred by the restrictive administration of American immigration laws. Undoubtedly, it took nurture from the decision of the Roosevelt administration in 1944 to begin "rescue" operations in Europe and to bring a small contingent of those rescued "temporarily" to the United States.[22] Yet its principal impetus came during the spring of 1945, when stories began circulating that conditions in the DP camps for death camp survivors were intolerable. A broad spectrum of American Jewish leaders, including Rep. Emanuel Celler, Rabbi Stephen S. Wise, and Nahum Goldman, began pressing for an investigation.[23] Working in tandem with Robert Morgenthau, the Secretary of the Treasury, they persuaded President Truman to dispatch Earl Harrison, a former Commissioner of Immigration, to Europe in July 1945 to "inquire into the condition and needs of displaced persons in Germany who may be stateless or non-repatriable, particularly Jews."[24]

Harrison sent back a searing account of how the victims of Nazi persecution were faring in occupied Germany. Among the hardships he catalogued were continuing deaths by starvation of those who had been rescued from concentration camps,[25] acute shortages of food, shelter, and fuel, and a clothing situation so bad that for months "many of the Jewish displaced persons . . . had no clothing other than their concentration camp garb . . . while others, to their chagrin, were obliged to wear German S.S. uniforms."[26] In a phrase that caught President Truman's special attention, Harrison asserted that "we appear to be treating the Jews as the Nazis treated them, except we do not exterminate them."[27]

4

Harrison's report drew a sharp rejoinder from General Eisenhower, who pointed to a number of special measures taken on behalf of Jewish survivors, who were generally better housed and fed than their German counterparts. Yet questions of food and shelter aside, the Jewish situation was especially desperate. A small percentage of European Jews wished to return to their former homes from which they had been forcibly removed. Most were absolutely and irrevocably disaffected, a cultural remnant precariously quartered among their recent oppressors, cut off even from news of "wives, husbands, parents, children."[28] Their great desire was to leave Germany and Austria as soon as possible. Harrison's chief recommendation was that this desire be honored. He encouraged the President to put pressure on the British to open up Palestine, where most of the Jewish survivors wished to settle. In addition to suggesting that an additional 100,000 resettlement slots for Palestine were needed, Harrison urged that the United States reestablish immigration from occupied Europe and "permit reasonable numbers . . . of Europe's persecuted Jews" to come to the United States.[29] Only if the United States reopened its doors, Harrison implied, could the devastated countries of Western Europe be expected to accept any significant number of Jewish migrants.

The Harrison report strengthened the resolve of American Zionists to wrest Palestine from the British. Many were not interested in resettlement in the United States and took no action to support it. However, other Jews who were not Zionists—or who believed that the Palestine issue would not be resolved quickly—found in the Harrison report a powerful argument for attacking the nation's restrictive immigration policy. President Truman's initial response to the Harrison report had been a public letter to General Eisenhower endorsing its findings and demanding that the army improve conditions for Jewish DPs.[30] He was sympathetic to their plight and clearly disposed to be helpful. Thus those American Jews who favored freer immigration to the United States directed their attention, first, to convincing the President to use existing immigration law to the fullest extent possible to aid Jewish DPs, and, second, to opening Palestine to Jewish immigration.

Whether prompted by their efforts or by his own humanitarian instincts, Truman acted quickly. On December 22, 1945, he directed the Secretary of State to reestablish consular offices in American zones of occupation "at or near displaced person and refugee assembly center areas."[31] He also ordered visa numbers to be allotted out of existing but unused annual quotas; as a consequence up to 39,000 people would be admissible from Central Europe, approximately 27,000 of whom could enter as German or Austrian nationals.[32] In order to defuse anti-Semitic criticism, the President did not specifically state that all the visas to be issued would be given to victims of persecution. Instead, he said that "common decency and the fundamental comradeship of human beings require us to see that our established immigration quotas are used to reduce human suffering."[33] Nor did he declare that Jewish migrants would be favored. Instead, his directive was framed in blandly neutral terms. No ethnic or religious group was mentioned by name. Those to be aided were described as "natives of central and eastern Europe and the Balkans."[34] The President indicated that "visas should be distributed fairly among persons of all faiths, creeds, and nationalities."[35] The only groups singled out for special consideration were "orphaned children" and the small group of refugees temporarily admitted in 1944 and still interned near Oswego, New York.[36]

Despite this careful rhetoric, it is clear that the early commitment of the Truman administration to resettlement focused exclusively on the problems of the holocaust survivors. Bound by the terms of a secret pact with the Soviet Union forged at Yalta to promote repatriation,[37] the U.S. was slow to acknowledge that many of the Soviets, Poles, and Balts who resisted being sent back home faced possible persecution, and deserved to be treated as a permanent part of the DP population.[38] However, the Truman administration already believed that most Jews were "non-repatriable."[39] Thus it found it easy to agree with the Harrison report, which had identified the postwar refugee problem as one most seriously affecting a single religious and ethnic group, surviving European Jews. The other conclusions reached in the report were also accepted at face value. The administration recognized that those survivors were not merely "displaced" but were also the victims of an extermination campaign that had left between 5 and 6 million of their brothers and sisters dead. It acknowledged the moral and practical impossibility of requiring them to live indefinitely among the people responsible for that campaign.

Not surprisingly, the President accepted the Harrison findings and renewed pressures on Britain to admit more Jews to Palestine.[40] Britain, however, resisted, and Truman realized that the only possible alternative was more migration to the United States. The program established to implement the President's December 22 directive reflected that perception. From the spring of 1946 through June 1948, approximately 40,000 people were issued visas under the Truman directive. By the best available estimate, 28,000 of these visa recipients were Jewish.[41]

However, those advocating more Jewish immigration quickly discovered that the President's program was, at best, a stop-gap and limited measure. The U.S. admissions system classified visa seekers according to their country of birth and imposed rigid limits on the migration of nationals from most of the countries which had generated a large number of refugees. Only 6,524 visas were available for Polish migrants, and 2,798 for natives of the U.S.S.R. The numbers admissible from the Baltic countries were derisory: 236 from Latvia, 116 from Estonia, 386 from Lithuania.[42] The exclusionary provisions of U.S.

immigration law, which limited the entry of the ill, the destitute, and the "undesirable," imposed further practical limits on entry. Despite administrative attempts to diminish some of the exclusionary barriers, only 50 to 60 percent of the visas technically available were actually issued.[43]

Under any circumstances, these barriers to entry might have encouraged an attempt to get at the underlying legal problem and liberalize the immigration statute. In 1947, however, a deteriorating situation in Europe and fading hopes for any quick opening of Palestine made legislation permitting easier immigration seem imperative to those who favored more Jewish immigration. Thus the DP problem did not vanish after the President's directive; instead it got notably worse. Some of the new difficulties not only involved Jewish refugees, but also threatened their future well-being.

The most immediate difficulty involved the displaced persons population, which, instead of continuing to shrink, began to expand rapidly. The repatriations of 1945 slowed and then came almost to a complete halt as the United States military command grew increasingly sensitive to the fears of the Eastern Europeans remaining in custody and became increasingly reluctant to return them to areas under Soviet domination or control. Procedures adopted late in 1945 ensured that DPs who feared persecution would be carefully screened and would not be required to return to territories which had been annexed by the Soviet Union after the outbreak of World War II.[44] Others were selected for repatriation only if it was determined that they belonged to certain unprotected classes, such as "war criminals" or "traitors."[45] Selective repatriation continued until mid-1947;[46] but after a series of suicides by DPs informed that they would be involuntarily returned to the Soviet Union and several bloody confrontations early in 1946 between the U.S. military and Russian DPs resisting such involuntary repatriation, the rate of return fell dramatically.[47]

As the rate of repatriations fell, millions of new arrivals poured into the American zone. Among them were hundreds of Eastern European gentiles who migrated west as their homelands fell under Communist rule, and an additional cohort of Eastern European Jews who had survived the war in hiding and made their way slowly to the west. This late influx of Jewish refugees was substantial. As many as 10,000 Jews entered the western zones of Germany in a single week during the summer of 1946.[48] A census taken in the second half of 1945 estimated that the total number of surviving European Jews was "slightly over 90,000, of whom 68,000 are in Germany."[49] Perhaps 190,000 additional Jewish survivors reached the displaced persons camps in 1946, with the majority entering the American zone of Germany.[50] However, the vast majority of those streaming into the American occupation zones were ethnic Germans who, under the provisions of the Potsdam Agreement,[51] had been expelled from Eastern Europe soon after the war ended or, finding life in Soviet-occupied

Germany intolerable, had crossed into British-, French-, or American-occupied territory. All told, between 9 and 10 million ethnic Germans entered the western zones between 1946 and 1951.[52] Approximately half of the German ethnics entered during the chaotic years of 1946 and 1947,[53] when relief operations were still rudimentary, the economies of Germany and Austria lay in ruins, and their own populations faced near starvation.[54] The ethnic Germans were not considered DPs by the Allies, but their arrival in the western zones immensely complicated the relief situation. The new arrivals, despite their German roots, were regarded as "foreign" and resented for their inevitable demands on the local economy.[55] The increase in xenophobia that resulted inevitably affected the DPs, who were even more foreign and who were obtaining subsidized food, shelter, and clothing at a time when virtually no aid was available for formerly hostile Germans. It also became increasingly difficult to find shelter for late-arriving DPs, and impossible to find any sort of employment for them.

Faced with this immense crush of numbers, the American military command threatened to close the DP camps. Planning for such a shut-down began in the spring of 1946.[56] Official intentions to stem the flow of new arrivals were announced in September 1946, and the camps were officially closed to newcomers in April 1947, although assurances were given that those fearful of persecution would still be permitted to enter the American zone.[57] The right of entry was of scant benefit to those who had been subjected to an extermination campaign by the German people, and now faced the possibility of being forced to live, virtually without protection, in their midst. Some relief from these fears was afforded by illegal immigration to Palestine, which took place with the tacit approval of American UNRRA personnel.[58] Yet despite a positive recommendation by the Anglo-American Commission of Inquiry, which had been created upon Truman's urging, the British government refused to open Palestine to Jewish refugees.[59] As a consequence, at a time when the situation for all DPs looked bleak, it looked especially bad for the Jews.

However, what made that situation seem intolerable—and provided the strongest motive for a wholehearted lobbying campaign—was a new outbreak of virulent anti-Semitism in Poland during the spring and summer of 1946. The targets were Jews who had come out of hiding or survived the concentration camps, and attempted to reestablish themselves in their former dwellings. They were set upon by mobs in dozens of Polish towns. The worst incident occurred in Kielce. Forty-one Jews were killed, and seventy-five badly injured. According to one commentator:

> The Poles in Kielce—men, women, and children—beat Jews mercilessly, squeezed their genitals, crushed bones, broke legs, tore off limbs, and mutilated bodies in the most barbaric fashion.[60]

Many of the late Jewish arrivals in the American zone of Germany were survivors of these attacks. They were the people most endangered by threats to
close the camps.

Responding to the worsening situation, the leaders of the American Council on Judaism (ACJ) and the American Jewish Committee (AJC) decided late in
1946 to organize and substantially underwrite a major campaign to change the
law so that an additional 100,000 European Jews would be eligible for visas.[61]
Yet they were fully aware that traditional restrictionist attitudes remained potent in Congress, and that considerable anti-Semitism existed both on Capital
Hill and in the populace at large. They were familiar with public opinion polls
taken at the height of the holocaust which opposed proposed American rescue
initiatives, and which consistently demonstrated that a large percentage of the
American population had an unfavorable view of Jewish immigrants.[62] They
also knew that the high percentage of Jews admitted under President Truman's
directive had already drawn sharp criticism from some powerful members of
Congress, including Sen. Richard Russell, the chairman of the Senate Judiciary
Committee.[63] And they knew that fears generated during the Great Depression
about unemployment and unproductive migrants had not been completely
allayed, and could scuttle any statutory plan to admit more DPs.

In view of these restrictionist attitudes, the two Jewish groups determined
that they would seek to build broad public and Congressional support by con-
sciously downplaying the special nature of Jewish claims, subordinating them
to more general concerns about the fate of the DP populations as a whole. They
also decided to advocate legislation so substantial that even after a politically acceptable number of gentiles had been designated for admission, sufficient visas
would remain available for endangered Jews. In light of concerns about
employment and economic impact, they fashioned a lobbying effort which
would focus at least as heavily on skills the DPs possessed, and their general
ability to be assimilated, as they would on persecution in Eastern Europe.

They began, then, a broad campaign to pass special DP legislation. One
authority describes it as a campaign which purposely enlisted a broad spectrum
of non-Jewish supporters to promote an "emergency" admissions program of
limited duration which would be perceived as only incidentally promoting
Jewish migration. According to that authority:

> . . . in the classic tradition of lobbying, a narrow humanitarian interest (aiding
> Jewish DPs) would take on an expanded focus (helping all DPs, 80 percent of
> whom were Christian), and would strive for widespread support.[64]

Toward these ends, early in 1947 the ACJ and AJC launched a new, well-
financed lobbying organization, the Citizens' Committee on Displaced Persons. Placed under the nominal leadership of Earl Harrison and given a board

of directors dominated by Protestants and Catholics who were nationally prominent businessmen, labor leaders, and churchmen,[65] the Citizens' Committee advocated legislation which would benefit every type of displaced person and would make hundreds of thousands of new visas available. Its propaganda consistently identified the displaced persons in intentionally general language which downplayed Jewish and Eastern European origins and emphasized Christian and anti-Communist characteristics. A typical press release identified the "displaced persons" thus:

> More than 75 percent of them are victims of one or another of European dictators, no matter under what cause or name the dictatorship flourished—communist or fascist. They are, those 80 percent, of the Christian faith, a good many of them Polish and Baltic Catholics. Another portion of them, by far the smallest number, only one out of five is of the Jewish faith. Some of them are political exiles, and since fascism is nominally dead in Europe today, this means that some of them are exiles from countries now controlled by communists.[66]

Similar generality characterized the DP legislation which the Citizens' Committee drafted. The first DP bill introduced on the floor of either House was one written by the Citizens' Committee and presented by Representative William Stratton of Illinois on April 1, 1947.[67] A model of ethnic neutrality, it proposed a special four-year program under which 100,000 displaced persons a year would be admitted to the United States as nonquota immigrants. It defined a displaced person as "any person in Germany, Austria, or Italy at the time of the passage of this Act who (1) is outside of his country of former residence as a result of events subsequent to the outbreak of World War II; and (2) is unable or unwilling to return to the country of his nationality or former residence because of persecution or fear of persecution on account of race, religion, or political opinions."[68] Representative Stratton explained that the bill bearing his name applied to victims of Nazi terror and to those who had entered the American zone "when the Balkans and parts of Germany were overrun in turn by the Communist army."[69] The DP population thus included a variety of "unsettled and homeless people who dare not return to their former homes where they would meet persecution, abuse, and even death at the hands of Communist-dominated governments."[70] That population was composed "primarily of Christians—Poles, Latvians, Lithuanians, Yugoslavians, Estonians, and Ukrainians."[71] Of the 20 percent who were Jewish, most, according to Stratton, "were going or lived in hope of going to Palestine."[72]

Representative Stratton's remarks may have been somewhat disingenuous. Many of the strongest supporters of displaced persons legislation believed that the problem was a largely Jewish one, and that the promise offered by Palestine was a faint one. It was also commonly believed among American Jews after

World War II that a large percentage of the Baltic and Ukrainian DPs, far from being victims of persecution, were war criminals who had collaborated with Nazis.[73] However, such remarks, by attracting the support of non-Jewish ethnics in the United States who were concerned about their relatives in Eastern Europe, clearly were calculated to enhance the bill's chances for eventual passage.

Similar efforts to reach a broad constituency characterized the Citizens' Committee lobbying and publicity campaign. Thus the Committee enlisted a staff of over seventy people to secure organizational endorsements, establish local support groups, publicize the DP problem, and engage in liaison work with the Congress and the Truman administration.[74] Thanks in part to the entrée provided by its blue-ribbon board, which included such luminaries as Eleanor Roosevelt, James A. Farley, Edward Stettinius, Herbert Lehman, Fiorello LaGuardia, and Marshall Field, it was able to exert considerable national influence very quickly. It exerted similar influence at the local level by forming more than 150 local committees in areas which were deemed familiar with "persons of foreign ethnic background"[75] and likely to be sympathetic. The national committee also coordinated a massive publicity campaign. It produced its own newsletters, documentaries, panel discussion shows, docudramas, and commercials, many of which featured prominent public figures and show business personalities. According to William Bernard, the Committee's staff director:

> The CCDP staff wrote articles and news items and their efforts were frequently expanded by prominent authors and journalists who donated their time and talents. Magazines, newspapers, Sunday supplements, newsletters, all were reached. Consultation and advice was given to producers of movies dealing with DPs. For a special group of some 3,000 opinion makers, composed of editors, columnists, commentators, broadcasters, et al., special fact sheets were prepared, objectively and succinctly outlining the details of various bills, legislative proposals, organization stands, and other pertinent developments.[76]

The targetted audience for this intense and exceptionally well-organized campaign included those Congressmen and the large body of Americans who were disposed to be generous to the DPs but were fearful of the economic and social impact they might have if admitted to the United States. To allay these fears, accounts of hardship and persecution were carefully balanced with descriptions of the benefits the DPs would bring to this country. Earl Harrison observed these priorities when he testified before Congress on the Stratton bill. Although noting that passage of the bill would help meet "the nation's humanitarian and moral obligations,"[77] his principal emphasis was on the contributions that the DPs were likely to make to America. Refugees were thus characterized as "seed population" whose entry would stimulate production and contribute to economic growth. The scientific accomplishments of those who had entered before and during the war were emphasized, as were the contributions they had made to American artistic and cultural life. With more enthusiasm than accuracy, Harrison predicted that those likely to seek admission would migrate to rural areas in large numbers, thus helping to relieve the acute shortage of agricultural labor which America experienced during the war.[78] Rejecting point by point all of the principal objections to the DPs (including the assertion that many were Communists), Harrison insisted that the United States possessed the geographical capacity, the ability to overcome a tight housing situation, and the social maturity to resettle many more refugees than the 400,000 special entrants whose admission was sought under the Stratton bill. The United States was threatened, he claimed, not by a Malthusian catastrophe, but by a shortage of the skilled workers necessary to insure America's continuing development. Refugees, far from being unnecessary or useless people, were vital if postwar economic recovery was to continue.[79]

The emphasis on the potential economic contributions of the DPs was especially heavy, not only in Harrison's Congressional testimony, but in the entire Citizens' Committee campaign. Mindful of the strength which the Depression had lent to restrictionism, DP advocates took special pains to educate the public about the improvement of the American economy. In 1946 and 1947, the unemployment rate stood at 3.9 percent.[80] Thus the labor market was better than it had been at any time since the late 1920s, except for the period during the war when virtually full employment was achieved. Strong employment, coupled with strong production in an economy starved for consumer goods, demonstrated that the Depression had fallen victim to the war. The Citizens' Committee regarded it as essential to convince uncommitted Americans that the reentry into the labor market of large numbers of returning servicemen would not revive it.

The primary targets of this component of the lobbying campaign were unions. Organizational liaison with labor organizations was a high priority:

> Particular attention was paid to labor unions, and specialists with extensive experience with labor were used to elicit labor support for DP legislation. This was forthcoming despite labor's historic opposition to immigration, and labor leaders such as William Green, President of the AF of L testified that the admission of the DPs was in the national interest.[81]

Undoubtedly, many labor leaders and union members continued to fear the effects of a massive DP influx. Yet by enlisting the support of over a dozen separate national unions, the Citizens' Committee neutralized the residual restrictionism of organized labor, converting a traditional opponent into a more than nominal ally. Similar efforts were made to convince the major veterans' organizations that the DPs posed no threat to the well-being of their members. Although that campaign was not entirely successful, the American Legion was induced to drop its opposition to the Stratton bill, thus removing one of the chief obstacles to its passage.[82]

By pursuing this sort of campaign, the Citizens' Committee managed to generate significant public support for the displaced persons and exert considerable pressure on Congress to enact special immigration legislation on their behalf. Endorsements of the Stratton bill were obtained from more than 250 national organizations, including labor unions, ethnic associations, religious groups, and a wide range of charitable, educational, and fraternal organizations. A letter-writing campaign was also initiated. According to William Bernard, "in early 1946 and early 1947, mail to the White House was running 7 to 1 against special DP legislation."[83] By the summer of 1947, when a variant of the Stratton bill was introduced in the Senate, that ratio had been reversed, and Congress was besieged by constituents urging it to do something specific for the DPs.[84]

Yet the 80th Congress which convened in 1946 was a very conservative one. For the first time since the advent of the New Deal, Republicans controlled both the House and the Senate. On many issues, they saw eye to eye with Southern and Western Democrats, who were also well represented. Restrictionism was a common creed.[85] Generally representing predominately rural areas with small foreign-born and Jewish populations, most Republicans and many Democrats from the less populous states were not amenable to the same ethnic pressures that affected their Northern and Eastern Democrat colleagues. Some were also blatantly anti-Semitic. Chapman Revercomb, the Republican Senator from West Virginia who served as Chairman of the Senate Judiciary Committee's Immigration and Naturalization Subcommittee during the 80th Congress, consistently slanted his remarks against additional Jewish immigration. For example, in 1947, speaking on the floor of the Senate, Revercomb rejected the view that surviving Jews were "stateless" and that there were genuine limitations on their ability to dwell safely in postwar Europe. In an exchange with Senator Leverett Saltonstall, he characterized the Kielce pogrom as "a local riot" and labeled the Jews, not as persons "who were compelled to flee," but as "those who migrated and moved simply because they felt they could improve their economic condition."[86] Similar views were expressed by Ed Gosset, a Texas Democrat who sat on the House Immigration and Naturalization Subcommittee. He frequently stated that most Jewish DPs were Communists or potential spies,[87] that they actively supported social revolution in Europe and consequently had nothing to fear from Russian domination, and that they were therefore "voluntarily displaced persons" rather than true refugees.[88]

Most members of Congress were more moderate—and more easily reached by the arguments of the Citizens' Committee. Yet conservatives remained powerful in Congress for several decades after World War II, and anti-Semitism did not evaporate overnight. The restrictionists, using parliamentary tactics, were able to delay all substantive consideration of the DP bill during 1947. They might well have been able to secure further delay if the Truman administration had not thrust itself into the middle of the DP debate and profoundly influenced the Congressional—and the public—perception of refugee politics.

Truman has sometimes been faulted by scholars for not making greater efforts on behalf of the DPs, and particularly for not involving himself strenuously enough in the legislative campaign to secure passage of a generous DP act.[89] Certainly, Truman's direct efforts on behalf of such legislation were limited. Despite urging Congress in his 1946 State of the Union address "to find ways whereby we can fulfill our responsibilities to these thousands of homeless and suffering refugees of all faiths,"[90] he did not publicly endorse the Stratton bill in 1947, and did not involve himself very actively in the legislative process when the bill was taken up again in 1948.[91] Although his staff maintained close contacts with the Citizens' Committee and informed the Committee of the President's support, he did not assume a leadership role in the campaign to push the bill through Congress. Arguably, more involvement in the domestic political arena might have promoted faster Congressional action—and fairer results—in 1948, when a substitute for the Stratton bill was enacted.

Yet despite the President's limited time in the legislative trenches, his administration's approach to the DP problem had the effect of opening a major second front where the battle could be fought with different weapons and on much more favorable terms. Thus the Truman administration's lasting contribution to the politics of refugee admission was its recognition that refugees had become part of the political landscape overseas, and that they had to be dealt with if the United States was to forge an effective foreign policy in the postwar world. It acted on that recognition late in 1946 and 1947 when it began to treat the problem of non-Jewish displaced persons as a permanent one, threatening the economic stability of Europe and demanding some sort of international resettlement response. At the same time, it confronted the Soviet Union on the refugee issue, taking an increasingly firm stance on forced repatriation and leading the successful effort to replace UNRRA, which it regarded as pro-Soviet, with the western-dominated and resettlement-oriented International Refugee Organization (IRO). By taking these steps, the Truman administration converted the refugee issue into an aspect of the emerging cold war, and thus provided a new basis for conservative support which was only marginally related to traditional interest group politics.

That transformation was not something that was carefully planned. It developed slowly as U.S.-Soviet relations worsened and the cold war emerged. Thus when the administration concluded sometime in late 1945 or 1946 that a large residual population of DPs was likely to remain in Germany indefinitely, its initial focus was on the backlash that their presence appeared to be generating among the German people. Its first concern was a possible revival of Nazism. It was not until late in 1946 that the DP issue became a serious bone of contention between the East and the West.

When conflict did erupt, UNRRA was in the middle of it. Charged with repatriating DPs and with providing rehabilitation assistance to all of the Allied powers devastated by the war including those in the Soviet orbit, UNRRA quickly incurred the wrath of the State Department. Dean Acheson described it as a badly managed and immensely wasteful agency which misdirected much of its aid: "due to the roles built into its charter, the great bulk of relief, largely supplied or paid for by the United States, went to Eastern Europe and was used by countries bitterly hostile to the United States."[92]

His sentiments were echoed by other diplomats who monitored UNRRA affairs on a regular basis and found themselves embroiled in continual quarrels with their Soviet counterparts over every funding question.[93] UNRRA was thus already in poor repute in September 1946, when a major controversy about its repatriation role erupted. The controversy was sparked by Soviet complaints that the western powers were refusing to fulfill their obligations under the Yalta agreements and were encouraging Soviet nationals to resist repatriation.[94] Pointing to the limited mandate of UNRRA, the Soviet Union objected to the grant of UNRRA aid to any displaced person resisting repatriation.[95] An immediate blow-up was temporarily avoided when the United States acquiesced to a plan which permitted such aid to be continued for a maximum of six months, but which acknowledged that UNRRA was entitled to repatriate DPs and would be permitted to do so in the future.[96] However, by December 1946 the battle lines were clearly drawn. Responding to intelligence reaching the West which indicated that many of those who returned to the Soviet Union were being treated as "war criminals" and to reports from the annexed Baltic states describing mass deportations to Siberia,[97] the military began actively hindering the efforts of UNRRA repatriation teams and brought the delivery of prisoners into Soviet hands to a virtual halt.[98]

Toward the end of 1946, the United States took action in the United Nations to kill UNRRA, refusing either to grant it additional aid or to extend its life.[99] Instead, in the face of adamant Soviet opposition, it committed itself to the creation of a new International Refugee Organization (IRO), which had as one of its chief functions the resettlement of refugees and displaced persons created by World War II. And it insisted that the mandate of the IRO be broad enough to offer protection to individuals with "valid objections" to repatriation, including objections based on "persecution, or fear, based on reasonable grounds, of persecution because of race, religion, nationality or political opinions" and objections "of a political nature, judged by the organization to be valid."[100] Other language in the IRO constitution paid lip service to Soviet, Polish, and Yugoslavian objections by asserting that the organization's principal objective was "to encourage and assist in every way possible early return [of refugees and displaced persons] to their countries of origin," and that "no international assistance should be given to traitors, quislings and war criminals, and nothing should be done in any way to prevent their surrender and punishment."[101] Despite this palliative language, the eastern bloc, which had been consistently outvoted in the UN General Assembly, responded angrily. The Soviet Union reiterated its charges that "the refugee camps of the West had become centers of anti-communist propaganda; that the refugees were being used as forced laborers and as mercenaries; and that the West intended to enrich itself by resettling the so-called refugees to the countries of the world making the highest bid for their labor."[102] In concert with other nations of Eastern Europe, it took the then unprecedented step of refusing to join the new organization, and made no contribution of any kind toward its operations. Thus from its creation in 1947,[103] the IRO was treated by the Soviets and their allies as a tool of the U.S. bloc, and bitterly resented.

By siding against the Soviet Union on the IRO, the United States implicitly committed itself to supporting a very expensive organization which had as its principal goal the resettlement of refugees. From the beginning it was clear that much of that support would have to be financial, since only the U.S. was capable of substantially underwriting the IRO's $161 million annual budget.[104] But because the IRO was dedicated to resettlement, and because the war-torn countries of western Europe were incapable of accepting all the DPs, immediate pressure was also put on the United States by its allies to make at least some admissions slots available. Thus, it was widely understood that U.S. membership in the IRO would have as its practical result some concrete commitment to refugee resettlement. The Citizens' Committee and the restrictionists were both aware of the force of this potential commitment. Thus the Citizens' Committee purposely delayed the introduction of the Stratton bill in the Senate until after the favorable precedent of a positive IRO vote had been established.[105] The restrictionists in both Houses of Congress insisted, however, that any authorization of U.S. IRO membership unequivocally state that no change in U.S. immigration law would result without further, positive legislation.[106]

The joint resolution authorizing U.S. membership in the IRO did leave American immigration law intact.[107] All of the principal supporters of the IRO insisted, in the words of Rep. Jerry Vorys, that IRO membership "had nothing to do" with the pending DP legislation.[108] In a technical sense, they were right. Yet, as Vorys also noted, the primary mission of the IRO was to care for those "who cannot go home . . . because [to do so] means to go to slavery or to death" and "to resettle as many as possible."[109] The Congressional debate on the IRO was notable for its lack of attention to where those resettled might eventually go.[110] In this respect, it mirrored the testimony of State Department and military personnel who testified in House and Senate hearings on the IRO that resettlement was necessary for humanitarian and foreign policy reasons but avoided discussing every domestic implication of resettlement except cost. For example, in the House IRO hearings, Assistant Secretary of State John Hilldring noted that few of the remaining DP's would voluntarily accept repatriation—and renounced any American intent of forcefully returning those who were unwilling to go home—yet insisted that the United States, by joining the IRO, made no "commitment of any kind or character . . . to permit [additional] immigration."[111] The "second alternative," leaving the displaced persons in place, was rejected for reasons enunciated by Secretary of State George Marshall:

> The displaced persons know the Germans are responsible for their present plight. The Germans regard the displaced persons as an uncomfortable burden and a constant source of annoyance. To turn them back to the Germans would be to perpetuate grave tensions and an ever present threat of internal conflict. . . . The western zones of Germany are already overcrowded with millions of Germans and people of German stock who have fled or have been transferred into Germany since the end of the war. If we should in addition throw these displaced persons onto the German economy, we should have to continue our contributions to their support, though indirectly, as an alternative to their starvation.[112]

Marshall also concluded that maintaining the displaced persons camps indefinitely was impossible because it would demoralize those held in the camps, would thus "have disastrous effects on the larger problem of the reconstruction of Europe that will alone make possible a peaceful world,"[113] and would also be extremely expensive. Major John Hilldring, Assistant Secretary of State for the Occupied Areas, also pushed the economic argument hard, arguing that a multilateral resettlement effort, with the costs distributed among all the IRO members, would reduce U.S. refugee expenditures from a current $130 million to $73 million.[114]

Promised savings were probably more important to most Congressmen than the East-West conflict which had led to the creation of the IRO. Perhaps because they testified immediately before the announcement of the Truman Doctrine and thus before the administration had established anti-Communism as its chief foreign policy priority, administration spokesmen promoting the IRO avoided hard anti-Communist rhetoric. Nevertheless, overt anti-Communism emerged in the Congressional IRO debates as a strong secondary reason for supporting the organization. Thus the pro-Western bent of the IRO was presented as one of its major assets and, not incidentally, as a way of distinguishing it from UNRRA, its predecessor. Representative Jerry Vorys assured the House that the Soviet Union would not be likely to join the IRO because it "has its own solution for the DP's problem."[115] In the Senate, Senator Arthur Vanderberg rejected the possibility of Soviet membership as a "hypothesis" and "fantastic notion" totally inconsistent with its record of "constant, persistent, relentless" and "bitter" opposition.[116] Representative Alvin O'Konski described IRO support as a moral responsibility to people who "were robbed of their lands by secret agreements at Yalta, Potsdam, and Tehran in which our government participated."[117] In O'Konski's view, the IRO was worthy of support because it would aid individuals who would contribute to the eventual liberation of Eastern Europe. He rejected the idea that the DP's were merely disguised immigrants. Instead, he quoted a young Estonian:

> I do not want to come to the United States; I want to go back to Estonia. I want to go back there and shoot up the damned Communists.[118]

Most Congressmen, at least in 1947, were more moderate than Representative Alvin O'Konski. Yet as Soviet-American confrontation became more apparent in 1947 and 1948, poisoning East-West relations in Germany and promoting fears of a new Soviet military offensive, the DP issue became more firmly enmeshed in cold war politics. Thus by May and June of 1948, when Congress moved from a consideration of IRO membership to final consideration of the DP act itself, it was widely understood that the legislation, by providing a haven for those who resisted return to the Soviet-dominated regimes of Eastern Europe, also contributed to the broader anti-Communist objectives of U.S. foreign policy. Even moderate Congressmen supported those objectives, though they tended to express them in moral, rather than instrumental, terms. Representative Harold Donohue spoke for a number of his colleagues when he stated:

> We are engaged in, and planning to extend, an ambitious program of aid to European nations resisting the imposition of communism. Let us implement this program by concrete evidence of willingness to assume a just obligation toward refugees in Europe already communist controlled. . . . In world leader-

ship we can speak more convincingly for freedom everywhere when we have done our fair share to bring real freedom to those who have suffered most.[119]

Thus a persistent theme of those arguing for the passage of the DP act was that the United States was engaged in "a battle of ideologies abroad,"[120] and "that we do ourselves and our democracy a great deal of good by show[ing] to all the world that we are in truth champions of freedom and that we shall aid all those who rally to our cause."[121]

The development of these foreign policy arguments and the continuation of the Citizens' Committee campaign forced a reluctant Congress to act. In April 1948 the House passed a bill introduced by Representative Frank Fellows considerably more restrictive than the original Stratton measure. The Fellows bill cut the number of authorized DP admissions in half, reducing the allocation from 400,000 entrants to 202,000, of whom 2,000 were to be recent political refugees from Czechoslovakia.[122] It also specified that admissions under the DP act were to be charged against the admission quotas of originating countries in future years.[123] Technically, the bill authorized no new admissions,[124] but it permitted substantial "borrowing against" numbers that would otherwise become available in the future—a practice which was termed "quota mortgaging." The Fellows bill further provided that visas be made available to various national and religious groups without discrimination, with the number of visas issued to each group proportionate to their respective populations in the western zones.[125] It linked eligibility for DP visas to three conditions: entry into the U.S., French, or British zone of Austria or Germany no later than April 21, 1947, when the DP camps were closed to new arrivals; registration with the International Refugee Organization (IRO) as a "displaced person" or "refugee"; and lack of prior membership or participation in "any movement which is or has been hostile to the United States or the form of government of the United States."[126] Finally, it required that each DP family provide an "assurance" of an available job and available housing in the United States, and established a set of preferences for admission, with first priority going to aliens "qualified as farm laborers, physicians, dentists, medical nurses, household, construction, clothing and garment workers; or aliens possessing educational, scientific, or technological qualifications."[127]

Supporters of Stratton's original bill objected to the "quota mortgaging" provision but generally regarded the Fellows substitute as an acceptable compromise. They knew that they stood no chance of getting the full 400,000 slots originally requested, regarded the "assurance" requirements as a political necessity, believed that the nondiscrimination language in the bill adequately protected Jewish interests, and lent their active support to the employment preference, which, in its provision for "clothing and garment workers," took into account a trade which had traditionally employed many Jews. However, restrictionists in the Senate were adamant: unless the Fellows bill was substantially modified, they would let the measure die. They acceded to the House limit of 202,000 entrants. But they insisted in conference committee on four major changes which the Senate had adopted. The most important arbitrarily restricted eligibility for DP visas to those who could demonstrate they had entered the western zone on or before December 22, 1945, the date of Truman's original Presidential directive. The effect of that cut-off date was to disadvantage two principal categories of migrants: Jews, most of whom had left the Soviet Union or fled Poland after Truman's announcement; and a growing number of non-Jewish, "new" refugees, who had left Poland, Hungary, Yugoslavia, and other Eastern European countries after the establishment of pro-Soviet regimes. With the exception of the provision for Czechoslovakians, no provision was made for any of these "late" migrants.

Two other changes also had the effect of reducing Jewish eligibility. One set aside 40 percent of all displaced persons slots for applicants from areas "de facto annexed by a foreign power."[128] As the legislative history made clear, this provision was meant to afford an absolute preference to applicants from areas annexed by the Soviet Union during and immediately after World War II, including Baltic countries and Poland east of the Curzon line. It embraced an area where anti-Semitic persecution had been most intense and where there were few Jewish survivors. The other change required that 30 percent of all visas for displaced persons be reserved exclusively for "persons who have been previously engaged in agricultural pursuits and who will be employed in the United States in agricultural pursuits."[129] Those with other needed skills were assigned a subordinate preference. Many of the Jewish concentration camp survivors who were in Germany on the December 22, 1945, eligibility date lacked the requisite agricultural background.

Despite repeated assertions to the contrary from the senators most responsible for these provisions, it is clear that their anti-Semitic effect was both foreseen and intended. Throughout the displaced person debates, Jews had been characterized by hard-line restrictionists as people who sought admission to the United States for the sole purpose of obtaining employment. They were regarded as urban, socialist troublemakers. The Balts, on the other hand, were characterized as genuine refugees who desired nothing more than steady work on America's labor-starved farms. Marvin Klemme, a former UNRRA official, presented all of these stereotypes when he testified before Congress in 1947. Advocating special preferences for Baltic migrants, he described them as "skilled agricultural and forestry workers" whose "only crime was that they actively opposed communism in their own countries."[130] Klemme stated, "The peasant type of immigrant is, in my opinion, the best type of worker that can be brought into this country."[131] Farmers were preferable, he claimed, "to the mostly urban workers who entered the United States after World War I and promptly went on relief," and the "so-called intellegensia that we took in," who "have very definite ideas of their own which are still alien to our ways of thought."[132]

The discrimination lying behind the agricultural and Baltic preferences was apparent, yet both provisions had some plausible justification. There was an acute shortage of agricultural labor in the United States. Some preference for Baltic displaced persons could also have been justified on humanitarian grounds. The Soviet annexation of Lithuania, Latvia, and Estonia had been marked by particular brutality. During the years immediately following World War II, more than 400,000 Baltics were deported to the Soviet Union, and an estimated 90,000 others executed or killed in an ongoing guerrilla war.[133] Yet no moral or pragmatic justification existed for the other change the Senate demanded and got. That change reserved 50 percent of the ordinary German and Austrian quota to "persons of German ethnic origin who were born in Poland, Czechoslovakia, Hungary, Rumania or Yugoslavia residing in Germany or Austria . . . on the effective date of the Act"[134]—that is, on June 25, 1948, thirty months after the Truman directive, and thus thirty months after the ordinary displaced persons cut-off date. Although the authors insisted that the provision was a humanitarian measure designed to aid victims of Soviet persecution, its adoption was clearly attributable to lobbying by Congressmen from states with large German-American populations and the efforts of extreme restrictionists to kill the act by loading it down with unacceptable amendments.[135]

Thus the DP act that Congress passed was fraught with restrictions, and appeared purposely designed to favor groups other than surviving European Jews. Predictably, it produced an angry outcry from the Citizens' Committee and its supporters. President Truman reluctantly signed the bill on June 25, 1948, but characterized it in an accompanying message as "form[ing] a pattern of discrimination and intolerance wholly inconsistent with the American sense of justice."[136] The victims of that discrimination, he claimed, were Jewish displaced persons, more than 90 percent of whom would be denied the act's benefits, and "many displaced persons of Catholic faith who fled in the American zones after December 22, 1945, in order to escape persecution in countries dominated by a Communist form of government."[137] No rationale, other than "abhorrent . . . intolerance," could explain the "wrongful exclu[sion]" of almost all recent arrivals.

As soon as this Displaced Persons Act of 1948 was passed, lobbying commenced immediately to amend the act and strip it of its most offensive provisions. That lobbying produced results, although not quickly enough to satisfy those demanding liberalization. Substantial support for amendments giving the advocates of more liberal legislation nearly everything they sought surfaced immediately; but those amendments took two full years to pass. The delay was attributable primarily to the influence of Senator Pat McCarran, who reassumed the chairmanship of the Senate Judiciary Committee when the Democrats regained control of Congress in the 1948 elections. As dedicated a restrictionist as Senator Revercomb had been, he diluted the effect of the new Democratic—and generally more liberal—majority by employing a variety of delaying tactics to keep the amendments favored by the Citizens' Committee off the Senate floor for nearly two years. Those amendments did not eliminate the "assurance" requirements. But the Baltic and agricultural preferences were dropped, "quota mortgaging" was liberalized, the number of DPs admissible under the act was raised from 202,000 to 341,000, and the period during which DPs would be permitted to enter the United States was extended by a full year to July 1, 1951.[138] Most importantly, the cut-off date for most DPs, marking the latest date they could have entered the western zones and still remain eligible for DP visas, was advanced to January 1, 1949, in recognition both of the substantial Jewish migration in 1946, and of the continued influx after that date of "political and religious dissenters from the regimes now ruling most, if not all of the eastern European countries, including the Soviet Union."[139]

The Congressional concern with "recent refugees" from Communist countries was explicit. Thus the House report on the new amendments stated that "the recent refugees constitute a part of the difficult problem of displaced persons just as much as [the] pre-1945 refugees."[140] While the 1949–1950 campaign to liberalize the Displaced Persons Act continued to be directed by the Citizens' Committee, and was motivated primarily by concern about the original act's anti-Semitic features, the overwhelming public and Congressional support for the amendments derived largely from an intensifying concern about the victims of Communist oppression. One effect of the later cut-off date was to make more Jews eligible for admission. Yet the establishment of the state of Israel in 1948 made the Jewish immigration issue somewhat less urgent. Meanwhile, an intensifying cold war and news about virulent persecution behind the Iron Curtain created a new groundswell of sympathy for Eastern European refugees.

Anti-Soviet sentiment, which had surfaced in the IRO and DP debates during the previous session of Congress, assumed a new importance as East-West relations grew progressively worse between 1948 and 1950. The Berlin blockade began in June 1948, the same month that the original Displaced Persons Act was signed. The struggle for control of Berlin spurred the western alliance into vigorous action. Over the course of the following year, the Congress authorized $5 billion in Marshall Plan aid,[141] the NATO alliance was formed, and the Federal Republic of Germany was created. The Soviets countered by establishing the German Democratic Republic, tightening their grip on the governments of Hungary and Czechoslovakia, and, perhaps most alarmingly, exploding their first atomic bomb. Mao's triumph in the Chinese civil war and a series of highly publicized subversion trials in the United States, including the infamous libel and perjury litigation involving Whittaker Chambers and Alger Hiss, helped quicken the strong anti-Communist fervor already so prevalent in America.

People fleeing the communist regimes established after World War II—the recent "escapees"—were the principal beneficiaries of this sentiment. In a 1948 broadcast deploring McCarran's dilatory tactics and the slowness of Senate action to amend the DP Act, Edward R. Murrow gave it eloquent voice:

> No one has produced a name for what is happening in the countries bordering Russia. It is, quite literally, a nameless terror. For the moment it is worst in Czechoslovakia. No one knows how many people have been taken in the night, how much property has been confiscated, or who will be the next to go. It may be that ten thousand have been arrested, or the number could be five times that number. . . .
>
> It is true that we can do nothing effective to free the miserable millions in eastern Europe from the nameless terror . . . they can't get out. It is also true that on Saturday the Senate decided not to do more than we now are doing to save those who had the courage or good fortune to find themselves on the sunny side of the Iron Curtain.[142]

Murrow's remarks, prompted by the purges in Eastern Europe which occurred as the Communist parties there tightened their grip on power, were hardly apolitical. Yet in their emphasis on the victims of persecution and their acknowledgment of the limits of American power, they presented the refugee problem in humanitarian rather than instrumental terms.

Others who shared Murrow's perception of inhumanity behind the Iron Curtain believed that there was no reason to distinguish between welcoming anti-Communist refugees and using that welcome to promote American cold war goals. Thus the large majority of Democrats who favored a more liberal DP act were quickly joined by Republicans who subscribed to John Foster Dulles' view that liberation from the yoke of Moscow will not occur for a very long time, and "courage in neighboring lands will not be sustained, *unless the United States makes it publicly known that it wants and expects liberation to occur.*"[143] Chief among the converts was Alexander Wiley of Wisconsin, the nominal author of the restrictive provisions in the DP Act demanded by the Senate in 1948 Testifying before the House Judiciary Committee the following spring, he stated:

If we revise this law speedily and equitably, it will be a real inspiration to all free people. It will be an ideological weapon in our ideological war against the forces of darkness, the forces of communist tyranny.[144]

The Truman administration was equally committed to resisting "Communist tyranny" and at least as definitive in its plans for using recent "escapees" to attack despotism. Thus an administration-sponsored provision of the 1949 House amendments set aside 15,000 DP slots for recent refugees who might not be eligible under the IRO constitution.[145] According to its advocates, authorizing the admission of such refugees, many of whom were characterized as "outstanding anti-Communist leaders" who were "still risking their lives behind the Iron Curtain," would "represent an important element in our foreign policy."[146] That argument was similar to one which was employed to secure authorization in the 1949 Central Intelligence Agency Act of up to 100 special visas each year for aliens whose entry would promote "national security" or "the furtherance of the national intelligence mission."[147] The Conference Committee, meeting in June 1950, endorsed the administration's proposal, stating, "granting authority to issue a limited number of visas to such persons [will give] strong encouragement to anti-Communist elements."[148] Yet it cut the authorization from 15,000 to 500 on the grounds that "these visas should be issued only to cases of unusual appeal."[149]

Increasingly often after 1950, however, cases of "unusual appeal" began cropping up as the CIA got its program into high gear and began recruiting agents overseas for intelligence, propaganda, and guerrilla operations. Those operations developed more fully in the intensely anti-Communist atmosphere of the early 1950s. But it is clear, looking back over thirty-five years of subsequent history, that the novel emphasis in 1949 on the role "escapees" could play in the "ideological struggle" with the Soviet Union was a turning point in the evolution of America's refugee admissions policy. In ways not then foreseeable, the DP act amendments transformed refugees into objects of permanent political concern. Although part of that concern continued to focus on the special hardships and fears that distinguished many DPs and "escapees" from other migrants, another, very important part focused on the various uses to which anti-Communist migrants could be put in an increasingly bitter cold war. As refugees were employed to wage psychological warfare, their individual ability to demonstrate a personal "fear of persecution" was customarily regarded as less important than the collective message their exit from "behind the Iron Curtain" carried to those left behind and to the world.

Chapter 2

The Politics of Escape

ON SEPTEMBER 23, 1950, three months after President Truman signed the DP amendments into law, a more controversial statute—the Internal Security Act of 1950[1]—was enacted over his veto. Among the sweeping powers it gave the federal government to combat "the world Communist movement"[2] were an expanded authority to screen aliens and a mandate to exclude all subversives including those who belonged or had ever belonged to the Communist Party.[3] In his veto message, the President stated:

> It must be obvious to anyone that it is in our national interest to persuade people to renounce Communism, and to encourage their defection from Communist forces. Many of these people are extremely valuable to our intelligence operations. Yet under this bill the government would lose the limited authority it now has to offer asylum in our country as the great incentive to such defection.[4]

Truman's fears were well-founded. In the month following the passage of the Internal Security Act, rigorous screening of refugees overseas was directed not only at high-level defectors but also at DPs already in the resettlement pipeline.[5] Yet within six months the administration, supported by DP advocates inside and outside of government, had convinced a reluctant Congress[6] that foreign policy considerations demanded less restrictive security provisions.

"Involuntary" Communists were made eligible for visas in March 1951.[7] A year later, certain formerly active members of the Communist Party who had repudiated their subversive views were declared admissible by Congress.[8]

A similar sequence of events occurred during 1952 and 1953. Again Congress took the lead in passing restrictive legislation over the President's veto. On June 21, 1952, it enacted the Immigration and Nationality Act of 1952, otherwise known as the McCarran-Walter Act. The McCarran-Walter Act recodified all of American immigration law but retained the national origins quota system.[9] Two groups of special interest to the President were adversely affected: escapees who continued to stream out of Eastern Europe, and Southern European ethnics, who had been campaigning heavily for more admission slots.[10] Again, Truman used specifically anti-Communist arguments in his veto message:

> Today we are protecting ourselves, as we were in 1924, against being flooded by immigrants from Eastern Europe. This is fantastic. The countries of Eastern Europe have fallen under the Communist yoke; they are silenced, fenced off by barbed wire and mine fields; no one passes their borders but at the risk of his life. We do not need to be protected against immigrants from these countries; on the contrary, we want to stretch out a helping hand, to save those who have managed to flee into Western Europe, to succor those who are brave enough to escape from barbarism, to welcome and restore them against the day when their countries will, as we hope, be free again. . . .
>
> Today, we have entered into an alliance, the North Atlantic Treaty, with Italy, Greece, and Turkey against one of the most terrible threats mankind has ever faced. We are asking them to join with us in protecting the peace of the world. We are helping them to build their defenses, and train their men, in the common cause. But, through this bill, we say to their people: You are less worthy to come to this country than Englishmen or Irishmen; you Italians, who need to find homes abroad in the hundreds of thousands—you shall have a quota of 5,645; you Greeks, struggling to assist the helpless victims of a Communist civil war—you shall have a quota of 308; and you Turks, you are brave defenders of the eastern flank, but you shall have a quota of only 225.[11]

Again, Truman's arguments initially failed. From December 31, 1951, when the Displaced Persons Act expired,[12] until the summer of 1953, the restrictive quota system was the only vehicle for bringing immigrants—including refugees—to the United States. Once again, lobbying orchestrated by the White House produced remedial legislation. A special Commission on Immigration and Naturalization established by President Truman held extensive hearings in which dozens of witnesses from the ethnic communities, the voluntary agencies, and the U.S. government agencies involved with European reconstruction and DPs echoed a common theme: admitting more anti-

Communist refugees and admitting more ordinary immigrants from countries threatened by Communism were essential if the United States was going to win the cold war.[13] Their efforts failed to convince Congress that the national origins quota system should be abandoned.[14] But they led directly to the passage on August 7, 1953 of another piece of "emergency" legislation, the Refugee Relief Act of 1953.[15] Under its provisions, 209,000 special immigrant visas were made available outside of ordinary quota limits. Some were reserved for Italian, Greek, and German ethnics who claimed no specific hardship; but half were reserved for recent "escapees" and "refugees" who had fled the "Communist-dominated or Communist-occupied areas of Europe."[16]

The pattern revealed in each of these examples was typical of refugee policy making during the period from 1950 until the Hungarian uprising in the autumn of 1956. During that period, Congress continued to play an essentially restrictionist role. It held the keys to the nation's door and was reluctant to turn them on behalf of refugees. Part of its reluctance stemmed from the security mania of the period, which cast suspicion on all Eastern European immigrants.[17] Part stemmed from a desire to maintain the dominance of Northern and Western European culture and political power,[18] which it believed was threatened by attempts to modify or circumvent the national origins quota system. Despite these attitudes, Congress paid some heed to ethnic pressures, and proved remarkably responsive to pleas made by both the Truman and Eisenhower administrations to admit more "friends of freedom," more "able and courageous fighters against Communism."[19] Responding to both influences, it sometimes confused refugees, who had been pushed out of their native countries, with ordinary immigrants, who had left voluntarily. For both, Congress offered more expansive immigration opportunities than those customarily available under American immigration law.

The idea that refugees posed a potential security risk was an old one, deeply rooted in the restrictionist fear of "races who have known no liberty at all." At the beginning of World War II, concern about "fifth column" spies led to the almost immediate abolition of visa slots for Jewish refugees fleeing the holocaust.[20] Throughout the DP act debates, Senators Revercomb and Gossett, abetted by a number of like-minded colleagues, laid heavy emphasis on the suspect origins and politics of the "Russian Jews" and other Eastern European migrants. As the cold war intensified, Senator McCarran played on these fears, devoting a considerable amount of time and effort to demonstrating that most DPs had falsified their visa applications and were, in all probability, Communist "sleepers" whose entry would further the Soviet Union's objective of infiltrating American society.[21]

Despite evidence that many DPs had in fact evaded the rigid preference system of the original Displaced Persons Act by misrepresenting their background to American investigators, there was virtually none to suggest that any significant percentage were Communist agents. Although McCarran estimated in 1949 that 75 percent of all DPs were security risks[22] and the Senate Judiciary Committee calculated in 1953 that "at least 40 percent of the refugees from the Soviet . . . and satellite countries had subversive or criminal backgrounds,"[23] few facts were produced to support either allegation. In the years from 1950 through 1953, for example, only forty-three people were excluded as criminals, and sixty-one as subversives from Iron Curtain countries.[24] The Senate Internal Security Subcommittee claimed in 1953 that "approximately 1200 displaced persons who have been admitted into the United States have warrants for arrest for deportation against them for fraud or criminal or subversive activities."[25] Yet the allegation made no attempt to differentiate between charges of deportable offenses and actual findings that they had occurred. Nor was any attempt made to distinguish among "technical" crimes, serious criminal offenses, and actual acts of espionage or subversion. Finally the Internal Security Subcommittee failed to note that the number of alleged security risks constituted approximately one-third of 1 percent of the 350,000 displaced persons who had already entered the United States.

However, in the overheated atmosphere of the early 1950s fear predominated over reason, and naked allegations that particular groups were heavily infiltrated with Communists had the power to sway opinion at every level of society. In an era when even the courts were reluctant to protect aliens from unsubstantiated charges of subversion,[26] Congress had a field day. Already engaged in far-reaching inquiries into "un-American activities" which treated with special suspicion those with Russian origins, it proved totally willing in 1950 to identify Iron Curtain refugees as special threats. The Senate Judiciary Committee, engaged in writing new restrictive immigration legislation, explained its reasoning this way:

> Since the rise of Soviet Russia during the past three decades, the problem of subversives has become a vital consideration in any evaluation of national immigration and naturalization policies. . . . As an international conspiracy, Communism has organized systematic infiltration of our borders for the purpose of overthrowing the democratic government of the United States by force, violence and subversion.[27]

Such "infiltration" was essential to any Communist success, the Committee believed, because it was inconceivable that "native Americans" (other than those "of, or married to, Russian stock")[28] could be trusted to cooperate:

> Communism is, of necessity, an alien force. It is inconceivable that the people of the United States would, of their own violition [sic] organize or become part of a conspiracy to destroy the free institutions to which generations of

Americans have devoted themselves. The tremendous political freedom and the corollary standard of living of the United States have given this country a national entity and heritage far superior to anything which human society has created elsewhere. . . .

In the light of these facts, it is not strange that a vast majority of those who would establish a Communist dictatorship in this country come from alien lands; and it is easy to see that the forces of world Communism must have or find ways and means of getting their minions into this country if they are to maintain the effectiveness of their organization here.[29]

The immediate effect of the Internal Security Act on refugee flow to the United States was devastating. Many of those remaining in camps in Europe were "new" refugees, who had spent some time living under Communist rule before migrating to the West. Some had joined the Communist Party freely but had quickly grown disillusioned with it. Others had joined as teenagers, or had been pressured into joining so that they could continue to practice their prewar occupations. All were forbidden entry. From the fall of 1950 into the spring of 1951, visa denials to displaced persons because of Communist affiliation rose dramatically.[30] As they rose, DP admissions slowed to a trickle. The United States Displaced Persons Commission estimated that between September 1950 and March 1951, more than 100,000 refugees were adversely affected by the Attorney General's interpretation of the Internal Security Act.[31] Had the situation been permitted to continue, the full quota of visas generated by the 1950 amendments to the Displaced Persons Act would never have been filled.

The slow-down of DP processing put Congress into direct conflict with the Truman administration, the Citizens' Committee on Displaced Persons, and the governmental organization created in 1948 to administer the DP act, the United States Displaced Persons Commission. McCarran and his supporters were vigorously attacked for ignoring the suffering of those who had fled Communism only to find their pathway to America blocked.[32] Reluctantly Congress gave way. After first reporting out bills that would have benefited only former Fascists and Nazis—not former Communists[33]—it amended the Internal Security Act to permit the entry of those whose membership in the Communist Party or in other prohibited organizations (including the Nazi Party) demonstrably had been "involuntary."[34] Partly to cure the delay in admissions occasioned by the Internal Security Act's original blanket exclusion of Communists, Congress also passed a final amendment to the Displaced Persons Act in June 1951, extending its life for six additional months.[35]

The Internal Security Act, because it mandated the exclusion of formerly active, "voluntary" Communists, created other problems for the Truman administration which the 1951 amendments did not solve. Those problems arose because the American government committed itself during the early 1950s to a vigorous campaign of "psychological warfare" to encourage defection from behind the Iron Curtain as a means of destabilizing the Communist regimes of Eastern Europe, but lacked the legal authority to bring many of these defectors to the United States.

Given the broad scope of psychological warfare, the heavy emphasis put on covert action, and the continued classification of many government documents dating from the immediate postwar period, it is impossible to date the initial use of DPs and escapees as surrogate soldiers. Extensive debriefing in the DP camps was common immediately after the war, although prior to 1947 or 1948, the predominant objective of American intelligence personnel was not information about life in the eastern bloc or plotting counterrevolution, but assurance that those claiming DP status were not former Nazi collaborators.[36] Nevertheless, western intelligence agencies did make contact with anti-Communist guerrillas in the Baltic states as early as 1945, and Jouzas Luksa-Daumantas, one of their leaders, was brought out of Lithuania in 1946, trained in the United States, and several years later parachuted back in by the CIA.[37] During 1945 and 1946, sporadic contact was apparently also maintained with other indigenous resistance movements, including a fairly extensive guerrilla movement in the Ukraine.

Despite these ventures, American intelligence was not in the position to make extensive use of refugees in the immediate postwar period. Between September 1945, when OSS was disbanded, and September 1947, when the National Security Act was passed, creating the National Security Council (NSC) and the CIA, American intelligence was divided, poorly funded, and essentially passive. Even if it had an interest in exploiting anti-Soviet refugees, it lacked the capacity to do so effectively. Within three months of the CIA's creation, however, the new agency had been granted "exclusive jurisdiction to carry out secret intelligence operations"[38] and the mandate to initiate them.[39] Seven months later, as the final debates on the first DP act raged in Congress, the CIA outlined a broad agenda for conducting "psychological warfare." As defined by the NSC in 1948, it encompassed

all . . . activities which are conducted by this government against hostile foreign states or groups, but which are so planned and executed that any U.S. governmental responsibility for them is not evident to unauthorized persons and that if uncovered the U.S. government can plausibly disclaim any responsibilities for them. Specifically, such operations shall include any covert activities related to propaganda, economic warfare, preventive direct action, including sabotage, anti-sabotage, demolition and evacuation measures, subversion against hostile states, including assistance to underground resistance movements, guerrillas and refugee liberations [sic] groups, and support of indigenous anti-Communist elements in threatened countries of the free world.[40]

Direct military operations were specifically excluded from the definition, as were espionage and counterespionage.[41] However, secret information gathering from refugees appears to have been included to the extent that it promoted other covert activities.

The campaign was aided immeasurably by the passage of the Central Intelligence Act in July 1949, which gave the Director of Central Intelligence a large budget and virtually unlimited authority to spend it on projects for which there was no outside accountability.[42] It took another great leap forward during the early 1950s, when American involvement in the Korean War led to greater emphasis on national security, and new intelligence and propaganda operations in Asia. Frank Wisner's covert operations fiefdom, the Office of Policy Coordination (OPC), which was affiliated with the CIA but remained administratively independent until 1951, was one of the principal beneficiaries. In 1949, OPC had a budget of $4.7 million, employed 302 people, and ran seven overseas stations. By 1952 its budget had risen to $82 million, 74 percent of the CIA total. It employed 2,812 people as regular staff and another 3,142 as contract personnel, who were directed out of forty-seven overseas stations. In the words of one commentator, it was transformed "from an organization that was to provide a limited number of *ad hoc* operations to an organization that conducted continuing, ongoing activities on a massive scale."[43]

Many of those activities were conducted in Korea and China, and had little relationship to refugee flow. Yet operations in Europe also increased, and in April 1950 the National Security Council endorsed a major, nonmilitary counteroffensive against the Soviet bloc "including covert economic, political, and psychological warfare to stir up unrest and revolt in the satellite countries."[44] These operations, which ranged from elaborate attempts to sow discord through disinformation to actual acts of sabotage and guerrilla warfare, involved American agents and an extensive network of bureaucrats, soldiers, professional people, and ordinary citizens who had been recruited in Eastern Europe and had agreed to work covertly for the United States. They also involved a smaller but still significant number of refugees, some of whom were already waging guerrilla war in Eastern Europe, or had banded together in the United States in order to pursue policies of eventual "liberation." According to one commentator:

> During his term in the State Department Wisner had spent much of his time on problems involving refugees in Germany, Austria, and Trieste. In addition, his service with OSS had been oriented toward Central Europe. The combination of State's continuing interest and Wisner's personal experience led to

OPC's immediate emphasis on Central European refugee operations. OPC representatives made contact with thousands of Soviet refugees and emigres for the purpose of influencing their leadership.[45]

However, some of the OPC contacts involved more than influencing exile leadership. Working with "emigre groups from Poland, the Baltic states, Yugoslavia, Albania, Soviet Georgia, and the Ukraine,"[46] OPC organized extensive paramilitary and sabotage operations "behind the Iron Curtain," and began activating them in 1949. Thomas Powers has described these operations in some detail:

> Hundreds of agents were trained and air-dropped or sent in over the beach along the Baltic Coast. Large caches of arms and munitions were established in Western Europe, to be air-dropped in the event of war. Supplies, including military supplies, and funds . . . were provided to resistance groups in Russia-occupied territory. In no way was this a reluctant or half-hearted effort.[47]

Available information does not reveal how many of these agents were in fact Eastern European nationals. Yet the Psychological Strategy Board (PSB), a subcommittee of the National Security Council, estimated in December 1951 that of 18,000 "escapees from the Soviet orbit" still under IRO custody, or likely to "cross the Curtain during 1951,"[48] at least 1,000—and perhaps double that number—could be "exploited" by the United States in a combination of military, intelligence, paramilitary, and psychological programs.[49]

These figures understate the importance of the part refugees played in intelligence gathering during the late 1940s and 1950s. For the sort of "exploitation" being described involved the direct involvement of escapees in U.S. psychological warfare programs. A relatively small number of "professional" defectors were brought to the United States by what the PSB euphemistically described as "selective inducement."[50] Recruited because of their positions of importance and special knowledge, they were a select group, closely monitored by the Department of State and the Department of Defense. However, other escapees who possessed a less sophisticated understanding of Eastern European politics and security matters, and had not been selectively recruited, were customarily interviewed about conditions in their homeland. During the late 1940s and early 1950s, they were generally believed to be the best sources of general information about life "behind the Iron Curtain."

The debriefing of important defectors was conducted by the CIA itself. But from 1950 until 1956, much of the interviewing of "ordinary" escapees was under the nominal control of their brethren who earlier had fled to the West. The information generated was passed directly to the CIA. But it was also used to promote another important refugee function, that of spreading anti-Soviet propaganda. Thus a substantial number of escapees were employed as interviewers and propagandists by the National Committee for Free Europe (NCFE), a CIA front, supposedly founded at the behest of the State Department by private citizens worried about Communism, and supposedly financed by voluntary contributions. Founded in 1949, NCFE became operational early in 1950.

The NCFE had actually been created at the behest of OPC, and promoted official governmental objectives. Its centerpiece was a network of propaganda radio stations broadcasting exile statements into the satellite countries of Eastern Europe, and later into the Soviet Union itself. Broadcasting into Eastern Europe was conducted by Radio Free Europe (RFE), and broadcasting into the Soviet Union by Radio Liberty. Another set of stations, located in West Germany and nominally controlled by the U.S. military, Radio in the American Sector (RIAS), carried very similar broadcasting, which was beamed into East Germany. Each of these stations was staffed heavily by exiles. Each sought to convey the illusion that they were in fact the "genuine voice" of the people whose countries they were being beamed into. They featured interviews with famous exiles and with recent escapees, and transmitted cryptic personal messages from such escapees to their relatives who remained at home.[51] The Eastern European employees of these clandestine and semiclandestine stations were required to generate a massive amount of information from refugee interviews, interviews with recent travelers from western countries, and mail carried into the West and hand-delivered to them. The station employees channeled this information to the CIA as a matter of course. And they also served as a reverse conduit, regularly sending coded messages in their broadcasts to agents-in-place in the East.[52]

Yet the principal business of RFE and its sister stations was in fact propaganda. The basic message conveyed by all the stations was very similar: life in the United States was abundant and free; life in Eastern Europe was desperate, bereft of economic hope, of political and religious freedoms, of all popular support, and of any saving grace which could elevate it above the level of slavery and terror. From an early date, that basic message was directed not only at the victims of Communism "behind the Iron Curtain" but also at the citizens of other countries and the American people.[53]

This propaganda had two contradictory aims. One aim was confrontational, and demanded keeping dissatisfied Eastern Europeans in place, where they could stir up trouble. Particularly during President Eisenhower's first term, when "liberation" broadcasting was most overt, the propaganda stations publicly disclaimed any intent of luring more refugees across the border, since if mass exodus occurred, "the Russians would rejoice, for they would have [Eastern Europe] to themselves."[54] On the other hand, during the entire 1950–1956 period American broadcasting, both on the official Voice of

America (VOA) and on the unofficial "exile" stations, devoted extensive coverage to stories of escape, and implicitly encouraged it by consistently hammering on the horrors of life behind the Iron Curtain and the contrasting attractions of the West. Foy Kohler, in charge of the Voice of America in 1952, told the House that the United States should do more to "exploit the great resources of the defectors."[55] His example of how best to do this detailed the coverage given the "Czech freedom train" when it crashed through barriers to enter West Germany in September 1951, carrying an engineer and thirty-two passengers who decided to stay in the West. Within hours, the story was headline news on the Voice of America. Similar use was made by VOA during succeeding years of dozens of stories involving the defection of Polish Mig pilots, of disaffected seamen, and of high party officials who had grown disenchanted with Communism. In the last days of the Korean War, the Psychological Strategy Board launched a successful campaign to "exploit . . . signed-in-blood petitions of [Korean] prisoners resisting repatriation."[56] The defection of Josef Swiatlo, a colonel in the Polish security service who expressed revulsion with the Communist system, was extensively covered until Polish authorities discovered, and then demonstrated, that he had long been a CIA agent.[57] According to C. D. Jackson, President Eisenhower's adviser on psychological warfare, late in 1954, on the eve of an expected anti-American speech by Andrei Vishinsky, the Soviet Ambassador to the UN, American propaganda officials, with the "blessing of Defense, State, and Justice," and presumably the CIA,

> carefully worked out [a] plan to give asylum to a considerable number of Polish seamen, and possible Soviet seamen, and the plan went beyond just giving them asylum and included shipping them to the United States by air to arrive as early as possible, preferably just before Mr. Vishinsky's speech.[58]

Jackson was enraged when, due to a bureaucratic foul-up, the plan was never put into execution.

The interest of the Voice of America in using escapees to make propaganda points primarily to a western or neutral audience was matched by the efforts of Radio Free Europe and its sister stations. After his resignation as Deputy European Director of Radio Free Europe, Allen A. Michie recounted in considerable detail RFE programs emphasizing the same dramatic escapes that were featured on the Voice of America. After the Czech "freedom train" incident, for instance, the engineer went on the air to explain that "thirty-two of us have chosen freedom. . . . We are all here in the West—and the climate is wonderful!"[59] Similarly, in 1953 the Mig-15 pilots were put on the air. After his defection in 1954, during one three-month period Josef Swiatlo was featured on the RFE Polish broadcast 101 times, and was mentioned in 146 separate news items.[60] A policy guidance memo issued to the RFE Czechoslovakian station emphasized that if party officials were not willing to act against their superiors, they should at least be encouraged to "defect to the west."[61] A similar secret directive, approved by James B. Conant, the U.S. High Commissioner for Germany, authorized RIAS to broadcast the following message to the East German People's Police (VOPOs):

> Special message to VOPO's
> Fellow Germans, Germany is certain once again to be united and free. We know that with God's help that day is coming. How can you risk shooting and maltreating other Germans whose only crime is that they are hungry? They will not (repeat not) forget. Come over to the side of freedom. You are welcome here.[62]

The effect of this sort of propaganda on the people of Eastern Europe is not easy to measure. However, it is clear that a significant percentage of each broadcast day was devoted to tales of escape and to the accomplishments of exiles in America. Several studies conducted for the American intelligence community during the early 1950s measuring the effectiveness of radio propaganda have recently been declassified. Although largely anecdotal, they indicate that such programs had a large audience, were particularly popular with Eastern European listeners,[63] and were directly responsible for some defections.[64]

By consistently contrasting the drabness, regimentation, and poverty of Eastern Europe with the wealth and opportunity of the "free world," these broadcasts highlighted the economic incentive for migration, which in many individual cases was probably more important than personal fear of persecution. Life in the Communist satellite nations was economically and politically harsh. The standard of living was only a fraction of that available in the West. Adequate housing and consumer goods were nearly nonexistent. Of course, political compulsion did engender considerable dissatisfaction. Based on hundreds of refugee interviews, one early study concluded that particular resentment was aroused by "attendance at various Communist meetings," the forced collectivization of farms and requisitioning from peasants of agricultural products, strict industrial sabotage laws, and "the omnipotence and omnipresence of secret police, which create an atmosphere of fear and suspicion and which, combined with other hardships, make life behind the Iron Curtain generally unhappy and miserable."[65] Yet the same study explicitly noted that

> current refugees from Poland, Hungary and Czechoslovakia do not defect because of ideological or political dissatisfaction with Communism but because of the poor living conditions in the Satellite countries. . . . Only a handful of those now arriving in the West can be considered to be escaping from Communism as a political system or from actual persecution. The usual story is rather one of disaffection and general tiredness with the material and physical

conditions of life in the satellite countries. The story is also one of great expectations with respect to conditions of life in the West.[66]

Similar conclusions were contained in a study prepared for the State Department in 1951.[67]

Thus the American propaganda program was at least partially responsible for the continuing movement of escapees into the West. As their numbers increased, immigration problems became more evident, and pressures to liberalize the DP act further grew. Some of these immigration problems involved the unresolved question of how to treat fully "voluntary" Communists and formerly committed Nazis with intelligence information. As of the spring of 1952, all—with exception of 100 aliens a year admissible under the CIA act—remained technically ineligible for visas. During the early years of the psychological warfare campaign, most defectors were assigned to Europe, and others were brought to the United States without the required screening.[68] Included were hundreds of Byelorussians and Ukrainians formerly associated with the Nazis—and in some instances, deeply implicated in Nazi war crimes against Jews and other civilians.[69] Wisner, working outside of ordinary channels, secured fraudulent visas for them, as he did for "important Nazi collaborators from the Baltic states and the Balkans."[70] According to the most thorough published account:

> Frank Wisner designed a program to smuggle his "Freedom Fighters" into the United States, where he could prepare them for the coming war of liberation. He instructed OPC to concentrate on refugees who had been high-level political collaborators. They were to be brought to the United States to set up "national committees for liberation" for each country behind the Iron Curtain. . . .[71]

Wisner's focus on former Nazi collaborators provided few immigration opportunities for more moderate defectors who had worked cooperatively with Eastern European Communist regimes, but now sought to enter the United States. Although Wisner had little personal interest in encouraging their escape, others anxious to liberate Eastern Europe did. Thus a legal means of obtaining visas for such defectors was required, as were better accommodations in Europe for those escaping, and a new immigration program which would permit more Eastern European migrants to enter the United States.

The early pressure for legislative reform came from those in the administration most committed to the escapee program—and from private voluntary agency personnel and segments of the national press with close links to those running that program. Harry N. Rosenfield, a member of the United States Displaced Persons Commission, was one of the more active proponents of new, generous legislation. He argued that the United States was "spending millions of dollars to encourage resistance from behind the Iron Curtain and defection from Communism," but "fail[ing] to make good on its word to the victims of the propaganda war with the Soviet Union."[72] Rosenfield supported a program which included not only aid but also "amendment of our immigration law to permit migration to the United States of some of these Iron Curtain Refugees."[73]

John McCloy, then U.S. Commissioner for Germany, struck a cautionary note. A December 1951 memorandum by Rosenfield indicated that McCloy

> has considerable misgivings as to the wisdom of encouraging defection from behind the Iron Curtain. He believes that the U.S. should put more effort inside the countries behind the Iron Curtain and less on encouragement of emigration to the Western Zones. [He believes] that once defectors came out, their efforts were diluted and their influence behind the Iron Curtain diminished. He put it very succinctly: "The more defectors, the less potential resistors."
>
> If despite these views, there were to be any special defector program, McCloy urged that the U.S. limit its effort to persons with special information or special talents. All others, he felt—and repeated several times—should be discouraged. Frankly, he said, few of the defectors have been of much use to us. Mass defectors, he insisted, would do harm, especially if nothing is done for such people; they cannot be given a "pretty easy life," as he put it, and therefore might become a source of counter-Western propaganda.[74]

However, Walter J. Donnelly, the American Ambassador to Austria, and General LeRoy Irwin, Commanding General, U.S. Forces in Austria, "firmly and vigorously espoused encouraging defection," and supported a defector program which would widen the immigration channels to the United States.[75] Their views were vociferously seconded by Ellis Briggs, the American Ambassador to Czechoslovakia, who argued that "nothing contributes more substantially to West and U.S. objectives than successful escapes, particularly spectacular ones like Freedom Train."[76] In Briggs' view:

> . . . it would be unthinkable for us publicly to discourage escapes or to permit widespread belief we are only interested in "important defectors" (whereas small fry had better stay and bear it or, if they escape, anticipate lengthy sojourns in refugee camps). Furthermore, the idea that the flow of refugees other than those technically defined as defectors represents a drain on elements constituting potential resistance movement within Czechoslovakia is opposed to facts as seen from here.[77]

The voluntary agencies also supported a more generous admissions policy. Most accepted the link between such a policy and overt anti-Communism. Associated with churches, emigré groups, and exiled intellectuals, all served clienteles which had been specially singled out for persecution. All came into daily contact with horrific stories of border crossings cut short by land mines, bullets, and barbed wire. They found it easy to believe that every escapee, through flight, was voting not only for a better material life, but for more political freedom. These reasons, and the desire to obtain governmental support for rescue and relief endeavors, help to explain why they permitted themselves to be used by those waging psychological warfare. Even today, it is not clear whether in being used, they understood or accepted the central role of the CIA and Frank Wisner's Office of Policy Coordination. Yet at least in the case of the International Rescue Committee (IRC), which took the lead in promoting escapee programs, strong circumstantial evidence suggests an awareness of intelligence involvement. Thus in October 1949 IRC launched its "Iron Curtain Refugee Campaign." Admiral Richard E. Byrd and General Carl Spaatz, men with close ties to the Truman administration, the intelligence community, and the National Committee for a Free Europe (NCFE), directed that campaign. At its inaugural luncheon, flanked by "refugee leaders from all the Iron Curtain countries,"[78] Byrd declared that refugees from Eastern Europe "are a symbol of the spirit we would like to mobilize to hold back totalitarian darkness."[79] Lt. Gen. Walter Bedell Smith also spoke to the gathering. Two months later, Smith was appointed Director of Central Intelligence by the President. Even stronger evidence of an IRC–intelligence community link emerged in 1951, when the Psychological Strategy Board established its top secret "Psychological Operations Plan for Soviet Orbit Escapees."[80] That plan called for the erection of a new escapee program which would bring refugees to the United States under some rubric which would be operationally sound and legal under U.S. immigration law yet would still make important defectors available to the intelligence and propaganda communities.[81] The Board considered putting the entire escapee program under the direction of IRC, which it believed "would be willing to work closely with NCFE."[82] Its reason for not pursuing the idea further was the view that "the present Executive Director of IRC has not been reliable in dealing with the U.S. Government and is not fully supported by the State Department."[83]

However, those reservations proved to be temporary. The ailing Reinhold Niebuhr was replaced by a new executive director, Leo Cherne.[84] When President Truman established the new United States Escapee Program (USEP) as a State Department operation in 1952,[85] the IRC worked closely with it to promote aid and resettlement.

A national press exceptionally sympathetic to anti-Communist escapees— and to the foreign policy objectives their migration would promote—also played an important role in getting the legislative ball rolling once again. Supplied with background information by the intelligence agencies, some of its principal constituents—the major television networks and the weekly and monthly news magazines—laid heavy emphasis on the difficulties ordinary citizens faced behind the Iron Curtain, and adopted the general line that all were victims of overt persecution.[86]

Such an approach owed something to the general tenor of the time. But it probably owed at least as much to the elaborate ties which linked the news media to American intelligence. Thus Edward Barret, who, as Assistant Secretary of State for Public Affairs, was responsible for America's official propaganda effort, was a former editor at *Newsweek;* C. D. Jackson, who assumed the directorship of the National Committee for a Free Europe and later served the Eisenhower administration in a number of capacities, was the former editor of *Fortune;* Henry Luce, the publisher of *Time* and *Life,* and DeWitt Wallace, the publisher of the *Reader's Digest,* served as members of NCFE; and David Sarnoff, a brigadier general in the U.S. Army Reserve and president of RCA, the parent of the National Broadcasting Company, served as the chairman of the "Crusade for Freedom," the public relations and fund-raising arm of NCFE. The involvement of the American press in psychological warfare was thus not limited to a few reporters who also worked for the CIA; it was epidemic and most visible in the board rooms of the largest and most influential news organizations.

The political power of these advocates of escape was sufficient to win several important concessions from Congress. In 1951, the Mutual Security Act authorized an expenditure

> not to exceed $100,000,000 . . . for any selected persons who are residing in or are escapees from the Soviet Union, Poland, Czechoslovakia, Hungary, Rumania, Bulgaria, Albania, Lithuania, Latvia, or Estonia, or the Communist dominated or Communist occupied areas of Germany and Austria . . . either to form such persons into elements of the military force supporting [NATO] or for other purposes, when it is . . . determined by the President that such assistance will contribute to the defense of the North Atlantic area and to the security of the United States.[87]

An amendment to the Mutual Security Act sponsored by Rep. Charles Kersten, a vigorous supporter of "liberation," was immediately approved which appropriated $4.2 million for these purposes.[88] That money was immediately channeled into President Truman's new escapee program.[89] Finally, as part of its sweeping revisions of the nation's immigration law, Congress approved the granting of visas to formerly subversive aliens, provided they "completely defected" from the Communist Party or other banned organization and demonstrated "active opposition" to the doctrines and programs of the party or organizations for at least five years, and provided their admission served the "public interest."[90]

Yet the McCarran-Walter Immigration and Nationality Act, which became law in June, 1952, provided no mechanism for creating any additional visas for refugees. Instead, it left the national origins quota system intact and did nothing to lift the quota "mortgages" imposed by the Displaced Persons Act. This conservatism was attributable to a variety of factors. The intensive ethnic lobbying which had been such an important influence on policy making between 1947 and 1950 diminished greatly after the passage of the DP act amendments. Senator McCarran, as Chairman of the Senate Judiciary Committee, retained considerable power to shape legislation affecting immigration. By limiting hearings on comprehensive immigration reform[91] and by carefully selecting those permitted to testify, he managed to fashion a legislative agenda which focused almost exclusively on popular domestic issues.[92] Months were spent fashioning a "preference" system which would grant visa priorities to those with needed skills or with close relatives in the United States.[93] The exclusionary provisions of the law were substantially reworked—and significantly strengthened.[94] Relying heavily on arguments that the United States should maintain its existing ethnic balance to promote social stability, the lawmakers adjusted the existing quota system only slightly.[95] Thus the census of 1940 was used to determine the percentage of Americans belonging to each alien nationality. And in response to the urgings of the Asian community in the United States—and the tireless efforts of Rep. Walter Judd,[96] who had spent years as a missionary doctor in China—the absolute barriers to the entry of most Asians were dropped, although the quotas they were afforded numbered only a few hundred.[97]

The change made on behalf of Asians clearly reflected Representative Judd's concerns about America's waning influence in the Far East in the wake of Mao's successful October 1949 revolution.[98] Yet Congress displayed no willingness to institute sweeping changes in the basic immigration statute on the basis of general Truman administration assertions that such changes would generally make the United States "look good" in the eyes of the world[99] or were necessary to solve an overwhelming refugee problem. The reluctance was probably due as much to the Truman administration's approach to immigrants and refugees during 1950-1951 as it was to Congress' own latent restrictionism. Thus, despite early support for an escapee program, neither the President nor his close advisers gave any indication that they favored international efforts to resettle any significant numbers of new refugees in the United States. Nor did they make any demands for changes in the quota system, or indeed for any new special refugee legislation during the period when the McCarran-Walter bill was being drafted.

The new caution which the Truman administration displayed toward international resettlement efforts manifested itself as early as 1949, when the United States made it clear it would not support an indefinite extension of the IRO's life.[100] Although it permitted the IRO to remain in operation until the end of 1950, American officials resisted Western European and Third World pressures and insisted that its successor, the Office of the United Nations High Commissioner for Refugees (UNHCR), be given no resettlement and virtually no relief responsibilities.[101] In the months that followed, the United States refused to contribute any funds to UNHCR emergency operations, withholding all financial support until 1955.[102] The Truman administration also refused to sign the 1951 Convention Relating to the Status of Refugees, promulgated by the UNHCR, which would have imposed a positive duty on the United States to avoid the involuntary repatriation of any person who faced probable persecution in Europe[103] on account of race, religion, national origin, or political beliefs.[104]

Part of the reason for America's lukewarm support for UN refugee operations was cost. UNRRA had been phenomenally expensive, and the IRO, despite the early assurances given to Congress, had proven to be a costly operation which, three years after its inception, had managed to resettle only a fraction of the world's refugees. By 1950, the United States was leery of making any open-ended commitments to refugees. Events in India, Korea, Indonesia, China, and the Middle East, where new refugees had been created by the millions, and along the perimeter of the Iron Curtain, through which escapees continued to stream, convinced American officials that the world refugee problem was virtually limitless. They were not willing to pledge unlimited support to those displaced by oppressive regimes. Instead, Mrs. Roosevelt, who had again been selected to speak for the nation in the United Nations, laid special emphasis on the limits of American generosity, warning against an

> increasing tendency to drive the United Nations into the field of international relief and to use its organs as the source and center of expanding appeals for relief funds.[105]

Yet the principal American objection to an expansive UNHCR was not that it would be an expensive operation, but that its expenditures might benefit refugees who were of little political interest to the United States and might create more demands for their resettlement in the United States. The United States was willing to pour millions of dollars each year into two UN agencies which it was chiefly responsible for creating. The first, the United Nations Relief and Works Agency (UNRWA), enhanced stability in the Middle East by providing aid—but no resettlement opportunities—to Palestinian refugees.[106] The second, the United Nations Korean Reconstruction Agency (UNKRA), provided a similar limited service to several hundred thousand people driven from their homes by the Communists during the Korean War.[107] The United States was also willing to extend considerable financial support to another agency, purposely established in 1951 by the United States outside of the United Nations, which addressed the problem of overpopulation in Western Europe. That agency, the Intergovernmental Committee for European Migration (ICEM), reflected beliefs commonly held in the United States during the early 1950s that West Germany—as well as perhaps Italy, Greece, and the Netherlands—was afflicted with the endemic problem of "surplus population" because of post-World War II involuntary migration and high birth rates. Anti-Communists in Congress, including Rep. Francis Walter, the Chairman of the House Immigration Subcommittee, feared that the press of a large, unemployable, and discontented population threatened European recovery. As importantly, they feared that the "surplus population" of West Germany was ripe for Communist exploitation. Thus they supported *in principle* the movement of up to a million Germans to other countries facing significant labor shortages.[108] In advocating the creation of ICEM as a means of moving such people, however, they sought to encourage migration to Latin America, Canada, and Australia and to minimize demands that the United States provide extra immigration opportunities.

The Truman administration initially shared this view. Its early silence on the McCarran-Walter bill was matched by a lack of effort to bring any segment of the "surplus population" to the United States. However, during 1951 and 1952 the Greek and Italian communities, convinced that the existing restrictive quota system was going to be retained by Congress, began clamoring for a special admissions program. Only then did the Truman administration link the problems of European overpopulation to its concerns with escapees and propose temporary legislation which would bring members of both groups to the United States as "emergency migrants."

Facing certain defeat in his attempts to kill the McCarran-Walter bill, President Truman launched his new legislative initiative on March 24, 1952. In a message delivered to Congress on that date, he asserted that overpopulation in parts of Western Europe was "one of the gravest problems arising from the present world crisis."[109] He declared that "this situation, aggravated by the plight of refugees escaping from Communist tyranny behind the Iron Curtain, is of great practical importance to the United States because it affects the peace and security of the free world."[110] He therefore advocated a program which would provide aid to "refugees from Communism," continue U.S. participation in existing international programs for migration and resettlement, and initiate a three-year special authorization which would permit up to 100,000 migrants a year to enter the United States outside of the national origins quota system.[111] The intended beneficiaries of this program were the USEP and the refugees it was designed to serve, ICEM, and members of the "surplus population" of Greece, the Netherlands, West Germany, and Italy, who would be brought to the United States under the auspices of ICEM.

The effect of the Truman proposal was to yoke provisions which would give aid and limited entry opportunities to genuine refugees to other provisions which appeared to give "back door" immigration preferences to members of particular nationalities. By tying immigration provisions to politically-popular training of anti-Communist resistance forces, the administration hoped to generate additional support for the admission, not only of refugees, but also of migrants from Western European countries threatened by Communism. This strategy was especially popular with those in government seeking to maximize immigration, but was resisted by those anxious to preserve the integrity of the escapee program. Reporting confidentially on the message before it was delivered, the Department of State expressed strong reservations about including refugee and overpopulation questions in a single package. It acknowledged that concern about surplus population was entirely consistent with the State Department's "international efforts to stimulate migration,"[112] but it identified the provisions relating to the "*admission* to the United States of persons who are residents of overpopulated European countries" as "essentially a matter of domestic internal policy."[113] On the other hand, it expressed the belief that "the proposals for the reception, care, and training of refugees from a Soviet orbit country are essentially matters of important foreign policy."[114] Its apparent concern was that the administration, by tying the "surplus population" issue to the objectives of the escapee program, endangered the Congressional support which already existed for USEP. That support had recently been manifested in the $100 million authorization for NATO-related refugee operations under the Mutual Security Act of 1951 and was considered too valuable to jeopardize.[115] However, other government agencies were more positive about the proposed message, and the Displaced Persons Commission, in one of its last official acts, strongly endorsed combining the escapee program provisions and those relating to the surplus population problem. Thus it argued that

> the deletion of the proposal concerning training for leadership [of exiles] would limit the President's program substantially to immigration and would narrow the broad base of the President's message as an anti-Communist measure. The current mood of the Congress is to do all possible for refugees from Communism; on the other hand, its mood is to restrict rather than extend immigration. . . . If training for leadership is retained, the program becomes a natural development of the President's "bold" program to counter Communist lies with democratic truths.[116]

The Displaced Persons Commission won the exchange, and for the remainder of the Truman administration the attempt was made to promote more immigration for refugees *and* the residents of specific European countries by emphasizing that in *either* case, more admissions would promote the goals of a vigorous anti-Communism. Truman was almost certainly aware how little time remained in his presidency to reshape immigration policy. Yet by pursuing change, he was able to shape a party policy that would appeal to the interests of specific ethnic groups, give evidence that the Democrats were not "soft on Communism," and skirt the political dangers of attacking the national origins quota system head-on during a period when restrictionism was again ascendant. Thus in June 1952 Truman appointed a Presidential Commission on Immigration and Naturalization, which was charged with developing the arguments for an immigration policy consistent with the President's March 24 message. Composed primarily of former supporters of the displaced persons program, the Presidential Commission held extensive hearings which strove to gather testimony from groups which had been systematically excluded during the 1951 McCarran Act hearings. Ethnic and religious leaders, voluntary agency personnel, the entire past and present leadership of the Displaced Persons Commission, U.S. foreign aid officials, and most of the members of the President's cabinet were called to testify. Almost all called for more American generosity. Their common refrain was that more admissions—of recent escapees, of residual World War II displaced persons, of unemployed Greek or Italian or German workers—would promote the image of America as a liberal society while at the same time striking a blow against Communism.

The Truman approach was anathema to some Democrats and many Republicans, who continued to regard refugees and other migrants as undesirable aliens unusually prone to subversion. However, when President Eisenhower assumed office in 1953, he followed Truman's policy with scarcely any deviation. Despite Republican resistance to any amendment of the McCarran-Walter Act and the strong influence of Sen. Joseph McCarthy in the State Department's Bureau of Security and Consular Affairs, which served as a consistent brake on Eastern European admissions, Eisenhower supported and helped push through a bill in 1953 which embraced most of the suggestions made by President Truman in his March 24, 1952 speech.

President Eisenhower's willingness to support a new "refugee relief act" undoubtedly owed something to the efforts of Arthur Bliss Lane, who sought to convince the President first to pursue a more active "liberation" policy and then to actively woo voters of Eastern European origin by adopting a more generous Republican approach to immigration.[117] Yet Eisenhower's own political attitudes also favored more immigration. Neither a committed "liberationist" nor an old-line "restrictionist," he did not believe that Communism would be quickly uprooted from European soil or that all aliens posed a threat to America's safety. He was willing to publicly endorse the rhetoric of "rollback," yet foresaw a long-term political struggle in Europe and a continuous outflow of people from behind the Iron Curtain. Unlike President Truman, he did not invest much political capital in campaigning for immigration reform, nor was he willing to exert his authority to curb the State Department's vendetta against escapees it regarded as being subversive. Yet his general instincts, expressed in speeches he made during his 1952 campaign[118] and during his presidency, were to support the admission of anti-Communist migrants. Likewise, he was aware that an immigration policy which favored Greek and Italian migrants might prove to be a political asset.

Almost immediately after assuming office, President Eisenhower sent a message to Congress requesting emergency legislation for the admission of more European migrants.[119] His principal claim was that growing population pressures in Europe necessitated immediate action. Pointing particularly to the situation in Greece, he warned that failure to act could nurture Communism and seriously endanger the western alliance. Gen. Walter Bedell Smith, serving as Acting Secretary of State, explained the situation to the House of Representatives in by-now familiar terms, insisting that the proposed legislation was temporary and specific, and that it addressed important American foreign policy concerns:

> We are now . . . faced with problems which have an important impact upon the health and stability of friendly countries in Europe. These are problems arising in part out of the war and in part out of totalitarianism. They are problems both of population pressures and of escapees, escapees from persecution. And they are creating situations in certain parts of Europe which gravely endanger the objectives of American foreign policy.[120]

As originally submitted in the House, the legislation which embodied the President's recommendation was entitled "the Emergency Migration Act of 1953." That title accurately reflected the priorities of the bill, which after significant changes was passed into law on August 7, 1953, as the Refugee Relief Act of 1953. Of the 209,000[121] special nonquota immigrants permitted entry during the act's three-year term, only a small percentage, including some 5,000 Far Eastern migrants, 2,000 Palestinian migrants, and 10,000 "escapees" residing in other NATO countries, were both stateless and fearful of persecution, and thus "refugees" in the limited sense recognized by the UNHCR. However, due to the definitions employed by the drafters of the 1953 statute, nearly half of those covered by its terms were officially categorized as "refugees." Thus the Refugee Act of 1953 defined the term "refugee" to include any person in a country or area which is neither Communist nor Communist-dominated, who because of persecution, fear of persecution, natural calamity or military operations is out of his usual place of abode and unable to return thereto, who has not been firmly resettled, and who is in urgent need of assistance for the essentials of life or for transportation.[122]

That definition, as it was applied in Western Europe, effectively eliminated the need to distinguish so-called "economic migrants" from "political refugees." Those displaced and rendered destitute by recent "military operations" (including World War II, which had ended eight years earlier) were rendered eligible for visas, as were a certain number of their immediate relatives.

Thus, in addition to providing 4,000 visas for orphaned children and 7,000 for Dutch immigrants, the act set aside 55,000 spaces for German expellees from Eastern Europe residing in West Germany, West Berlin, and Austria; 35,000 spaces for "escapees" in those areas; 60,000 spaces for Italian immigrants; and 17,000 for Greeks. All of these migrants, with the exception of some of the German and Austrian "escapees," were nationals of the state from which they sought entry, although some—like the German expellees, persons of Italian ethnic origin who had been displaced from land annexed by Yugoslavia, and persons of Dutch ethnic origin who had been displaced from Indonesia—had obtained their nationality only after World War II.

The open-endedness of the definition of the term "refugee" caused some in Congress, including Representative Walter, to attack the act on the grounds that it had destroyed the numerical limits imposed by the McCarran-Walter Act.[123] As importantly, the spectre of risks to national security was again invoked to challenge a generous admissions policy. Because the distinction between refugees and other migrants was so vague, traditional restrictionists and those whose chief concern was national security were spurred to seek greater control in the implementation of the act. One means of imposing that control was to rigorously enforce the act's security requirements, which fell with particular severity on those who had arrived most recently in Western Europe, i.e., those most clearly fleeing persecution. Thus each alien covered by the act was required to undergo a thorough security check and to provide a complete and verifiable history of his or her activities during the two years prior to visa application.[124] Recent arrivals had the most difficulty establishing the facts of their recent personal history, and were systematically denied entry by the State Department's Bureau of Security Affairs, under the direction of Scott McLeod. Through the spring of 1955, out of some 108,000 aliens admitted under the act, only 1,044 qualified under the sections granting entry to "refugees."[125]

The restrictive element of the 1953 act's refugee provisions was revealed to the nation in a well-publicized scandal which erupted when Francis Corsi, who had been hired by the State Department to administer the act, was unceremoniously fired by John Foster Dulles. Corsi blamed his firing on McLeod, Representative Walter, and Senator McCarran and claimed that they had worked systematically to scuttle the act because they were obsessed with national security, indifferent to the plight of genuine refugees, and were overly protective of the national origins quota system. Congressional hearings held in 1955 on the administration of the Refugee Relief Act substantially bore out Corsi's story, although they did not win him back his job.[126] Nevertheless, they prompted the President to move McLeod out of the chain of operational command. This led to a more evenhanded administration of the act and largely put to rest the concerns about national security which had plagued immigration and refugee policy during the 1950s. In a real sense, they signaled the end of McCarthyism, which had survived uncommonly long in the immigration and security offices of the Department of State.

Corsi's moral victory had significant implications for Republican immigration and refugee politics. Pierce Gerety, who assumed responsibility in the State Department for administering the Refugee Relief Act of 1953, advocated more sensitivity to ethnic politics when considering immigration legislation. A similar position was taken by the Republican National Committee, which, despairing of winning the Eastern European vote through the pursuit of overt "liberation" policies, turned to immigration reform as an alternative method of winning that vote. According to one commentator:

> If Yalta and liberation were not going to be Republican issues of the campaign, how would the party appeal to the ethnic groups? On July 31, the *New York Herald-Tribune* supplied the answer. According to staff reporter Earl Mazo, the Republican party, in its attempt to get the nationality vote, would have a platform plank promising the easing of immigration restrictions. "The foreign policy plank," Mazo wrote, "is expected to appeal to those whose native lands are now dominated by Russia."[127]

Implicit in this strategy was the belief, held by most in the Republican Party, that Europe would not rise up in spontaneous revolt, and that there were limits to how much aid the United States could give to local uprisings, such as the one that occurred in Berlin during June 1953. Refugee policy was thus assimilated back into the mainstream of immigration politics, where generosity was measured out according to its potential domestic political effect.

However, "liberation" activists in Congress, in the CIA, in private voluntary organizations, and on Eisenhower's staff had a different view. They continued to regard admissions questions in exclusively cold war terms. Some, like Ambassador Ellis Briggs, believed that mass escape had enormous propaganda value, while others, like C. D. Jackson, believed that the eventual revolution would have to be won by brave anti-Communist partisans willing to remain home and do battle. The more moderate of these "hard-liners" encouraged escape because of the message it would send back "behind the curtain."

Typical of their efforts was the launching in late 1955 and early 1956 of a program to counter the so-called "Soviet Redefection Campaign," which sought with some success to persuade escapees to abandon the West and return to their native lands. "Redefection" had been a concern of the CIA since at least 1952, when Allen Dulles warned the House Foreign Affairs Committee meeting in executive session that failure to provide better facilities and a warmer welcome for escapees would promote their return.[128] That concern intensified in the middle 1950s, when more Eastern Europeans began to "redefect." Whether promoted by the CIA or inspired by their own anti-Communist views, Leo Cherne and the IRC again took the lead in marshaling public opinion in favor of "escapees." The IRC's criticism of the Soviet campaign, focusing on instances of blackmail, threats to family members, kidnapping, and even murder, spoke of the "iron hand . . . beneath the velvet glove."[129] Yet its principal concern, in common with that of American intelligence officials, was with the campaign's propaganda effects, which it concluded could serve

> (1) to break the back of the liberation movements in exile, (2) to discourage others behind the Iron Curtain who were disposed to consider escape, (3) to deprive the West of the priceless propaganda element inherent in the mass escape of refugees from the Communist "paradise," (4) to provide the Communist propaganda apparatus with a steady supply of redefectors, whose stories of "disillusionment" in the West were most useful for general consumption at home and for broadcasts to the uncommitted countries of Asia and Africa.[130]

To avoid those negative effects, the IRC helped launch a counterpropaganda effort, and helped persuade Congress and the federal bureaucracy to be more generous to those who had fled. However, the hardest of the "hard-liners," men like General James Doolittle and Frank Wisner, were not content with symbolic victories that a more generous policy could bring. Convinced that the cold war required opponents of Communism to do more than flee, they helped initiate projects which contributed to the tragedy in Hungary in 1956 and to a brand new American way of responding to refugees.

Chapter 3

Finding Room
for the Freedom Fighters

IN THE MIDDLE of Eisenhower's first term, the President initiated a review of the CIA's covert operations. Gen. James Doolittle, who had gained fame by leading bombing raids over Tokyo during World War II, and who was well acquainted with Frank Wisner[1] and the OPC, was put in charge of the review panel. The Doolittle report endorsed existing operations, and bluntly recommended that they be extended:

> It is now clear we are facing an implacable enemy whose avowed objective is world domination by whatever means and at whatever cost. There are no rules in such a game. Hitherto acceptable norms of human conduct do not apply. If the United States is to survive, long-standing American concepts of "fair play" must be reconsidered. We must develop effective espionage and counterespionage services and must learn to subvert, sabotage and destroy our enemies by more clear, more sophisticated, and more effective methods than those used against us.[2]

The President concurred. On March 12, 1955, the National Security Council issued Memorandum 5412/1 with his approval. NSC 5412/1 had as its principal objective "creat[ing] and exploit[ing] problems for international communism."[3] It approved

Subversion against hostile states or groups including assistance to underground resistance movements, guerrillas, and refugee liberation groups.[4]

By endorsing and acting on the Doolittle report, the President accepted personal responsibility for America's part in the secret war which continued to be waged in Eastern Europe. Despite significant doubt about that war's possible success,[5] he allowed Wisner to continue plotting counterrevolution, and to continue recruiting and training the exiles who were waging it. He therefore bore a heavy burden of blame when "liberation" failed in Hungary and tens of thousands of Hungarian refugees streamed into Austria and Yugoslavia. He shouldered that blame by stretching American immigration law almost beyond recognition, admitting some 32,000 Hungarians to the United States who were not eligible for visas under the restrictive national origins quota system and were not the beneficiaries of special legislation. He was able to do so because of a small loophole in the law which gave the Attorney General authority to temporarily "parole" aliens into the United States "for emergent reasons or for reasons deemed strictly in the public interest."[6] Congress understood that this loophole was being expanded, but out of sympathy for the "freedom fighters" took no immediate steps to reassert its own authority to regulate immigration. Nor did it take remedial action a few years later when the Kennedy administration, engaged in a secret and similarly unsuccessful war in this hemisphere, used parole to admit anti-Castro Cubans. Thus the politics of failed liberation yielded as their surprising fruit a new, executive-dominated method of bringing refugees to the United States.

On November 4, 1956, the link between a generous refugee admissions policy and American hopes for the liberation of Europe was shattered. On that day the Soviet army entered Hungary in force, toppling the week-old government of Imre Nagy, which had come to power on the heels of a popular uprising, had introduced multiparty rule, and had announced Hungary's withdrawal from the Warsaw Pact. Even before the decisive Soviet military assault, hundreds of Hungarian nationals—including some associated with the Kadar regime which Nagy had displaced—had begun moving toward the Austro-Hungarian border. By far the greatest number, however, were those who left after the Soviet invasion. Between November 3, 1956, and mid-February 1957, when the Austro-Hungarian border was effectively closed,[7] approximately 180,000 Hungarians entered Austria. An additional 20,000 Hungarians crossed the Hungarian-Yugoslavian border, which remained open for another month.[8]

Of these 200,000 migrants, probably only a small percentage were "freedom fighters." Paul Tabori, a post-World War II Hungarian immigrant to the United Kingdom who played a key role in British resettlement in the winter of 1956, wrote:

. . . the vast majority were not political refugees, had not taken an active part in the revolution, but had simply left a life that was drab and hopeless. For the first time in almost fifty years the frontiers were open *both ways*—you could get out and other countries would let you in—so anybody who had a second cousin in Auckland or an uncle in Sydney got going. This did not detract from the severe judgment the people who voted with their feet had passed on their homeland—for if [Hungary's] borders had remained open a little longer, some 10 percent of Hungary's population would have left.[9]

James A. Michener, the American novelist, who accompanied a team from the International Rescue Committee to the Austro-Hungarian border, reached a similar conclusion. Thus he identified three waves of Hungarian migrants: the small group that left before the Nagy government had fallen, composed, in his view, primarily of "prostitutes," "young adventurers," and "cowards who could not face up to the requirements of a free Hungary";[10] and two larger groups with stronger credentials. Quoting "certain Austrian immigration officials," Michener noted:

. . . the first wave of adventurous young people numbered not more than three thousand. . . . The second wave of real refugees totalled about twenty-five thousand. But remember, even of this select group not more than two thousand had played any vital role in the revolution. That leaves around one hundred and seventy thousand who came out in the third wave, and practically none of them ever fired upon a Russian or committed himself in any way during the revolution. You've seen them. They're fine clean, healthy, middle-class people who hated communism and saw a good chance to escape. No doubt many of them wanted to get out ten years ago. This was their chance.[11]

According to Michener, many in the second wave fled Hungary because to have remained behind would have been to invite execution or deportation to slave labor camps in Russia."[12] Yet he believed that the "members of the third wave neither participated in the revolution nor had any reprisals to fear therefrom."[13]

In the narrow legal sense, then, it seems certain that most of the Hungarians who fled their homeland in 1956 and 1957 possessed no "well-founded fear of persecution" and were not technically refugees when they left Hungary—although it seems likely that because of their departure and subsequent activities in the West, some would have faced harsh treatment had they elected to return.[14] Yet the reaction to the Hungarians did not turn on fine distinctions between the merely dissatisfied and the patently fearful. The brutality and cynicism of the Soviet assault, which occurred after a partial withdrawal of Soviet forces in October and early indications that a peaceful solution might be accepted by the Soviet government, was everywhere apparent. Austria opened its borders to all comers, and most of the countries of

Western Europe immediately began to provide resettlement opportunities. France and Great Britain announced their willingness to take an unlimited number of Hungarians.[15] Aided by ICEM and by the UNHCR (which played an especially active role in the movement of Hungarians out of Yugoslavia), Great Britain took approximately 21,000 Hungarian migrants; West Germany, 15,000; Switzerland, 13,000; France, 13,000; Sweden, 7,000; and Belgium, 6,000.[16] Similar generosity was displayed by some of the less heavily populated countries of Europe, such as Denmark and Norway, and was quickly matched by the actions of a number of non-European nations. Thus Canada accepted 37,000 Hungarians; Australia, 11,000; and Israel, 2,000.[17] And several thousand more were brought to Latin America by the governments of Honduras, Guatemala, Venezuela, Argentina, and Brazil.[18]

The U.S. response was more complex. Ultimately it would accept more Hungarians for resettlement than any other nation—38,121 by final count.[19] The reasons for such generosity were largely similar to those which had prompted so many other countries to accept Hungarians. During the height of the uprising, the American television audience had been provided with same-day coverage of students hurling paving stones and Molotov cocktails at Soviet tanks. One study of their reception in the United States concluded that "the Hungarians were viewed as heroes, easily the most popular group of refugees in U.S. history, because of their battle with Communism."[20]

This popularity was augmented in official Washington by guilt over the disparity between the rhetoric of liberation and America's passive response when the uprising was crushed. The "liberationist" wing of the Republican Party, their ideological allies in private organizations such as the International Rescue Committee, and the CIA's covert action arm, the Office of Policy Coordination (OPC), had all invested heavily in the hope that news of Khrushchev's denunciation of the Stalinist era at the Soviet Twentieth Party Congress would help shake the Eastern European satellites loose from Soviet rule. According to one commentator:

> Khrushchev had been brutal in his denunciations of Stalin and seemed to promise that the future would be different, that a relaxation of Communist Party controls inside Russia would be matched by a moderation of policy toward the satellites. It was even hinted that there might be a modicum of true independence for the satellites in the near future. It was, in short, an explosive document, and the Soviets had kept it a closely guarded secret.[21]

When to reveal the contents of the speech became a matter of controversy within the CIA. Frank Wisner, head of the OPC, and James Angleton were in charge of an operation—called "Red Sox/Red Cap"—which, according to Stephen Ambrose, involved training refugees from Hungary, Poland, Rumania, and Czechoslovakia for covert and paramilitary operations inside their homelands. Angleton and Wisner wanted to hold the secret speech until the Red Sox/Red Cap forces were "up to snuff," and then release it to promote national uprising.[22]

Nevertheless, Allen Dulles, siding with others in the agency who sought a more immediate propaganda advantage, ordered the publication date pushed up. The appearance of the Khrushchev speech in the *New York Times* on June 2, 1956, created a furor in Eastern Europe. Rioting in Poland during October 1956 led to the reconstitution of the Polish government, the accession to power of Wladyslaw Gomulka, and "substantial independence" from the Soviet Union which, according to Ambrose, "set an example for the other satellites."[23]

Clearly, Hungary was following that example when on October 23, 1956, its students took to the streets demanding reform and the installation of Imre Nagy as head of government. Yet despite official secrecy and the predictable denials which occurred in the aftermath of defeat, it is now clear that Hungary—to some extent, at least—was also following the lead of Frank Wisner's agents-in-place, and was egged on by American propaganda. One of Michener's Hungarian sources stated:

> Hungarians are bitter about the lack of interest you Americans showed in our struggle for freedom. For years now, as part of your battle for the possession of men's minds, you have been saying to us, "You are not forgotten. America's ultimate aim is to help you win your freedom. To achieve this, we will support you to the best of our ability."[24]

He noted that long before the uprising began,

> young Hungarians who had been abroad began mysteriously to appear among us and they promised, "If trouble starts, don't worry. America will be on hand to give you support. But you don't have to wait for the other side to begin. Do something yourself. You've got to prove that Hungary deserves the freedom you claim for her."[25]

Prior to the uprising, arms were smuggled into Hungary either by the CIA or the CIA-supported Gehlen organization in West Germany.[26] During the uprising itself, even after it had become clear that the Soviet army was again in control, Radio Free Europe repeated the slogan "America will not fail you . . . America will not fail you . . ." over and over again.[27] Thus the President, who had approved the Red Sox/Red Cap operation, who had proclaimed liberation "a major goal of American foreign policy,"[28] but who resolutely resisted the urgings of the "liberationists" in his own party to take immediate military action on the side of Hungarian freedom fighters,[29] was confronted, not only with tens of thousands of people fleeing Soviet aggression, but with the knowledge that they were also the victims of false expectations about U.S. policy. Eisenhower quickly came under pressure from his supporters to provide refugee relief in lieu of the military aid that had been withheld.

Probably the first advocate of this position—and certainly one of the most forceful—was Leo Cherne, chairman of the IRC. Immediately upon learning of the outbreak of the revolution in Hungary, he traveled to Vienna with the IRC's president, Angier Biddle Duke,[30] and then on to Budapest, where, as the first American to enter the city since the uprising began, he interviewed the recently freed Cardinal József Mindszenty, who stressed the need for Western help.[31] On October 29, 1956, a week *before* the Soviet Army reestablished control, Cherne and Biddle cabled their New York headquarters:

THEY MUST HAVE ASSURANCES FREE WORLD SUPPORT AT THIS DECISIVE MOMENT WHICH MAY WELL BE TURNING POINT WORLD HISTORY. BEST WE CAN DO TO DEMONSTRATE OUR SYMPATHY, SOLIDARITY AND TOTAL IDENTIFICATION WITH HUNGARIAN LIBERATION FORCES IS TO RUSH AT ONCE MASSIVE QUANTITIES RELIEF SUPPLIES.

. . . WE ARE PREPARING, TOO, FOR TRAGIC POSSIBILITY SOVIET RECAPTURE CONTROL, WHEN COUNTLESS ESCAPEES WILL FLOOD INTO AUSTRIA, AND THUS MUST BE READY WITH RESOURCES.[32]

Biddle remained in Austria to organize relief and possible resettlement efforts. Cherne returned home to the United States to drum up support, both moral and financial, for the freedom fighters. He appeared on the Ed Sullivan Show "to tell the story of Hungary's glory and need"; he also participated in a massive rally at New York's Madison Square Garden held shortly after the uprisings had been crushed, which protested America's failure to act, demanded sanctions against the Soviet Union,[33] and "succeeded in emphasizing the need to rescue those who could still make their escape."[34]

It appears certain that even without this pressure, Eisenhower would have reacted favorably to the plight of the Hungarian "escapees," although the scope of the U.S. resettlement program might have been smaller. While the situation in Budapest was still fluid and it appeared possible that the freedom fighters might prevail, the President authorized the expenditure of $20 million in emergency funds "to help provide food, shelter, and medical supplies for those refugees crowding into Austria and for people still inside Hungary."[35]

The emphasis in the administration shifted immediately to resettlement when it became clear that the uprising had failed. Thus on November 7 Scott McLeod, taking a position far more generous than any he had assumed during the controversy over the Refugee Relief Act (RRA), called for the United States to begin offering asylum to the Hungarians.[36] To do so, however, required the surmounting of two problems, one legal and one political. The legal problem derived from the fact that the Hungarian quota for 1956, which was still burdened by the "mortgage" imposed in 1948, was already oversubscribed, and in 1957 would have permitted the entry of only 865 applicants from Hungary.[37] Congress was out of session, and unless reconvened on an emergency basis could not formally authorize any additional immigration numbers. Pierce Gerety advocated using some of the special visas which remained available under the RRA, which was due to expire in less than two months. But the assurance and security provisions of the RRA, if scrupulously applied, would have made it virtually impossible for any recent Hungarian refugee to obtain a visa before the act expired. Thus the administration was forced to choose between abandoning the RRA as an entry vehicle and expediting the security procedures mandated by that act by waiving its requirement that each applicant fully document his security fitness, or spend two years establishing a clean record before being permitted to enter the United States. It chose the latter course on November 8, 1956, when it announced that 5,000 RRA visas would be made available to the Hungarians.[38] However, as the flow out of Hungary continued and as domestic pressures for generosity built, it became apparent that 5,000 visas were not sufficient. And so, on November 26, the President announced his decision to use 1200 more RRA visas and in addition to "parole" 15,000 Hungarians into the United States on a temporary basis, pending the next Congressional session and the passage of "emergency legislation which will, through the [authorization of the] use of unused numbers under the Refugee Relief Act, or otherwise, permit qualified escapees who accept asylum in the United States to obtain permanent residence."[39] Subsequent announcements raised the total number of parole authorizations to more than 32,000.

The waiver of the RRA's security requirements raised some legal questions, although such a waiver may have been technically permissible under a little-used provision of the McCarran-Walter Act which provided for "temporary admission" despite "nonadmissibility" if the Attorney General and the Secretary of State concurred in waiving a particular ground for exclusion.[40] More significant legal concerns were raised by the President's assertion that he possessed the authority to "parole" large numbers of aliens into the United States pending Congressional action. That assertion was based on an equally obscure section of the immigration code which permitted the Attorney General to allow aliens to physically enter the United States (but not obtain any of the legal benefits of formal admission) "temporarily under such conditions as he may prescribe for emergent reasons or for reasons deemed strictly in the

55

public interest."[41] The legislative history of that provision made it clear that it was intended to serve very narrow objectives, and was designed to address such cases as those involving "an alien who requires immediate medical attention before there has been an opportunity for an immigration officer to inspect him [or situations] where it is strictly in the public interest to have an inadmissible alien present in the United States, such as, for instance, a witness or for purposes of prosecution."[42]

Since the passage of the first federal immigration legislation in 1875, it had been universally understood that Congress—and not the President—possessed the constitutional authority to set conditions for entry and to fix quota numbers. It was precisely this understanding that had forced President Truman to approach a restrictionist Congress in 1947 when he had sought to institutionalize the displaced persons program. To use the parole statute to secure the entry of over 30,000 otherwise inadmissible migrants was the sort of action which, under other circumstances, could have provoked a major constitutional confrontation.

But the political environment, at least in the first weeks after the Soviet invasion, was remarkably nonconfrontational. Representative Walter, the Chairman of the House Immigration Committee, who after Senator McCarran's death had become the most powerful voice in Congress on immigration matters, was consulted by the President, and responded initially by advocating that *all* Hungarians seeking entry be paroled in as freedom fighters fleeing Communist aggression.[43] He proposed raising the first parole allocation from 5,000 to 17,000 slots, and in a letter to the Washington, D.C. *Post–Times Herald,* expressed the view that Eisenhower's exercise of the parole power was fully consistent with the original intent of Congress.[44] Senator James O. Eastland, the Mississippi Democrat who chaired the Senate Judiciary Committee, through which all immigration legislation was funneled, was similarly supportive. Temporarily abandoning his customary restrictionist stance, he urged the Eisenhower administration to stretch the immigration statute to admit a fair share of the Hungarians who had so valiantly fought Communism.[45] It was only after the initial pro-Hungarian refugee enthusiasm had begun to wane, and the traditionally restrictive elements in Congress again began to perceive the new arrivals as immigrants rather than as anti-Communist symbols, that their admission began to be seriously questioned. By that time, parole as a precedent had already been established.

The first stirrings of anti-Hungarian sentiment were apparently heard after November 21, 1956, when the first refugees began arriving in the United States. By November 29, the President was already receiving significant amounts of mail objecting to a more generous admissions policy.[46] However, little evidence of serious opposition to the Hungarians was seen in the almost universally favorable press coverage of their arrival at Camp Kilmer, New Jersey, where they were brought before being redirected to sponsors and jobs. Thus many of the stories were about orphaned children and brave anti-Communist rebels who had fled across the border pursued by Soviet troops. When an early entrant stabbed a guard at Camp Kilmer, the episode merited only a small and inconspicuous story in the *New York Times*.[47] Representative Walter, convinced that most Hungarians would return to fight the Soviet troops as soon as it was safe to do so, advocated the use of ships to bring more Hungarians to the United States.[48] Yet the administration was clearly concerned about behind-the-scenes negative reaction. According to Arthur Markowitz, one of the President's chief purposes in dispatching Vice President Nixon to Vienna in mid-December was "to head off mounting criticism by dramatizing the seriousness of the problem."[49]

Nixon's report to the President on his return laid heavy emphasis on the quality of the Hungarians as potential immigrants, on their "political" motives for departure, and on their general trustworthiness. Thus it indicated—accurately—that

> the large majority are young people—students, technicians, craftsmen and professional people.[50]

Less accurately, it suggested that almost all were active "freedom fighters" who risked active persecution if forced to return:

> For the most part they were in the forefront of the fight for freedom and fled only when the choice was death or deportation at the hands of foreign invaders or temporary flight to a foreign land to await the inevitable freedom for Hungary. . . .

> The majority of the refugees who have been interviewed say that they left Hungary because of fear of liquidation or of deportation. The number of [Communist] floaters and of those who left Hungary purely for economic reasons is relatively small.[51]

Finally, it asserted that by cross-checking the stories and identities of those seeking admission with other refugees, U.S. personnel overseas were able to establish "the identity of spies and agents," and as a consequence, continued admission of Hungarian refugees would "present no significant risk of internal subversion in this country."[52] Similar points about the Hungarians coming to the United States were made by those entrusted with their resettlement. On November 29, the President appointed Tracy Voorhees as his personal representative to coordinate refugee problems. One of Voorhees' first acts was to hire a private public relations firm, Communications Counselors, a division of the McCann-Erickson Advertising Agency, which was entrusted with the task of creating a positive image of the Hungarians.

The effort to resettle Hungarians was completed successfully. Yet it could not and did not abolish all anti-Hungarian sentiment in the United States. A Roper poll conducted during the spring of 1957 revealed an America divided about the wisdom of admitting the Hungarians. Thus in response to the question "What do you think the effect of the refugees will be on this country?" 24.1 percent of the respondents were undecided, 21 percent said that they would have "no appreciable effect," 32 percent believed that they would be "a bad influence," and only 26 percent thought that the country would be "better off."[53] Views such as these revealed more uncertainty than antagonism. By themselves, they would not have been sufficient to bring the Hungarian program to an end. But they revealed no great enthusiasm for prolonging or expediting it.

By February 1957 the outflow from Hungary had slowed considerably. Other nations had pledged to take the majority of the remaining refugees. The hope that any Hungarians would return home to fight the foreign invaders had vanished. Stories were reaching Washington with increasing frequency that a significant percentage of those who had left Hungary were not in fact devout anti-Communists. Thus it was not surprising that Representative Walter, after a trip to Austria where he claimed he saw refugees destroying their Communist Party cards,[54] developed a sudden change of heart, began asserting that the use of the RRA visas and the parole provision were both illegal, and demanded that the United States "close the crack in the Iron Curtain" through which thousands of people he regarded as potential security risks continued to stream.[55] Nor was it surprising that the House Judiciary Committee, following his lead, rejected the recommendations of Nixon and Eisenhower that Hungarian parole be converted into "permanent residence," and that American immigration law be rewritten to set aside a certain number of visas each year for refugees fleeing Communist or Communist-dominated countries.[56] The curtailment of the Hungarian admissions program in April 1957 was probably chiefly attributable to the easing of the refugee crisis overseas. Yet it also revealed that parole, while it had circumvented restrictionist politics, had not rendered them completely irrelevant.

The Hungarian program not only changed the way that decisions affecting the entry of refugees were made but also affected the way they were resettled after they got here. Prior to 1956, government involvement with refugees had been confined to assisting them overseas prior to resettlement, making certain that they met the various security, employment, and housing assurance provisions stipulated in the relevant law before issuing them visas, and, on occasion, lending them the money needed to secure transportation to the United States. The principal responsibility for refugees under the traditional approach fell to private sponsors and voluntary agencies that could guarantee refugees jobs and immediate care in the U.S. before they ever embarked.

Under the Hungarian program, the voluntary agencies continued to play an active role. In Austria, they divided up responsibility for the Hungarian migrants, selecting for their particular care those who shared a particular characteristic, such as religion or ethnic background or student or professional status. They also played a significant role in the United States, helping to match particular refugees with particular sponsors. Yet in several important ways, their role—and that of the federal government—increased during the Hungarian crisis.

To a large degree, those changes were attributable more to the suddenness of the Hungarians' arrival than they were to any federal intention to assume greater financial and administrative responsibility for U.S. resettlement operations. According to the best recent account, "the Federal Government was explicit about its reliance on the private sector to resettle the Hungarian refugees. There was no provision for Federal resettlement expenditures beyond providing some health care funding and paying transportation costs."[57] The enthusiasm of a significant percentage of the American population for the Hungarians, particularly during their first weeks in America, made it uncommonly easy to obtain private sector support. Thus much of the Camp Kilmer operation was staffed by volunteers, and they had virtually no difficulty finding sponsors or job opportunities for the migrants entrusted to their care. The entire program was almost completed in ninety days, with all but 1,600 of the 27,000 migrants who passed through Camp Kilmer established in new communities by early March.[58]

Undoubtedly, some of the success in resettling so many refugees so quickly was attributable to the personal qualifications of the Hungarians, their ties to a preexisting Hungarian community in the United States, and the favorable economic conditions which prevailed when they arrived. At the end of 1956, the male U.S. unemployment rate stood at 3.8 percent.[59] The Hungarians were a predominantly male group, over a quarter of whom were craftsmen with immediately saleable skills. Most were young, and virtually all were educated, although most had no university training.[60] A large, well-dispersed Hungarian community already existed in the United States when they arrived;[61] in general, the new arrivals chose to settle in areas where that community was already concentrated.[62] Although they experienced some difficulty in learning English, many, because of their vocational skills and their choice of resettlement locations, found that the difficulties this entailed were not incurable. By the end of 1957, fully 65.7 percent of the Hungarian refugees were gainfully employed, compared with 40.7 percent for the U.S. population as a whole.[63]

Yet despite the generosity of the American people and the characteristics of the Hungarians themselves which promoted assimilation, their movement into the United States and their integration into the larger community was due more to direct governmental intervention than had been the case for any prior refugee group. Because the immediate pressures on Austria were so great, overseas screening was minimal, the time spent in camps overseas was generally limited to a few weeks, and the United States government became immediately involved in insuring—and in some cases, providing—transportation to the United States. Camp Kilmer was heavily staffed with volunteers; yet directing their efforts were a number of governmental agencies, including the Public Health Service, and the U.S. Employment Service of the Department of Labor, which "interviewed and classified" refugees according to occupational skills, training, and resettlement preferences, maintained an inventory of jobs and available housing, and matched Hungarian arrivals by computer with available positions.[64] Meanwhile, a highly visible President's Committee for Hungarian Refugee Relief, somewhat like the Displaced Persons Commission in the late 1940s and early 1950s, worked to secure broad community support for the new arrivals and initiated a substantial public relations campaign to drum up jobs and housing.[65] Thus the same administration which had discovered new methods for bringing refugees into the United States without express Congressional approval also discovered new means of insuring their successful resettlement.

The lessons the nation learned from the Hungarian experience about admission and resettlement were understood more thoroughly and more quickly than the lesson about the limits of American power. The Hungarian defeat convinced the Eisenhower administration that no practical or moral reason supported the continuation of "liberation" as either a policy or a promise in Eastern Europe. In 1957, Frank Wisner sought to launch a new round of "special operations" in Czechoslovakia, using CIA-trained exiles.[66] Predictably, C. D. Jackson and some of the other members of the "liberationist" faction urged approval of the plan. Yet the President remained firm in opposing any renewal of covert operations designed to destabilize Eastern Europe. In the words of William Colby, former Director of the CIA:

> It was established, once and for all, that the U.S., while firmly committed to the containment of the Soviets . . . was not going to attempt to liberate any of the areas within their sphere.[67]

But no similar policy was established for the rest of the world. During the late 1950s and early 1960s, the CIA remained heavily involved in operations to "destabilize" or overthrow regimes in Asia and Latin America which it regarded as either Communist or leaning heavily in the direction of Moscow. Emboldened by its early successes in Iran and Guatemala, where it had played a key role in the removal of the Mossadegh and Arbenz regimes, it continued or initiated large-scale covert operations in Indonesia and Laos,[68] and began training Tibetan exiles in Colorado, with the apparent aim of promoting anti-Chinese guerrilla war in the Himalayas.[69] Nowhere, however, was American involvement with guerrilla movements, or with the exiles who manned them, more extensive than in Cuba. That involvement, which had as its consistent goal the removal of Fidel Castro from power, contributed directly to the *laissez faire* policy which permitted tens of thousands of Cubans "temporarily" to enter the United States during 1960 and the early months of 1961.

On January 1, 1959, Fulgencio Batista fled Cuba and Fidel Castro established a revolutionary government. Slowly at first and then with increasing rapidity, Cubans dissatisfied with the new regime began entering the United States. Some came legally, admitted with immigrant visas. Others arrived with nonimmigrant visas but refused to return home when their terms expired. Still others came with no documentation at all. Between January 1, 1959, and April 1961, approximately 125,000 Cubans arrived in the United States. At least 40,000 of them—perhaps as many as 90,000—settled in southern Florida.[70] There had been extensive planning and elaborate immigration controls regulating the entry and final settlement of some 38,000 Hungarian refugees in 1956–1957, but no similar program was instituted for the larger and more concentrated Cuban flow. Instead, for nearly two years the United States government permitted Cubans to settle haphazardly in Florida, even though there was significant local unemployment. Many of the Cubans arrived without adequate means of support, and their children quickly overwhelmed the Dade County schools.

The government pursued a passive policy designed to let virtually any Cuban enter the United States without legal formalities. No sponsorship or guaranteed employment was required. The consular office in Cuba remained open until January 1, 1961. Initially, it insisted that all the usual visa procedures be followed—including the required check with local police officials to determine if applicants had criminal records.[71] But as U.S.-Cuban relations worsened, the consular office began issuing visas in an expedited and apparently *pro forma* manner. The Coast Guard made no attempt to turn away undocumented Cubans, who even during this early period were arriving quite regularly in small boats. And the Immigration and Naturalization Service (INS) avoided instituting deportation proceedings against those arriving illegally or remaining in the United States after the expiration of their visas, and began the process of granting "extended voluntary departure" as a deportation avoidance device.[72]

These liberal admissions practices[73] were explicable on humanitarian grounds as well as on grounds of long-established political ties and geographical affinity. Executions and public trials of members of the old regime occurred soon after Castro assumed power.[74] The earliest arrivals were *Batistianos* who had good cause to fear the same fate. They were soon followed by other Cubans not directly implicated in the former government. These were political exiles who were clearly pushed out of Cuba, where they held positions of wealth, privilege, and power, but who had no place in the new revolutionary world.[75] A final group arriving in the first twenty-eight months of Castro's rule were some of his disaffected followers, veterans of the Sierra Maestra campaign. Like the *Batistianos*, they had reason to fear for their personal safety. During this period there were relatively few restraints against emigration, and commercial flights continued to operate out of Havana.

However, the informality of the early U.S. response to the Cubans cannot be explained without taking into account the special perception of them shared by the Eisenhower and Kennedy administrations. Both regarded the Cuban flow as temporary—a view embodied in the frequent use of the word "exile"[76] to describe those fleeing from Castro's Cuba prior to late 1962 or early 1963. From the very beginning, those settling in Florida were united by a common goal: to return to their homeland as quickly as possible.

During 1959, the Eisenhower administration restrained its hostility toward Castro. Nevertheless, tensions between the two countries intensified. The United States reacted negatively to a wide range of events in Cuba, including the public trials and executions of several Americans; land reform and nationalization programs that affected or threatened U.S. economic interests; and the development of a close political, economic, and military relationship between the Soviet Union and Cuba. The Eisenhower administration particularly feared communist subversion in the Caribbean and initiated a series of policies designed to pressure and harass the Castro regime. Cuba was directly threatened by the U.S. decision to slash its sugar quota and by the repeated incursions of counterrevolutionaries flying into Cuba from sanctuaries in southern Florida. Ever mindful of the overthrow of the leftward-leaning Arbenz regime in Guatemala in 1954 and an extensive program of CIA covert activities throughout the Western Hemisphere, Castro was spurred into anti-American hysteria in March 1960, when *La Courbe*, a French ship docked in Havana harbor, inexplicably exploded with considerable loss of life.

American training of exiles for a possible future invasion of Cuba did not occur until March 17, 1960.[77] However, such a use of the exile community was officially contemplated a full year earlier, when it was urged privately by then

Vice President Richard Nixon.[78] By the autumn of 1959, the CIA was not only in contact with the exile community but had helped ferry Cubans from Cuba to Florida. Such ties may in fact date from March 1959 or earlier. Whatever the date, it is clear that President Kennedy inherited from President Eisenhower not only an invasion plan but also two correlative beliefs: that Castro could be overthrown with the help of Cubans in the United States,[79] and that once he was overthrown, these Cubans would—as they so often publicly proclaimed—return home. These beliefs did not necessarily entail enlisting large numbers of Cubans in the revolutionary brigade training in Guatemala; but they did tend to discourage federal policy from treating the exile phenomenon as potentially long-standing or permanent, particularly if such policy meant removing the exiles from their staging area for impending return, southern Florida.

Nevertheless, some federal action was required, since many of the Cubans arriving in southern Florida lacked the resources to support themselves, were ineligible for local welfare benefits, and found it extremely difficult to find jobs and housing at a time when unemployment in the Miami area exceeded 7 percent,[80] and affordable lodging was extremely scarce. Beginning in the summer of 1960, the *Miami Herald* began to run daily stories on the Cuban refugees, as well as frequent features about their impact on the region. The stories were generally sympathetic, yet the image they presented was in large part one of an American community which found it difficult to cope with a flood of immigrants, who entered at the rate of at least 500—and later at least 1,000—per week and made significant demands on the local school system and on all of the charitable resources available in the region. On November 10, 1960, President Eisenhower dispatched Tracy Voorhees, who had coordinated Hungarian resettlement, to Miami to address the problem. Voorhees' ensuing report to the President noted that the welfare needs of the Cuban exiles

> run the gamut of personal and family necessities, including food, clothing, medical treatment and education. In view of the very bad housing conditions . . . it is a tribute to the courage of these distressed people that the least frequent request . . . has been for housing assistance.[81]

Even before the release of the Voorhees report in January, 1961, the President acted, and thus on December 7, 1960, the first organized federal response to the Cuban influx emerged with the opening of the Cuban Refugee Emergency Center in Miami. Yet Voorhees, who designed that program, indicated that resettlement out of Florida, which would have alleviated some of the problems of the refugees and the communities where they settled, might prove to be difficult to achieve. He reported to the President that Cubans in Florida were convinced that it would soon be possible to return to their homeland and would not willingly relocate in significant numbers unless granted "assurance from an authoritative source . . . that they are not losing their chance to return home."[82] Those assurances had not been given by January 1961, when President Kennedy established a successor Cuban Refugee Program designed to meet the same two fundamental objectives as the Voorhees program: provision of welfare benefits to Cubans in need and resettlement of some of the thousands of Cubans already straining the resources of southern Florida to other parts of the United States.

Voorhees' concern proved to be justified. As of the end of March 1961, 13,122 Cubans out of an exile population of approximately 125,000 had registered at the Cuban Refugee Center in Miami; only 2,011 had been re-settled.[83] Kennedy's decision on March 11 "to let the Cubans go where they yearned to go—to Cuba"[84] thus fulfilled a long-standing expectation of the exile community and brought a series of political decisions affecting that community to a logical close. However, when the decision was implemented on April 17, 1961, the Bay of Pigs invasion failed.

The Bay of Pigs fiasco was a watershed event in the Kennedy administration and a key moment in the development of U.S. policy toward Cuba and toward the Cuban exiles. Nevertheless, the politics of exile, characterized by the expectations and the implicit promise of repatriation, did not die an immediate death. Instead, repatriation became suddenly a more distant prospect, and the United States was forced to regard the exile community as a fact that would not disappear overnight. One response might have been to close the border to Cuban entrants, most of whom were arriving on regularly scheduled airline flights at the rate of 1,500 to 1,700 per week. No consideration at all appears to have been given to this alternative. Instead, Cuban migration continued at approximately the same rate until October 22, 1962, when in the aftermath of President Kennedy's Cuban missile crisis speech, it was unilaterally terminated by Castro. In the aftermath of the Bay of Pigs, it would have been politically suicidal and highly questionable morally to shut the door on potential Cuban entrants.

The United States had planned, equipped, and then, through its half-hearted support, helped to botch an invasion that left over 100 exiles dead and nearly 1,200 in the hands of Castro's army. However critical the U.S. press was of the planning and execution of the Bay of Pigs, it was clear that there was widespread support for driving Communism from the Western Hemisphere and general admiration for those abandoned on the beaches of Cuba. Typical of the press coverage of the time was an editorial in the *Washington Post* entitled "Invasion of Cuba."[85] It began, "Most Americans will make no secret of their sympathy with the efforts of Cubans to overthrow the Communist-dominated regime of Fidel Castro." Later it asserted, "There is no law or treaty which precludes American help to those who are seeking to regain their freedom." U.S. perception of the exiles as victims and opponents of Castro's Communist government did not change after the Bay of Pigs; what changed was the perception of their strength, the strength of the revolution in Cuba, and the role that Cubans who had already fled—or might flee in the future—could realistically have in reversing it.

These new perceptions and the shape of U.S. policy to come were signaled on April 20, 1961, in President Kennedy's first public statement after the Bay of Pigs. Entitled "The Lesson of Cuba,"[86] it conceded that Communism was firmly entrenched in Cuba and would not be easily overthrown. It recognized that the threat Cuba posed to Latin America was partly ideological, and depended not only on military force but also on the "legitimate discontent of yearning peoples."[87] Yet it argued that refugee flow revealed the bankruptcy of Communism's promise.[88] In order to meet the threat of Castro's Communism, therefore, the United States, together with other nations in Latin America, would have to assert its own will in "a struggle in many ways more difficult than war":

> If the self-discipline of the free cannot match the iron discipline of the mailed fist—in economic, political, scientific, and all the other kinds of struggles as well as the military—then the peril to freedom will continue to rise.[89]

While engaged in that struggle, however, it would have to maintain its generosity toward Cuban refugees.

Kennedy's speech provided the blueprint for U.S.-Cuban relations for the next thirteen years and gave a good indication of the role that Cuban refugees would play in the second stage of the struggle. Significantly, it did not renounce the use of force, although it precluded any "unilateral American military intervention in the absence of an attack on ourselves or an ally."[90] CIA intervention in Cuban affairs, either direct or through intermediaries, continued into the Nixon era,[91] if not beyond. Included were several attempts to assassinate Castro commencing in late 1961, although not made public until 1975.[92] Exiles continued to receive on-the-record financing with CIA funds until May 1963, when it was announced that the annual stipend to the Cuban Revolutionary Council, a group dedicated to ousting Castro, would be terminated.[93] Circumstantial evidence suggests that radical anti-Castro Cubans continued to receive secret U.S. government aid for at least another decade.

Despite this aid, the United States took considerable care to distance itself from another possible invasion, specifically renouncing all intention of participating in such an exercise as part of the agreement it reached with the Soviet Union in October 1962 which brought the Cuban missile crisis to an end.[94] Nor would it commit itself to supporting a government in exile. Instead, the

American "struggle" to rid the hemisphere of Castro's influence increasingly was fought with economic and propaganda weapons. Beginning in 1962, the United States began the policy of isolating Cuba from its neighbors, instituting what George Ball was later to call the "program of economic denial".[95] Part of that denial involved cutting off trade to Cuba. But another part involved cutting Cuba off from its best-educated and most productive people—doctors, lawyers, teachers, skilled craftsmen. Each defection helped to turn the screws a little tighter, while proclaiming to the world the failures of Castro's revolution.

As in the case of the Hungarian revolution, the exodus from Cuba thus proved to be permanent. Like the Hungarians, who were granted permanent resident status in 1958, all of the Cubans were eventually permitted to regularize their status and seek U.S. citizenship.[96] Yet the Cubans, unlike the Hungarians, came from an island only 90 miles from the Florida Keys, and continued to be actively welcomed by an American government still interested in promoting flight. The Cuban missile crisis, which was to bring emigration to a halt for three years, did not permanently undo the pattern of flow which emerged in the early 1960s. The United States remained attractive to the Cubans, not only because of the greater political freedoms it offered but also because, for many Cubans, it had become the home of friends and relatives. And its attractiveness was enhanced by the Cuban Refugee Program, which did not wither away and die after the Bay of Pigs invasion.

Most of the Cubans coming to the United States found work quickly and became productive citizens. Yet they were able to do so, in part at least, because they remained special favorites of the federal government. Describing the situation in Miami in 1961, Juanita Greene, a reporter for the *Miami Herald* testifying before a Senate Committee, noted that the community had responded to the Cubans with "great sympathy".[97] Nevertheless, she also noted a "growing resentment," which she attributed not only to mindless xenophobia but also to a number of more legitimate concerns:

> First of all, in Dade County, Cuban refugees are eligible for more relief than are our own American needy. . . . Cuban relief goes to any Cuban refugee in need, and he does not have to wait weeks and months before receiving his first check, as our American needy must. . . .
>
> The second legitimate complaint, as I see it, is that Cuban refugees are taking away the jobs of some American workers. . . .
>
> The third complaint involves our school systems. In many classrooms, the number of Spanish-speaking students—who speak no English—outnumbers the number of English-speaking students. . . . Otherwise tolerant parents call the *Herald* to complain that their children are being held back scholastically because of the flood of refugee children into their classrooms.[98]

Perceptions of this sort were not uncommon in Florida during the early 1960s.

However, it took almost two full decades and the coincidence of a new and uncontrolled migration from Cuba with the massive influx of refugees from Indochina to convert backlash into a major policy issue, either in Dade County or in the nation as a whole. Yet there was something prophetic in Ms. Greene's remarks, including her observation that "resentment in Miami appears highest among our Negro population. . . . While they fight to achieve full freedom, they say they see strangers welcomed with open arms and given respect and assistance still denied the Negro."[99] For the Cuban migration of the early 1960s not only foreshadowed the arrival of asylum seekers from other nations in the Western Hemisphere but also introduced concerns about aid and equity which have colored the public perception of later groups of refugees.

Chapter 4

Asylum and the Emergence of a Double Standard

P RESIDENT EISENHOWER'S parole of nearly 40,000 Hungarians into the United States, and the subsequent use of the parole authority by President Kennedy permitting several hundred thousand Cubans to either enter the United States without appropriate visas or to remain after those visas expired, radically altered the nation's refugee politics. Decisions which had always required prior Congressional approval suddenly became matters of executive prerogative. President Eisenhower's informal consultations with Representative Walter prior to admitting the Hungarians established a pattern which was to continue until 1980, when a new refugee act was adopted. According to that pattern, most decisions to admit refugees were initiated in the Department of State to meet specific foreign policy concerns approved by the President and then were submitted to key Congressional leaders for rubber-stamp approval. No votes were taken. Only after admissions decisions had created specific problems, such as the need to find funds to support a Cuban Refugee Program in Florida, or the creation of immigrant groups in the United States with uncertain legal status, was actual legislation sought. Presented with a series of *faits accompli*, the Congress sometimes delayed but always acceded eventually to Presidential demands. Thus refugee centers for Cubans in Dade County were funded, the Hungarians were permitted in 1958 to seek permanent resident status, and the same privilege was afforded to Cubans in 1966.

The pattern established in 1956 would not have survived for over twenty years if it had not proven generally acceptable to Congress. The elimination of the national origins quota system in 1965 demonstrated that the overt restrictionism which had played so strong a role in the passage of the McCarran-Walter Act was no longer as potent a force in American domestic politics. Admission of some refugees outside of the limits formally established by law was accepted as an expedient practice, if not an entirely legal one. Presidential initiatives to afford special immigration opportunities to the victims of Communist regimes remained ideologically appealing, and encountered no strong Congressional opposition until the late 1970s, when new fears about the impact of Indochinese refugees on American society began to be expressed.

However, despite the general acceptability of parole, Congress did attempt to play a more active role in the formulation of refugee policy than it had during the aftermath of the Hungarian uprising and the Communist takeover in Cuba. In the interval between the Cuban missile crisis in October 1962 and the fall of Saigon in April 1975, it attempted to bring refugee admissions within the general framework of immigration law by creating a new category of quota immigrants, refugees fleeing from "Communist or Communist-dominated lands." It also took some steps to restrict the use of parole, particularly when certain groups who benefited from it, such as the Cubans who arrived on the last "freedom flights," began to be regarded more widely as the source of significant social burdens. Most importantly, for a variety of humanitarian and political reasons, it began advocating an admissions policy which would benefit groups such as Chileans and Soviet Jews who were not well served by the parole process during the Nixon and Ford administrations..

Thus Congressional initiative played a major role in gradually transforming America's commitment to refugees from an artifact of the cold war into something with broader humanitarian roots. Yet that transformation was gradual, and not free from contradictions. Despite gradual Congressional acknowledgment of new, nonideological standards for granting refugee status, Congress made no serious efforts to reform American asylum policy, which continued to permit anti-Communist Cubans to enter the United States freely yet imposed new restrictions on the entry of Haitian "boat people." A clear "double standard" which governed the acceptability of migrants from particular countries emerged as the principal feature of American refugee policy. Cubans were the principal beneficiary of this double standard. The Haitians were the principal losers. Hurt by their lack of ethnic support in the United States, and by the perception that they were poor, black, and difficult to resettle, they were dealt a deathblow by the reluctance of successive American administrations to antagonize François Duvalier or contribute to the success of his domestic opponents. The politics of asylum, grounded in the experiences of the 1950s and in the pragmatism of the Department of State, remained essentially immune from Congressional influence.

The Cubans who entered the United States from 1959 through 1962, arriving hard on the heels of the Hungarian freedom fighters, from the beginning were perceived as brothers and sisters of the European and rare Asian "escapees" who had fled Communism after World War II and sought liberty in "democratic America." Great attention was paid to the general ideological import of their departure, little to the individual motives of each entrant. Many, under any definition of the term, had risked or experienced persecution in Castro's Cuba. Yet even those whose motives appeared to be general dissatisfaction with the new regime or a desire to be united with family members were specially welcomed. Occasionally, that welcome extended to Cubans who sought admission from a third country, such as Spain or Mexico.[1] It also reached nearly a thousand victims of the Bay of Pigs who had been captured by Castro's army and remained in custody until ransomed by "private" American contributions. But in the main, it was afforded to those who departed Cuba without appropriate visas, and came directly to the United States. Thus a *de facto* asylum policy emerged, characterized not by the selection of refugees overseas and the conscious choice to treat them as immigrants, but by an unwillingness to deport people who shared the nation's anti-Communist sentiments. Unlike the asylum policy of the United Nations—which required a commitment from all the signatories of the 1951 Refugee Convention that they would not return those genuinely fearful of persecution at the hands of *any* regime to their place of origin[2]—the U.S. approach was rooted in a clear anti-Communist ideology, and favored only those who appeared to share it.

The significance of this emerging policy as a source of future political problems was not understood during the early 1960s. The preference for migrants from Communist countries reflected no bias against other potential entrants; concerns about an ideological "double standard" made sense only when opponents of right-wing regimes began—as was not initially the case—being turned away. Nor was there any immediate reason to fear an unmanageable immigration problem. Although nearly one-quarter of a million Cubans entered the United States between 1959 and October 1962, and although the United States, through broadcasts on the Voice of America and other propaganda means, sought to entice others to come,[3] Castro's suspension of flights to the United States during and after the Cuban missile crisis and his exercise of tight border controls brought Cuban immigration to the United States to a virtual standstill. Affecting only the passengers of the occasional small boat which reached Florida after a clandestine departure from Cuba,[4] "asylum" ceased to be a major issue until the autumn of 1965, when Cuban emigration resumed in earnest.

The shutdown of the Cuban flow late in 1962 created a lull, which was made more visible by the very low level of refugee acceptance from anywhere in the world during the period. The displaced persons problem, which had remained a nagging concern of the United States and the European countries of first resettlement throughout the 1950s, finally had been brought to a close in 1961, the "World Refugee Year." A successful international effort, sponsored by the United Nations, was made to resettle all remaining "hardcore" DPs and to close down the few remaining care and resettlement centers in Europe. Approximately one-quarter of the remaining DPs in Europe—the percentage specified by Congress in a special resolution—were brought to the United States. Other movements toward the United States were minimal. The large-scale refugee flows in Africa which erupted in the late 1950s and 1960s were regarded by the United States as essentially local phenomena with few cold war implications, and therefore virtually no African refugees were resettled in the U.S. In Europe, the United States Escape Program (USEP) remained operational, but with the exception of Germans crossing into West Berlin, the number of new arrivals from Eastern Europe declined significantly after the Hungarian uprising. Movement out of Germany, with the exception of infrequent, well-publicized escapes, virtually ceased after the Berlin Wall was erected in August 1961. Only in the Far East, where the United States responded to British pleas to ease some of the immigration pressures in Hong Kong by instituting a small Far Eastern Refugee Program (FERP),[5] did new refugee problems lead to any increase in the waning American commitment to resettlement. But even when refugee inflow into the U.S. was almost nonexistent, the Kennedy and Johnson administrations, in their advocacy of special refugee programs and fundamental changes in American immigration law, assumed implicitly that refugees would continue to find their way to the United States, and that some would be asylum seekers from countries in this hemisphere.[6]

Thus the Kennedy administration secured passage in June 1962, of the Migration and Refugee Assistance Act.[7] That act, although "in no way chang[ing][8] the law pertaining to the admission of aliens to the United States," made express provision for ongoing assistance for "refugees [who] are continuing to find their way out of Cuba."[9] It also established an emergency fund of $10 million which would permit the President "to meet unexpected refugee and migration developments."[10] According to the Senate Committee on Foreign Relations, such a provision was necessary because

> Experience since World War II teaches that international tensions and Communist efforts to increase such tensions will result in escapee and refugee problems. These situations may rise suddenly and it is impossible to predict where trouble may come. The bill recognizes the necessity of being prepared for such eventualities. . . .[11]

Other changes proposed during the Kennedy and Johnson years, but having their roots in proposals first made by the Eisenhower administration, resulted in 1965 in specific legislation to provide special immigration opportunities for refugees fleeing "Communist or Communist-dominated" lands.

The source of that legislation was continuing controversy between the executive and Congress about the use of parole, which had been widely used since the Hungarian uprising to admit thousands of refugees without regard to existing quota limitations and without formal Congressional approval. Although Kennedy and Johnson wanted to keep parole or its equivalent so that the government could respond quickly and flexibly to refugee crises, many in Congress resisted what they regarded as the usurpation of an inherent Congressional right to regulate immigration. Yet most also believed that enacting ad hoc legislation for every emergency was a time-consuming and repetitive task, and thought it preferable to make permanent changes in the immigration statute which would finally bring refugee admissions within the general framework of ordinary immigration law.

Faced with these Congressional concerns, the Executive Branch presented Congress with two options for reforming the refugee admissions system. The first option, which President Eisenhower had strongly urged in 1957, was to put parole on a more secure legal footing by establishing a specific statutory authorization which would permit the Secretary of State to afford entry to "escapees . . . who have fled or in the future flee from communist persecution and tyranny."[12] A similar proposal, introduced as a joint resolution of Congress by Sen. John F. Kennedy and Rep. Walter in 1959, would have "vest[ed] in the Attorney General permanent authority to cope with the continuing problem of the admission of refugees into the United States"[13] and put the Congress on record as approving the use of the "parole authority to admit refugees and escapees."[14] The second option presented to Congress sought to provide more immigration opportunities for designated classes of refugees by adjusting the existing quota system. In 1956, President Eisenhower suggested that the national origins quota system be substantially revised, that 5,000 numbers be "set aside . . . for admission of aliens without regard to nationality or national origins,"[15] and that the "quota numbers that are unused by countries to which they are allocated should be made available for use elsewhere."[16] One purpose of these changes, the President suggested, would be to provide "greater assistance to persons abroad who have undergone suffering and hardship resisting Communist aggression."[17] After the Hungarian uprising, Vice President Nixon, in his official report, recommended the provision of "flexible authority to grant admission to this country of additional numbers of Hungarians and other refugees from Communist persecution, through the use of nonquota visas within the annual ceiling."[18] And in July 1963, President

Kennedy sent a special message and draft legislation to Congress recommending that the national origins quota system be phased out entirely, that visas within the overall ceiling be issued on a "first come, first-serve basis,"[19] and that up to 20 percent of the annual total be reserved for "refugees whose sudden dislocation requires special treatment."[20] A revised version of the Kennedy bill was reintroduced by the Johnson administration in 1965.

These proposals finally resulted in specific legislation on October 3, 1965, which abolished the national origins quota system and provided special immigration opportunities for refugees fleeing "Communist or Communist-dominated" lands. In place of the quotas, the 1965 amendments to the Immigration Act instituted a complex preference system for countries in the Eastern Hemisphere. Six preference categories were established for immigrants with relatives already in the United States and immigrants who had talents and skills needed by the United States. The feature of the Immigration Act amendments of 1965 most relevant to refugees was the creation of a new "seventh preference," which reserved 6 percent of the visas made available under the new system for Eastern Hemisphere

> aliens who . . . because of persecution or fear of persecution on account of race, religion, or political opinion have fled . . . from any Communist or Communist-dominated country or area, or . . . from any country within the general area of the Middle East . . . or are persons uprooted by catastrophic natural calamities as defined by the President who are unable to return to their usual place of abode.[21]

By adopting an ideologically based refugee definition, the Congress thus institutionalized the American practice of admitting refugees according to cold war preferences. Thus the 1965 amendments to the Immigration Act officially endorsed the practice, common since the late 1940s, of equating "refugee" with someone turning his or her back on Communism. Having created the new "seventh preference" to deal with refugee admissions, Congress elected to leave the parole statute alone. Rather than amend the statute, it contented itself with expressing general disapproval of its further use on a widespread basis to benefit refugees. Specifically, the Judiciary Committees of the House and Senate reiterated in their respective reports on the 1965 amendments their belief that the use of parole, at least for aliens eligible for "seventh preference" consideration, should be restricted. According to those reports:

> Inasmuch as a definite provision has now been made for refugees, it is the express intent of the Committee that the parole provisions of the Immigration and Nationality Act, which remain unchanged by this bill, be administered in accordance with the original intention of the drafters of that legislation. The parole provisions were designed to authorize the Attorney General to act only

in emergency, individual, and isolated situations, such as the case of an alien who requires medical attention, and not for the immigration of classes or groups outside the limit of the law.[22]

This expression of legislative disapproval did not, however, constitute a formal prohibition. Describing the prevailing Congressional attitude, Abba Schwartz, a State Department official who helped guide the immigration legislation through Congress, noted that each time a parole action was taken, "a number of Congressmen object to this use of the Attorney General's parole power even though many support the actual entry of the refugees themselves."[23] By 1965, the convenience of leaving the primary decision for refugee admissions in the hands of the President had become apparent, as had the flexibility that the parole power afforded.

The flexibility inherent in parole proved exceptionally convenient when dealing with the Cubans. The 1965 legislation affected only "Eastern Hemisphere" refugees, and in no way addressed the situation of any person from any Latin American or Caribbean nation who arrived in the United States without adequate papers and sought relief from deportation on the ground that persecution was likely. Thus when Castro, responding to pent-up emigration demands, announced in late 1965 to all who desired to leave Cuba that they were free to do so, it was probably inevitable that President Johnson would welcome them unreservedly and initiate a new parole program. What could not have been predicted was that the program would last nearly eight years and result in the admission of more than 200,000 additional Cuban migrants.

The new wave of Cuban migration began in October 1965. It was ushered in by two speeches—one delivered in Havana by Fidel Castro inveighing against his domestic critics, inviting them to leave, and the other delivered by President Lyndon Johnson at the foot of the Statue of Liberty proclaiming the United States a land of freedom with room for all the Cubans who might seek to enter. Johnson declared, "I have directed the Departments of State, Justice, and Health, Education and Welfare to immediately make all the necessary arrangements to permit those in Cuba who seek freedom to make an orderly entry into the United States of America."[24] Castro took the President at his word. Almost immediately, he opened up Camarioca harbor, permitting several thousand of his disaffected countrymen to board small boats there and set sail for the United States. As was again to prove to be the case in 1980, some of the boats were provided by members of the exile community in Florida anxious to bring friends and relatives out of Cuba.

The departure of the boats from Camarioca caused considerable distress in the Department of State, where some regarded it as a direct affront to the territorial integrity of the United States.[25] It also engendered rumblings in Miami, where memories of the problems associated with the disorganized Cuban influx in the early 1960s were still fresh. Responding to these concerns, the Johnson administration entered into negotiations with the Castro government to convert the chaotic boat lift into something more closely resembling a controlled refugee flow. An agreement was reached in late 1965 which provided for daily flights from Havana to Miami. It also established criteria for departure which favored those who had relatives in the United States.

The majority of the Cubans who left after 1965 did not do so for explicitly political reasons. The "Memorandum of Understanding" between Cuba and the United States excluded all political prisoners and all draft-age men, who might have sought refuge as conscientious objectors, from becoming potential immigrants under the program.[26] Undoubtedly some individuals who left Cuba had political motives, but it is difficult to dispute Virginia Dominguez's general characterization of the post-1965 Cuban arrivals as "consumer refugees" and her explanation in testimony before Congress that they were

> people who left Cuba largely because they were used to a standard of living they could no longer have in Cuba. Many consumer goods were not easily available after the revolution. Many of those who came after 1965 were housewives and children, and were not actively political. They were not necessarily poor, or the victims of political persecution. The people who really do qualify as political refugees . . . are those who left within the first two years after the revolution and not those thereafter.[27]

During this period and until 1980, Cubans were welcomed without close examination into their motives for departure. The United States made no effort to involve the UNHCR in its Cuban admissions program. The "freedom flights" served important symbolic purposes. The departure of Cubans was viewed as a demonstration of the economic and political repression of a Communist regime and was treated as a "ballot for freedom."[28] Further, it was believed or at least argued as late as 1970 that a generous U.S. refugee immigration policy might encourage continued resistance to Communism in Cuba. Thus, defending the continuation of the freedom flights that had begun in December 1965, Robert Hurwitch, Deputy Assistant Secretary of State for Inter-American Affairs, testified in July 1970,

> In addition to the humanitarian considerations involved and the fact that we have entered into an international agreement, there is additional sound basis for the airlift. Experience has indicated that as long as hope for escape to freedom exists, people living under oppression resist committing themselves to the regime's goals; but when escape routes are sealed, accommodation to the inevitable becomes the prevailing attitude. Illustrative of this phenomenon is the case of East Germany where the beginning of economic recovery can be said to date from the erection of the Berlin wall: when the wall barred future escape to the freedom of the West, the East German population had no real

alternative but to accommodate to the Communist regime there. The refugee airlift, a route to freedom, forestalls the certainty of accommodation to communism by the Cuban people.[29]

In sum, it was an article of faith that the ultimate repudiation of Communism was the spectacle of people "voting with their feet." That type of vote, UN Ambassador Arthur Goldberg argued in 1965, is a "criterion of how people really feel:"[30]

> Many thousands of Cubans have seized every available means of transportation which will take them from Cuba to the United States, but no crowds are pounding on Cuba's gates and seeking admission.[31]

Had Ambassador Goldberg continued, he might have noted that the unidirectional flow from Cuba was perceived by policy makers in the United States as having an instrumental as well as a symbolic effect. As U.S. resistance to a UN decision to grant Cuba agricultural development funds illustrated, economic denial was linked to an attempt to deprive Cuba of technical expertise.[32] Increasingly in the late 1960s and early 1970s, Castro complained of the negative effect on the Cuban economy wrought by the departure of so many well-educated and skilled people to the United States. Cuban unwillingness to let the freedom flights continue indefinitely was undoubtedly influenced by this brain drain.[33] However, in ways apparently not foreseen by anyone in the Department of State, some significant benefits accrued to the Castro regime from the outflow. Potential dissidents were exported in large numbers, their property redistributed, and the socialization of the Cuban economy hastened. It is thus not clear that the 1965–1973 migration was of more lasting benefit to the United States than it was to the Cuban government. But the contemporary view, expressed frequently by politicians and State Department officials, was that the freedom flights furthered U.S. foreign policy objectives.

That view dominated Cuban refugee policy until the early 1970s. Parole decisions made in the Executive Branch and only cursorily and informally reviewed by key members of Congress provided an ongoing method of admitting Cuban migrants outside of the ordinary parameters of immigration law. Foreign policy imperatives controlled, although domestic political concerns undoubtedly played some role in keeping the gates open. Thus it is clear that the parole policy of the Johnson and Nixon administrations gained credit with the Cuban community nationally, and enhanced their position with an important segment of the south Florida population. President Kennedy's welcoming address to the returning Bay of Pigs veterans in 1963 established a precedent which succeeding Presidents and presidential candidates have usually followed. Speeches to the Cuban community in Miami praising its courage and devotion to freedom and deploring the conditions in Havana became as much of a staple of American politics as the obligatory Columbus Day address to an Italian audience, or the St. Patrick's Day address to an Irish one. The continuing Cuban Refugee Program guaranteed that a regular flow of new Cuban immigrants into Dade County—for the great majority of those airlifted eventually settled there—would pose no unacceptable welfare or social service strains. And the equity issue was partially defused during the late 1960s by a generally strong economy which enhanced Cuban—and, to a lesser extent, American black—employment and thus reduced the competition between the two groups.

Yet the domestic payoffs from a generous Cuban admissions policy remained highly problematical. Until 1966, no mechanism existed for granting Cubans who had entered the United States without immigrant visas permanent resident status.[34] Not all Cubans eligible to apply for that status when it became available chose to do so, and those that did generally were not able to secure American citizenship immediately.[35] Thus the Cubans, particularly in 1965, did not constitute a significant voting bloc. And the entry of their fellow countrymen continued to create tensions in south Florida, where the relative prosperity of the newcomers was resented by the indigenous poor, and where the spread of Spanish from the schoolyard to the marketplace created new employment problems for those who were not bilingual.

The lack of broad-based public support for continuing the freedom flights became more apparent in the early 1970s, when those flights began bringing more elderly people to the United States who immediately became eligible for welfare benefits but contributed little to the local economy. The press in Miami began to report that the Cuban admissions program had outlived its usefulness.[36] From a foreign policy perspective, this judgment was undoubtedly correct. The Cuban government had eased its population pressures, lessened the amount of visible popular dissatisfaction, and grown increasingly unhappy with its brain drain to the United States. For its part, the American government had discovered that as the Cuban migration progressed, the practical and symbolic value of the new arrivals diminished. Cuba remained one of America's favorite whipping boys; but under Nixon, the lash was applied more sparingly. After a dozen years, massive Cuban emigration had few new lessons to teach about the failed promise of Castro's revolution. Nor had it proven to be an effective way to weaken the Castro regime.

Pressures from Congress to end the freedom flights therefore proved difficult to resist. Those pressures reflected a growing belief that Cuban migration had lost its original political character, that it was bringing to the United States larger numbers of people less easily assimilable to the domestic labor market and more dependent on welfare aid, and that the money spent on the airlift and related resettlement programs might better be spent on the American poor. In

June 1971, the Appropriations Committee of the U.S. Senate voted to cut off funds for the airlift because it believed the continuing influx was adding to U.S. welfare rolls.[37] Similar attempts to cut off airlift funds and use them to aid U.S. urban poor occurred in 1970.[38] Whether Congress would have acted eventually to stop the flights by cutting off the funds needed to continue them cannot be stated with any certainty. For in 1973, after several earlier suspensions, the Cuban government unilaterally cancelled the airlift.

The American reception of Cuban migrants between 1965 and 1973 demonstrated how far the concept of asylum could be stretched when those seeking admission were regarded as ideologically valuable. The Cubans who entered the United States during this period arrived after an earlier wave had achieved some permanency in the Miami area, and they were afforded the benefits of the Cuban Refugee Program. Thus, despite their numbers, the Cubans posed no insuperable problems to policy makers, who continued to use parole to further cold war objectives and achieve better relations with the growing Cuban-American community. Yet even under these favorable circumstances, the open-ended nature of the American commitment, the awareness that it was being used as a substitute for ordinary immigration, and concerns about its economic impact resulted eventually in Congressional demands that the freedom flights be halted. Even for Cubans, there were practical limits on entry.

However, for those whose entry served no cold war purpose, but instead tended to illustrate the imperfections of American allies, the limits were geopolitical rather than practical. Thus the Haitians, the only other significant group of asylum seekers from 1965 through 1975, after a brief period of wary welcome, discovered that they were automatically excludable or deportable. The reasons had little to do with their possible impact on southern Florida or the urban centers of the Northeast, where many settled. They had even less to do with the difficulties of proving a well-founded, personal fear of persecution, a non-ideological standard that the United States Senate in 1968 made a part of American treaty law when it ratified the 1967 United Nations Protocol Relating to the Status of Refugees.[39] Haitians—and the churches, the voluntary agencies, and the public interest law firms which became their chief supporters—found that the principal barrier to formal or informal asylum was the progressively cozier relationship between the United States and the government of Haiti which emerged during the 1960s and 1970s.[40] Attempts to shift American official attention to the actual plight of particular Haitian boat people, and to the conditions in Haiti which brought them here, were remarkably unsuccessful.

The Haitians began to enter the United States in significant numbers in 1957, when François Duvalier transformed Haiti into a personal instrument of power, self-aggrandizement, and terror.[41] Those who resisted Duvalier's tyranny were systematically silenced, and tens of thousands of Haitians fled for their personal safety. Although never the beneficiaries of the strong rhetorical support which the Cubans received, the Haitians who arrived in the United States between 1957 and 1971 were generally tolerated. Most were businessmen or professionals who had arrived in the United States on nonimmigrant visas. Entering with thousands of fellow countrymen and women of a similar background who had left Haiti because of a general dissatisfaction with conditions there and a hope for a better and more rewarding life in America, they were distinguishable only because of their special tales of oppression and terror. Yet the U.S. Immigration Service took a permissive attitude toward all Haitians, did not actively pursue those who remained illegally, and rarely deported them. As a consequence, virtual refugee status was granted to Haitian entrants without any examination of individual persecution claims. However, none were ever officially categorized as refugees, and the formal steps to relax immigration rules for Cubans, including the practice of waiving the visa requirement altogether, and the passage of legislation to grant earlier arrivals "permanent resident" status were not taken for the Haitians. Consequently, even the most "political" of the Haitians, active opponents of the Duvalier regime like former President Magloire, were denied the certain asylum granted most Cubans. Unlike Cubans, Haitians were never characterized as voting with their feet against an oppressive regime, nor was there any U.S. effort to portray the Duvalier regime as one of the most abusive in the world. There was no sense that it was in the U.S. national interest to characterize Haitians as victims of persecution. Thus under Eisenhower the State Department view was that Duvalier "had given more stability to Haiti than any exile coalition could, and that his overthrow might plunge Haiti into chaos."[42]

Although the U.S. publicly maintained under the Kennedy administration that there continued to be no viable alternative to Duvalier, it tried to develop such an alternative by channeling financial assistance to Haitian opposition figures such as Magloire. Such aid was meant to convey the message to Duvalier that there were limits to American tolerance of his regime. While Kennedy wished to remove Duvalier or bring about radical improvements in his methods of rule, he feared creating a "second Cuba" in the Western Hemisphere. Hoping to ensure a stable, friendly government as a successor to Duvalier, the Kennedy administration, in the words of Secretary of State Dean Rusk, "used persuasion, aid, pressure and almost all techniques short of the landing of outside forces" to bring about changes in Haiti.[43] Such pressures included nearly a total cut-off of American economic and military aid, withdrawal of the American Ambassador from Port-au-Prince, and secret funding of Haitian exile groups; and there were ties between U.S. intelligence agencies and the exile groups that invaded Haiti in 1963.[44] However, Duvalier was able to exploit his position as a military and political ally of the U.S. in a broadening hemispheric campaign against Castro to avert an open breach until the very end of Kennedy's term.

U.S. ostracism of Haiti was short-lived. President Johnson moderated the policy of economic and diplomatic sanctions against Haiti and adopted a less critical stance toward Duvalier. In the years that followed, official and unofficial American support of the Haitian regime grew, though no evidence was presented that Duvalier had ceased his campaign of repression. The U.S. adopted measures to prevent U.S. territory from being used as a base by Haitian exiles, provided Haiti with radio-jamming equipment to counter the broadcasts of anti-Duvalier exiles, and initiated a vigorous law enforcement effort to stop exile activities based in the U.S. and aimed at Haiti. During this entire period, the U.S. continued to allow Haitians to remain on sufferance, but without special programs or secure legal status. Thus the earliest recorded Haitian boat people, a contingent of some two dozen persons who landed on Florida's coast in 1963, were denied the political asylum they sought and returned involuntarily to Haiti.

Jean Claude Duvalier's accession to the presidency of Haiti in 1971 was marked by a significant increase in Haitian migration to the United States. Beginning in late 1972, a virtually continuous flow of boats with Haitians seeking political asylum began to land in south Florida. In contrast to previous flows to the U.S., greater numbers of those arriving were poor, uneducated, and of rural origin. The increase in emigration did not result from a sudden worsening in political conditions, but neither did it reflect any great popular approval of Baby Doc's regime or of the quality of life available in Haiti. Instead, it reflected spreading dissatisfaction with every aspect of Haitian existence—its grinding poverty, its lack of opportunity, its corruption, its lack of political freedom, its failure to provide the average man or woman with any protection, legal or otherwise, against the avarice and the brutality of the state.[45]

In the eight years prior to the passage of the Refugee Act of 1980, as many as 30,000 Haitians entered the United States by boat. Thousands sought asylum. The best information available suggests that between 25 and 50 of these applicants were granted political asylum or its equivalent.[46] The rest were subjected to treatment totally unlike that afforded Cuban migrants, and totally inconsistent with the explicit terms and the underlying objectives of international refugee instruments. Initially, the INS denied "excludable" Haitians—generally, those apprehended in the water or immediately after reaching shore—the right to any formal hearing on their asylum claims, although informal procedures adopted late in 1970, after the Coast Guard had returned a

Lithuanian seaman to Russian authorities without giving him a chance to seek asylum, were employed.[47] Nevertheless, return to Haiti was automatic and immediate. New INS regulations adopted in 1974 provided for hearings but permitted the summary disposition of most asylum cases.

The problem with such procedures, and with the virtually certain deportation that followed, was not that they always worked to deprive deserving asylum applicants of the right to enter the United States, but that they revealed a clear double standard which an increasing number of Americans objected to on ideological, legal, and moral grounds. Senator Edward Brooke, a Republican from Massachusetts who had the distinction of being the only black to be elected to the Senate since reconstruction days, conducted a personal inquiry into the Haitian refugee situation in April 1974. He concluded that those departing Haiti left for a variety of reasons:

> No one can deny that some of the exiles living in the United States and elsewhere were forced to flee Haiti because of their political leanings. They can properly be classified as "political refugees" although it is impossible to determine their exact number.
>
> Many of the Haitian exiles, however, are more "economic" than political refugees. Conditions in Haiti are such as to create a desire in the educated classes to migrate to the United States and elsewhere to improve their standard of living. However, entry visas are difficult to obtain. The only other way to gain entry is to claim to be a "political refugee" as "economic refugees" are not accorded sanctuary. Hence, the only alternative is to claim "political refugee" status even though the true reason for leaving Haiti is an economic one.[48]

Brooke's position represented a middle ground between that of INS and the Department of State, which collectively concluded that virtually no Haitians were genuine "political refugees," and that of concerned church groups, which concluded that conditions in Haiti were so universally bad that virtually all who departed, however much they hoped to improve their lot in the United States, were in fact fleeing "persecution." The latter view was the converse of the traditional post-World War II perspective, which held that all those migrating from Eastern European countries were fugitives from an innately evil political system and for that reason alone deserved to be considered refugees. In general, the proponents of the latter view, then and now, have been to the political left of the traditionalists. Yet certain individuals and organizations closely identified with the equation of "Communism" and "persecution" in the 1950s and 1960s—including Leo Cherne and the International Rescue Committee—expressed the belief that Haiti was a "totalitarian state" and that those leaving it were generally deserving of asylum.

No system of evaluating asylum claims can eliminate the effect of such ideological presumptions. "Persecution" is not an easily definable term, and always derives some of its meaning from the political perspectives of those employing it. The belief that all Cubans—or all Haitians—are automatically "refugees" may seem unfair to those that do not benefit from the presumption, but does not necessarily imply bad faith among those doing the categorizing. However, the difficulty the Haitians faced was of a different order. For the effect of the prevailing cold war ideology was not merely to favor Cuban asylum seekers, but to make it virtually impossible for any Haitian, on an individual basis, to demonstrate that he or she was genuinely fearful of persecution. Thus a negative presumption, built into the summary asylum procedure itself, deprived particular applicants of the opportunity to prove that they belonged in Senator Brooke's first category because particular experiences or threats had forced them to flee in fear of their lives or personal safety.

Congressional hearings held in 1975 and 1976[49] demonstrated that untrained American immigration officials systematically denied Haitian asylum seekers any meaningful opportunity to present their claims or to receive individualized evaluation of their purported fear of persecution. They also revealed the primary role that the Department of State played in the asylum decision process. Although the INS has always been entrusted with the duty of evaluating individual asylum claims, prior to 1980 it was required to seek an "advisory opinion" from the State Department on doubtful cases and on those which the INS considered to be without substance. The hearings showed that State Department officials within the Office of Refugee and Migration Affairs (ORM) customarily rendered opinions on applicants whom they had never interviewed and whose files were woefully incomplete. They also demonstrated the key role played by the Haitian desk officer who automatically reviewed the applicant's claim before the Department of State issued its advisory opinion. Such review was crucial, because the applicant was required to demonstrate that his fear of persecution was due to political conditions inside Haiti and resulted from his activities or organizational affiliations. Yet the determinations of the desk officers were often based on the unexamined assumption that Haitian asylum claims were not valid. In very few instances were cases ever referred to the U.S. Embassy in Port-au-Prince for further verification or investigation, nor was much effort expended to monitor returnees. Moreover, the Embassy had no guidelines for review of such asylum claims and did not have enough personnel to carry through a monitoring effort.[50] Thus decisions were made on the basis of considerations having little to do with individual fear of persecution and much to do with relations with countries accused of persecuting.

It might have been possible to hide the politics of asylum if they had surfaced in some other city. But the fact that Cubans and Haitians both came to Miami, and that the former were welcomed unreservedly while the latter were imprisoned and then deported, revealed the contrast too starkly. In the 1975 and 1976 Congressional hearings, the State Department emphasized the "constructive" changes in Haiti since Jean Claude Duvalier had assumed power from his father in 1971, and the Commissioner of the INS, ignoring entirely the actual circumstances of recent Cuban migration, argued:

> Unlike other large alien nationality groups which have fled sudden and intolerable political changes in their respective countries—for example, Hungary, Cuba, and Vietnam—almost all of the Haitian claimants seek to enter the United States or to remain here for the purpose of obtaining employment.[51]

The Miami District Director of the INS explained, "We feel that any relaxation of the rules could produce a flood of economic refugees from all over the Caribbean." But other witnesses, who had involved themselves with the reception and care of the Haitian boat people, told another story. Thus the Rev. Jack Cassidy, associated with the local Haitian relief efforts, detailed a growing involvement of the Protestant churches in Miami with the Haitian situation as the misery of the immigrants and the disparity of the treatment they received became apparent. Unlike the Cubans, he noted, the Haitians had not been "received with open arms and given every assistance and welcome that was possible."[52] Ira Gollobin, a lawyer brought into Miami by the National Council of Churches to represent the Haitians, quoted the Archbishop of Miami, who stated, "I have a dog who receives better treatment than these Haitians."[53]

Gollobin went beyond canine comparisons and the issues of fairness and compassion they raised. As a lawyer, he fought for legal remedies, and claimed to discern the outlines of one in an action of the Johnson administration and the 90th Congress which had occurred nearly six years earlier and then fallen into oblivion. That action was President Johnson's transmittal of the 1967 United Nations Protocol Relating to the Status of Refugees to the Senate for approval and its subsequent ratification in October 1968. Exactly why the United States acceded to the protocol is far from clear. The sparse legislative history suggests that it was primarily a symbolic gesture, a manifestation of solidarity with the United Nation's humanitarian mission timed to coincide with the "International Year for Human Rights," which the U.S. and the UN had both proclaimed.[54] Supporting that gesture were the UNHCR, which had as one of its statutory responsibilities the promulgation of international conventions relating to refugees, and a large number of American voluntary agencies, which advocated continuing U.S. involvement with refugees but apparently had no interest in broadening the refugee definition which the United States had adopted in 1965. Certainly the Department of State, in its testimony advocating ratification of the protocol, believed that nothing in it would significantly alter the nation's obligations to refugees or require any changes in U.S. administrative practice.[55]

Nevertheless, the 1967 protocol contained all the operative language of the 1951 convention except the former document's temporal limits and its optional limits on territorial scope. Its central provision, like that of the earlier document, was the guarantee that each "contracting state" was obliged to give that it would not "expel or return a refugee in any manner whatsoever to the frontiers of territories where his life or freedom would be threatened on account of his race, religion, nationality, membership of a particular group or political opinion."[56] As was the case in the 1951 convention, the definition of refugee spoke of "well-founded fear of persecution,"[57] but not of a particular political system giving rise to that fear. Thus by adopting the 1967 protocol, the United States, perhaps unknowingly, had formally committed itself to a policy of sending no genuine refugee, no matter what his nationality, back to a country where actual persecution was likely.

Quoting President Johnson, Gollobin asserted that the protocol constituted a "Bill of Rights" for every refugee.[58] Those rights, he argued, were not restricted simply to refugees from Communism, but extended also to those fleeing Mr. Duvalier's tyranny. That argument had no immediate effect. The hearings ended, Congress took no action, and the INS continued its campaign of Haitian deportation. Yet the argument Gollobin made in front of Congress was made increasingly often in the courts during the early and middle 1970s. By November 1975, twenty-one separate lawsuits involving 509 Haitians had been filed in the federal courts.[59] None were immediately successful. But all paved the way for more extensive litigation in the years to come. During the Carter and Reagan years, the courts would be used often by human rights organizations and public interest law firms in an attempt to counter the cold war "double standard" which governed American asylum policy and to secure more liberal and evenhanded treatment for asylum seekers entering the United States from Haiti, El Salvador, and other countries governed by right-wing regimes. However, during the early 1970s, the primary focus of these groups—and of the ethnic lobbies, which still played a major role in determining who would be admitted—was on political action dedicated to creating more admission slots for overseas refugees from the Soviet Union, Chile, and Uganda. Some of that action was directed at the Nixon and Ford administrations. But even in the age of parole, refugee advocates learned that Congress still had an important part to play.

Chapter 5

Congress and the Choice of Victims

DURING THE DECADE after the passage of the Immigration Amendments of 1965 and before the fall of Saigon in 1975, U.S. refugee admissions policy continued to be dominated by the President rather than the Congress, and refugee choices increasingly reflected not only the perceived benefits of admitting anti-Communists, but the perceived foreign policy advantages of denying refugee status or political asylum to the increasing number of migrants who entered, or sought to enter, the United States from authoritarian regimes which the United States regarded as allies. This development was partly the result of the ideological bias which was built into the "seventh preference" of the 1965 immigration amendments, which specifically provided for the admission of refugees from "Communist or Communist-dominated" countries but made no provision for those fleeing other sorts of tyranny. However, during the Nixon and Ford administration, ideological bias was balanced with Henry Kissinger's *real politik* vision and a desire for détente with the Soviet Union. Thus, during the decade 1965–1975, favorable treatment continued to be granted Cubans but was resisted for Jewish emigrés from the Soviet Union. And restrictive policies were adopted for applicants from Haiti and Chile and a host of other countries—such as South Korea and the Philippines—with which the U.S. was closely aligned. To the extent that countries closely bound to the U.S. by mutual security interests produced dissatisfied and desperate migrants, the State

Department, with only minor exceptions, recommended against using the special discretionary refugee quota for their admission into the United States. And when nationals of such countries entered the United States, State played a key role in the administrative process of denying them political asylum.

During the decade, however, Congress did listen to ethnic and humanitarian voices that objected to the double standard and the pragmatism of the Executive Branch. Despite obdurate opposition from the Nixon and Ford administrations, it began reshaping American policy to take those interests into account. Increasingly, during the late 1960s and early 1970s, churches, human rights organizations, and public interest law firms began to champion the causes of refugees who lacked broad ethnic support, and whose admission into the United States either served no clear foreign policy interest or ran counter to the prevailing cold war ideology. They were joined by conservative and Jewish lobbyists who believed that pragmatic decisions about foreign policy had resulted in executive unwillingness to address human rights abuses in the Soviet Union. Humanitarian considerations were also moved to the forefront when Congress examined the conduct of U.S. foreign policy in the early seventies. Disenchanted with the *realpolitik* priorities of the Nixon and Ford administrations, Congress passed several resolutions calling on the State Department to increase the priority given to human rights in American foreign policy and to suspend military and economic aid to governments that persistently abused the rights of their citizens.[1] Simultaneously it also expressed greater concern about refugee policy and became more involved in the actual framing of refugee admissions choices.[2]

Between 1965 and December 31, 1972, approximately 68,000 migrants were admitted to the United States under the "seventh preference."[3] That figure was composed entirely of aliens who had departed "Communist or Communist-dominated" countries and either had obtained a "conditional entry" visa after "satisfy[ing]" an Immigration and Naturalization Service officer at an examination in any non-Communist or non-Communist dominated country" that they were in fact eligible for that visa or had obtained a similar visa after entering the United States.[4] Under either procedure, the refugee's ability to reach the West and a presumption by the State Department that the refugee's homeland was in fact Communist-dominated ordinarily were the only things necessary to obtain admission. The 10,200 "seventh preference" visas available each year—later raised to 17,400 when Western Hemisphere migrants were brought within the preference system—generally met the needs of the applicants.

Apart from Cubans, the only major group to enter the U.S. during the period 1965 to 1972 consisted of Czechoslovakian refugees. During 1968, the Soviet authorities again mobilized their forces to put down a liberalization movement in Eastern Europe. In the "Prague spring" of 1968, approximately 80,000 Czechoslovakian nationals were permitted to travel abroad. When the Soviet Union and four of its Warsaw Pact allies militarily occupied Czechoslovakia during the summer of 1968, a significant percentage who had been granted travel permits refused to return.[5] At least 40,000—and perhaps as many as 60,000—Czechoslovakians eventually sought asylum. According to Louise Holborn:

> This group of refugees differed from [earlier Czech refugees. It] was composed of much younger people—students, teachers, scientists, journalists, and doctors. Many of them spoke English, French, and German. They were in possession of valid passports, and often had financial means.[6]

Not surprisingly, they were generally welcome in Western Europe and were the recipients of resettlement offers from a number of other countries, including Canada, Australia, South Africa, and Iran. Although the U.S. government established no special program for them, voluntary agencies did bring some to the United States, and others found their way here on their own. All told, as many as 12,000 Czechoslovakians may have entered the United States either as "seventh preference conditional entrants" or as ordinary immigrants. Unlike the entry of the Hungarian "freedom fighters," their resettlement went virtually unnoticed.

Special problems arose, however, when people seeking to emigrate were not able to leave their countries or could not demonstrate to U.S. authorities that they had fled a Communist political system. During the period from 1972 through 1975, the Nixon and Ford administrations felt increasing pressure to take action on behalf of refugees who fell through the cracks of the new law. Initially, that pressure came mainly from the British government, which sought in 1972 to "internationalize" the problem it faced when Uganda, under the ruthless leadership of Idi Amin, summarily expelled over 50,000 East Asians, many of them holders of British passports. Over the objections of Joshua Eilberg, who had assumed the chairmanship of the House Immigration Subcommittee, and who objected to any extension of parole to aliens who did not meet the definition of "refugee" contained in the "seventh preference," the Nixon administration temporarily admitted over 1,100 Ugandan Asians.[7] It also refused to deport other Ugandan nationals who, it believed, would face immediate persecution if returned.

Most of the pressure to offer protection to refugees who fled authoritarian states or who did not serve larger U.S. foreign policy interests originated from an emerging coalition of human rights organizations, churches, ethnic groups, and activist lawyers, in alliance with members of Congress concerned about human rights violations abroad. By the early seventies, Congress had become increasingly critical of the geopolitical vision and policies of Henry Kissinger, who served as the principal foreign policy architect to the Nixon and Ford administrations. Preoccupation with power politics during the Kissinger years frustrated liberals who felt American foreign policy should reflect national ideals and values. It also frustrated conservatives, who felt that Kissinger, in his pursuit of détente, was too reluctant to criticize human rights problems in Communist countries. In short, the *realpolitik* of Kissinger was judged morally deficient by liberal and conservative opinion alike, and strong support emerged in Congress for a more humanitarian American foreign policy and for more generous treatment of human rights victims abroad.

As part of the broader struggle with the Nixon and Ford administrations over the issue of executive versus Congressional authority in the making of foreign policy, Congress began to confront the Executive Branch on human rights issues. With surprisingly little publicity, Congressman Donald Fraser, Chairman of the Subcommittee on International Organizations and Movements of the House Foreign Affairs Committee, held extensive hearings to examine the role of the U.S. government in the protection of international human rights.[8] This landmark series of hearings, comparable in many ways to Senator William Fulbright's Foreign Relations Committee hearings on U.S. policy in Vietnam in the 1960s, outlined an alternative idea of the national interest in American foreign policy. The Subcommittee summarized its findings thus:

> The human rights factor is not accorded the high priority it deserves in our country's foreign policy. Too often it becomes invisible on the vast foreign policy horizon of political, economic and military affairs.
>
> An increasingly interdependent world means that disregard for human rights in one country can have repercussions in others. . . . Consideration for human rights in foreign policy is both morally imperative and practically necessary.[9]

During the next several years, Congress initiated action in support of these findings and, over strong objections by the Ford administration, incorporated human rights provisions into major economic and security assistance legislation.[10] Some members of Congress went further and translated their several concerns about human rights into special efforts to aid the victims of human rights violations. They focused particularly on groups who stood some chance of escaping danger, but had been offered no welcome by the Johnson, Nixon, or Ford administrations.

The roots of Congressional action on behalf of Soviet Jews lay in institutional perceptions which began to emerge in the mid-1960s, when Senators Birch Bayh, Jacob Javits, Robert Kennedy, Abraham Ribicoff, and Hugh Scott began making public appeals for their cause.[11] To some extent, such appeals were meant to demonstrate to the world the unacceptability of the Soviet political system. Thus New York City Mayor Robert Wagner stated in 1965:

> We do not say that the Soviet Union has a monopoly on persecution. There are other places in the world where men, women and children live in fear and suffer the repression of their faith and their freedom of worship. And there are persecutions of other kinds, too. There is darkness in many parts of the world. But nowhere is that darkness more tragic than in the Soviet Union. . . . Hence, in this city of 8 million free Americans gathered from every corner of the globe, we have a right to join in protesting the persecution of Jews behind the Iron Curtain. As we believe in freedom, we must uphold its causes and denounce its repression.[12]

Many of the individuals who supported these declarations did so for no other reason than to affirm the human rights of Soviet Jews. Yet these appeals also reflected deeply held assumptions about Communist states and their methods of rule—namely that the denial of certain rights, including the right to vote and limitations on travel, the press, free assembly, and complete religious freedom, was equivalent to persecution per se; that Communist regimes were growing progressively more restrictive; and that those escaping could never return without facing significant retribution. Such assumptions had provided the ideological rationale for admitting virtually all Eastern European escapees during the 1950s and early 1960s, had enabled the U.S. to admit several thousand Czechs after the 1968 Soviet invasion, and continued to dominate Congressional opinion in the late 1960s and early 1970s.

External pressures on the Soviet Union to permit more migration coincided in the late 1960s with strong internal demands within the Soviet Union for a liberalized emigration policy and the initiation by Soviet Jews of a lobbying campaign for exit visas. Initially, Soviet authorities reacted negatively. In the wake of the 1968 invasion of Czechoslovakia, the internal political climate of the Soviet Union became increasingly militarized and earlier economic reforms were abandoned. The Soviet Jewish movement doubted that further liberalization in the U.S.S.R. was possible, yet stepped up its activism. The Brezhnev regime permitted more than 2,000 Jews to leave in 1969, but as more Soviet Jews applied to emigrate in 1970, the Soviet leaders cracked down, holding a series of show trials aimed at deterring other Soviet Jews from leaving. The first show trial, in December 1970, involved a group of Soviet Jews who, having been refused exit visas to Israel, allegedly conspired to hijack a plane. The severe penalties imposed on them caused an international outcry and brought the Soviet Jewish emigration question to the forefront of public attention in the United States and Europe.

As a result, the international campaign on behalf of Soviet Jews intensified. An international conference on Soviet Jewry in Brussels in February 1971 and the large demonstrations appealing for emigration that greeted Kosygin on his trip to the West in the early fall of 1971 proved highly embarrassing to the Soviet Union. In the United States, a series of resolutions was passed in Congress calling on the Soviet Union to liberalize its emigration policies,[13] and Congressman Edward Koch of New York introduced legislation to provide 30,000 special nonquota visas for Soviet Jews permitted to leave the Soviet Union.[14] Speaking for many of his colleagues in Congress, Koch explained:

> Enactment of this bill . . . is both a real invitation and an expresson of conscience. And in a real sense it is a challenge to the Soviet Union to open wide her doors and permit the Jews who are vilified there to leave. It will contrast sharply with the neglect of the Jews by mankind 30 years ago when so many countries, ours included, refused sanctuary to many of those Jews who escaped or would have been permitted to leave Nazi Germany through negotiations had visas been available. . . .[15]

Under considerable pressure from Congress to act forcefully on the emigration issue, the Nixon administration responded by promising a liberal admissions policy for Soviet Jews. On September 30, 1971, Attorney General John Mitchell sent a letter to Emmanuel Celler, Chairman of the House Judiciary Committee, promising to use the parole provision should large numbers of Soviet Jews want to come to the U.S.[16]

The Soviet Union responded to these pressures for a liberalized policy by granting thousands of exit visas in the spring of 1971 and then permitting a massive increase in the emigration of Soviet Jews during the last three months of 1971. Allowing approximately 2,500 Jews to emigrate each month was unprecedented, yet that trend continued into 1973. Soviet policy makers wanted to defuse internal dissent and to make a gesture to Western public opinion for the purpose of expanding trade relations, securing economic and technical assistance, and concluding the strategic arms limitations agreements it was negotiating with the Nixon administration. It seemed that the Soviet leadership believed that as long as the issue of the right to leave occupied a central place on the agenda of the Western world, discussions leading to détente would be strained, and that it was therefore in Moscow's interest to defuse the Jewish emigration issue while East-West negotiations proceeded.[17]

The Nixon administration was also interested in pursuing détente and was anxious to reduce the importance of the issue of Soviet Jewish emigration. Yet that anxiety did not translate into immediate condemnation of Soviet internal policies or lead to an executive-sponsored immigration program. Kissinger believed that in order to reach a more constructive relationship with the Soviet Union, a minimum amount of trust and cooperation had to be established between the superpowers. An important element of achieving better relations was, in Kissinger's view, mutual restraint by the superpowers, including non-intervention in the domestic affairs of the other. Kissinger refused to criticize the Kremlin for its repression of Eastern Europe and its refusal to liberalize the Soviet political system. This position was most evident during the negotiations over the Final Act of the Conference on Security and Cooperation in Europe, the Helsinki Agreement. Kissinger was extremely reluctant to attach much importance to human rights issues for fear of delaying or jeopardizing progress on the security and cooperation provisions of the Helsinki Agreement, which had important bearing on the balance of power between East and West. President Nixon and Secretary Kissinger consistently eschewed all types of human rights intercession with the Soviets—unless domestic political pressure forced them to act.[18]

Congress and the Jewish community strongly believed that Soviet Jews should not be ignored in the pursuit of better relations with the Soviet Union, that the United States should pressure Moscow to allow more Jews to emigrate, and that the U.S. immigration authorities should allow more admissions places for those Jews who were allowed to leave. In response to this sentiment, executive officials emphasized the importance of "quiet diplomacy." In testimony before Congress, Richard Davies, Deputy Assistant Secretary for European Affairs, indicated that such diplomacy consisted mostly of presenting lists of names of individuals who were of humanitarian interest to the United States to Soviet officials. Regarding the official administration position on Soviet Jewry, Davies told Congress that "a small number of outspoken Jewish activists has been dealt with arbitrarily and unusually harshly. . . . Individual applicants for emigration are sometimes harassed. We deplore this."[19] But the State Department was reluctant to do other than to deplore, and Davies strongly implied that most Soviet Jews were not singled out for persecution. He said that the United Nations was the best "regular forum for focusing world attention on the situation of Soviet Jews," and he sought to deflect criticism by noting two American protests lodged by the United States Representative to the United Nations Human Rights Commission, Rita Hauser, in March 1970 and February 1971. As for Jews wishing to go to Israel—in contrast with Jews wishing to reunite with American families—Davies flatly asserted, "we cannot be of direct assistance in cases of persons seeking emigration to other countries."[20]

Davies' testimony did not satisfy Congress, but only strengthened Congressional opposition to what it perceived was official indifference to the plight of Soviet Jews. Most members of the Jewish community and of the Congress believed that Soviet Jews were being persecuted, and that the United States had an obligation to aid them. Many legislators feared that détente was being pursued without enough concern for human rights questions. On June 18, 1971, a letter to Nixon signed by forty-two Congressmen asked him "to speak forcefully on the subject to the Soviet government."[21]

During the next several months, a variety of public and private pressures were exerted on the Nixon administration which had the effect of shifting control of the Soviet Jewry issue from the executive to the legislative branch. The year 1972 was a presidential election year, and Senators Henry Jackson and Edmund Muskie, both aspirants for the Democratic nomination, spoke out for Soviet Jewry. The American Israel Public Affairs Committee (AIPAC), a 12,000-member organization which since 1951 had served as an umbrella for all pro-Israeli lobbying by the major Jewish-American organizations, lobbied actively to switch American policy from passivity to firm and vocal support for Soviet Jews. Selecting Jewish emigration as a major AIPAC issue for the years 1972–1974, AIPAC Director Isaiah Kenen focused on persuading Congress to pass the Soviet Jewish Refugee Assistance Act of 1972, which authorized $85 million to help with the cost of resettling Soviet refugees in Israel.[22] He also sought to raise public consciousness about the plight of Soviet Jews. The Jewish community responded quickly to AIPAC initiatives. According to the *American Jewish Yearbook,* "in thirty-five different states, there was legislative action, gubernatorial proclamations, denunciations of Soviet persecution of Jews, and appeals asking the President to raise the question of Soviet Jews."[23]

Despite the growing pressures on Nixon to take a public stance on human rights in the Soviet Union, the President and Kissinger resisted and refused to include Soviet Jewry on the agenda of discussion topics for the upcoming Moscow summit. Jewish leaders met with Nixon and Kissinger before and after the May 1972 summit in Moscow. According to William Safire, Nixon's speechwriter, "the Nixon men impressed on the Jewish leaders the need to let the Soviets back off without losing face. Kissinger kept pointing out that they were not telling us to solve our own race problems before dealing with them. . . . Kissinger did not want détente jeopardized by the admission of impediments like internal policy to the marriage of true minds."[24] If the issue of Soviet Jewry was raised at the summit at all, it was done in a most discrete manner. Kissinger counseled Safire and Presidential aide Robert Haldeman in Moscow to "say nothing while we're here. How would it be if Brezhnev comes to the United States with a petition about the Negroes in Mississippi?"[25] The impression left on most Jewish activists and lobbyists was that Nixon and Kissinger were concerned exclusively with not jeopardizing Soviet-American relations and that détente was being pursued without enough concern for the plight of Soviet Jews.

Congress and those supporting AIPAC continued to believe that only through sustained pressure would the Soviet Union liberalize its emigration policy. Their belief was confirmed in August 1972 when the Soviet Union suddenly imposed an "education tax," which required Soviet Jewish emigrants to pay a considerable sum compensating the state for the costs of higher education. This action was seen by Soviet Jewish and world public opinion as an almost insuperable obstacle to emigration and caused an international outcry. In the United States it precipitated legislative action in Congress which sought to link the economic benefits of détente to freer emigration.

Congress fastened onto the only leverage it had at its disposal and demanded a change in Soviet emigration practices as a condition for favorable trade terms. Most of the initiative for this action originated with Senator Henry Jackson. An important part of détente for the Soviet Union was the economical benefits they hoped to gain from improved relations with the United States. Advocates of the Jackson proposal assumed that Moscow always weighed the gains to be derived from a particular action against losses. Senator Jackson and his supporters believed increased East-West trade through the granting of most-favored-nation tariff treatment and large-scale credits would outweigh the Soviet loss of skilled Jewish emigrants and the possible destabilizing effects on Soviet society of easing emigration structures. In the fall of 1972 the U.S. reached a trade agreement with the Soviet Union. At about the same time, Senator Jackson introduced his proposal, which would tie trade benefits to Communist nations including "most-favored-nation" tariff treatment, credits, credit guarantees, and investment guarantees, to the removal of obstacles to emigration.[26]

Senator Jackson's legislation attracted the support of numerous interest groups, including Jews, who were concerned about their persecuted brethren in the Soviet Union, and organized labor, which opposed the granting of trade concessions to the Soviet Union for fear of losing more jobs abroad. Congressional support for the Jackson proposal quickly blossomed, due in no small part to the extraordinary lobbying efforts of AIPAC, working in close collaboration with three senior Jewish aides to Senators Henry Jackson and Abraham Ribicoff and Representative Charles Vanek.[27] Threatening to run hostile election-year mail campaigns against reluctant Senators, AIPAC quickly secured the support of seventy-six Senators who cosponsored the Jackson amendment. In response to this pressure, the Nixon administration relaxed its opposition to raising human rights issues with the Soviet Union and indicated that it would not proceed with any lowering of U.S.-U.S.S.R. trade barriers without legislative authorization. The Soviet Union also indicated its receptivity to Congressional concerns by temporarily suspending collection of the "education tax" and by allowing emigration to reach its highest level during the closing months of 1972. These gestures, however, did not stem the rising tide of Congressional support for the Jackson amendment, and Representative Vanek's companion amendment making the same proposals quickly garnered

237 cosponsors in the House of Representatives. Despite subsequent assurances from Moscow that it would drop the "education tax" and end its harassment of Jewish emigrés, Senate and House Committees took favorable action on the Jackson and Vanek amendments. As a result of intensive negotiations between Kissinger and the Soviets, however, the amendments were modified so that the President, by indicating that he had assurances about future performance of the U.S.S.R. in respect to emigration, could waive the restrictions on "most-favored-nation" status and credits for eighteen months.

By December 1974, when the combined Jackson-Vanek amendment to the Trade Reform Act of 1974 came up for a vote and passed, a deteriorating international climate, prompted largely by Soviet actions during the Yom Kippur War of October 1973, led Congress to further limit its trade concessions. Led by Senator Adlai Stevenson, Congress placed sharp limits on financial credits to the U.S.S.R. The restrictions imposed by the parallel Stevenson amendment could be overcome only by a Presidential declaration of national interest and prior Congressional approval. In debate on the amendment, Stevenson explained that Congressional approval would depend on moderation in a variety of foreign policy areas. While the Soviet leaders appeared willing to live with the Jackson-Vanek amendment and to make compromises on Jewish emigration, these concessions were predicated on Moscow's access to sizable American economic credits. The amount permitted under the Stevenson amendment, in Kissinger's words, was "peanuts in Soviet terms." Thus the Soviets, not surprisingly, concluded that it was a bad bargain for them. A few days later they repudiated the trade agreement they had reached with the Nixon administration in October of 1972, and the economic pillar of U.S.-Soviet détente virtually collapsed.

As U.S.-Soviet relations deteriorated during the Ford administration, Soviet Jewish emigration fell to 13,000 in 1975, about one-third the record level of 1973. During the following decade, as those relations went on a roller-coaster ride, emigration from the Soviet Union fluctuated wildly. When bilateral relations became generally bad, conditions for Jews tended to become worse, and when relations were generally stable or Moscow had potential benefits to gain, Soviet Jews were permitted greater freedom and larger numbers were allowed to emigrate.

Support for those who did manage to emigrate remained remarkably stable. Parole was used automatically to admit those migrants desiring to enter the United States. Even in 1979, when the number of Jewish entrants reached 50,000 and the resources of the voluntary agencies responsible for resettling them were strained substantially, there was virtually no public resistance to continued entry. Soviet Jews, particularly in Congress, where their advocates were legion, remained a politically popular immigrant group. Their popularity was chiefly attributable to American sensitivity about its conduct toward Jewish refugees during the Nazi era and the well-organized lobbying campaign which made advocacy of Jewish emigration a precondition for AIPAC support. Yet it also owed something to the awareness that those seeking to emigrate were fleeing the Soviet Union, which American conservatives regarded as an innately evil land.

No similar network of support for the backers of President Salvador Allende existed in the United States in 1973 when General Augusto Pinochet staged a successful coup d'état, and ousted the democratically elected but avowedly Marxist Chilean government. The Nixon administration, which had used the CIA in an unsuccessful attempt to keep Allende out of office, felt little immediate pressure to extend aid, protection, or resettlement opportunities to Allende's constituents or to any of the residents of other Latin American nations with leftist views who Allende had welcomed. The Chilean refugees, in particular, were regarded as enemies of the state by Pinochet and his military supporters. The U.S. ignored diplomatic entreaties from the UNHCR and other Western governments and maintained a studied "neutrality" which accepted widespread and manifest persecution without public demurral. Yet as that persecution intensified, new voices urged greater compassion and generosity. Included were members of Congress, such as Rep. Robert Drinan of Massachusetts and Sen. Edward Kennedy, various religious groups in the United States, and a number of human rights organizations, of which Amnesty International was perhaps the most notable. Initially they had great difficulty convincing the rest of Congress that humanitarian considerations should take precedence over deep-seated antagonisms to "leftist radicals," and they were not able to influence executive conduct directly. However, their persistence, buttressed by a continuing stream of detailed stories of human rights violations from Chile, contributed to a growing national awareness of an intolerable situation, which eventually resulted in a series of small parole programs for Chileans and other Latin-Americans facing persecution under Pinochet.

The initial concern of the international community when General Pinochet seized power centered on the 10,000 to 15,000 refugees who had fled right wing regimes in Brazil, Argentina, Uruguay, and other Latin American countries and had been granted asylum in Chile during Salvador Allende's presidency. In the tense atmosphere after the coup, many of these foreign refugees were detained and tortured; others were forced to seek political asylum in foreign embassies in Santiago or go underground. Large numbers were executed. In addition, thousands of Allende supporters were summarily imprisoned, and many were tortured or shot. Thus an acute refugee problem surfaced in Chile which necessitated an emergency international response.[28]

As signatories of the Treaty of Caracas, most Latin-American nations upheld the practice of granting "diplomatic asylum" and these nations responded by filling their embassies to capacity with Chilean and foreign refugees. In view of the exceptionally grave circumstances, many European governments, departing from ordinary practice, provided asylum in their Santiago embassies. The United States, on the other hand, did not alter its traditional policy despite State Department guidelines on asylum policy which state that "immediate temporary refuge [in embassies] may be granted in extreme or exceptional circumstances wherein the life or safety of a person is put in danger."[29] The U.S. Embassy did what was necessary to avoid being accused of total neglect of the human rights and refugee situation, but U.S. Ambassador David Popper received no encouragement from the Executive Branch to take a more activist role. This position was consistent with the Nixon administration's antagonism toward the former Allende regime.[30] That antagonism was comparable only to the pressure against Fidel Castro of Cuba early in the Kennedy administration. After the 1970 Chilean election, the abrupt decrease in U.S. foreign assistance, multilateral lending, and private foreign investment—as well as the destabilizing efforts of U.S. intelligence agencies and U.S. corporations—contributed to the downfall of Allende. Thus it came as no surprise when the Nixon administration made no outward protest to the Chilean government concerning human rights violations within Chile after the violent overthrow of Allende. Jack B. Kubisch, who was at that time serving as Assistant Secretary of State for Inter-American Affairs, explained the administration's position:

> Most countries still regard references to domestic activities involving human rights as improper involvement in their internal affairs. This is true of all sorts of governments, and it is a reality which we must face in our dealings with foreign governments on human rights issues.[31]

Thus the U.S. government publicly ignored human rights violations in such countries as Chile. Pragmatic considerations—the risk of antagonizing foreign governments or their friends, the risk of losing a source of raw materials or opportunities for foreign investment, the likelihood that protests or other actions would have little practical effect, and the limited approval Washington could expect from other states for a moral stance—were deemed by the United States to outweigh any humanitarian considerations. Kissinger believed that opposition to another nation's human rights violations would only make it difficult to achieve more important political, military, or economic objectives. Under the assumption that U.S. security still demanded the support of avowedly anti-Communist regimes, the U.S. continued to underwrite its allegiance to a wide variety of repressive but strategically important governments with extensive programs of economic and military aid. In terms of the short-run national interest, there seemed little to be gained and much to be lost by taking a pro-human rights stand.

When Ambassador Popper did raise human rights issues with Chilean officials in 1974, he was severely reprimanded by Kissinger, who said, "tell Popper to cut out the political science lectures." Instead of censuring Chile, the administration made every effort to enhance General Pinochet's legitimacy. Direct U.S. bilateral aid to Chile rose from $10.1 million in 1973 to $177.3 million in 1975 despite indisputable evidence of massive human rights violations authorized at the highest levels of the Chilean government. In Fiscal Year 1975, Chile received $57.8 million in assistance under the American Food for Peace program. The rest of Latin America, with thirty times Chile's population, received only $9 million.[32] Economic aid, however, was not matched by any commitment to accept those threatened by the Pinochet government.

The initial response of Congress to the Chilean refugee problem was not much more positive than that offered by the Executive Branch. Although Congressman Robert Drinan, only a few days after the coup in Chile, urged in the House "that the United States give the same treatment to those suffering persecution in Chile as we have given to Hungarian freedom fighters and the refugees from Fidel Castro's Cuba,"[33] Congress took no initiative to alleviate the refugee problem. Bills to admit Chilean refugees into the U.S. introduced by Drinan and Senator Edward Kennedy were unsuccessful, primarily because Congress strongly resisted admitting Marxists and Communists who had been aligned with Allende.[34]

The resettlement effort on behalf of Chilean refugees and detainees was led by international organizations, particularly the United Nations High Commissioner for Refugees (UNHCR), the Intergovernmental Commission for European Migration (ICEM), and the International Committee of the Red Cross (ICRC).[35] UNHCR efforts initially concentrated upon aiding those refugees falling within its mandate, which extended to the foreign refugees stranded in Chile but not to Chilean nationals who remained there. Two days after the coup, the High Commissioner cabled the Chilean Foreign Minister expressing grave concern that the lives and safety of refugees within UNHCR's mandate were seriously imperiled. He appealed for their protection and requested permission for UNHCR access to Chile. A few days later the UNHCR representative for Latin America was permitted to enter Chile and to establish an emergency office there. As a result of negotiations between the UNHCR and the Chilean government, a National Committee for Aid to Refugees was established.

After the initial siege, which involved the widespread detention and torture of former Allende supporters, the Pinochet regime worked to rid Chile of its dissidents and improve its image abroad. Believing that the best way to handle the problem was to involve the international agencies, the Chilean government requested ICEM and ICRC intervention on behalf of those Chileans who sought to emigrate. Over the next several months, ICEM, ICRC, concerned churches, and the Chilean government negotiated arrangements to move the thousands of individuals in prisons and detention centers who wanted to leave Chile. Unlike its European and Latin American allies, the U.S. expressed no interest in this program, and provided no funds to ICEM to finance the resettlement of Chilean refugees until 1976.[36] Prior to 1976, all such funds were raised by non-U.S. sources, and the largest donors were Sweden, the Federal Republic of Germany, Italy, and the German Democratic Republic. The U.S. was the last government to cooperate with the ICEM program for Chileans,[37] and American assistance came after the majority of Chileans had already been resettled abroad.

The U.S. did contribute to UNHCR care and maintenance programs for non-Chilean refugees, but ignored appeals from UNHCR to resettle refugees from Chile. When General Pinochet declared that all foreign nationals remaining in Chile had to leave the country by February 1974, the UNHCR urgently appealed for help from UN member states. While the Federal Republic of Germany, France, and Sweden each took in between 800 and 1,100 refugees, the U.S. accepted only 26 out of about 150 people who had applied for admission to the U.S. through UNHCR. A year after the coup, in August 1974, the UNHCR appealed to the U.S. to grant asylum to a substantial number of the 4,000 Chilean exiles who had been temporarily accepted by Peru on the condition that they later be resettled. In September 1974, the Chilean government also announced that it would release most of its political prisoners if foreign governments would offer them asylum. In response to these appeals, the Office of Refugee and Migration Affairs urged its superiors in the State Department to take positive action. The State Department, however, receiving no firm guidance from the Nixon administration, decided to consult with the House and Senate Immigration subcommittees before it submitted a formal proposal to INS to establish a Chilean parole program. Thus it was not until late April 1975 that the State Department formally proposed a group asylum program for the Chileans to the Attorney General. It took Attorney General Edward H. Levi another two months to respond with qualified approval to the State Department's parole program proposal, and the program which was finally approved was limited to 400 parole cases. The U.S. indicated it would accept only those currently in prison for political offenses and would not accept any persons outside of prison whose claims reflected only a fear of future persecution. It also announced that it would not consider under the program any detainees or refugees found to be ineligible under the provisions of the INA because of membership in the Communist Party, in leftist revolutionary movements, "or [in] other terrorist groups," or who had criminal records. Furthermore, all applicants would be required to undergo a "rigorous" security screening and a "detailed" medical examination.[38] Of all the resettlement countries involved in the Chilean program, the U.S. had the strictest admissions criteria.[39]

The Nixon and Ford administrations and Congress all resisted the establishment of a comprehensive parole program to meet the humanitarian needs of Chilean refugees. Many members of Congress privately expressed misgivings about the parole program, fearing that it would result in the admission of "leftist radicals" into the United States or that it might burden the already existing unemployment situation. In the words of one analyst:

> State Department representatives went to great lengths trying to overcome these objections. They assured the doubters that the immigration act would be complied with and that no communists or "subversives" would be admitted. There would be no "blanket admission" of Chileans. Finally, they argued that the number of admissions contemplated was only about 400 families—hardly enough to have a serious effect on the economy. In the end, though, congressional attitudes were still mixed:

> Chairman Eastland in the Senate . . . and . . . Edward Hutchinson, the ranking Republican on the House Judiciary Committee, appear to be opposed to a parole program for those refugees in Chile and those in Peru. . . .

> Chairman Kennedy of the Senate Subcommittee enthusiastically supports a program of parole for both groups. . . .

> The House Subcommittee has indicated support for parole of refugees physically in Chile, but [has] declined to indicate support for those in Peru.[40]

This lack of Congressional consensus helps explain in great part the bureaucratic resistance within State and the INS that occurred both prior to and after the implementation of the Chilean parole program. Senator Edward Kennedy complained that

> Foot-dragging and excuses have characterized our government's approach to the Chilean refugee program. We have heard a litany of promises but have seen very little action. For two years, letters from the Department of State, in response to my inquiries . . . and the testimony of department officials before this subcommittee, have given assurances of an intent to provide generous parole for refugees from Chile. Those assurances were not fulfilled. Press releases were issued announcing a willingness to receive Chilean refugees. But that willingness has been contradicted by the lack of positive action. And then

only when we were engaged in requesting those same international organizations and agencies for help in resettling Vietnamese, the red tape barriers suddenly were broken and the Chilean parole program was suddenly established in early June.[41]

Further delays occurred after the June 1975 establishment of the Chilean parole program as the Executive Branch moved slowly on the processing of cases. Few Chilean refugees applied to the U.S. parole program because of their antipathy toward the U.S., which had opposed Allende and continued to support Pinochet. Many were Communists or socialists and would not have been eligible for admission under U.S. law. Nevertheless, it was not until more than four months after the initiation of the program and only after hard-hitting hearings held by Senator Kennedy that the first Chilean parolee entered the United States on October 17, 1975. Even then, the screening process by INS officials was unprecedentedly long, and security screening exceptionally thorough.[42] Each Chilean parolee had to be personally approved by the Director of the INS.[43] It took months and sometimes years to secure INS approval, locate a sponsor for each refugee and his or her family, and receive an exit decree from the Chilean government. By January 1976, seven months after the program began, only seventy-six people had been approved for the parole program and only twenty-seven people had arrived in the United States.

The situation of the Chileans would probably have been even more untenable without Senator Kennedy's advocacy and a network of other supporters in the U.S. A coalition of human rights organizations, including Amnesty International and religious agencies, repeatedly lobbied for a change in U.S. policy toward the Chilean government and better treatment of that regime's victims. Concern about human rights violations in Chile led Congress to make cuts in aid to the Pinochet regime. Section 35 of the 1973 Foreign Assistance Act provided that the President require Chile to protect human rights, support United Nations and Red Cross activities to aid political refugees and investigate detention centers, support and aid voluntary agencies in emergency relief needs, and request the Inter-American Commission on Human Rights to investigate recent events in Chile.[44] Section 25 of the 1974 Foreign Assistance Act prohibited all military assistance to Chile and limited economic assistance to $25 million during 1975.[45] In the end, the combined pressures from Kennedy's Judiciary Subcommittee, Amnesty International, and other human rights groups did force the U.S. to make good on its Chilean parole program, but it came too late to be of any real benefit.

The efforts of private voluntary organizations and certain public officials to make America's response to refugee problems less overtly political and more explicitly humanitarian often ran up against obdurate governmental opposition and the prevailing geopolitical ideology of the Kissinger period. The admission of Chileans did not have broad ethnic support nor did it serve clear foreign policy interests. The United States not only had encouraged destabilization in Chile, but felt no obligation to resettle those persons endangered by the overthrow of Allende. No significant progress was made in securing the actual admission of Chileans until the Carter administration assumed office and began promoting concern for human rights as an explicit element of U.S. foreign policy. By 1977, out of 20,000 Chileans moved by ICEM for resettlement, about 1,100 had resettled in the United States. In March 1978, the "Hemispheric 500 Program" was announced by the Carter administration with strong support from Senator Kennedy and others. It provided for the parole of several thousand additional Chilean prisoners to the U.S. and the parole of a similar number of Argentinians imprisoned by the military dictatorship in Buenos Aires.

Thus, by the middle and late 1970s parole had reemerged as an admissions device in Latin America and Eastern Europe. Its most significant flowering, however, occurred in Indochina. There, its initial impetus came not from a Congress concerned with admitting groups the President had chosen to ignore, but from a profound foreign policy failure which demanded immediate executive action.

Chapter 6

Flight from Saigon

In April 1975, the United States faced the result of a failed foreign and military policy in Southeast Asia. Despite the fact that over two and a half million American soldiers had fought in Vietnam and 58,000 had died there, the regime of Nguyen Van Thieu was collapsing and hundreds of thousands, if not millions, of South Vietnamese, whom successive administrations from Eisenhower to Ford had promised to defend, feared for their safety under a new Communist government. These potential victims of a Communist takeover vividly symbolized America's failed crusade in Vietnam and bore witness to the end of America's long, frustrated involvement in Indochina. The United States felt a profound sense of obligation to the Vietnamese and initiated an admissions program which would rescue 130,000 of them.

The fall of Saigon precipitated an instantaneous refugee crisis which demanded immediate attention in the Executive Branch. American policy makers were presented with an emergency in which a large number of people with whom the U.S. had been allied were threatened with harm. Regarding the crisis primarily in humanitarian and political terms rather than as an ideological opportunity or as a means of promoting ethnic immigration interests, the White House, the military, and the State Department all committed themselves to a program of limited scope and duration dedicated to rescuing America's Vietnamese allies.

Despite the anti-Vietnam War sentiment that existed among the public and the generally restrictionist attitudes of interested Congressional committees, the decision to admit Indochinese refugees was made relatively quickly. The pattern of executive-dominated refugee admissions which had prevailed since the 1950s, despite recent Congressional initiatives on behalf of Jewish and Chileans refugees, remained intact. The backing of the Ford administration, the dominance of the Department of State in the decision-making structure, media support, and the lack of serious resistance among the public permitted the rescue policy to proceed with a minimum of political fallout. This commitment to admit Indochinese refugees began as an attempt to rescue a limited number of former allies who could be safely evacuated. However, the long-term Indochinese admissions program which was to extend over the next ten years was a far more extensive and ideological operation than its antecedent.

By early 1975, military defeat was imminent for the non-Communist Indochinese states. In Cambodia, the Khmer Rouge had control of the Mekong River, which was used to convey supplies to Phnom Penh, the last stronghold of Gen. Lon Nol's forces. In South Vietnam, the North Vietnamese forces were gearing up for a spring offensive in the highlands in order, in veteran Politburo member Le Duan's words, "to create conditions for a general uprising in 1976," with a bid for complete victory sooner "if opportunities present themselves."

These ominous signs in early 1975 caused the State Department's refugee office to begin planning for an evacuation of Americans from the Indochina states in early 1975. Top secret telegrams were sent out to all embassies in the Southeast Asian nations inquiring whether their governments would be willing to receive Cambodians and Vietnamese in the event of Communist military victories.[1] For the most part, however, American officials were not yet ready to confront the problem of planning an evacuation from Vietnam. Despite the unpopularity of the war, no one wanted to be responsible for losing Indochina after over fifteen years of American involvement and considerable loss of life. The Ford administration and those in charge of the U.S. Embassies in Saigon and Phnom Penh focused their efforts on shoring up the rapidly failing pro-American regimes through supplemental aid packages they hoped Congress would approve. In the case of Cambodia, last minute aid was not forthcoming. Despite a Congressional mission to Phnom Penh which witnessed the desperate military situation there, Congress refused to restore military assistance. The refusal hastened the fall of the Cambodian government.

The rapid closing down of the war in Indochina and the refusal of Congress to come to the rescue of America's allies by granting the President the military aid packages he wanted caused many U.S. and Indochinese officials to complain that Washington was abandoning its allies in their moments of greatest need. To the American Ambassador to Cambodia, John Dean, Congress had betrayed a small nation "with whom the American people had mingled their blood and had died."[2] Many believed that the U.S. had not kept its promises to Cambodia and was acting in an inhumane and cowardly fashion by leaving the country to the brutal Khmer Rouge. In the final hours before his departure, Ambassador Dean offered to take with him any Cambodian cabinet minister who wanted to leave. In response, Dean received this letter from one prominent cabinet member, Prince Sirik Matak:

> Dear Excellency and friend. I thank you very sincerely for your letter and for your offer to transport me towards freedom. I cannot, alas, leave in such a cowardly fashion.
>
> As for you and in particular for your great country, I never believed for a moment that you would have this sentiment of abandoning a people which has chosen liberty. You have refused us your protection and we can do nothing about it. You leave and it is my wish that you and your country will find happiness under the sky. But mark it well that, if I shall die here on the spot and in my country that I love, it is too bad because we are all born and must die one day. I have only committed this mistake of believing in you, the Americans.
>
> Please accept, Excellency, my dear friend, my faithful and friendly sentiments. Sirik Matak.[3]

The poignancy of Matak's remarks underscored for many American officials the sense of shame they felt at America's failure to support a small and vulnerable ally. In the years to follow, Matak's message would also haunt many who thought the U.S. should have rescued more Cambodians when they abandoned Phnom Penh to the Khmer Rouge. This sense of obligation to a people the United States had supported and then abandoned would also be the rationale for opening up a U.S. admissions program for Cambodians in 1980.

As the Khmer Rouge encircled Phnom Penh, Ambassador Dean closed the American Embassy and left Cambodia by helicopter on April 12, 1975. In all, only 800 Cambodians were evacuated with the American Embassy staff in Operation Eagle Pull. Most were flown into Thailand by the U.S. Air Force. However, several thousand additional Cambodian refugees arrived about the same time on foot in the border areas of eastern Thailand. No more were taken at the time because few Cambodians had worked directly for the U.S. military. Unlike the situation in South Vietnam, the American war effort in Cambodia had been largely conducted by U.S. and South Vietnamese bombers and Cambodian ground forces. Although the evacuation from Cambodia was hastily planned, Ambassador Dean took an active role in arranging for the departure. Those few who chose to be evacuated were high-level Cambodian officials and others who would have been executed by the victorious Khmer Rouge. Most of those Cambodians reaching Thailand were subsequently resettled in the

U.S. or France. Many tens of thousands of Cambodians with Western ties were left behind, however, and would soon become the first victims of the Khmer Rouge reign of terror.

The prowestern government in South Vietnam fell three weeks later. Despite the chaos of the American departure from Cambodia and the feeling of unease over abandoning an ally and its people, the United States was caught almost entirely unprepared for the unraveling of South Vietnam. The downfall of Thieu and the speed with which the final collapse occurred were not anticipated. Many U.S. government officials, in particular Ambassador Graham Martin, had expected the South Vietnamese army and the Saigon government to survive longer, despite U.S. intelligence reporting to the contrary. Less than two months before the fall of Saigon, U.S. Secretary of Defense James Schlesinger proclaimed that there would be no major Communist military offensive against the Thieu government that year.[4] But in March, several South Vietnamese highland cities fell to a Communist military offensive, and panic ensued when President Thieu responded by ordering his army to retreat. Over 1 million refugees retreated from the highlands and headed for the coast.[5]

Disorder spread when the cities for which many refugees were bound fell in rapid succession. Da Nang, South Vietnam's second largest city, was evacuated under chaotic conditions. In the panicky rush to escape, people were pushed off overcrowded barges and drowned. Soldiers fought civilians for scarce Air America seats. The weak or helpless did not escape or survive the evacuation from Da Nang. It was mainly soldiers, civil servants, and merchants who made it safely all the way to Saigon.[6] After Da Nang, other coastal cities quickly fell, leaving only a perimeter around Saigon under the South Vietnamese government's control.

Throughout the crisis, Ambassador Martin had as his objective the preservation of the Thieu regime, and he refused to plan for evacuation from Vietnam which would include Americans and Vietnamese.[7] With the nightmarish experience of Da Nang in mind, Martin believed that the moment word got out that an evacuation was being planned, there would be a stampede to leave, and the entire government would collapse. Martin and Secretary Henry Kissinger believed there was a danger that frenzied South Vietnamese government troops might massacre the Americans and their Vietnamese cohorts to prevent them from departing. Moreover, Martin hoped that an interim government might take power, buying the U.S. the time it needed to arrange a massive and orderly evacuation from South Vietnam. Until then, Martin opposed drawing up evacuation plans on the grounds that any overhasty planning might bring on Thieu's downfall. He did not want this at a time when the Ford administration was attempting to offer full support in the form of increased American military aid to Saigon.[8] He believed that the key to holding firm and stabilizing the military situation was $722 million in supplemental American aid to Thieu's forces, a recommendation advanced by Gen. Fred Weyand, the last U.S. military commander in Vietnam.

The chaos at Da Nang, however, had a catalyzing effect on a number of U.S. Foreign Service officers and Agency for International Development (AID) officials who felt a deep commitment to their Vietnamese co-workers. They believed the U.S. government had a moral obligation to help persons who had supported U.S. policies. They felt personally dishonored that the U.S. had abandoned its Vietnamese employees and associates in Da Nang, and they were determined that no similar betrayal would occur in Saigon. A small group began to develop an unofficial evacuation schedule for both Americans and "high risk" Vietnamese. At the same time, Foreign Service officers in the American Embassy began to draw up lists of potential evacuees, including in-laws of present and former Embassy staffers who had married Vietnamese, and to prepare safe houses and covert communication links for the final evacuation. None of these activities received any encouragement or guidance from Martin. As a result, senior-level State Department planning for a full-scale evacuation of Americans and Vietnamese began only in the second week of April and by the third week had not progressed beyond the preliminary stage. It was not until Saigon was encircled by Communist troops that Assistant Secretary of State Philip Habib agreed to convert the informal working group in the operations center at the State Department into a task force to coordinate State's evacuation planning.[9]

Until the last moment, the Ford administration worked hard to persuade Congress to approve its proposed aid package to Thieu, but the President was unsuccessful. Included were last-ditch efforts to gain American sympathy for the South Vietnamese cause and to paint as alarming a picture as possible of the fate facing the South Vietnamese people in a postrevolutionary Vietnam. In an April 3 news conference, President Ford stated that the fact that South Vietnamese people were "fleeing from the North Vietnamese" was clearly "an indication that they don't want to live under the kind of government that exists in North Vietnam."[10] Ford characterized the refugee situation in Vietnam as "a tragedy unbelievable in its ramifications."[11] Operation Babylift,[12] an emergency program whereby over 2,000 Vietnamese orphans would be flown to foster homes in the U.S. under a new parole program, was launched on April 4.[13] Commenting on Operation Babylift at the time, Dr. Phan Quang Dan, Deputy Prime Minister for Social Welfare, wrote Prime Minister Khiem after meeting with Ambassador Martin:

> The departure of a considerable number of orphans will cause a profound emotion in the world, and especially in the United States, that will be all to the

benefit of South Vietnam. The American Ambassador will assist us in every way possible, since he himself is convinced that the evacuation of thousands of war victims will help to sway American public opinion in South Vietnam's favor. When the children arrive in the United States, the press, television and radio will give ample publicity to the matter and the impact will be enormous.[14]

President Ford greeted the first planeload of orphans to reach the U.S. and was photographed on the ramp, smiling and holding in his arms the first arrival.

One of the principal concerns of U.S. policy makers was the mistreatment they expected the new Communist government to visit on its former opponents. There was a widespread belief that there would be a bloodbath if the revolutionary forces took over in South Vietnam. For twenty years South Vietnamese citizens had been taught by their leaders that the Communists would massacre them should the North prevail. The execution of landlords in North Vietnam in the 1950s, the 1968 Hue massacre, and the Viet Cong assassinations of village leaders during the war constituted proof enough that Communist terror was far from imaginary. However, Saigon's fears were reinforced by numerous dire warnings from Washington. On April 15, Secretary Schlesinger, testifying before the Senate Appropriations Committee for additional military aid to South Vietnam, warned that over 200,000 Vietnamese would face death if the Communists seized power. The rumors of a bloodbath were rampant, and atrocity stories abounded in the South Vietnamese press, including third-hand reports of Communists tearing out women's fingernails and murdering local officials.[15] It was hoped that such news reports would help influence Congress to vote for major funding to continue the war. In the end, Congress was not influenced. Dire warnings about a slaughter in Vietnam seemed to many Congressmen an easy line of propaganda spread by American and Vietnamese officials to justify and perpetuate an increasingly unpopular war. Congress voted down the Ford request for military aid to Thieu. In taking this action, Congress simply reflected the opinion of the overwhelming majority of Americans who favored no further aid to Saigon. The major effect of American dire predictions was to convince large numbers of South Vietnamese that they would suffer at the hands of the advancing Communist forces if they did not flee.

In several public statements in early April,[16] President Ford expressed the need to develop an American plan for evacuating Vietnamese and the need to request the authority to parole Vietnamese into the U.S. However, as the testimony of Assistant Secretary Philip Habib before the Senate Judiciary Committee's Subcommittee to Investigate Problems Connected with Refugees and Escapees on April 15 made clear, the U.S. still did not have a detailed plan for an evacuation. The potential victims of Communist reprisals numbered, in addition to 6,000 Americans, more than 100,000 Vietnamese then or formerly employed by various American agencies—who, with their kin, swelled the total to nearly a million. U.S. officials had only focused on plans to evacuate Americans and U.S. government employees. Fourteen days before Saigon fell, it was unclear how many Vietnamese the U.S. would help evacuate, how these Vietnamese would be selected, whether all those whom the U.S. helped evacuate would be allowed to enter the U.S., and what status those admitted would have. Furthermore, the U.S. had made no provisions by that time for receiving large numbers of Vietnamese into the country. The voluntary agencies, which had considerable prior experience in the resettlement of refugees into the U.S., had not been consulted, and virtually no consideration had been given to how the U.S. was going to resettle those Vietnamese it did evacuate. At the April 15 hearing, Habib made a commitment to evacuate only American citizens and their dependents (3,839 people) and about 17,600 Vietnamese currently employed by the U.S. government. This evacuation was to be achieved through the use of the parole authority, which had been used in the past to admit large numbers of Hungarians and Cubans. Congress authorized use of the parole for dependents of American citizens in Vietnam. But no decision had been made on whether the U.S. would assume responsibility for the dependents of its Vietnamese employees or Vietnamese whom the U.S. considered to be in "high risk" categories, i.e., previous U.S. employees who were vulnerable to Communist retribution.[17]

It was only after the Senate Armed Services Committee actually voted down the $722 million supplemental aid request which signaled the last hope for a military reversal in Vietnam that the administration belatedly set the evacuation in gear. President Ford formed an Interagency Task Force headed by Ambassador L. Dean Brown, who was called out of retirement to coordinate the evacuation from Vietnam. On the same day, April 17, Kissinger ordered the phased evacuation of Americans from Vietnam and requested the still reluctant Ambassador Martin to submit a plan for evacuating as many as 200,000 Vietnamese. As originally planned, the Vietnamese were to be removed to neighboring Southeast Asian countries. However, Ambassador Brown, sensing regional opposition to the granting of long-term asylum, shelved this plan and decided instead to transport them directly to the United States. For command and control reasons, Brown requested the U.S. military to administer the evacuation and resettlement effort. According to Frank Snepp's account:

> From the outset [Ambassador] Brown accepted as a "given" that large numbers of Vietnamese would have to be included in any evacuation program. The main questions were how many and under what kind of immigration authority. There was also the subsidiary problem of where to put all the refugees. With so few practical alternatives available, it quickly became ap-

parent that the United States itself would have to absorb the vast majority of them. But who was to take charge of this potentially mammoth enterprise? After some debate, the White House decided to give the job to the Army, Navy and Air Force. Each branch of the Armed Forces was promptly invited to "volunteer" an installation as a temporary resettlement center.[18]

The decision to evacuate Vietnamese through U.S. bases and Guam would make later efforts to internationalize the subsequent resettlement of Indochinese refugees more difficult.

Most of the world perceived the evacuation from Saigon as an apt conclusion to the U.S. debacle in Vietnam and the refugees who were escaping Saigon as America's responsibility. Although the U.S. Mission in Geneva had requested assistance from the United Nations High Commissioner for Refugees (UNHCR) and the Intergovernmental Committee for European Migration (ICEM) in locating third countries willing to accept refugees from Indochina, there was little indication from the beginning of the crisis that efforts at internationalization, or "burden sharing," would be successful. The UNHCR and most third countries viewed the Indochina crisis as an American problem and as the almost inevitable aftermath of years of American involvement. From a legal and political standpoint UNHCR doubted that the Indochinese were *bonafide* refugees.[19] Rather it was UNHCR's perception that the evacuations were American operations, and it was not UNHCR policy to take care of America's allies to the exclusion of other refugees, such as the Chileans. The UNHCR also did not want to overextend itself. It wanted to maintain good relations with the new Communist regime in Vietnam, apparently because it expected to play a reconstruction and development role in the postwar era. Although nearly all the Southeast Asian nations had originally expressed a willingness to accept the Vietnamese, they had agreed to provide asylum on the condition that the refugees be admitted only temporarily and be resettled abroad as quickly as possible. Senior members of the Interagency Task Force visited European capitals to solicit resettlement offers, but nearly every major nation except France viewed the Vietnamese refugees as an American responsibility. Thus, despite early pleas from Congressman Joshua Eilberg and others on the House Judiciary Committee encouraging other nations to take Vietnamese refugees,[20] it was clear that the U.S., if it intended to rescue any Vietnamese, had little choice but to employ the President's parole authority and bring them to the United States.

The decision to parole Vietnamese was taken amidst a crisis atmosphere. The Thieu government lost its last battle at Xuan Loc on April 21, and Thieu resigned as President on the same day. With fifteen North Vietnamese divisions massed against the six South Vietnamese divisions that were left to defend Saigon, the end seemed imminent. Testifying before the House Appropriations

Committee, Kissinger described the military situation in Vietnam as "very grim" and said that "the range of choices is extremely limited."[21] The parole request was extended to include other relatives or U.S. citizens of permanent resident aliens who petitioned for immigration visas. Congress urged the State Department to evacuate "nonessential" Americans and drastically reduce those remaining in Vietnam.

The crisis atmosphere contributed to the perception that the U.S. had a humanitarian and political obligation to "rescue" its former allies. In his resignation address, President Thieu complained, "This is an inhumane act by an inhumane ally. Refusing to aid an ally and abandoning it is an inhumane act."[22] President Ford responded in a television interview on the same day that the U.S. had an obligation to evacuate large numbers of South Vietnamese,[23] and a *New York Times* editorial a few days later asserted that the U.S. could not shed its moral responsibility for thousands of Vietnamese who had trusted the U.S. in the past.[24] Responding to these pressures, the Senate Judiciary Committee unanimously approved, and the Justice Department made public, a new parole for over 150,000 Indochinese, including 50,000 Vietnamese in the "high risk" category. This was done on April 22. The same day, the Interagency Task Force ordered civil and military authorities on Guam to prepare for the care and maintenance of an estimated 50,000 refugees. The Pentagon took immediate action, positioning twenty-five ships, including aircraft carriers, destroyers, and amphibious ships, at sea in the Gulf of Thailand and the South China Sea in anticipation of the evacuation.

As the war in Vietnam drew rapidly to a close, any thought of carrying out a well-planned evacuation and resettlement program had to be put aside. Instead, the emphasis was placed on rescuing as many of America's Vietnamese associates as possible in the short time remaining before Saigon fell. This task was made difficult because during the past two months the U.S. had been trying to bolster confidence in the remaining South Vietnamese government and could not be seen to be evacuating Saigon government personnel while holding the disintegrating government together. The more quickly the U.S. evacuated senior Vietnamese government officials, the more likely was the complete collapse of all resistance to the advancing Communist forces. Because the minimal planning that had been done received so little official support from Martin and others in the Embassy, there were few official controls over the actual refugee selection process. To a large extent, U.S. officials in the field set up their own guidelines for selecting evacuees, and those guidelines varied according to the individual Americans making decisions. Many Americans involved in selection had spent years in Vietnam and had developed close personal ties with Vietnamese. It was not surprising, therefore, that they worked hard to evacuate any

Vietnamese who wanted to leave the country if they thought their lives or livelihoods would be endangered.[25]

Their efforts to evacuate U.S. government employees had limited success. Approximately 130,000 Vietnamese left the country during April 1975. Among these refugees were government officials and members of the military who feared Communist reprisals; but such was the disorder in the final days that many with less valid claims of fear of persecution managed to depart. Those who could not get on the departing airplanes sometimes pushed their children on, believing they were sending them to a better life. In the last week of April, masses of people jammed the Tan Son Nhut Airport and the American Embassy, climbing fences and trying forcibly to enter compounds and airplanes. American transport planes rolled off the runway day and night at the rate of nearly two every hour. Few of those leaving had valid travel documents or exit permits, but the Vietnamese police who controlled the air base didn't enforce emigration regulations during these final days. The controlled evacuation that had been envisioned became a chaotic and traumatic event.[26] In all, between April 21 and 29 the U.S. provided the means for about 65,000 Vietnamese to leave the country by air and by boat.[27]

The other 65,000 Vietnamese who fled in April arranged their own transportation. Many had access to planes or boats or were armed and could commandeer transportation. Vietnamese air force pilots took their planes, loaded them with family, girlfriends, or mistresses, or hired out space at more than $10,000 per person, and flew to U.S. bases in Thailand. Vessels of the Vietnamese navy evacuated families of crew members and friends and headed for Subic Bay in the Philippines. Other Vietnamese fled by sea in small fishing boats, barges, rafts, and floats and were picked up by friendly ships. Still others fled overland through Laos and Cambodia to Thailand.

On the last day before the fall of Saigon, Ambassador Martin ordered the evacuation of 10,000 Vietnamese by fixed-wing aircraft the following day. That night Tan Son Nhut Airport was shelled by Communist forces who had reached the city's perimeter, and the airport was closed. On the 29th, an alternative plan was entertained. An attempt was made to evacuate by river barge but was abandoned when the buses which were to take people to the Saigon docks never showed up at the agreed meeting point in the city. On that day the U.S. Embassy in Saigon closed. During the final hours, helicopters engaged in Operation Frequent Wind plucked people from the rooftop of the U.S. Embassy compound in Saigon while Marine guards beat back hysterical mobs of Vietnamese trying to escape. All but a handful of Americans, along with thousands of Vietnamese, were rescued and flown to U.S. naval vessels offshore.

In the confusion and disarray, large numbers of Vietnamese designated as "high risk" were abandoned. They included hundreds of senior Communist defectors, several thousand operatives of the American CIA, and as many as 30,000 agents trained by the CIA for the Phoenix program, which had been designed to capture and kill Viet Cong. In addition, over 1.5 million soldiers, police, and civil servants of the defeated Thieu regime were left behind.[28] On April 30, Communist tanks rolled into Saigon and the flag of the Provisional Revolutionary Government of South Vietnam was hoisted over the presidential palace. On May 1, U.S. rescue operations were officially terminated.

In the following days, Vietnamese refugees straggled into ports throughout Asia. Most Vietnamese were channeled into the U.S. resettlement effort, Operation New Life, which took them first to Guam for initial processing and later to receiving centers at military bases in the United States itself.[29] The camps were run jointly by the Interagency Task Force (IATF) and the U.S. military, whose responsibilities and goals often overlapped and conflicted. Once the refugees had been interviewed and given a medical examination, they were quickly assigned to one of the nine voluntary agencies (volags) which assumed the task of finding sponsors for the refugees and resettling them in the mainstream of American society.

The decision to resettle the Vietnamese evacuees involved no conflict with the prevailing nexus between anti-Communism and refugee admissions. The chief concern of U.S. policy makers was the mistreatment they expected the new Communist government to visit on America's former allies. Vietnamese refugees were assimilated into the prevailing cold war rhetoric that people inevitably oppose Communism by voting with their feet.

Editorial support for the refugees was broad, was based on a sense of obligation to former allies, and was not restricted to the prowar press. Instead, it also reflected the concerns of those who regarded the refugees as part of America's legacy of guilt. The press ran stories that placed the Vietnamese within the context of earlier refugee movements to the U.S. and emphasized family reunification and the past role of many with the U.S. government. U.S. public relations officials portrayed the Vietnamese as persons who, like Hungarians and Cubans in the past, were "voting with their feet" against Communism and who were entering the U.S. looking for freedom and democracy.[30] President Ford also put the Indochinese refugee program within the context of the prior refugee flows to the U.S.:

> After World War II, the United States offered a new life to 400,000 displaced persons. The generosity of the American people showed again following the Hungarian uprising of 1956, when more than 50,000 Hungarian refugees fled here for sanctuary. And we welcomed more than a half million Cubans fleeing tyranny in their country.

Now, other refugees have fled from the Communist takeover in Vietnam. These refugees chose freedom. They do not ask that we be their keepers, but only, for a time, that we be their helpers.[31]

However, there was surprisingly little attempt to exploit the propaganda value of the Indochinese refugees, particularly in comparison with the Eastern European and Cuban situations. The difference was in the perception of the Vietnamese evacuation as a "rescue operation" precipitated by military defeat, rather than as a traditional "refugee" situation involving demonstrated victims of past persecution. The Ford administration chose to emphasize the traditional image of America as the nation of immigrants and attempted to mobilize the humanitarian impulse of American society.

President Ford invoked America's "long tradition of opening its doors to immigrants of all countries," and on May 19 he stated:

In one way or another, all of us are immigrants, and the strength of America over the years has been our diversity; diversity of all kinds of variations—religion, ethnic and otherwise.

I recall very vividly a statement that seems apropos at this time, that the beauty of Joseph's coat is its many colors. The strength of America is its diversity.

The people that we are welcoming today, the individuals who are in Guam or in Camp Pendleton or Eglin Air Force Base, are individuals who can contribute significantly to our society in the future. They are people of talent, they are industrious, they are individuals who want freedom and I believe they will make a contribution now and in the future to a better America.[32]

George Meany of the American Federation of Labor–Congress of Industrial Organizations stated at a separate news conference that refusal to absorb the Vietnamese would be a denial of "our own heritage."[33]

In an effort to overcome the traditional restrictionist arguments of unemployment, housing shortages, and the threat to national security, the President repeatedly offered public support for the resettlement program, asked the nation's governors and leaders to welcome the Vietnamese, and appointed a President's Advisory Committee on Indochina Refugees which assisted in focusing public attention on the refugee resettlement effort and in establishing liaison with labor unions, national civic organizations, and professional associations.[34]

Congress, although responsive to a general lack of public enthusiasm for massive Indochinese migration, felt no strong pressure from its constituents to buck the Executive Branch or drastically limit migration. Opposition to the Indochinese admissions program was generally not overt, and was not perceived by the Congress or the Ford administration as an important political issue. The prevailing sentiment in Washington was that the U.S. had just lost a war and still had a responsibility to the victims of that war. The willingness to admit so many refugees and to provide them with large-scale assistance were perceived as part of U.S. postwar responsibility to its former allies and outweighed any restrictionist sentiment then present in the Congress. Therefore, Congress moved quickly to pass legislation to fund the Indochina resettlement program. On May 22, a little more than three weeks after the final evacuation of Saigon, the Indochina Migration and Refugee Assistance Act was passed, authorizing a massive federal role in reception and resettlement for a period of two years.[35]

Pro-admissions sentiment in Congress, however, was limited to the rescue mission. Several Congressmen, including Joshua Eilberg, the influential Chairman of the House Judiciary Committee's Subcommittee on Immigration, Citizenship, and International Law, were anxious to end the Vietnam "nightmare" and turn away from Indochina once and for all. Eilberg felt that once the Indochinese left the camps, the U.S. responsibility was fulfilled.[36] Congressional concern also reflected an unwillingness to test further the capacity of the U.S. to absorb culturally diverse newcomers. For the U.S. government, therefore, the issue was how to integrate this diverse group of immigrants rapidly into American society with the minimum of domestic impact. In the hearing which approved the Indochina Migration and Refugee Assistance Act, Representative Paul Sarbanes warned the Interagency Task Force that the assimilation of Indochinese refugees had to proceed quickly, before the mood of Congress and the U.S. public became less sympathetic to the resettlement effort.[37]

The remarks of Congressman Sarbanes reflected the existence of an emerging public opposition to the Indochinese resettlement program. In mid-1975, the U.S. was in the midst of an economic recession. Unemployment was high, particularly among racial minorities, and there was some resentment toward the new arrivals from those who were competitors for limited social services. A Gallup poll taken in May 1975 indicated that Americans were opposed to admitting Vietnamese by 54 percent to 36 percent.[38] A front-page article in the *Wall Street Journal* cited the high 8.9 percent unemployment rate, the language barrier, and residual public opposition, among other factors that would substantially frustrate resettlement efforts.[39] In addition, the long and costly U.S. military involvement in Vietnam made the American public apathetic, if not hostile, to anything that reminded them of Vietnam and military defeat.

Hostility was particularly pronounced in the communities where the Vietnamese refugees were temporarily housed. California Governor Edmund Brown, Jr. publicly expressed his concern that Vietnamese refugees would take jobs away from Americans in his state,[40] and urged Congress to insure that "jobs for Americans first" would be a priority in pending legislation to aid the Vietnamese. The Seattle City Council turned down by a vote of seven to one a resolution that would have welcomed the Vietnamese. Residents near Fort Chaffee, one of the resettlement camps, publicized plans to protest at a town council meeting, circulated petitions calling for an end to the resettlement effort, and picketed in front of Fort Chaffee's main gate, carrying signs reading "Let's start helping Americans" and "How long is temporary?"[41]

Congress, too, offered only a wary welcome to the Indochinese. Several Congressmen expressed concern about a number of issues, including the effect of Vietnamese refugees on the U.S. labor market, the distribution of refugees within the U.S., particularly areas that already had high unemployment, and the extent to which there were criminal elements among the Vietnamese arrivals.[42] However, the limited scope of the operation, coupled with the formation of the Interagency Task Force to promote resettlement, alleviated Congressional concerns that the impact of Indochinese admissions on particular American localities and on the economy would be intolerable. Moreover, from the beginning of the resettlement program, IATF objectives focused on moving the Indochinese out of Guam and the U.S. military bases quickly and minimizing the impact of domestic resettlement. The key to leaving camp and assimilating into the mainstream of American society was for each refugee to have a sponsor. As was traditional practice, the IATF contacted American voluntary agencies (volags) to find individual and group sponsors who would assume fiscal and personal responsibility for the refugee families for a period of up to two years. The volags initially had to work under a great handicap. They had only been informed of the role they would play after the formation of the IATF and had insufficient time to plan for such a major resettlement effort. However, the public response to the appeals of President Ford, churches, and civic organizations to help resettle Vietnamese refugees was surprisingly enthusiastic. Positive media coverage of the refugees helped focus on the need for sponsors and new homes for the refugees. More than 20,000 offers of assistance from individuals flooded the IATF's toll-free line during the first few weeks of operation, and by early autumn the voluntary agencies had more sponsors than refugees.[43]

Inevitably the pressure to resettle refugees as quickly as possible to avoid public antipathy created anxieties among the voluntary agencies[44] and problems for the resettlement effort. Senior government officials, including Julia Taft, who had succeeded Ambassador Brown as director of the Interagency Task Force (IATF), believed that prolonged confinement in camps would make resettlement in America more difficult, and therefore they had little alternative but to integrate the refugees as quickly as possible.[45] The pressure from the IATF to speed up refugee processing and resettlement was perceived by voluntary agencies to be both unseemly and unwise because their experiences with resettling other groups of refugees had demonstrated that successful resettlement was a time-consuming effort and had to be geared to the particular needs of the refugees themselves.[46] The agencies argued that the Vietnamese who were arriving in America were principally from the educated, urbanized elite of Vietnam and successful assimilation depended on their adjustment to a lower social and occupational status within American society than they had held in Vietnam. For those Vietnamese who came from rural backgrounds, assimilation required their adjustment to western, urban, industrial society.

The IATF objective of minimizing the domestic impact of so many Vietnamese resettling in the U.S. over a short time span led to the establishment of a number of operating guidelines. Most importantly, the decision was taken to disperse the Vietnamese throughout the country rather than to allow the concentration of these refugees in ethnic enclaves. To this end President Ford sent a letter to all state governors indicating his strong support for the resettlement program and suggesting that they become involved, not only as a sponsoring agency but also as a coordinating mechanism along with the voluntary agencies. Dispersal directly involved the states and minimized the possibility that a handful of communities would have to shoulder an overwhelming proportion of the costs of receiving the refugees. The IATF also stipulated that

> states should not suffer any fiscal impact. Thus 100% of the costs for cash assistance, medical care and social services would be funded by the Federal Government.

> The program should continue for two years and not develop into the protracted Federal effort which characterized the Cuban refugee program.

> The voluntary agencies should be responsible for ensuring that refugees were not placed on welfare, except in particular hardship cases.

> The incremental educational costs to school systems should be covered by Federal funds for the first year.

> Special English language and social services programs should be available to refugees to assist them in achieving economic self-sufficiency.

> To the extent possible, refugees in need should be served by the mainstream human service programs, rather than by creating new institutional service mechanisms.[47]

Even with these precautions, not enough attention was subsequently paid to community relations. The Vietnamese often encountered hostility in areas where unemployment was high or housing was scarce. In Maine, unemployed young people occasionally roughed up and robbed the Vietnamese. In Denver, Mexican-Americans reacted violently when twenty-four Indochinese families were given apartments in a housing project that had a long waiting list of Hispanics. The efforts on the part of voluntary agencies to get the Vietnamese jobs and to become self-sufficient as quickly as possible often placed refugees in direct conflict with other minority groups. Thus when Vietnamese shrimp fishermen were moved to Galveston, Texas, they were perceived as a threat to the livelihood of local fishermen and were terrorized by members of the Ku Klux Klan. Also, despite efforts to distribute the Vietnamese equitably around the nation, secondary migration occurred after arrival, often away from the frost belt and toward other locations with large groupings of Indochinese and toward states with more generous cash assistance arrangements. Thus refugees clustered in California, Louisiana, and Texas, resulting in the kind of adverse impact the IATF had hoped to avoid.

Despite some nativistic and racist hostility to the Indochinese, public reaction to the refugees was mostly muted and constituted a low-level concern to the Ford administration. The executive was able to secure Congressional cooperation and funding, and, given the large number of entrants and the short resettlement period, this first wave of Indochinese assimilated quickly into American society. As a group, the 130,000 refugees were relatively well educated and accustomed to the American way of life. Within two years of their arrival, 94.5 percent of employable Indochinese had jobs, compared with 93.1 percent for the United States as a whole. With low-paying jobs and large families, they sometimes had to supplement their incomes with public assistance programs such as food stamps or Medicaid, but they presented no major welfare or economic problems. Generally, the Indochinese were hailed as model refugees: hardworking, well motivated, and eager for self-sufficiency.[48]

Because other countries viewed the refugee problem as Washington's special responsibility, not their own, U.S. efforts to divert the flow of Vietnamese to other countries after the collapse of Saigon were less successful than domestic resettlement. In order to placate Congress and to soften the impact of so many refugees streaming into the nation, the U.S. government encouraged Vietnamese in the camps to consider resettlement in other countries. Facilities were provided for other countries to set up offices at the camps to recruit refugees, and camp newspapers ran articles encouraging resettlement elsewhere. In the end, only a few thousand refugees opted to reemigrate to other nations. There was a general lack of international interest in resettling Indochinese.[49] Although Congress complained about the lack of internationalization, U.S. domestic resettlement problems were not significant enough to generate strong political pressures on other countries. Moreover, Congress believed that once the 130,000 were resettled, the Indochinese problem would disappear. As it had with Cuban migrants, the U.S. had singlehandedly managed the Indochinese evacuation from the beginning and had limited the role of the international agencies, particularly UNHCR. Insofar as international involvement was sought, Congress and the State Department believed that they needed to demonstrate to the American public that others in the international community were doing "their fair share" in order to insure domestic support for the resettlement program. Although France accepted a relatively large number of Indochinese from the beginning, no country was willing to grant them blanket acceptance. Admissions criteria were almost the same as those applied to ordinary immigrants and were highly selective. Usually only professionals, those with relatives in the prospective host country, or those who could speak the language of that country were taken by other nations. Moreover, some countries, such as West Germany, agreed to accept only Indochinese directly from the U.S. It was not surprising that once Indochinese were on U.S. soil, very few would choose to leave to resettle elsewhere. By December 1975, about 6,000 refugees were resettled in third countries, far fewer than the 20,000 who were originally expected to depart.

Some U.S. officials believed that repatriation was neither possible nor desirable, despite the fact that a small number of refugees sought to return to Vietnam. In the minds of many American military people administering the camps on Guam and in the U.S., the idea that anyone would want to go back to Vietnam seemed incredible. There were instances of U.S. officials trying to dissuade those who wanted to return to Vietnam voluntarily.[50] This attitude was a source of conflict with UNHCR, which agreed to negotiate with the Communist authorities in Vietnam to arrange for voluntary repatriation and to send personnel to Guam and to the U.S. to interview Vietnamese indicating a desire to return. Subsequently, over 2,000 Vietnamese asked to be repatriated and the Vietnamese application forms were reviewed by Vietnam. The IATF officially encouraged repatriation from the beginning, and all refugee camps and resettlement centers were instructed to post notices and to run regular announcements in the camp newspapers informing the refugees of the possibility of returning home to Vietnam should they want to. But repatriation was held up for months as Hanoi, not eager to receive back potential malcontents, failed to respond quickly to UNHCR inquiries.

Some 1,500 Vietnamese persisted with their demands to go home, and after several months, the Ford administration provided the repatriates with a 20,000-ton Vietnamese freighter, the *Thuong Tin I,* which had come with the original evacuees. President Ford and Secretary Kissinger felt that if Hanoi wasn't going to respond quickly to UNHCR inquiries, the U.S. should act even without UNHCR cooperation.[51] The U.S. Navy helped select a captain among the former South Vietnamese sailors and assumed responsibility for repairing and provisioning the freighter. Finally, on October 16, 1975, the *Thuong Tin I* sailed from Guam with 1,546 repatriates aboard bound for Vietnam. Upon arrival in Vietnam, the repatriates were detained and sent to reeducation centers, where they remained for several years. This incident confirmed for many U.S. officials their belief that repatriation of Vietnamese refugees was not a humane option.

By December 1975, when the U.S. processing camps were closed, some 80,000 Indochinese refugees were still located in camps throughout Thailand. Included were Cambodians who had escaped the brutal savagery of the Khmer Rouge takeover, Vietnamese who were still trickling out of Vietnam, and Laotians. The Laotians comprised members of the former non-Communist regime centered in Vientiane and the Hmong who had been used by the American Central Intelligence Agency to fight the Communist Pathet Lao for over a decade and a half and who were now in full retreat after being abandoned by their CIA sponsors. In late 1975, two additional U.S. parole programs were authorized, one in August for 528 Vietnamese and Cambodians who had left their countries between March 15 and July 1 but were not covered in the earlier parole program and one in December for 3,466 Laotians, who had been totally excluded from the earlier parole program and who, like the Hmong secret army, were closely associated with the U.S. government. These parole programs, like the one in April were perceived as saving the lives of people out of humanitarian and political obligation.

The original Indochinese admissions program was perceived as a "rescue operation" precipitated by military defeat, rather than a traditional "refugee" situation involving demonstrated victims of past persecution. The program began as a reflexive executive response to a situation regarded primarily as a humanitarian and political crisis, rather than as an ideological opportunity or as a means of promoting ethnic immigration interests. In the immediate aftermath of defeat, no U.S. strategy for continuing American influence in Indochina had yet emerged, nor was there a sense that Vietnamese refugees, like their Cuban counterparts in the past, had a substantial instrumental role to play on behalf of the United States. The tradition of executive parole, although subject to Congressional attempts to limit its practice from 1965 on, was still the primary vehicle for refugee admissions, and was especially well suited for handling emergencies of the Vietnamese type. Congress, although mindful of possible domestic backlash to massive Indochinese migration, felt no strong pressure from its constituents to challenge the President or drastically limit migration so long as the admissions program would be limited and would fulfill America's responsibility to Vietnam once and for all. Contrary to expectations, however, the 1975 programs did not resolve the Indochina refugee situation. Increasingly, a new phenomenon arose—that of the "boat people"—and the United States found itself under heavy pressure to admit additional refugees.

Chapter 7

Providing Safe Harbor for the Boat People

T HE FALL OF SAIGON, like the American military disengagement which preceded it by two full years, did not mark the end of U.S. involvement with Indochina and its people. From the middle 1950s through 1975, the United States had involved itself politically, economically, and, in the end, militarily in the life of South Vietnam. It had also recruited and trained agents in Laos, and engaged in an intense bombing campaign in Cambodia. America's responsibility to the people of Indochina did not stop suddenly in 1975.

The final Communist triumph in the region generated intensely ambivalent feelings. On one hand, the Congress and many American officials, reflecting the attitudes of the great majority of the American people, sought "to put the war behind us." Their desire for total disengagement in the wake of a humiliating defeat led them to regard the partial evacuation of Saigon in April 1975 as an act which "wiped the slate clean," relieving the United States of further responsibility for former allies who remained in Indochina. On the other hand, for many Americans, the circumstances of American withdrawal seemed shameful. The sense of betrayal expressed by Prince Sirik Matak in his letter to Ambassador John Dean or by Nguyen Van Thieu in his final remarks to his nation was felt by many who had supported the war in Indochina and were convinced that the consequences of defeat included the punishment and persecution of thousands who had made the mistake of believing American promises.

Particularly disturbed were Americans who had been most closely involved with the Vietnamese and Laotians: CIA operatives who had trained the "secret army" in Laos and supervised Operation Phoenix in South Vietnam; AID officials who had spent years establishing the American presence in Indochina; diplomatic service representatives who had helped make the promises which the United States found itself unable to keep. The latter group, composed primarily of mid- and lower-level Foreign Service officers who had spent years in the field in Vietnam, were vocal in their expressions of outrage and guilt and were determined to secure the admission to the United States of as many Indochinese as possible. Their efforts, given a substantial boost by some of their superiors, by the lobbying of a coalition of nationally prominent businessmen, labor leaders, and churchmen, by the widespread publicity afforded the boat people by the media, and by the willingness of the Carter administration to stand behind a new refugee program, were probably the chief factors in the gradual conversion of a short-term American rescue operation into a long-term international commitment which has resulted to date in the resettlement of some 1.5 million Indochinese, over 750,000, in the United States.

The need for a long-term commitment to the resettlement of Indochinese refugees was not immediately evident to U.S. policy makers, and their response to the evolving human tragedy in Southeast Asia did not come readily or adequately at first. After the rescue of Vietnamese from Saigon in 1975, the American public lost interest in Indochina. There was a public desire to turn away once and for all from the "Vietnam problem" and to end the long tragic chapter of America's involvement there. However the "Vietnam problem" would not simply go away. Although no revenge killing or bloodbath took place in Vietnam, the Communist Party relied on incarceration and indoctrination to bring the country under its control. Over 200,000 members of the former South Vietnamese government and army and former members of political parties and organizations who were classified as reactionary after 1975 were imprisoned without trial for indefinite periods in "reeducation camps."[1] In 1976 the government also embarked on an unpopular program of population relocation under which hundreds of thousands of Vietnamese were forcibly resettled on previously uncultivated land designated "New Economic Zones." Those who resisted these population transfers and those who were eventually released from reeducation camps found themselves and their families with no legal status or means of livelihood in the new society. Large numbers of people soon became nonpersons and had little choice but to seek to leave Vietnam.[2] Little by little an exodus by boat began—to southern Thailand, Malaysia, Hong Kong, the Philippines, Indonesia, Singapore, and even lands as far away as Brunei, Japan, Korea, and northern Australia.

Similar though less harsh political and economic developments occurred in neighboring Laos.[3] Of considerable importance to the U.S. was the situation of the Hmong, who had been recruited by the United States during the Indochina war as the CIA's "secret army" to fight against the Pathet Lao. With the end of the war, the Hmong refused to abandon their resistance and continued to fight against the Pathet Lao and their Vietnamese allies. The departure of the Americans, however, interrupted their supplies. The main resistance collapsed, and the Hmong began to flee Laos in large numbers. During the next three years, poor human rights conditions, loss of personal freedoms, and desperate economic hardships led to the eventual flight of over 300,000 lowland Lao and Hmong, 10 percent of the country's population, across the Mekong River into Thailand.

Vietnamese boat people and Laotians captured much of the international attention given to refugees during this period. The terror in Cambodia which began in 1975 when the Khmer Rouge assumed power was not widely reported in the West and received little official attention until 1979, when hundreds of thousands fleeing Cambodia became part of the Indochinese refugee problem. From 1975 through the first half of 1979, almost all of America's attention was on the Vietnamese and Laotian refugees who remained unsettled after the fall of Saigon.

The U.S. response was deliberately kept limited at first, and only grew slowly and reluctantly as the extent of human tragedy and suffering in Southeast Asia unfolded. From 1976 to 1978, apart from a bitter controversy within the former antiwar movement over human rights violations in Vietnam, there was a surprising lack of domestic concern about Indochinese refugees. A similar lack of concern about events in Indochina was exhibited by the State Department. No strategy for continuing American influence in the region had yet emerged, nor was there a sense that Indochinese refugees had any substantial role to play on behalf of the American government. Unlike earlier refugee movements, such as the Eastern Europeans or the Cubans, the United States sought little political advantage beyond a reaffirmation of the horrors of Communist rule from the developing refugee crisis in Indochina. As a result, the Department of State focused on the problem of solving the "residual" refugee problem remaining in Southeast Asia after the rescue mission from Saigon ended. As with past refugee emergencies, executive parole was the primary vehicle used for admitting Indochinese. State Department requests for additional parole authorizations[4] were successful because the paroles being urged upon Congress were small and each one was presented as "final" and as part of the continuing overall American responsibility to the victims of the Vietnam War and its aftermath. Congress, although unenthusiastic about massive Indochinese migration, felt no strong domestic pressure to buck the Executive Branch or drastically limit migration, particularly after the world press began recording the plight of the Vietnamese "boat people." Moreover, the parole process involved considerable concentration of power in the hands of a few committees and principal Congressmen, including the chairmen and ranking minority members of both House and Senate Judiciary Committees and the key members of the refugee subcommittees. In the Senate, the key decision makers included Senators Strom Thurmond, James Eastland, and Edward Kennedy, and in the House, Peter Rodino, Joshua Eilberg, and Hamilton Fish. The major opposition to the paroles came from Eilberg, who resisted reopening America's borders on the grounds that the Vietnamese would not be easily assimilated into American society and that the widespread use of parole undercut the basic principles of American immigration law.

Most of the impetus for the Indochinese admissions program came from a small group of junior Foreign Service officers—Sheppard Lowman, Hank Cushing, and Lionel Rosenblatt—supported by a number of senior State Department officials. Many of these people were simultaneously affected by the misery of the Indochinese and by geopolitical concerns about the political future of all of Southeast Asia if the thousands of migrants who sought protection there were not resettled. All had previously served in Vietnam and had personal and emotional attachments to the country. Most had been evacuated from Saigon in April 1975, and had helped to rescue South Vietnamese just before the city fell. Lowman had served for six years in Vietnam, had married a Vietnamese, and had many good friends there. In 1975, he had served as chief of the internal political reporting unit of the U.S. Embassy. In the final days of the evacuation he personally arranged for the departure of hundreds of South Vietnamese, including the mayor of Saigon, with whom he was airlifted from the country on April 29. In April 1975 Rosenblatt was serving on the personal staff of the Deputy Secretary of State. Without official leave, Rosenblatt took off at his own expense for Saigon and spent the final weeks in South Vietnam helping to evacuate a substantial number of his former Vietnamese colleagues before he was required to leave the country himself. Cushing had served many years in South Vietnam and in 1975 had been Deputy in the Consul General in Can Tho, the administrative capital of the Mekong delta. During the final evacuation, he took a barge down the Mekong River filled with Vietnamese and his staff and proceeded out to sea to meet the U.S. fleet offshore. These men, who came to be part of the group nicknamed the "Saigon cowboys," were impelled not only by a humanitarian concern for refugees but also by a deep sense of guilt and personal involvement. They expressed strong support for what became a main principle underlying American refugee policy—that the U.S. had a special responsibility toward those Indochinese who could not or would not remain behind after the Communist victories. They were also strongly anti-Communist and believed that future stability of America's remaining allies in Southeast Asia would be threatened by the presence of large numbers of refugees.

These officials were instrumental in persuading a sometimes reluctant Congress to keep immigration channels open for Vietnamese and Laotians after the fall of Saigon. They largely succeeded because they developed symbiotic relationships with their superiors, with sympathetic voluntary agency personnel, and with the press. They had powerful sponsors at pivotal positions within the State Department. During the early years, Philip Habib, first as Assistant Secretary of State for East Asian Affairs and later as Under Secretary for Political Affairs, was the most senior supporter of the program. Frank Wisner, Jr., as Deputy Executive Secretary of the Department, controlled the flow of information to the Secretary of State, had major input into the content of the Secretary's submission to the President's evening reading, and thus sensitized the President and the Secretary to the Indochina refugee crisis and the need for greater U.S. admissions. During a later period, David Newsom, as Habib's successor as Under Secretary for Political Affairs, and Richard Holbrooke, the Assistant Secretary for East Asian Affairs in the Carter administration, became crucial bureaucratic supporters of the program. Because of America's long involvement in Vietnam, most of these senior men also had prior experience and commitment to Vietnam and therefore were sympathetic to the initiatives of their junior staff.

Utilizing these high-level contacts, Lowman and Cushing had exceptional control over refugee policy development and operations. They controlled their budget and personnel, enabling them to place strong supporters of an Indochinese admissions program—principally Americans who had formerly served in Indochina—in key positions both in Washington, D.C., and in Southeast Asia. From this strong position they were able to directly influence U.S. refugee admissions policy at first within the State Department and later within the Carter administration.

The first major parole request for Indochinese after the evacuation occurred in early 1976.[5] Some Congressmen, in particular Representative Joshua Eilberg, were intensely dissatisfied with the continued use of executive parole by the Ford administration to admit refugees outside of ordinary immigration law. Questioning the State Department attempt "to justify [the] parole request on humanitarian concerns, when it is really based on foreign policy considerations," Eilberg expressed dismay at the almost limitless numbers of Indochinese whom the U.S. had an "obligation" to save. In response to Eilberg's pleas—"I am . . . concerned with how long the compassion and patience of the American people will continue, as we come in with these continued requests on an *ad hoc* basis"—the State Department witness, Philip Habib, replied that this parole would allow the U.S. to bring the refugee problem under control and to "clean up" the region of refugees. Moreover, he promised that this would be State's "final request" and promised not to come back to Congress "for an increase in parole authority in this category." Over Eilberg's objections, Representative Peter Rodino, Chairman of the House Committee on the Judiciary, concurred with the parole request for 11,000, and it was finally authorized on May 5, 1976. But concern for the use of executive parole as the primary vehicle for handling refugee admissions was rising in Congress, and it would not be the last time the State Department would bear the wrath of Eilberg.

Initially, American officials had thought the May 1976 parole of 11,000 Laotions would be the last and that any subsequent flow from Indochina would be small and could be handled by normal refugee numbers under the 1965 amendments to the Immigration Act. Although the bulk of the annual 17,400 "Seventh preference" conditional entries were reserved for Soviet refugees, about 100 admission places per month were allocated for Indochinese, principally for boat refugees. Since the flow of boat people ran below a few hundred per month in mid-1976, the U.S. believed it had sufficient numbers to keep pace with the magnitude of new arrivals, and a small follow-up program was set up to handle those who would continue to leave Vietnam and Laos.

Almost as soon as this program was in place, however, a substantial increase in boat refugees from Vietnam occurred as Hanoi tightened its grip on South Vietnam and increasing numbers of its citizens realized they had a bleak future there. The conditional entry program could not keep up with the burgeoning number of new arrivals, and a backlog of several thousand boat people and tens of thousands of Laotians accumulated in Southeast Asian countries without opportunities for permanent resettlement.

Indochinese refugees were not welcomed in neighboring Southeast Asian countries because they were viewed as a potential threat to economic and political stability in the region.[6] Thai authorities, particularly the military, saw the refugee influx as having immense potential for disruption and as an increased security threat. Thus Bangkok was unwilling to adopt an open asylum policy and not only refused to officially resettle refugees in Thailand but also made efforts to discourage new arrivals.[7] Malaysia was concerned that the flow of Vietnamese boat people, who were primarily ethnic Chinese, could upset the delicate domestic racial and political balance, particularly since they landed on the east coast of Malaysia, where the population was overwhelmingly rural Malay, devotedly Islamic, and poor. The refugees were pictured as a subtle invasion force from Vietnam and as a potential fifth column for a renewed Communist insurgency.[8] Refugees in general were viewed as a domestic political liability, and the Malaysian government came under increasing pressure from local state and political leaders to take a firmer stance against them.

In the face of this growing refugee crisis, the U.S. found the Office of the

United Nations High Commissioner for Refugees (UNHCR) woefully un-prepared in the field and unwilling to take an active resettlement role for Indo-chinese refugees.[9] Prior to October 1978, the UNHCR regional office in Thailand had only four field representatives to monitor fifteen camps in that country. In Malaysia there were only three UNHCR staff. Camp conditions were notoriously poor. Moreover, Thailand, Malaysia, and Singapore were not signatories to the 1951 UN Convention Relating to the Status of Refugees or its 1967 protocol and therefore, in the absence of strong commitments from those governments, UNHCR lacked leverage in persuading them to provide temporary asylum to the Indochinese. Aware of their lack of enforcement powers and limited mandate, UNHCR representatives opted in favor of trying to work quietly to get the Thais and Malays to change their attitudes rather than publicize openly violations of the principle of first asylum by the members of the Association of Southeast Asian Nations (ASEAN).

The United States felt that the UNHCR not only failed to offer adequate protection to the Vietnamese refugees but also failed to take the initiative to find resettlement places for the refugees. The U.S. believed that there existed no possible solution to the refugee problem other than third country resettle-ment and constantly pressured UNHCR to obtain more resettlement places for Indochinese refugees. UNHCR initially resisted actively promoting resettle-ment to third countries because it believed such programs would only open a migration channel to the West. In order to prevent migrants from being "pulled out" of Vietnam, UNHCR thought it necessary to provide aid to displaced persons inside Vietnam and maintain good relations with Hanoi.[10] Under intense pressure from the U.S., the High Commissioner nevertheless did make several special appeals for resettlement places. Although some twenty countries responded to these appeals, the majority of resettlement states felt no responsibility to take boat people, while others were willing to help only by providing funds. Only France, because of its past colonial ties to Indochina, ac-cepted relatively large numbers. The U.S. felt that UNHCR showed little or no initiative to persuade others to share the burden. No real attempt at interna-tionalization was made until late 1978, when large numbers of boat people had arrived in first asylum countries in Southeast Asia.[11]

The U.S. also disagreed with UNHCR over the possibility of repatriating some of the refugees, particularly those from Laos.[12] UNHCR felt, for exam-ple, that many Laotians had fled their country because of temporary economic hardships and believed that it might be possible to repatriate them in large numbers. The U.S. refused to believe that any Laotian could safely return home and live there without fear of persecution, and therefore continued to push UNHCR to find resettlement places for them. During 1976–1978, UNHCR field representatives successfully resisted U.S. pressure to resettle large numbers of Laotians, but UNHCR was less successful in preventing America's own initiatives on behalf of its former allies. Thus when U.S. Ambassador to Thailand Charles Whitehouse telephoned Cesare Berta, the UNHCR regional representative, in early 1976 to give him the news that the U.S. had decided to parole an additional 11,000 Indochinese refugees, mostly Laotians, Berta reportedly replied, "This is a catastrophe. This is disastrous, Mr. Ambassador." The UNHCR representative in Laos believed this program acted as a magnet and could only further contribute to the hemorrhaging of Laos.

Because of the lack of international support for the resettlement of Indochinese and because refugees were continuing to flee into neighboring Southeast Asian countries, the State Department felt it had no choice but to utilize the parole provision once again.[13] Although the Ford administration had made a commitment to Congress in May 1976 not to request additional parole authorizations before the enactment of new refugee admissions legislation, the newly elected Carter administration did not feel bound by the promises of a prior administration and requested parole for a further 15,000 Indochinese refugees. Despite the predictable opposition of Congressman Eilberg, the reluctance of Attorney General Griffin Bell, who felt uncomfortable using the parole provision to admit groups of refugees, and hesitation on the part of the Office of Management and Budget for financial reasons, this parole was approved in August 1977.

Under this, the fifth Indochinese parole program in two years, the U.S. declared its intention to admit 7,000 Vietnamese boat people and 8,000 land refugees, primarily from Laos. As with earlier Indochinese parole programs, those with relatives in the U.S. or formerly associated with the U.S. government, American organizations, or the former non-Communist governments of Vietnam, Laos, or Cambodia were given preference for admission. In addition, an admissions category was established for the first time for refugees who were not accepted by any third country, and presented "compelling humanitarian reasons." Thus, admissions criteria for boat people were extremely liberal. The only provisions were that refugees not have resettlement commitments from other countries, and that they not be excludable from the U.S. under immigration law. Vietnamese and Laotians were seldom denied entry to the U.S., and the parole was quickly oversubscribed.

The number of refugees arriving by sea and by land in Southeast Asia rose sharply and demonstrated the need for a much larger and longer-term U.S. response. By fall 1977 it was apparent that the number of U.S. resettlement opportunities was not keeping pace with the growing number of boat people. By November, effectively all of the 7,000 U.S. parole numbers available for boat people had been committed and new arrivals were coming ashore in Southeast

Asia at the rate of over 2,000 per month. Thai and Malaysian authorities became increasingly hostile, refused refugees permission to disembark, and pushed boats back to sea. These actions endangered the lives of many refugees, added to the growing number already losing their lives at sea, and served to prejudice the willingness of captains of passing ships to rescue refugees from the many foundering boats. At the same time, Lao refugees continued to escape by land to Thailand at the rate of nearly 2,000 per month, and voluntary agency prescreening indicated that over 20,000 appeared to be potentially qualified for the American program and willing to be considered for admission.[14] It was evident that thousands more were eligible for admission to the U.S. than the 8,000 places allotted for land refugees. In late November, Robert DeVecchi, who headed the Indochina desk for the International Rescue Committee, reported on these developments after a visit to Thailand:

> . . . an additional response is needed to those refugees who wish to come to the United States and who qualify under our criteria. . . .
> The United States involvement in Indochina over a quarter of a century is unprecedented. . . . We as a nation will never be able to completely discharge the obligations our involvement created until we have responded fully to the pleas of those Indochinese refugees who risk their very lives in the hope of beginning a new life.[15]

There evolved a gradual recognition in both the Executive Branch and the Congress that an ongoing and substantial commitment to resettle Indochinese in the United States or in other willing countries was needed. In consultations with Congress, State Department officials began to stop speaking of the Indochinese refugee program as a "clean-up" operation. In testimony before Eilberg's subcommittee, Habib said that he would not promise that this parole was the administration's final one; instead, he called it part of a continuing U.S. response to a build-up of refugees in Southeast Asia.[16] By mid-1977, there was an increasing recognition that the U.S. refugee effort was part of a stabilization effort in the region and that there existed strong foreign policy reasons for developing a long-range refugee program. U.S. officials were keenly aware that Southeast Asian governments felt their countries were threatened by the large and growing numbers of refugees flooding into their territories. Increasingly, Southeast Asian officials drew attention to the extent of difficulties facing them and gave dire warnings of what they would do to the refugees if the U.S. refused to relieve them of some of their burdens. Accordingly, higher-level decision makers began to take an active interest in the issue.

In the fall of 1977, the White House requested the State Department to form and head a new interagency task force to develop a comprehensive refugee policy. The interagency committee, which was run out of Philip

Habib's office, recommended that the U.S. Indochina refugee policy be based on two underlying principles, namely that admissions criteria be established on the basis of family or employment ties to the U.S., as well as on humanitarian grounds, and that the U.S. admit sufficient numbers of refugees to alleviate pressures on ASEAN allies and preserve the principle of asylum in Southeast Asia. The work of this committee was continued at a higher level on the National Security Council at the White House, and basically the same recommendations were made to President Carter in March 1978.[17]

While U.S. refugee policy engaged the attention of higher U.S. officials, the Carter administration resisted adopting an open-ended refugee program. A Harris Survey opinion poll taken in late July 1977 had indicated that admitting more Indochinese refugees into the U.S. would be politically unpopular and that public opinion had already turned against the refugees. Of those polled, 57 percent had opposed the August 1977 parole while only 31 percent had supported it. The public anticipated that newly arriving refugees would compete for jobs with America's unskilled workers and that the language training and resettlement costs for the refugees could be more usefully spent on poor Americans. The Carter administration perceived that a Democratic administration, which was traditionally dependent on the support of blacks, Hispanics, and blue-collar workers, had to be sensitive to the potential impact and competition from the influx of refugees, and that a political price would have to be paid for establishing a virtually open-ended Indochinese refugee program. Consequently, the executive was reluctant to move far ahead of public sentiment on the issue of refugee admissions.

Responding to the increasingly desperate plight of Indochinese refugees and having reached the limits of their own resources to convince the Congress and the administration of the need for yet another parole program, a few individuals within the State Department decided in late 1977 to go outside the government to find an advocacy group to overcome the political impediments within the administration and to mobilize public opinion.[18] The subsequent formation of a special commission for Indochinese refugees, whose membership included a number of representatives of humanitarian and public and private agencies and individuals who spanned the gap between governmental and private interests, was part of a long tradition of close collaboration between the voluntary agencies and the State Department on U.S. refugee policy. Working together to influence admissions policy, both played a major role in subsequent decisions made by the Carter administration to admit hundreds of thousands of Indochinese.

In late November, Sheppard Lowman visited Leo Cherne, the chairman of the International Rescue Committee, and briefed him on the situation in Southeast Asia. Cherne had been a supporter of the Republic of South Vietnam and was an anti-Communist hard-liner who had been in the forefront of most major postwar refugee crises. He had been in Hungary in 1956 and in Czechoslovakia in 1968 for the IRC and had organized several successful commissions and coalitions in support of refugees fleeing Communism. He was an advocate for U.S. leadership in refugee affairs and believed that the U.S. had moral obligations to its former allies. To him, they were a concrete demonstration of the failure of Communist regimes.[19] Cherne was also a humanitarian who was concerned over the fate of thousands of Indochinese who risked their lives fleeing persecution, discrimination, and poverty. Both political and humanitarian motives influenced Cherne and many State Department officials who advocated the entry of refugees from the Communist countries of Indochina.

Cherne was fully aware that traditional restrictionist attitudes were still prevalent among some members of Congress and the populace at large. He was also familiar with recent public opinion polls which opposed the expansion of American rescue initiatives, and he knew that fears still existed, particularly among American blacks and the poor, that an infusion of refugees would exacerbate the unemployment problem. In order to overcome these impediments to increased admissions, Cherne agreed to duplicate what had been done so successfully in the past by the Citizens' Committee on Displaced Persons and other blue-ribbon refugee commissions. He would seek to build broad public, Congressional, and executive support for a large Indochinese refugee program through a public relations campaign and coalition building. Cherne told Lowman:

> ... there's one thing we have done a half-dozen times in the past in the face of a great refugee crisis in an effort to affect the U.S. government and public opinion. That involves assembling a group of prominent and experienced American citizens to form themselves into a citizens' commission to investigate the particular crisis and report back its findings to the press, the public and especially the White House, State Department, Attorney-General and the Congress. I believe I can get the IRC to finance such a commission initially. . . .[20]

At a subsequent IRC board meeting in early December, Cherne formed the Citizens' Commission on Indochinese Refugees. The Commission included representatives from the major religious groups, business, and organized labor, former government officials, and prominent persons across the political spectrum. Its membership ranged from persons such as Bayard Rustin, the black civil rights leader and president of Social Democrats USA, to William Casey, subsequently the CIA Director for the Reagan administration.[21] Most members were well connected in Washington, D.C., were part of the foreign policy establishment, had their own public constituencies, and also were respected by foreign leaders. As a group they formed a powerful public voice for the need to resettle more Indochinese.

In a separate action, Cherne sent strongly worded mailgrams to National Security Adviser Zbigniew Brzezinski and Attorney General Griffin Bell urging the immediate parole of 7,000 additional boat people into the U.S. A month later, on January 25, 1978, the Attorney General announced the new parole. What effect such pressure had on the resulting parole decision is impossible to gauge. What is certain is that Cherne's advocacy, in alliance with the State Department's proadmissions sentiment, had considerable leverage on U.S. policy makers. However, it was evident by this time that continuing use of the parole provision on an ad hoc basis was not going to be sufficient to meet the needs of the Indochinese refugees and that the Citizens' Commission had to convince the executive to establish a comprehensive admissions program.

The Citizens' Commission set about in early February 1978 to create the public awareness and support needed to make a long-term U.S. program for Indochinese refugees possible. With the encouragement and support of the State Department, the Commission visited a majority of the refugee camps in Southeast Asia and spoke with representatives from the U.S. government, UNHCR, and the voluntary agencies. On the final day of its mission in Bangkok, the Commission issued a set of recommendations which urged the U.S. to "adopt a coherent and generous policy for the admission of Indochinese refugees over the long-range, replacing the practice of reacting belatedly to successive refugee crises since the spring of 1975." The Commission also recommended that the U.S. accept greater numbers of Indochinese refugees under more liberal criteria than those prescribed in the past. It urged that the U.S. waive all existing admissions criteria and categories for boat people and Cambodians and that their admission for resettlement be accelerated. It also stated that in light of "the hidden and pervasive character of its role in 'the secret war' in Laos," the U.S. had an obligation to ease and apply more "generously and sensitively" the criteria for admitting refugees from Laos. Finally the Commission called on all shipowners and sea captains to pick up boat people who were in danger of drowning at sea. These recommendations were very close to those which had been urged in the interagency committee report at State and later at the NSC, and they prepared the way for the initiation of a formal U.S. admissions policy for Indochinese refugees.

Almost immediately upon return to the U.S., the Citizens' Commission, employing many of the lobbying and coalition-building strategies of the Citizens' Commission on Displaced Persons after World War II, engaged in an extensive and well-organized lobbying effort to reach as broad a constituency as possible. In the words of Cherne, "Stage one of our work was finished but the important but problematic part was yet to begin. How to reach our targetted audience."[22] This audience included not only the executive and legislative branches of the U.S. government but also the constituencies which mattered most to the Carter administration: organized labor and the black community. The Citizens' Commission regarded it as essential to convince reluctant Congressmen and the White House that the entry of large numbers of refugees would not take jobs away from Americans. In an effort to enlist the support of organized labor and thereby neutralize the arguments that Congressman Eilberg and others would make regarding the economic capacity of the U.S. to absorb large numbers of Indochinese, Cherne and Bayard Rustin flew to Miami to report to the AFL-CIO Executive Council meeting. George Meany and the AFL-CIO unanimously endorsed the Commission's recommendations and arranged for Cherne and the Commission to appear and present its recommendations before the Eilberg subcommittee.

In hearings before the House Subcommittee on Immigration, Citizenship, and International Law, the Citizens' Commission was repeatedly asked what assurances it could give that other countries would accept a proportionate share of the refugees and what would be the domestic impact of a larger admissions program. In response, the Roman Catholic Monsignor Ahearn and the civil rights leader Bayard Rustin proved to be strong proponents of an enlarged admissions program:

> Msgr. Ahearn. I find that the question which has been raised a number of times, what will other countries do, is acutely embarrassing, first because the Commission as such can only offer hopes, not guarantees.
>
> Secondly, it ignores a substantial current history. On Monday I interviewed a gentleman who is a Ugandan refugee in Kenya, one of 60,000. I am not aware that Kenya asked us how many we would take before they took any.
>
> Finally, the measure of what we do is not what others do, but what we are able to do. If we get into the situation in which we are waiting for others, it is almost the Kitty Genovese syndrome: who is going to call the police first, and the lady dies anyway.[23]

Bayard Rustin assured Eilberg that the Citizens' Commission's recommendations had the full backing of labor and particularly George Meany. He also argued that a rescue policy for Vietnamese "boat people" had the support of the black community and dismissed the notion that refugees would take jobs away from the poor, saying, "most Americans . . . will not . . . take the . . . ill-paying and dirty work that many of these refugees will take as they start the upward path to mobility, as all of us in the past, wherever we came from, had to take." These two statements had the effect of mitigating two areas of Congressional concern, the need to share the resettlement burden with other nations and the domestic impact of refugees, which had up to then been quite significant. In addition, members of Eilberg's subcommittee had close links with labor, and Bayard Roustin's testimony and a letter from the AFL-CIO Executive Committee supporting the Citizens' Commission's recommendations made Eilberg and others more receptive to the idea of larger Indochinese admissions.

Much of the success of the Citizens' Commission can also be attributed to intensive lobbying directed at key people in the Carter White House, the Congress, the State Department, and the INS. Largely as a result of the access provided by its prominent members, the commission was able to exert considerable national influence very quickly. The Commission called on Sen. Edward Kennedy, National Security Adviser Brzezinski and Vice President Walter Mondale. All three were receptive to most of the Commission's recommendations. The Commission met separately with Secretary of State Cyrus Vance and INS Commissioner Leonel Castillo. Both men agreed to waive normal immigration procedures and offer immediate sanctuary to any boat people who were picked up at sea and denied landing at their next port.

Having met with the top administration and Congressional leaders, Cherne and the Commission embarked on a massive effort to change the climate of public opinion and persuade President Carter to adopt a bold new approach to the Indochinese refugee problem. Combining humanitarian and political concerns, the Citizens' Commission was able to mobilize the traditional humanitarian impulse of American society. Most important, the Commission was able to dispel fears that the trade union movement, minorities, and civic groups would not react with generosity, compassion, and sympathy to Indochinese refugees because of economic and social concerns. The Citizens' Commission secured support from numerous national organizations, including labor unions, ethnic associations, religious groups, and a wide range of other organizations. Supporters ran the gamut from the National Council of Jewish Women, the American Council of Voluntary Agencies for Foreign Service, the U.S. Catholic Conference, the American Jewish Committee, Freedom House, the Anti-Defamation League of B'nai B'rith, and Social Democrats USA to the Coalition for a Democratic Majority. Undoubtedly, many blacks feared the effects of a massive influx of refugees.[24] Yet by enlisting the endorsements of over eighty prominent black leaders, including all the black mayors in the country, who called on the Carter administration to accept Indochinese refugees "in the same spirit that we have urged our country to accept the victims of South Africa's apartheid,"[25] the Citizens' Commission neutralized potential opposition. AFL-CIO Chairman George Meany hand-delivered both to Carter and Vance his own personal appeal urging that administration policy be based on the findings and recommendations of the Commission. The Commission recommendations were endorsed by 135 leading American citizens, and syndicated columns by William Buckley, Jr., Charles Bartlett, John Roche, and others, publicizing the Citizens' Commission's efforts, appeared in hundreds of newspapers throughout the country. The *New York Times* wrote a major editorial entitled "Our Vietnam Duty Is Not Over." Radio and television interviews were quickly arranged with various members of the Commission.

Simultaneous with this specific lobbying, journalists like Henry Kamm of the *New York Times* were reporting stories of Thai pirates who were robbing, raping, abducting, and murdering Vietnamese boat people with incredible brutality. Television viewers saw forcible boat push-offs from Malaysian and other Asian ports. These accounts stirred the consciences of many officials and the American public at large and helped create a more receptive audience for the Citizens' Commission's initiatives. So too did various Congressional and staff delegation trips to Southeast Asia during this period help build a constituency for a larger Indochinese admissions program. The U.S. Embassy in Bangkok paid extraordinary attention to making advance preparations for these delegations and insured that all necessary preparations, including advance visits to the camps, lining up people for interviews, and making certain that the visitors had full and emotional contact with the refugees, were undertaken so that sympathetic impressions would be taken back to Washington, D.C.[26] In particular, a mission by two senior staff members of Eilberg's subcommittee exposed them to the human misery in the region and the need for further U.S. action.

This extraordinary effort on the part of Cherne, the Citizens' Commission, and individuals like Lowman and Rosenblatt culminated on March 30, 1978, when President Carter approved a plan to put the Indochina refugee program on a long-term basis, including new refugee legislation and the use of parole in the interim to admit 25,000 Indochinese refugees over a period of a year.[27] Despite some resistance from the domestic policy staff of the White House and from the Department of Health and Human Services to the budgetary implications of a large admissions program, the Carter plan was very similar to the recommendations of the Citizens' Commission. Because of financing problems, the 25,000 person parole was not finally approved by the Attorney General until June 1978.

In a letter to individual members of the Citizens' Commission, Leo Cherne reflected on the crucial role played by the Commission in securing the 25,000-person parole:

. . . we have succeeded beyond anything we would have candidly acknowledged when we started. Even Henry Kamm's well-deserved Pulitzer in its citation noted not only his remarkable journalism, but specifically mentioned the beneficial human results which were stimulated by his coverage. You can't display it but you each own a piece of a Pulitzer Prize. And, after all, there will be 25,000 Indochinese resettled in the U.S. by next May who were not on their way when we left Bangkok, and there will be many lives saved at sea because we helped to inspire the Secretary of State. There is one other group which deserves enormous praise—the group functioning under Patt Derian [Assistant Secretary of the State Department's Bureau of Human Rights and Humanitarian Affairs], and especially her colleagues under Shep Lowman in the division of Refugee Affairs."[28]

Without the initiative provided by the Citizens' Commission, it is unlikely that the Carter administration could have secured this parole authorization so easily, nor would it have been possible to admit so many Indochinese in subsequent years. Following the traditions and patterns set by former commissions for refugees in the postwar era, the Citizens' Commission for Indochinese Refugees contributed its endorsements, testified before Congressional committees, rallied public opinion, and engaged in proven lobbying efforts to overcome the restrictionist concerns of Congress and to change U.S. admissions policy. In playing a catalytic role in the admission of Indochinese refugees, the Citizens' Commission confirmed a long-standing trend in U.S. refugee policy. Advocacy on behalf of refugees from particular countries has depended to a large extent on the formation of broad coalitions which represent humanitarian and political concerns. The success of such advocacy has depended on the formation of symbiotic relationships between governmental and private groups who have worked hand in hand to influence refugee admissions decisions.

In its lobbying for a larger U.S. admissions program, the Citizens Commission issued numerous warnings of a major humanitarian crisis in Southeast Asia. These warnings came true sooner than expected as Indochinese refugees began to flood into Southeast Asia in 1978 and again outpaced the number of resettlement offers in the West. Under mounting pressure, the Southeast Asian nations adopted harsher measures to turn away "boat refugees," reject at the frontier those who had made their way there by land, and expel those who had managed to enter their territories. The plight of the refugees and reports of a large number of drownings at sea, estimated by the *Times* of London in early 1978 as 100,000, began to attract international attention and concern. The media began to give extensive coverage to the boat people and acted as a catalyst to stimulate the Western public and governments to respond.

The immediate cause of the dramatic upswing in boat arrivals was the March 1978 economic decrees to nationalize private trade in Vietnam and the subsequent expulsion of Vietnam's Chinese minority. During 1977 and 1978, Vietnam also experienced severe economic setbacks due to inclement weather. Concurrently, Hanoi stepped up policies designed to achieve social and economic transformations by restructuring production and distribution. These measures affected the entire Chinese community in Vietnam, who were the country's entrepreneurs, as well as wealthier and middle-class Vietnamese. It made clear the truth that there was no longer an economic future for ethnic Chinese in Vietnam. A number of influential members of the Chinese community were subsequently arrested,[29] creating fears among the community of anti-Chinese persecution.[30] As political tensions between the Chinese and Vietnamese intensified, more than 160,000 Vietnamese of Chinese origin traveled overland into China between March and July of 1978, when China closed its border with Vietnam.

The number of refugees fleeing Vietnam to parts of Asia other than China reached dramatic proportions during the second half of 1978. From 2,829 refugees who arrived by boat in other countries of Southeast Asia from Vietnam in August 1978, the number leaped to 8,558 in September, 12,540 in October, and 21,505 in November, setting a record every month. These figures were startling both to the countries of first asylum and to the major resettlement nations.

It soon became evident that this exodus of refugees was not entirely spontaneous and was in fact being officially exploited by the Vietnamese government. By late 1978 a large-scale, well-organized scheme was established in which people wishing to leave Vietnam handed over their life savings, usually in gold bars, and were taken to small boats and thence to seagoing vessels. It was a very lucrative activity for the organizers. Those who profited were not only members of the tightly knit overseas Chinese community, who ran the refugee trade, but also Vietnamese officials, some at a high level, who were directly involved in arranging illegal departures by boat. The trade probably earned a high proportion of Vietnamese foreign exchange during the period 1978–1980, when the country's economy was in ruins and the foreign currency reserves exhausted.[31]

With the arrival of freighters full of refugees in late 1978, Southeast Asian sentiment hardened considerably against the boat people, and the policy of turning away overladen crafts was intensified. The Thai Prime Minister, Gen. Kriangsak Chamanand, declared on November 28, 1978, that Thailand would not accept any more refugees. He said that unseaworthy boats would be repaired and sick refugees given treatment, but Thailand would return them to the open sea. In Malaysia, coastal patrols started blocking the refugee boats and giving them supplies to continue their onward journey. Military helicopters provided early warning of approaching refugee crafts, coastal patrols fired over their bows to deter them, and warships kept them away from the Malaysian shore. Malaysia received heavy adverse publicity when it refused to allow 2,500 Vietnamese to disembark from a chartered freighter.

The tens of thousands of Vietnamese who managed to get ashore in Southeast Asia were sequestered in crowded and inhumane camps. One such camp was on the tiny, storm-swept island of Pulau Bidong, about 15 miles off the Malaysian coast. Over 40,000 Vietnamese were crammed into a quarter of a square mile of foreshore among coconut trees at the base of a towering hill. No proper toilets had been built, supply lines were not organized, storage facilities were nonexistent, and no steps had been taken to seal wells to prevent their contamination. As a consequence, all potable water had to be imported from the mainland. Refugees lived in makeshift shacks loosely constructed of scavenged timber, plastic sheeting, used bags, cardboard cartons, and flattened pieces of metal. The open latrines stank, especially on hot days. Other temporary camps, most not so primitive as Pulau Bidong but harsh nonetheless, sprang up all over Southeast Asia.[32]

The majority of these refugees were not being resettled fast enough in Western countries. Out of a total of 94,000 boat people who had been given refuge in Southeast Asia, only 38,000 had been resettled by November 1978, of whom 21,000 had gone to the United States, 10,000 to Australia, and 3,000 to France. The Southeast Asian governments, acutely sensitive to the need to maintain a delicate balance between their ethnic communities and reluctant to assume responsibility for refugees in such numbers as to affect the general economic and social development of their countries, felt that they were being unfairly saddled with a problem which was not their responsibility, but that of the United States and the international community.

By late 1978 the plight of the boat people could not be easily ignored by the Carter administration. The U.S. announced on November 27 that it would admit another 21,000 Vietnamese boat people before May 1979. With the large numbers of refugees still sequestered in camps throughout Southeast Asia and a larger flow from Indochina on the way, the Carter announcement was a palliative measure. The need for more effective and dramatic action was underscored by the *Washington Star*, which complained:

> Isn't there someone—at the U.N. High Commission for Refugees, or in the world's civilized capitals—who has the will to cut through the baffling red tape that keeps these people penned up in fetid ships, starving and diseased, while the technicalities of maritime law are endlessly disputed?[33]

As the numbers of refugees surged, the numbers of news and media stories about helpless boat people increased as well. Moreover, the Carter administration was criticized for not being open-hearted enough and was pressured to undertake more on behalf of the boat people. An editorial entitled "The Shame of '78" in the *Wall Street Journal* criticized the "buck-passers" in the international community and called on the United States to open its doors to the boat people: "America has a unique responsibility toward the refugees from Indochina . . . because America is the nation that can afford the most in material help, has traditionally opened its doors the widest to refugees, and has stood most steadfastly for freedom in the world."[34] Slowly the perception emerged within the Carter administration that only an American government deeply concerned about the Vietnamese and willing to share the burden of resettlement could use its prestige and power to get the international community to act.

Within the U.S. government, the State Department's Bureau of East Asian and Pacific Affairs (EA) assumed the leading advocacy role for a larger Indochinese admissions program. The most powerful advocate for greater admissions within EA was the U.S. Ambassador to Thailand, Morton Abramowitz, who had strong support from Lowman, Rosenblatt, and others. Alarmed at the deteriorating refugee situation in Southeast Asia, Abramowitz warned Washington in an October 1978 cable that the refugee crisis had taken a new, unpredictable turn, particularly since Hanoi was now facilitating departures from Vietnam. At the same time, he argued that the flow from Laos had increased dramatically and that without an enlarged resettlement program the Thais would be under considerable pressure to push back new arrivals and U.S. leverage on the Thai government to continue to offer asylum would be greatly reduced.[35] Over the next several months, the U.S. Embassy in Bangkok continually urged Washington to enlarge its program and to lobby other nations to increase their own admissions numbers. In addition to being convinced of the need for a greater worldwide effort to resettle the Indochinese, Abramowitz and others at EA urged the maximum condemnation of Vietnam and support for a campaign to show that it was Vietnam's policies that were forcing the Indochinese to flee.[36]

The policy position advanced by Abramowitz gained rapid support within the Carter administration. Part of that policy was directed at punishing Vietnam for the mass expulsion of its own citizens. Although a few members of Congress,[37] including Senator Edward Kennedy, recommended that the U.S. offer various inducements to Vietnam with a view toward resolving outstanding bilateral issues including the refugee problem, a majority in Congress believed that the U.S. should maintain a policy of economic and political coercion to try to force Vietnam to change its ways. Since 1977, Congress had prohibited bilateral aid to Vietnam and expressed strong opposition to loans by international financial institutions to Hanoi on the grounds that Hanoi violated human rights and that such aid would not serve U.S. interests or increase stability in Southeast Asia.[38] Attempts to resume relations with Vietnam during 1977 and the first half of 1978 had failed, principally because of Hanoi's insistence that the U.S. provide reconstruction aid before the establishment of diplomatic relations. By late 1978, geopolitical factors, such as U.S. concern over the growing influence of the Soviet Union in Hanoi, Vietnam's invasion of Cambodia in December 1978, and the American desire to move rapidly toward normalization of relations with China, made further negotiation with Hanoi a difficult, if not impossible, task.[39]

In addition to exerting leverage on Vietnam to force it to modify its mass expulsion policies, the U.S. attempted to increase the involvement of the international community in reaching a solution to the problem. Under great pressure from the U.S. and from the ASEAN nations, the UNHCR called for an international consultation meeting in Geneva on December 11 and 12, 1978, to which all governments interested in the problems of refugees in Southeast Asia would be invited. The Southeast Asian nations dominated most of the discussion at the meeting, drew attention to the difficulties they faced, and called on the international community to provide assistance to the countries of first asylum, especially by providing immediate resettlement opportunities to the refugees. The U.S. representative, Under Secretary of State for Political Affairs David Newson, emphasized the need for a direct and massive involvement of the UNHCR and the international community. He said that the UNHCR would need greatly increased financial contributions. Overseas resettlement was the cornerstone of the U.S. approach to the boat people crisis. The resettlement nations would have to offer more admissions places, and other Southeast Asian nations would have to share more equitably with Malaysia and Thailand the burden of first asylum.[40]

Unfortunately, the consultation meeting achieved few concrete commitments in regard to resettlement offers or more financial aid to UNHCR programs in Southeast Asia. The Deputy High Commissioner, Dale DeHaan, made the concluding remarks and noted "that there can be no humane or durable solutions unless Governments grant at least temporary asylum in accordance with internationally accepted humanitarian principles." He also emphasized, as a corollary, "that existing facilities in countries of first asylum in Southeast Asia were already overloaded and that for such countries temporary asylum depended on commitments for resettlement in third countries and the avoidance of residual problems in the area."[41] Despite these remarks, no new havens of refuge outside Southeast Asia were immediately made available. The resettlement nations made pledges of only another $12 million and offered only about 5,000 new resettlement places in addition to those that had been pledged prior to the meeting. The Malaysian representative described these pledges at a press conference as "a drop in the ocean." Furthermore, the Southeast Asian countries received no assurances from Vietnam that the refugee flow would be curtailed. The Vietnamese representative, Vo Van Sung, denied that his government was involved in any way with the mass exodus and claimed that Hanoi was powerless to prevent it.

The pressure to involve the international community in the Indochina refugee situation increased dramatically during the first half of 1979 as the growing outflow of refugees began to directly affect many more countries and as the media began to depict the boat people as victims of an "Asian holocaust." The international response grew slowly and reluctantly out of human tragedy and suffering on a vast scale. It emerged only after repeated threats by Southeast Asian governments to forcibly turn away refugees at the frontier or on the high seas. Sometimes these threats were actually carried out, and the publicity given the large numbers of drownings at sea finally galvanized the international community into action. The Carter administration exerted considerable moral leadership and played a major role in organizing the international effort to provide refuge to the boat people.

By spring 1979, the number of new boat arrivals overwhelmed the Southeast Asian asylum countries. The incidents of refugees from Vietnam arriving on large vessels increased and caused considerable paranoia throughout the region. The outbreak of direct war between China and Vietnam in February 1979 resulted in an even greater number of departures of Vietnamese citizens of Chinese descent to Malaysia, Thailand, Indonesia, and Hong Kong. From a March rate of 13,423, the numbers escalated to 26,602 in April, 51,139 in May, and 56,941 in June. The rate at which refugees were resettled in the West, however, failed to keep up with the pace at which they left Vietnam. While more than 51,000 Vietnamese arrived in Southeast Asian countries in May, only about 8,500 left for resettlement.

Southeast Asian governments made it abundantly clear to the Carter administration that their willingness to provide first asylum to the boat people depended entirely on firm commitments by the U.S. and other countries to resettle the Vietnamese outside of the region. They also gave warnings of what they would do if they did not receive the necessary assistance. In view of no new significant resettlement pledges from the West, Southeast Asian governments, in particular Malaysia, stepped up their efforts to deter boat people. Malaysian officials termed the refugees "scum, garbage, and residue" to be swept off the beaches and pushed back to sea. Threatening to put machine guns on the beaches, Kuala Lumpur made it clear that it was willing to let boat people die rather than let them stay permanently. The Malaysian navy systematically towed boats back to sea even though they knew many were unseaworthy and would sink. Western refugee officials estimated that in February 1979 about 25 percent of those who tried to land in Malaysia were pushed off, in April, 50 percent, and by mid-1979, 80 percent. During this period, Malaysian officials estimated that coastal patrols had pushed about 40,000 boat people back out to sea. In the process, large numbers of Vietnamese died of starvation, thirst, or exposure and many drowned when their boats were capsized. Others were murdered by Thai pirates, who repeatedly and brutally attacked the refugee boats. Many of those pushed off by Thailand and Malaysia ended up at the southern end of the South China Sea in the Annabas Islands in Indonesia. Some boats had to sail all the way to Australian shores. The Indonesians also pushed boats off, as did the Filipinos, who threw a naval blockade across Manila Bay to stop refugee boats from entering the harbor.

Only after such actions and after a Malaysian official announced that his government would continue its policy of driving the refugees back to sea and in the future would shoot (later modified in the face of international criticism to "shoo") boat people rather than let them land did a sufficiently strong sentiment for resettlement emerge in the international community. The world's conscience had been pricked, and a lifeline of help to the Indochinese refugees was slowly being lowered.

In the spring of 1979 the Carter administration threw its weight behind the emerging sentiment favoring the rescue of the boat people. That sentiment was undoubtedly spurred by East-West confrontation in the region and a residual feeling of guilt over America's past involvement in Vietnam. Yet the tremendous groundswell of sympathy that eventually made an almost open-ended admissions policy possible was prompted, not by ideology or guilt, but by fear of widespread persecution and mass murder. The tragedy of the Vietnamese refugees evoked memories of the suffering of Jewish refugees from Nazi Germany and sparked a demand by Jewish and Christian agencies for an immediate U.S. response. Terence Cardinal Cooke of New York issued an appeal on behalf of 100 million Catholics, Protestants, and Jews which called on President Carter, Congress, and UN General Secretary Kurt Waldheim to act. Elie Wiesel, chairman of the Carter administration's Commission on the Holocaust, expressed distress at the silence and apathy over the plight of the boat people: "We are outraged at the sight of people set adrift with no country willing to welcome them ashore. We are horrified at the imposition of quotas which exclude women and children in the full knowledge that such a policy of exclusion can be a sentence of death."[42] The memory of America's failure to help Jews in the 1930s was instrumental in the demands made in Congress to resettle Indochinese refugees. Appeals to "not repeat the history of the Holocaust" were made repeatedly. "We are all too familiar", said Sen. Robert Dole of Kansas, "with the painful remembrance of ships loaded with European Jews seeking refuge during the Nazi period and in the aftermath of World War II. Many people found death after being herded from one port to the other."[43] Representative Stephen Solarz, himself Jewish, whose father had suffered during the holocaust, expressed the view of many of his colleagues in Congress:

It would be nice if the Government of Vietnam were not the Government of Vietnam and it had the kinds of policies which enabled these people to remain, but it is what it is, and we have got to deal with the subsequent realities. In the 1930's somebody might have said that Nazi Germany should change its policies to accommodate the needs of the Jewish people in Germany so that they would not want to leave, but the reality of the situation was that the Nazis were not about to change their policy, and the only real question that remained to the rest of the world was, given the policies of the Hitler regime, whether we were going to open our doors to the people who were desperate to get out.

. . . a somewhat similar situation exists in Vietnam. . . .[44]

Despite the growing sense in Washington that the U.S. should act to save the boat people, the Carter administration was unable to move quickly enough to keep up with the flow out of Vietnam. A complicating factor was finding sufficient funding to pay for the large admissions program. In April, the U.S. approved a new parole for 7,000 admissions from Indochina per month, but the U.S. refugee program was only able to process about half that number during April and May. Congress, which was concerned about the budget implications of increased admissions, did not approve funds to bring refugees to the U.S. until June. In order to maintain at least a reduced refugee program, the State Department borrowed money from its emergency fund for refugees and deferred part of its contributions to the UNHCR and ICRC for their refugee operations. Finally, the voluntary agencies, which resettled refugees in the U.S., were asked to operate on a credit basis and temporarily forgo their replacement grants, which forced most of them to go heavily into debt.[45]

Throughout the spring of 1979, powerful advocates both inside and outside the executive branch continued to press Congress on the need to overcome these financial hurdles and make the humanitarian commitment necessary to turn the boat people crisis around. Appealing to Congress to allocate the necessary refugee funding, the Secretary of the Department of Health and Human Services, Joseph Califano, argued:

There are relatively few moments in our national life when a legislative issue touches the very heart of a moral issue, when what we choose to do about a political problem expresses what we really are as a nation.

Such moments are deeply important. And the issue of refugees now seeking haven in America brings us to precisely such a moment. By our choice on this issue, we reveal to the world—and more importantly to ourselves—whether we truly live by our ideals or simply carve them on our monuments.[46]

Leo Cherne warned Congress that "the volcano is about to blow" in Southeast Asia and called on the President and Congress to radically increase admissions authorizations. At the same time, he argued that restrictionism was out of place for a nation which aspired to moral and political leadership in the world:

> Despite our efforts and those of a few other countries—notably France, Australia, and Canada—the world's response is grievously inadequate. What is needed, and this clearly comes to the nub of the problem . . . is clearly leadership—leadership of the sort that Franklin Delano Roosevelt uncharacteristically did not provide in the late 1930's, leadership of the sort that Lyndon B. Johnson did provide in the 1960's. . . . The President and the Congress must clearly enunciate a national commitment to resolve this present human crisis and call on the rest of the free world to work with us. It seems to us that this present crisis is a test of this administration's ability to meet . . . human rights commitments. . . . We certainly will press as hard as we can for a meaningful American response to that crisis. This nation has done it in the past, there is no reason why we cannot do it now.[47]

Support for resettling the Vietnamese also appeared in editorial columns across the country. In a lead article entitled "Save Us! Save Us!" *Time* magazine called on the U.S. and other nations to rescue the boat people. In an attempt to overcome restrictionist sentiment, *Time* argued that "though there have been traces of resentment against them, as there have been against immigrants of the past, the Vietnamese as a group have shown themselves to be hardworking and proudly self-sufficient."[48] Prominent members of the former antiwar movement appealed to the Carter administration to rise to the moral challenge from Vietnam. Concerts were held in Washington and New York in support of the boat people and in an appeal to people's humanitarian consciences.

Responding to the broad sentiment to rescue the boat people, the Senate unanimously passed a "sense of the Senate" resolution calling upon the United Nations to immediately convene an emergency session to deal with the Indochinese refugee crisis. Senator Boschwiz from Minnesota, himself a Jewish refugee from Nazi Germany, got passed an amendment to the supplemental appropriations bill which made funds immediately available to finance relief and resettlement assistance to the Indochinese refugees. Senator Hayakawa and Congressman McCloskey wrote to President Carter asking him to send the Seventh Fleet to search for and rescue the boat people leaving Vietnam.

Such sentiments were also expressed at the international level, and Vietnam came under considerable pressure to moderate its policies. Sweden, Yugoslavia, and the French left—formerly strong supporters of Vietnam—criticized Hanoi. Old enemies among French intellectuals, like Jean-Paul Sartre and Raymond Aron, joined in public appeals to aid the victims of Hanoi's expulsion policy. At the urging of the United States, the European Common Market voted to divert its economic aid to Vietnam to refugee relief for the boat people.

But more than public sentiment and economic sanctions were needed. The massive build-up of refugees in the region necessitated a larger worldwide refugee admissions program. The UNHCR called upon the U.S. and other industrialized nations to assume responsibility for the resettlement of large numbers of the refugees. In the face of a rapidly deteriorating first asylum situation in Southeast Asia, UN Secretary General Kurt Waldheim announced an international conference on refugees and displaced persons to be held in Geneva in July 1979 to secure such pledges. The leadership for such an initiative could not be provided by UNHCR, which was incapable of either protecting the rights of the Indochinese refugees or providing for their safe return home, but had to come from the United States.

President Carter bowed to appeals by religious and refugee groups, as well as by many members of Congress, his own administration, and the international community, and took several important initiatives prior to the Geneva meeting to insure that the major industrialized nations would assume responsibility for the resettlement of large numbers of the refugees. In late June, President Carter met with the Japanese Prime Minister prior to the 1979 economic summit in Tokyo and persuaded the Japanese to join with the Americans in providing leadership on the Indochinese refugee problem. Japan agreed to step up its contribution to UNHCR's 1979 Indochina budget from 25 to 50 percent and also to fund half the cost of the refugee processing centers which were proposed to hold refugees until they could be resettled abroad. Carter, in turn, announced that the U.S. would double its intake of Indochinese refugees to 14,000 a month.

The U.S.-Japan announcement constituted a dramatic initiative and created sufficient momentum to encourage others to respond generously. At the conclusion of the Tokyo economic summit, the seven industrialized nations issued a special statement in which they declared that the plight of refugees was "a humanitarian problem of historic proportions" and a threat to the peace and security of Southeast Asia. Most importantly, they pledged "as part of an international effort, [to] significantly increase their contributions to Indochinese refugee relief and resettlement by making more funds available and by admitting more people. . . ."[49]

After the Tokyo summit, Carter dispatched Secretary of State Cyrus Vance to Bali, Indonesia, where the foreign ministers of the Association of Southeast Asian Nations (ASEAN) had just had their annual meeting and where they had declared their intention not to offer refuge to any more boat people. Vance assured the ASEAN ministers that a major international effort was underway to help them, and asked them to reconsider their refusal to accept any more refugees. Although the ministers agreed to reconsider their policy, an ASEAN spokesman said on July 4 that even the increased admissions of refugees announced by the United States and other Western countries in Tokyo were still too small to resettle them quickly.[50]

At the Geneva Conference on Indochinese Refugees in July 1979 a significant effort was mounted to build on the momentum provided by President Carter. Pressures were exerted by states which were substantial contributors to the UNHCR budget, by the bureaucracy of the UNHCR itself, by the network of voluntary agencies loosely affiliated with it, and by Southeast Asian countries of first asylum seeking aid and resettlement opportunities. The Foreign Minister of Indonesia called for "firm commitment" instead of "lofty words."

Much of the impetus for international action to rescue the boat people came from the United States. Vice President Walter Mondale reaffirmed that the U.S. was serious about rescue. He evoked the powerful image of the Evian Conference, which had been convened in 1938 to rescue Europe's Jews from the Nazi holocaust. The failure of that conference to offer resettlement places for Jews gave Hitler *carte blanche* to proceed with the slaughter of 6 million Jews. Mondale called on the delegates to the Geneva Conference to "not re-enact their error [and] not be the heirs to their shame."

Unlike the Evian Conference, a plan that met the immediate needs of the boat people crisis emerged. The industrialized nations backed up their expressions of concern with money and increased quotas for refugees. The sixty-five countries in attendance pledged resettlement aid totaling some $160 million, and scores of governments increased their resettlement commitments, raising the total number of pledged placements from 125,000 to 260,000. Through the active intervention of Assistant Secretary of State Richard Holbrooke, the Philippines also offered several new sites, including one on the Bataan Peninsula, for a refugee processing center to hold up to 50,000 Indochinese. Conference delegates also gave a "general endorsement" to the principles of asylum and *non-refoulement* to emphasize their concern about Malaysian efforts to turn refugee boats back to sea. Finally, conference members pledged international cooperation in effecting sea rescues, and President Carter ordered the Seventh Fleet to seek out refugees in distress on the high seas and guaranteed resettlement in the U.S. if no other opportunities were available.

Although significant positive steps were taken to alleviate the plight of existing refugees, the United States and other Western countries were faced with a serious human rights dilemma. UN Secretary General Waldheim announced at the meeting that Vietnam "for a reasonable period of time . . . will make every effort to stop illegal departures." That announcement contained neither a general condemnation of Vietnamese persecution of ethnic Chinese nor a reassertion of one of the principles of the Universal Declaration of Human Rights, which insures freedom of travel and the right to emigrate. Thus control over the outflow of people from Vietnam was restored by undercutting the right of peoples facing persecution to move out of danger and flee their country.

The boat people crisis reached a turning point in July 1979 when the number of displaced Indochinese in Southeast Asia declined for the first time in eighteen months. As the Vietnamese authorities clamped down on "illegal departures," the decline in new arrivals was dramatic. From a high of 56,941 boat people in June, the numbers tumbled to 17,839 in July, 9,734 in August, 9,533 in September, 2,854 in October, 2,209 in November, and 2,745 in December. With arrivals rapidly dwindling and camps emptying steadily, the first asylum countries soon abandoned their push-off policies and offered protection to incoming boat people.[51]

The need to assure first asylum countries that they would not be left with a residual permanent refugee population led the U.S. to process for resettlement all those who had made it to refugee camps in Southeast Asia. As a result, by late 1979 the U.S. was admitting over 14,000 Indochinese per month, and virtually any person who fled Vietnam or Laos was likely to find safe haven in neighboring countries and could expect fairly rapid resettlement. The number of refugees leaving Southeast Asian countries began to exceed the number arriving. Throughout 1979 and 1980, the U.S. was able to maintain a large refugee admissions program. However, as the numbers of new arrivals in first asylum countries declined and as dramatic "push-off" cases became less frequent, the impetus to sustain a large U.S. resettlement program diminished. Large admissions inevitably increased resettlement impact on the United States, and domestic pressures and backlash from local U.S. communities against Indochinese refugees led to new efforts by Congress to exert more control over the admissions process.

In the fall of 1979, another refugee crisis—that of the Cambodians—loomed large on the horizon. The 1979 Geneva Conference had focused almost entirely on the fate of the boat people and had ignored the situation of the Khmers. Increasingly, however, the world was forced to shift its attention to the hundreds of thousands of refugees pouring out of western Cambodia during late 1979 and 1980 and to consider the question of whether the Khmer people would survive as a civilization.

Chapter 8

Meeting the Crisis in Cambodia

BEFORE 1978, little news of the terrible suffering of the people of Cambodia reached the West. Information about the destruction of a people under Pol Pot's reign of terror, about forced marches and forced labor, starvation, disease, and vicious mass murder, was fragmentary. The only accounts available were a few dispatches for the handful of Western newsmen who retained access to Cambodia after the spring of 1975 and the stories of the few refugees who managed to escape across heavily guarded borders. The newspaper accounts could not compete with the televised agony of the Vietnamese boat people, and the refugee stories generally were dismissed as exaggerations or anti-Communist propaganda. Only after the Vietnamese invaded Cambodia late in 1978, when tens of thousands of emaciated survivors crossed the border into Thailand and mass graves were discovered, did the full horror begin to seep in.

Responding to that horror, the United States in 1978 and 1979 committed itself, first, to massive Cambodian aid, and then to significant Cambodian reset-tlement. It acted largely out of humanitarian considerations, but as it had fre-quently done in the past three decades, sought through its humanity to achieve specific results in the worldwide struggle with Communism. Its generosity was great but not unlimited. Thus for approximately two years, the White House, the State Department, the bureaucracy charged with bringing refugees into the United States, and the Congress worked harmoniously together to bring Cambodian refugees to the United States. But by the middle of 1980, as the pace of resettlement quickened, new strains had begun to emerge. Congress, jealous of its prerogative to control migration and anxious to test the powers it had been given under a new Refugee Act, grew increasingly restive as recently admitted Cambodians began to add to the difficulties of communities with large Indochinese populations. Those in the State Department charged with moving refugees to the United States began expressing fears that a short-term rescue effort was being transformed into a long-term immigration program with no visible end. They were joined by INS officials who argued that the crisis in Cambodia had passed, that the new Refugee Act protected only those with a current fear of persecution, and that many of those seeking to enter the United States in 1980 and early 1981 were motivated primarily by the desire to enter the new land of milk and honey, America, "the western Shangri-la." [1]

If America was "Shangri-la," Cambodia under Pol Pot was hell. For pure brutality the Khmer Rouge probably have had no equal in the postwar world. In three and a half years, from mid-1975 to the end of 1978, between 1 million and 3 million Cambodians—one-seventh to nearly one-half of the nation's entire population—died from executions or from preventable malnutrition, disease, or exhaustion after forced marches and compulsory labor under draconian conditions. The Cambodian experience was possibly the worst to befall a people since the Nazi holocaust.

When the Khmer Rouge assumed power in April 1975, they inherited a devastated country. American bombing during the war had destroyed Cambodia's economic infrastructure and its agricultural productivity. The Khmer Rouge were faced with a desperate food crisis and the overwhelming task of restoring the cultivation of rice in a war-shattered country. In a single-minded policy aimed at maximizing agricultural production, the new rulers of Cambodia emptied the cities and relocated the rural population. Almost immediately a curtain fell on Cambodia. The Khmer Rouge closed and mined Cambodia's borders, and the country remained largely isolated until the invasion and occupation by Vietnamese troops in December 1978. The only accounts of life under the new regime were derived from some very early observations by journalists who remained behind after Phnom Penh fell, from official Khmer Rouge radio broadcasts, and, above all, from the reports of refugees recounting their personal experiences.

Those accounts, which were picked up and amplified as early as 1977 by a few American and French reporters, presented the image of a brutal and totally despotic regime.[2] Collected in 1975 and 1976 by representatives of the Australian, British, and Norwegian governments and by representatives of the rights organizations Amnesty International and the International Commission of Jurists, they were handed over to the UN Human Rights Commission in

1978.³ A UN spokesman concluded that the Cambodian situation was "the most serious that had occurred anywhere in the world since Nazism," and was nothing less than "autogenocide."⁴ That conclusion was based on hundreds of separate interviews, each similar to the one recounted by Joel Brinkley, late in 1979, in the *Louisville Courier-Journal:*

> "It is very sad about my country," said Say Khol, a 30 year-old man who once taught English in Phnom Penh. He was sitting in Cambodia's Samet Mean-chey refugee camp a half-mile from the Thai border, drawing in the dirt as he talked.
>
> "Small boy, he no have anything to learn. Old man, he no have anything to eat. Cambodia is only here. This all that is left of my country. Soon this will be gone too."
>
> Like many Cambodians, Say spoke English often "until Pol Pot. Since then, I scared to speak one word or I be killed. I forgot so much."
>
> Pol Pot is the Communist commander whose Khmer Rouge soldiers overthrew the American-backed military government of Gen. Lon Nol in 1975. . . . After the overthrow, Pol Pot's soldiers began executing everyone with any hint of wealth or education—especially those who spoke a foreign language.
>
> The executions were supposed to purge centuries of Western influence and remake Cambodia into a self-sufficient, rural society.
>
> Death came swiftly from machetes and bullets, or slowly from prolonged torture. More than a million Cambodians died that first year.
>
> Some were hung upside down by their feet, their heads submerged in buckets of water. They remained alive as long as their neck muscles could hold their faces out of the water. Still others were publicly disemboweled.
>
> Children were chained together, then buried alive.
>
> Say, a handsome young man, had been a lieutenant in Lon Nol's army. But when the Khmer Rouge forces approached Phnom Penh, "I threw away my uniform, put on clothes to look like an ordinary farmer and tried to leave the city."
>
> The executions had already begun.
>
> "I saw many, many people killed, hit on the back of the neck with a bamboo knife. They threw the bodies into huge, big piles in the middle of the street. I saw my friends in those piles."
>
> He escaped the Khmer Rouge's notice. Then with the rest of Phnom Penh's survivors, he said, "I got pushed by Pol Pot into the country, to Kampong Speu Province" in southwestern Cambodia.
>
> Like other survivors, Say was forced to live on a commune and work as a rice farmer for several years, conscious every minute that he'd be executed the moment he betrayed his middle-class past.
>
> "They pushed me very, very hard. I worked every day, 4 a.m. to 11 p.m. with only two meals. No religious holidays."

At communes across the country, Khmer Rouge soldiers would, without warning or apparent provocation, grab workers and take them away. Sometimes weeks or months later, Say and other refugees said, workers would stumble upon mangled bodies in the corner of a rice field.

"Later Pol Pot pushed me to Battambang Province [in western Cambodia], where we built a big, big water tank," Say said. "No machines or tools. Just people. We worked 24 hours a day, seven days a week until it was finished. Many people, old people and young people, they died, dropped while we worked, and we worked around them.

"We have only a little bit to eat. Seven spoons of rice a day. Seven spoons, sir. That's all. Sometimes we eat only salt and little animals and the leaf of a tree."

Millions of Cambodians in other communes suffered along with him. . . .[5]

Despite stories like these, there was remarkably little reaction to what was happening in Cambodia except among relief and refugee workers and a handful of journalists and scholars. Eyewitness reports from Sydney Schanberg of the *New York Times* and others describing reports in subsequent years of Khmer Rouge atrocities from refugees in Thailand did not generate an international outcry similar to the one prompted by human rights abuses in Chile. One of the first persons to lament this lack of sensitivity was Leo Cherne of the International Rescue Committee. In June 1975 Cherne appealed to the Board of Trustees of Freedom House:

> . . . it is possible for the world to learn of monumental tragedy, tragedy beyond measure and ignore it. The blunt fact is that these "three to four million people" fell into a deep black echoless hole. They are silent, and we are silent. There are no enquiries underway. The International Red Cross has not been rushed to Phnom Penh. No protests have been lodged with the International Commission of Jurists. The United Nations has not been called into special session, nor has an agenda item even been suggested for this Fall's regular session of the Assembly. No advertisement carrying the names of concerned citizens has appeared in any U.S. newspaper. And this silence is not limited to the United States. . . .
>
> I appeal to you, fellow members of the board of Trustees of Freedom House, to take the first step so that this ghastly silence may end. If our voices are raised, there may be others who will add their cries. Then, in turn the High Commission for Refugees of the United Nations may request the government of Cambodia to permit an objective inquiry seeking to learn the truth.[6]

Despite Cherne's efforts, the media paid little attention to the situation in Cambodia, and refugee reports were met with skepticism, indifference, and hostility.[7] The refugees who emerged from Cambodia were considered to be unreliable informants, and few people and no governments were interested in their stories of hardship, of disease, and of vicious mass murder. Just as few people in the 1930s and 1940s had wished to believe in the Nazi elimination of Jews until the evidence was overwhelmingly presented to them, so many people wished not to believe that atrocities were taking place in Cambodia under Khmer Rouge rule. Until 1978, Vietnam attempted to establish close relations with the Khmer Rouge and had no interest in damaging these relations by calling attention to human rights violations in Cambodia. Hanoi dismissed the refugee accounts about Khmer Rouge conduct as "CIA stories," thus adding to disbelief in them, particularly among the Western left. Many former antiwar activists, having worked so hard to insure the withdrawal of America from Cambodia and the victory of the Khmer Rouge, now downplayed Khmer Rouge behavior, denigrated the refugee stories, and criticized the few journalists who reported them as falling prey to the CIA "bloodbath" theory. In addition, television reporters had difficulty conveying the horrors described by the refugees. Hanoi refused journalists access to South Vietnam, where 150,000 Cambodians had taken refuge, and in the absence of visual images the mass murder in Cambodia was deemed not newsworthy. Western political leaders were also hesitant to criticize the Khmer Rouge. The United States was weary of the war, and after an ignominious defeat, the Ford administration wanted to forget about Indochina. The Carter administration, despite its general advocacy of human rights and its belief that they should figure into the foreign policy calculus, proved to be more interested in supporting the government of Thailand, its principal ally in Southeast Asia, and in wooing China than it was in sounding an alarm about the situation in Cambodia. While it never condoned Khmer Rouge brutality, it perceived more important interests in promoting Thailand's stability, which the Thai government sought through negotiations with the Pol Pot regime, and in achieving better relations with the Chinese government, a strong supporter of the Khmer Rouge regime and a strong opponent of the government in Hanoi. Thus for geopolitical reasons it refrained from overt criticism of Khmer Rouge rule.

It was not until early 1978, nearly three years after the brutal seizure of power by the Khmer Rouge and hundreds of thousands of deaths, that the Western powers began to respond more aggressively to the situation in Cambodia. Public knowledge of Khmer Rouge atrocities had finally reached a point that no longer permitted the issue to be ignored. In 1978, CBS ran a special hour-long TV documentary on the plight of Cambodians and the ABC TV morning show and the McNeil-Lehrer Report also began focusing public attention on the situation. Reporting from the field by Henry Kamm of the *New York Times*, the *Far Eastern Economic Review*, and the American Ambassador to Thailand, Morton Abramowitz, alerted U.S. officials and policy makers to the fact that there was a problem of mammoth dimensions in Cambodia.[8] In the spring, President Carter called the Khmer Rouge "the world's worst violators of human rights." A group of Norwegian politicians, academics, and journalists held a hearing on Khmer Rouge atrocities. The Canadian Foreign Ministry compiled a dossier of human rights violations in Cambodia, and Britain asked for an inquiry into the situation in Cambodia at the UN Commission on Human Rights. Moreover, with the outbreak of open conflict between Vietnam and Cambodia, Vietnam, along with the Soviet Union, began for the first time to denounce Khmer Rouge atrocities.

The time was thus ripe for new efforts by the Citizens' Commission on Indochinese Refugees to secure parole slots for those Cambodians who had managed to flee into Thailand but had been virtually ignored by the United States and other Western nations for five years.[9] Disappointed that President Carter had not included any Cambodians in the parole of 25,000 Indochinese announced on March 29, 1978, the Citizens' Commission lobbied vigorously in Washington during the summer of 1978 for more admissions. At a session on Capitol Hill arranged by Georgetown's Center for Strategic and International Studies for members of the House, Senate, White House, and press, Leo Cherne made an impassioned appeal for action. Immediately following this briefing, members of the Citizens' Commission testified on Cambodia before the House Subcommittee on Asian and Pacific Affairs, and the AFL-CIO, the NAACP, the American Jewish Committee, and a large number of church and civic groups announced their support of a special parole for the Cambodians. Cherne and many voluntary agency personnel felt that the United States shared some of the responsibility for what had befallen Cambodia, and that that responsibility extended to resettling those Cambodians who could still be saved.[10] That view was shared by some in Congress. Much to the dismay of his colleagues, Sen. George McGovern even suggested the possibility of international intervention to remove the Khmer Rouge from power. Sen. Robert Dole and Rep. Stephen Solarz introduced legislation which stipulated that 15,000 places would be provided for Cambodians in the Indochinese parole program and directed the Attorney General to modify the parole criteria to admit more Khmer. Despite opposition in Congress from Eilberg and others who were not supportive of Indochinese migration, the Dole-Solarz joint resolution passed the House on September 29, due in part to Carter administration support and to extensive lobbying by Representative Solarz. It also passed the Senate, and the Attorney General subsequently included Cambodians as an eligible group in the December 1978 parole.

The support of voluntary agencies and key Congressmen for the Cambodian parole in 1978 revealed the initial significance Congress attached to the suffering of the Cambodian survivors at the time when the Pol Pot regime was crumbling and thousands of starving people were beginning to stream toward the Thai border. That support was to continue to grow unabated for nearly two years, and, in a much attenuated form, still continues today. By mid-1985 over 130,000 Cambodians had been admitted to the United States and American efforts had contributed to the resettlement of 60,000 more in other countries.[11] The gate, once opened, proved almost impossible to shut. Yet at the same time that Congress was urging the President to take second measures to admit more Cambodians, it was engaged in a major legislative effort to reassert its own gatekeeping authority.

While the Cambodian parole was being debated in Congress in 1978, discussions were already underway in the legislative branch to reform the tradition of executive parole and to grant back to Congress more of its traditional power to regulate refugee admissions. Many in Congress, including Sen. Edward Kennedy and Rep. Joshua Eilberg, the principal spokesmen in Congress on refugee issues, were united in believing that parole was an inefficient way of dealing with the continuing Indochinese refugee crisis. Eilberg believed that parole had been consistently misused since 1975 to evade the clear limits of the Immigration and Nationality Act. As an opponent of generous Indochinese parole, he advocated more Congressional opportunity to review the President's parole requests and more practical power to turn them down. He also complained that although it was apparent from the time of the 1975 evacuation of Saigon that a regular flow of refugees would be leaving Indochina for years to come, the ad hoc nature of the parole mechanism encouraged the Executive Branch to avoid planning for this refugee flow.[12] Senator Edward Kennedy concurred. In his words: "the Executive was put in the position of waiting repeatedly until the numbers of refugees in the countries of first asylum reached crisis proportions and then declaring an emergency which required yet another special program."[13] Between 1975 and 1979, at least ten separate paroles were used to admit over 300,000 Indochinese refugees. Each parole was limited in duration and numbers and responded to a specific crisis. Each parole was in turn overwhelmed by a new crisis, and required a successor.

The advent in 1977 of an administration sensitive to human rights considerations and the assumption by Edward Kennedy of the chairmanship of the Senate Judiciary Committee opened up the possibility of reform in immigration and refugee policy after a decade of resistance on the part of traditional restrictionists in Congress. A systematic approach to the broad range of immigration problems confronting the nation, including large-scale refugee flow and illegal migration, was contemplated by the Carter administration, which joined with Congress late in 1978 to appoint a blue-ribbon panel, the Select Commission on Immigration and Refugee Policy. The Select Commission was charged with making systematic policy recommendations.[14] But in the refugee area, it was quickly overtaken by independent executive and Congressional action.

The impetus for that action came not only from the latest Indochinese parole, of which the Cambodians were a significant part, but also from an increasingly heavy flow of Soviet Jews into the United States. During 1978 and 1979, Moscow approved over 50,000 exit visas for Soviet Jews in the expectation that concessions on the issue of emigration would make Congress more receptive to ratifying the SALT II agreement Moscow had negotiated with the Carter administration.[15] By late 1978, annual refugee admissions from overseas were 50,000 and were rising fast. It was clear that the "seventh preference," which, as a result of 1976 changes, now permitted a maximum of 17,400 annual refugee admissions, was not sufficient to deal with such large numbers. The pace of resettlement also outstripped existing governmental assistance programs. The Indochina Migration and Refugee Assistance Act of 1975 had to be repeatedly extended, and with each new parole the need for supplemental budget requests mushroomed. In 1978, the increased numbers of Soviet refugees also necessitated the passage of special federal assistance to the beleaguered voluntary agencies, which no longer had the funds to resettle all who came from the Soviet Union.[16] Thus Congress was forced to expand its thinking from a narrow concern about refugee admissions to a broader, more comprehensive approach which addressed the problems of resettlement in the United States.[17]

The crisis prompted the administration to undertake a revision of United States refugee policy without awaiting completion of the Select Commission's report. In February 1979, the Carter administration created the Office of the U.S. Coordinator for Refugee Affairs and appointed former Senator Dick Clark as the first coordinator to bring order and continuity to the handling of refugees and to help shepherd a new refugee bill through Congress.[18] Senator Kennedy and Representative Rodino introduced the administration's legislation, and after numerous hearings and intensive consultations between the Executive Branch and Congressional committee staffs, a new Refugee Act was passed in March 1980.[19]

The Refugee Act of 1980 was the first comprehensive refugee legislation in United States history and broke new ground in a number of areas. It explicitly abolished parole as a device for bringing large groups of refugees into the United States and provided that refugees, previously admitted in limited numbers as "seventh preference" immigrants, would now be admitted under a new and entirely independent quota. A baseline refugee quota of 50,000 individuals to be accepted annually for the first two fiscal years was established. The act also stipulated that Congress should have a limited but definite role in determining allocations or changing the quota. The annual allocation was to be determined by the President "after consultation with Congress," thus formally insuring an enhanced role for Congress in the formulation of United States refugee policy. The new law also afforded the United States Coordinator for Refugee Affairs more funding and the statutory authority to use it. The act was significant because it recognized that the problems of refugee admissions and of domestic resettlement were long-standing and of critical importance for public policy and because it provided for a major change in the formation of United States refugee policy.

One of the most significant changes involved the new definition of the term "refugee." Congress was concerned that the definition emphasize the humanitarian and nondiscriminatory aspects of the legislation, remove the ideological and geographical bias which characterized previous American law and conform closely to international standards. Thus it eliminated the "seventh preference" language which stipulated that refugees were those fleeing "from any Communist or Communist-dominated country" and replaced it with a more universal definition. That definition was basically the same as that employed in the United Nations 1951 Refugee Convention and 1967 Refugee Protocol and covered persons outside their own country who were not firmly resettled elsewhere and who had a well-founded fear of persecution based on race, religion, nationality, social class, or political opinion. By redefining "refugee" to conform to international standards, the 1980 act eliminated questions about the admissibility of persons subject to persecution in countries not in the Middle East or under Communist domination. The new definition also destroyed the former presumption that all those fleeing Communist lands were in fact refugees.

The Cambodians paroled into the United States in 1978, 1979, and early in 1980 benefited from this presumption. Seeking to avoid return to a Communist country just before the Refugee Act of 1980 went into effect, all were automatically regarded as refugees. Yet that fact did not immediately translate into a large resettlement program. Prior to the Vietnamese invasion of Cambodia late in 1978, there had been no large-scale refugee program involving Cambodians for the simple reason that most were prisoners in their own country. Yet even after the Pol Pot regime was driven from power and hundreds of thousands of Cambodians streamed toward the Thai border, the American response, like that of every other Western nation, developed slowly.

Some of this slowness was attributable to the massive effort which had already been launched on behalf of the Vietnamese boat people and the scarcity of trained international personnel in Southeast Asia capable of handling the needs of a new and substantial body of refugees. Some was undoubtedly attributable to America's greater sense of responsibility to the Vietnamese, who had served as America's battlefield allies in Indochina. And some was almost certainly due to the length of time it took for the principal dimensions of the Cambodian tragedy to be reported by the press and assimilated by the voluntary agencies, the Congress, and the American people. Thus as reports of another holocaust filtered into the national consciousness, American willingness to provide humanitarian assistance and, later, resettlement opportunities increased exponentially. Like the Vietnamese and Laotian programs which preceded them, the American programs for Cambodian refugees which developed in late 1979 and 1980 were marked by considerable selfless generosity. Like those earlier programs, they revealed the ability of a few dedicated people to shape public policy, the influence of humanitarian coalitions, and the importance of strong Presidential leadership. However, they also demonstrated how conscious those making policy were of the geopolitical significance of their actions.

The beginning of America's large-scale resettlement effort for Cambodians probably can be traced back to the lightning offensive against the Pol Pot regime which the Vietnamese government launched late in December 1978. The effect of that strike was to drive Pol Pot and his inner circle into the remote jungle near the Thai border, to establish a new pro-Vietnamese government headed by Heng Samrin, and to open up the Thai-Cambodian border for the first time since 1975. A year of unprecedented movement of people inside and outside Cambodia followed. Many Khmers set out to return to their pre-1975 homes but found only devastation and ruin, a barren countryside and towns without functioning services or administration. Masses of people, undernourished and worn out by four years of slavery, criss-crossed the nation seeking reunion with their families. Stocks of rice, including seed rice, were eaten and food supplies ran low. Thousands, therefore, decided to seek refuge and food, temporarily at least, on the Thai border.[20]

The Thais perceived the Cambodian influx, which began while large numbers of refugees continued to stream out of Vietnam and Laos, as having the potential for immense disruption. As a consequence, Thailand officially closed its border to the Khmers and treated all of them who attempted to cross as illegal immigrants. Some were incarcerated in border camps; many were denied access to UNHCR investigating teams. In April 1979, thousands of Cambodians were returned to Cambodia or forced back at the border, where untold numbers died of hunger, neglect, and personal violence.[21]

The news of this migration quickly reached the West; as importantly, the migration, by bringing Cambodians to the Thai border, brought them into contact with the Western nightly television news in the United States. Telecasts began to feature starving Cambodian women and children—wide-eyed, shrunken, bones draped with sagging flesh—struggling miles across mined borders to the relative safety of Thailand. These images competed emotionally with the continuing pictures of foundering Vietnamese boats and thus, at least to the extent that the broader American public was involved, did not lead to any immediate call for the opening of American borders. Instead, with the blessing of the White House, a major public relations effort, similar to those employed on several occasions in the 1970s and 1980s to secure relief for African famine victims, was launched. Rosalynn Carter made the Cambodians her special cause, and the Rev. Theodore Hesburgh of Notre Dame University was appointed the chairman of the Cambodian Crisis Center, an umbrella organization created to coordinate the fund-raising efforts of dozens of private charitable organizations.[22] The country was flooded with press releases detailing the "agony of Cambodia," starving children became a regular feature on the evening news, and millions of dollars for the purchase of food, shelter, and medicine were eventually raised.

Even as this public relations campaign was getting underway—and long before it reached its peak during the autumn of 1979—Morton Abramowitz, the United States Ambassador to Thailand, was reporting considerable Thai dissatisfaction with the increasing number of Cambodian refugees crossing Thailand's borders and with the failure of the United States to take any steps to deal with the situation.[23] Because the United States had few direct ties with individual Cambodians, its fervor for rescue was understandably limited. The United States, particularly after Malaysia began pushing Vietnamese boats out to sea, was under extraordinary pressure to select those Vietnamese stranded in Malaysia first. Prime Minister Kriangsak of Thailand complained constantly to American diplomats that the Western world was interested only in the boat people, and did not care what happened along the Thai-Cambodian border. Despite Ambassador Abramowitz' efforts to alert Washington to the needs of land as well as boat refugees, the U.S. made few concrete assurances to Bangkok about increasing Cambodian refugee admissions levels.[24] In the absence of such assurances, and becoming increasingly concerned that fighting between the Khmer Rouge and the Vietnamese forces in Cambodia might spill over the Thai border, the government of Thailand took matters into its own hands.

The Thai army stepped up efforts to keep Khmers out of Thailand and began to push back into Cambodia entire groups of refugees who had congregated on the Thai side of the border. Formal complaints about forced Thai repatriations were made by the High Commissioner for Refugees, Poul Hartling, by the U.S. Coordinator for Refugee Affairs, Dick Clark, by the Citizens' Commission on Indochinese Refugees, and by a number of U.S. Congressmen[25] who wrote directly to Prime Minister Kriangsak. Despite these protests, Kriangsak moved unilaterally to stop the Cambodian overland migration.

In June 1979, the military rounded up 40,000 Khmers encamped along the border, bused them away, and then forced them at night and at gunpoint across the border, pushing them down narrow trails on steep escarpments into heavily mined areas of Cambodia. Press reports stated that thousands died, both from exploding mines when they tried to move forward and from Thai gunfire when they tried to return to Thailand. Many more succumbed during the following weeks in the immediate border area to malaria and starvation.

Abramowitz and his Embassy staff believed that the forcible repatriation of Cambodians not only underlined the Thais' determination to deal with their refugee problem unilaterally but also revealed the "iron hand" of the Thai military, who felt that the Cambodian migrants posed an unacceptable security risk for the nation.[26] For fear of undermining Prime Minister Kriangsak in the eyes of the Thai military, thus inviting a possible military coup and the overthrow of an important regional ally, Abramowitz was reluctant to strongly criticize Thai actions. Yet the United States Embassy also believed that the situation of the Cambodians in Thailand was desperate, and had been rendered worse by the failure of early efforts of the UNHCR to provide them with either relief or protection. During this critical early period, UNHCR was badly understaffed in Thailand, and suffered from incompetent and inexperienced leadership in the field.[27] It proved incapable of mustering the material support necessary to keep refugees alive, and was not effective in motivating the Thais to be more humane. The UNHCR representative in Thailand hesitated to criticize Thai authorities openly, believing that external pressure would only embarrass the Thais and cause them to be even more restrictive. Lacking even a single protection officer for the period October 1978 to June 1979, the Bangkok office of UNHCR was almost totally ineffective in the field and was powerless to prevent the forcible repatriation of Cambodians or to provide decent camp facilities for the refugees who remained in Thailand. Betraying a tension between its general function to offer protection to refugees and the necessity to work closely with the country of first asylum, UNHCR headquarters in Geneva was also reluctant to irritate the Thai authorities by pressing too hard on protection problems in Thailand.

UNHCR's early failures were obvious; yet its institutional capacity to ameliorate the situation in Thailand was limited. The success of UNHCR's activities always depends on the willingness of national governments to cooperate with the regional office and the Geneva headquarters of UNHCR. UNHCR can call attention to the legal obligations undertaken by governments that have adhered to the Refugee Convention and Protocol, but it is without the ability to change the course of a determined government that intends either to violate treaty commitments to protect and aid refugees or to ignore the policies of the United Nations with regard to refugees. Thailand was not a signatory to the

Refugee Convention and Protocol and was clearly unwilling to respect these treaties or cooperate with the UN. In May 1979, UN Secretary General Kurt Waldheim visited Thailand and raised the issue of asylum for the Khmers with Kriangsak, but his visit had no visible effect. Because Thailand felt it could act harshly toward Cambodian refugees without much immediate disadvantage, UNHCR believed it had little choice but to temper its criticism and not loudly inveigh against Thai actions, in the hope of producing a more favorable response in the future.

The limited effectiveness of UNHCR to change Thai policy convinced Abramowitz that the United States was the only authority that might force the Thais to act more humanely toward the refugees. He believed a dual approach to the Cambodian refugee problem was needed. On one hand, it was imperative to stabilize the situation along the border and greatly improve the quality of relief efforts there while minimizing the impact of the Cambodians on Thailand. On the other hand, looking further into the future, it was necessary to reopen the United States resettlement stream, even if this meant that significant numbers of new refugees would eventually have to be accepted by the United States.[28]

Those goals, and the additional goal of maintaining Thailand's stability in a chaotic and potentially disruptive international environment, were not pursued in mutual isolation. It was understood that better relief, administered outside rather than within Thailand's borders, would lessen the security concerns within Thailand and offer additional protection to people who otherwise faced continued overt opposition from the Thai army. It was also understood that refugees who had already been permitted to enter Thailand could not morally be pushed back, given the civil war raging in Cambodia and the desperate food situation there. For most of the latter refugees, resettlement in the United States was the only practical solution, although the possibility existed that other Western nations could be persuaded temporarily to let down their immigration barriers and take a percentage of those in need.

To achieve better relief required the same basic thing necessary for a successful resettlement operation: broad awareness in Congress and among the American people that the Cambodians were truly desperate, and that they lacked the option of returning voluntarily to their homes any time in the foreseeable future. The immediate imperatives of border relief generated significant acrimony between the United States and the international agencies operating in the area and a significant breach between the U.S. and the UNHCR, which began to heal only after the UNHCR began dramatically to increase its staff in Thailand and dispatched Zia Rizvi, an experienced and competent administrator, as Regional Representative for Southeast Asia in October 1979.[29] The acrimony was attributable in large part to Abramowitz' insistence that food and other necessities be distributed through a special operational group established by the Embassy in Bangkok with military oversight and relief responsibilities. The group, called the Khmer Emergency Group (KEG),[30] was directed by Lionel Rosenblatt and Mike Eiland, a colonel in the U.S. Army who had gained considerable combat and intelligence-gathering experience during the war. The KEG was remarkably successful in bringing aid to the Cambodian people, and played a major role in getting international relief operations underway.[31] Some of the criticism it attracted was clearly attributable to territorial jealousy. Yet the perception, shared by many in the UNHCR and voluntary agencies, that the American program was an overtly political one cannot be dismissed out of hand.

According to one KEG document, the U.S. Embassy's three objectives in the Cambodian program were to provide humanitarian assistance, to lobby for resettlement places, and to "explore [the] desirability of assistance, military and or logistic, to Khmer resistance elements, including use of exits."[32] By providing relief assistance to the border, the U.S. intended to provide not only humanitarian aid, but also to feed and clothe the various Cambodian resistance groups, including the Khmer Rouge. Provision of "exits" was intended to assure the Khmer "freedom fighters" that they could seek refuge in Thailand if they had to flee across the border in the event of a Vietnamese attack. Throughout the campaign to assist Cambodians, the political and humanitarian aspects of the U.S. relief effort were almost impossible to disentangle. Yet one purpose, clearly understood by Abramowitz and apparently endorsed by the State Department's Bureau of East Asian and Pacific Affairs, was to use American generosity as a counter to Soviet-supported Vietnamese aggression. In a November 1979 cable to Washington in which he argued for the delivery of food to starving Cambodian refugees at the Thai border, Abramowitz emphasized the importance of using the refugee issue to Vietnam's political disadvantage:

> One, we must step up the international campaign against Moscow and Hanoi for permitting this scene to continue. In the past few years Hanoi for the first time has lost most of its diplomatic and international support. We must maximize their isolation on humanitarian grounds much as we did on the boat refugees.
>
> Second, and it will be enormously difficult for Thailand, we must encourage people to come to the Thai border. We are doing this already; the presence of food on the Thai border is already getting well known all over Cambodia. VOA broadcasts will further contribute to it.[33]

To certain members of the Executive Branch, however, and to many members of Congress, the political benefits of providing either relief or more resettlement places were problematical. Much of the policy-making bureaucracy in Washington initially resisted providing emergency relief aid to Cambodia. The National Security Council gave overriding priority to improving relations with China, and perceived relief aid to Phnom Penh as action that would help the Vietnamese.[34] Despite evidence as early as January 1979 of widespread famine, the State Department also hesitated to initiate a program inside Cambodia because it feared shipments of food and medicine could not be monitored and would be seized by Vietnamese troops before they ever reached starving Cambodians. Along with the NSC, State questioned the desirability of providing relief to a country occupied by the Vietnamese army.[35] The problem the Bangkok Embassy faced was therefore to find advocates back home powerful enough to promote additional relief and a more generous admissions policy.

It addressed that problem by being especially solicitous of the press and other potential supporters. In an effort to encourage U.S. public awareness and support for the entire relief effort, the KEG team met official and private U.S. visitors, including journalists and Congressmen, and briefed them on the refugee situation. KEG officials saw to it that all visitors contacted refugees and heard individual refugees' stories of personal hardship, thereby creating a human bond and helping to create a prorefugee constituency in the United States.[36] Such contacts helped generate a better understanding of the Cambodian problem and more sympathy for its victims. They thus helped further the concerted, and ultimately successful, lobbying effort pursued in the United States by individual members of Congress, voluntary agency personnel, and religious and sectarian leaders who feared an unparalleled disaster if more relief was not provided.

By late summer 1979, a groundswell of sympathy for the Cambodians had begun to develop in the United States and other Western countries. United States policy makers were affected by the desperate plight of a people whose very existence seemed to be in grave jeopardy. In August 1979, a House Study Mission on Indochina reported that

> the Cambodian refugee population in Thailand . . . could increase by hundreds of thousands within the next few months as predicted famine conditions spread in Cambodia. We therefore recommend that the United States seek creation of an internationally sponsored and monitored food relief effort in Cambodia to prevent such a famine. Such a program should be made available to all needy Cambodians and not through the auspices of any political regime. In addition, we recommend that the United States establish a special bilateral aid fund to assist the Thai government in caring for those Cambodian refugees in the Thai-Cambodian border area who would like to return to Cambodia as soon as famine conditions and hostilities cease.[37]

Throughout the fall, other warnings of impending mass starvation in Cambodia emerged. In September a UNICEF official, after visiting Cambodia, reported that few children under the age of five were still alive and more than 80 percent of Khmer children were starving. Eyewitness accounts from Phnom Penh coincided with a U.S. Embassy report from Thailand that "the physical conditions of newly arrived refugees over the past few days were among the worst we have witnessed. Assuming that only the strongest are able to make the trek into Thai territory, it appears that those still inside Cambodia are reaching the point where it is no longer possible for them to survive."[38] The director general of the British Red Cross said in October that up to 2 million Cambodians "could die before Christmas if the relief operation cannot be sustained." Thirteen major U.S. volunteer agencies appealed to Secretary of State Vance "to pursue all available bilateral and multilateral channels . . . to see that the United States moves quickly and effectively in responding to this crisis."[39]

The Cambodia crisis seized the conscience of the West. Political and religious leaders competed to show their concern, and there were calls to truck food across the Thai border into Cambodia and to begin a massive airdrop of food supplies over large areas of Cambodia. Pictures of emaciated and dying refugees were splashed across the world's newspapers, and numerous editorials appealed for action. *Time* magazine's cover story "Deathwatch: Cambodia" was representative of the press coverage:

> It is a country soaked in blood, devastated by war, and its people are starving to death. Every day numbed witnesses to the appalling tragedy that has consumed Cambodia trek across the border into Thailand. Stumbling on reed-thin legs through the high elephant grass that grows along the frontier, they form a grisly cavalcade of specters, wrapped in black rags. Many are in the last stages of malnutrition, or are ravaged by such diseases as dysentery, tuberculosis and malaria. Perhaps the most pathetic images of all are those of tearful, exhausted mothers cradling hollow-eyed children with death's head faces, their bellies swollen, their limbs as thin and fragile as dried twigs. Since early October, an estimated 80,000 Cambodians have made it safely across the border, and perhaps 250,000 others are clustered in the western provinces of the country, waiting for their chance to escape. They are the lucky ones. Relief agencies believe that as many as 2.25 million Cambodians could die of starvation in the next few months unless a vast amount of aid is provided soon.[40]

The immediate response was a massive outpouring of private aid and the development by KEG of a new relief delivery system which brought tons of food and other needed supplies to the Thai-Cambodian border, where they were trucked a few miles into Cambodia and distributed to tens of thousands of uprooted migrants.

When Sen. Edward Kennedy, Carter's challenger for the 1980 Democratic presidential nomination, complained that the U.S. had done nothing to alleviate the Cambodian crisis, President Carter, who had provided key leadership only six months earlier in the international initiative to rescue the Vietnamese boat people, announced a major U.S. relief effort on October 24, 1979. With Cardinal Cooke of New York and Father Hesburgh of Notre Dame University appearing at his side, Carter pledged $69 million, later pushed up to $106 million by various acts of Congress and the administration. Recalling the legacy of Auschwitz, Carter called Cambodia the new holocaust which had to be avoided at all costs. Within a week Rosalynn Carter left for Thailand to visit camps along the border, and while there was photographed with a dying baby in her arms, thus dramatizing the issue and conveying to the rest of the world that there was a great need to avert a crisis. Similar generosity was displayed by other Western countries. At an international conference in November, $210 million in aid to be evenly distributed to Phnom Penh and the Thai-Cambodian border was pledged by participating nations. Compared with the response to similar and nearly simultaneous emergencies of Afghan refugees in Pakistan and Somalian refugees in the Horn of Africa and a famine in Uganda, the Cambodia crisis evoked an extraordinary outpouring of giving in America and Europe.

Yet the magnitude of this international relief effort, although capable of staving off starvation, could not immediately overcome the long-term political problems occasioned by years of agricultural neglect. As importantly, it could not shake Thailand's resolve to close its borders to additional Cambodian migrants and to treat those already present as unwelcome visitors rather than permanent settlers. From October 1979 to January 1980, Thailand insisted that Cambodians not be defined as refugees or granted first asylum. Rather, they would be considered illegal entrants and placed in specially built, UNHCR administered holding centers inside Thailand to await return to Cambodia when conditions there permitted. In the meantime, the Thais denied resettlement countries, including the U.S., access to refugees inside the holding centers. Bangkok did not want the Cambodians who had arrived in 1979 to be resettled in the West, since the Thais believed that a resettlement program would only encourage more people to leave Cambodia.[41] The Thais feared that resettlement countries would not increase admissions quotas sufficiently to accommodate the large numbers of Khmers, and that even partial resettlement would make the remaining Khmers less willing to consider other alternatives. Of all the alternatives, voluntary repatriation of the refugees back to Cambodia seemed the most attractive to Thailand.[42]

The UNHCR holding centers for Cambodians inside Thailand were effectively closed to new arrivals by January 1980, and by the middle of the year the situation in the holding centers and along the Thai-Cambodian border had stabilized, with more than 160,000 Cambodian refugees in UNHCR holding centers inside Thailand, about 200,000 straddling the Thai-Cambodian border, and more than 300,000 Cambodians who would travel from the interior of Cambodia to the border to pick up food and medical supplies.[43] Concerned about the long-term impact of the Cambodians' presence, the Thai government decided to make a concerted effort to reduce the holding centers' population and announced a program of voluntary repatriation with UNHCR support in June 1980. Subsequently, 9,000 Cambodian refugees, the majority Khmer Rouge supporters who had used the holding centers as rest and recuperation centers, were given hastily arranged and summary interviews by UNHCR, taken to the Thai-Cambodian border, and released. Not surprisingly, the Vietnamese perceived the repatriation as an attempt by the West to use the intenational agencies to return thousands of Khmer Rouge troops to the border to fight inside Cambodia. Within a week, Vietnamese troops retaliated by attacking several border camps, driving thousands of refugees across the boundary line into Thailand and causing death and confusion. The repatriation program was never resumed, although Zia Risvi of the UNHCR continued to try to negotiate a repatriation agreement until mid-1982.[44]

The failure of these repatriation efforts convinced the United States Embassy in Bangkok—which had always favored some resettlement—as well as State Department officials in Washington that there was no humane alternative to admitting more Cambodians as refugees.[45] The Thai government finally relented on the resettlement issue in mid-1980 and decided to allow the United States and other resettlement countries to call selected refugees out of the holding centers to be processed for resettlement, with the proviso that it be done quietly and discreetly. Out of the holding center population of 160,000, the United States identified some 20,000 as having family or employment ties in the United States, thereby meeting the government's criteria for admission.[46] Throughout the fall of 1980, American officials debated whether to include all Cambodians in the holding centers in the United States admissions program. Abramowitz and Rosenblatt felt strongly that the relief effort alone was not going to solve the Cambodian problem and that Cambodians should be given the same resettlement opportunities as Vietnamese or Laotian refugees. They argued that the majority of Cambodians in the centers would not return to Cambodia until peace was reestablished and a new government which represented neither Vietnamese nor Khmer Rouge interests was created. Rather than perpetuate the camp life of refugees who resisted repatriation, they urged the Carter administration to include all Cambodians, regardless of United States connections, in the resettlement stream.[47]

The principal opponents to an increase in Cambodian admissions were the United States Coordinator for Refugee Affairs, Victor Palmieri, and his deputy Frank Loy, who was also head of the State Department's Bureau of Refugee Programs. Both men had been appointed to their positions in late December

1979 after the departure of Dick Clark. Palmieri's concern was similar to the one expressed by the Thai government. Thus he believed that if the U.S. offered broad resettlement opportunities to Cambodians, that would, in effect, magnetize the border and create a pole of attraction for farmers who might more profitably stay inside their own country. Making resettlement more readily available might also discourage those refugees in holding centers who would otherwise seek to be repatriated. In Palmieri's view, a large resettlement program would constitute a severe drain on the human resources of Cambodia and strip the country of the skilled personnel needed to make Cambodia self-sufficient again.[48] Palmieri's views also coincided with those of UNHCR officials in Thailand, who believed that substantial numbers of Khmers in the holding centers would be ready to return to their home villages in Cambodia if a safe means of transport could be found. The UNHCR, therefore, discouraged the U.S. from admitting large numbers of Cambodians until the results of repatriation negotiations with the Vietnamese authorities in Phnom Penh could be determined.[49]

The proponents of opening up the admissions channel for Cambodians, however, had powerful allies both within and without the U.S. bureaucracy. The Citizens' Commission on Indochinese Refugees again played a catalytic role. In a letter to members of the Commission, Leo Cherne outlined the Commission's objectives and targets:

> This brings us to what will undoubtedly be the next and perhaps final task of the Citizens' Commission—efforts directed toward international resettlement of those Cambodian refugees who will not return, and who clearly cannot be expected to remain indefinitely in Thailand. During the last 60 days, we have, without publicizing our efforts, brought our concern to the attention of the Administration as well as a number of members of Congress. Our plea has been to include a substantial number of these Cambodians who qualify under U.S. resettlement criteria among the 14,000 Indochinese refugees being brought to the U.S. each month. At present, only those with immediate relatives in the United States and a few select others are considered eligible for the U.S. program.
>
> . . . . There is no legal or numerical rationale for not quickly broadening resettlement opportunities for the Cambodians in the camps in Thailand. There are the strongest humanitarian reasons for doing so. No group which has fled any of the three countries of Indochina has suffered more than they. In addition, a large percentage of those in the camps are the survivors of the educated and trained population of Cambodia which survived the Pol Pot genocide. Among them are the remnants of the medical, teaching and other literate professions and activities which were singled out for destruction by the Khmer Rouge. Their background and skills thus make their resettlement as viable as it is politically and ethically compelling.

There is evidence of support in Congress for a broader application of resettlement criteria for Cambodian refugees. Recently two letters signed by concerned members of Congress were sent to President Carter expressing such sentiments. Copies of these letters are attached to this report.

The Commission intends to pursue this question vigorously in the period ahead.[50]

The resettlement and religious agencies and members of Congress joined forces with the Citizens' Commission in lobbying for a change in policy.

That lobbying again linked the Citizens' Commission to sympathetic State Department officials and local Congressional advocates of more resettlement. As had been the case during the recently concluded campaign to secure more admission slots for Vietnamese and Laotian refugees, Leo Cherne, Sheppard Lowman, Morton Abramowitz, Lionel Rosenblatt, and Assistant Secretary of State Richard Holbrooke, head of the Department's Bureau of East Asian and Pacific Affairs, shared common objectives and worked cooperatively to promote them. By maintaining close contract with the press, which always wrote movingly about the tragedy in Cambodia, and with the offices of Senator Kennedy and Representative Solarz, who were strong supporters of Cambodian admission, they were able to outflank Palmieri and Loy and convince the Carter administration and the Congress that more Cambodians should be admitted. Thus by late 1980 all traditional institutional opposition in the U.S. to opening up the resettlement stream for Khmers had been overcome. The formal decision to extend parole to a much larger group of Cambodians was taken in early 1981 by a new acting Coordinator for Refugee Affairs, Richard Smyser, who believed that the U.S. had an obligation to admit Cambodians who had been associated with the U.S.-backed Lon Nol regime and who faced special danger from both the Heng Samrin and Pol Pot forces.[51] After discussion and formal consultation between Smyser and Congress, the U.S. agreed to accept 30,000 Cambodian refugees. As one official from the U.S. Embassy in Bangkok described it, "We dumped them on Reagan's lawn."[52] Processing began in spring 1981, and refugees from this group began to arrive in the U.S. during the spring and summer months of that year.

Before the first of the later Cambodian parolees reached the United States, new questions about their welcome had begun to emerge. Those questions were raised by local communities which had experienced five years of Vietnamese migration and did not look forward to the new Cambodian flow with any great enthusiasm. They were also raised by some scholars and by INS officials, who warned that the creation of the new Cambodian program would tend to perpetuate economic migration to the United States. And in a tentative way, they began to be raised by some members of Congress, who, distancing themselves from the immediate aftermath of Pol Pot's genocide, started asking whether either humanitarian or cold war considerations justified the indefinite extension of a special admissions policy which had first emerged in April of 1975, had brought over 600,000 refugees to the United States, and appeared to stretch forward into the indefinite future.

By the beginning of 1981, it was apparent that many of the most recent Indochinese arrivals were finding it difficult to adjust to life in the United States. Unlike the earlier flows of refugees from Eastern Europe and Cuba and the "first wave" from Vietnam, few of the new arrivals had significant formal education, professional and occupational skills relevant to an industrial society, or familiarity with the English language and American way of life. Laotian hill people and Cambodian peasants, like many of the Haitians and some of the Mariel Cubans who came in 1980, arrived in the United States unprepared for Western urban life. Their difficulties were compounded by the problems they confronted in the American communities where they settled. The great majority of the Indochinese, either directly or through secondary migration, settled in a few densely populated areas—forty counties in ten states, with California, Texas, Florida, and the Pacific Northwest most heavily affected. Their high concentration in these areas put significant strain on the private and public agencies charged with their resettlement. Fear and hostility toward "foreigners" erupted. While most communities made a special effort to make the Indochinese welcome, inevitable conflicts arose. Some had nothing to do with the fact that many refugees were recipients of public aid, but centered on the fact that refugee children, because of their lack of English and need for remedial instruction, put heavy strains on the local schools. Similarly, hard-working Indochinese adults were sometimes resented because they competed with their American counterparts for increasingly scarce employment. Stories about the conflict between Vietnamese and local shrimp fishermen in Texas were reported nationally and bespoke powerful local resistance to new immigrants.

These perceptions did not trigger immediate or widespread resentment against the Cambodians. Most had not yet entered the United States, and those that had were still perceived as victims. Yet certain migration patterns already established for Vietnamese and Laotian refugees were considered likely for Cambodians if they were permitted to enter in large numbers. Several studies published in 1980 and 1981[53] indicated that a large number of those fleeing Indochinese Communist countries were no longer political refugees, at risk in their own countries, with close family ties in the United States, or associated with American programs during the war. These studies concluded, moreover, that generous U.S. resettlement programs meant that almost any person from Indochina who escaped to Thailand could expect fairly rapid resettlement in the West. In other words, the U.S. refugee program encouraged or "pulled" out some Indochinese who would not otherwise leave. In addition, there was no individual screening, as required by the 1980 Refugee Act, to determine if those leaving were likely to be persecuted if returned to their countries of origin. Critics of the U.S. refugee program argued, "The programs have . . . acquired self-perpetuating characteristics and encourage a continuous outflow from Laos and Vietnam that increasingly resembles a migration rather than a refugee flow."[54]

Concern within the U.S. government that the Indochinese refugee program had developed into a migration program was especially felt by the INS, in particular by its District Director in Hong Kong, Joseph Sureck. In a lengthy letter to U.S. Coordinator of Refugee Affairs Victor Palmieri in February 1980,[55] Sureck argued:

> It is time that we recognize that the outflow of refugees from Vietnam, with the possible exception of the Sino-Vietnamese refugee, has been given impetus by the major role being played by the U.S. in their resettlement . . . It has become an endless stream with the hoped-for destination for most being the U.S.—Shangri-La. The fact that the U.S. vociferously proclaimed to the world that it increased its quota for refugees from 7,000 to 14,000 a month—168,000 a year—has compounded the problem. This word filtered into Vietnam by letters, by Voice of America, by BBC. It provided hope to people whose day-to-day livelihood has been very difficult. Most never dreamed of a possibility to live in America. They are willing to take a chance, even at the risk of their lives, to seek a new mode of existence and opportunity for themselves and their families.

During the remainder of President Carter's administration, Sureck's views had no effect on official policy, which continued to be set primarily by advocates of generous admission in the State Department. Nevertheless, Sureck persisted. In a later cable to the INS in Washington, noting that INS officers believed that many Vietnamese were now departing for reasons other than persecution, he argued that

> with the passage of the Refugee Act of 1980, Congress indicated there shall be no more mass movement of refugees for "emergent reasons." In its place, Congress provided for a systemized program for selection of refugees, including for the first time a definition for refugee. If the applicants qualify as refugees, as defined, they must also be refugees of special humanitarian concern.
>
> As of the effective date of the 1980 act, we were in a new ball game with new rules, but with the same players—not as contended by the State Dept., a perpetuation of the old regime with the same policies. INS officers who were questioning applicants after the effective date of the 1980 act were now faced with legal requirement to determine whether the applicant qualified as refugee, as defined.[56]

Only a few members of Congress indicated that they shared Sureck's concerns, and their complaints tended to focus on the chaotic handling of Cuban and Haitian asylum claims, rather than on the blanket admission of Indochinese. Yet in a thoughtful article written in the middle of 1980, Rep. Don Bonker expressed many of the fears that were to prove endemic among his colleagues in the years to come. Claiming that "we are facing a refugee crisis without an effective policy," Bonker argued that the burdens imposed on "Federal, State, and local governments" by "the projected level of 234,000 refugees [allocated under the Refugee Act of 1980] for fiscal year 1980" was "staggering." He estimated that the cost of refugee resettlement would exceed $1.6 billion in 1980 and could exceed $2.5 billion in 1981. He also questioned why so many refugee visas were being given to Indochinese when the new Refugee Act prohibited blanket admissions and when the government was simultaneously deporting Haitians. His objective, he asserted, was a fairer policy with clear limits: "We need a policy which upholds the best of our humanitarian traditions, while limiting inflows to levels we all can realistically support."[57]

Representative Bonker's article was also occasioned by the mass migration of Cubans and Haitians to the United States during 1980. Faced with the sudden and uncontrolled arrival of more than 100,000 "boat people" from the Caribbean during a five-month period, the President, the Congress, and the American people were forced to confront the fiscal and political consequences of a refugee policy which appeared to have no clear limits. The crisis of mass asylum which emerged helped to reestablish restrictionism as the basic framework for future admissions decisions. In the long term, that crisis had a profound effect on America's willingness to accept additional refugees from Indochina. Its more immediate consequence, however, was to raise new questions about the nation's willingness to grant asylum to refugees from this hemisphere.

Chapter 9

Carter and the Politics
of Mass Asylum

THE MARIEL BOATLIFT from Cuba in the spring and summer of 1980 was perhaps the most extraordinary event in the history of U.S. refugee policy. Within a period of five months, nearly 130,000 Cubans arrived in Florida. During peak periods, more than 5,000 persons a day swarmed across the docks at Key West. Those who were not immediately resettled were detained in military camps across the nation. As their stay in army barracks stretched from days to months, the *Marielitos* became increasingly frustrated and angry. Riots broke out at Fort Chaffee, Arkansas, and at other installations. Substantial backlash occurred when it was discovered that the Cuban migration contained a number of criminals and other undesirables. As a result, U.S. policy makers and the American public questioned seriously the value of their country's continuing to provide asylum for the persecuted and other desperate migrants from the Western Hemisphere.

Although the mass exodus from Cuba was a unique event, it highlighted the growing problem of asylum in the U.S., which had been building up for years. During the late 1970s, hundreds of thousands of the Indochinese who entered the U.S. were joined by a continuing flow of asylum seekers who also sought to enter the country. American policies toward asylum seekers were essentially similar to what they had been in the early 1970s, with the few Cubans who still came welcomed and the Haitian boat people and "new" refugees from Central

America generally turned away. These decisions reflected foreign policy priorities, although there was some concern expressed by public officials over the negative social and economic impact on American society of Haitian immigrants. The level of asylum applications reached crisis proportions in 1980 at the same time that the refugee flow from Indochina had peaked. The principal crisis in 1980 was the Mariel boat lift along with the simultaneous arrival of thousands of Haitians. Initially, the U.S. responded favorably to the Cuban influx, and this positive welcome was also extended to the Haitians. But as resettlement problems grew, the mood of the American public shifted, first in Florida and then in the nation as a whole. Public resentment against Cuban "criminals" spread to Haitian "illiterates," and the principle of asylum, and indeed of refugee welcome in the U.S., was jeopardized.

Ideological discrimination, not domestic backlash, was the primary force which influenced U.S. asylum policy during the late 1970s. As in earlier periods, asylum decisions remained the prerogative of the State Department and the Immigration Service, both of which regarded asylum as a privilege to be accorded only to anti-Communists. Asylum seekers—with the conspicuous exceptions of important defectors and Cubans—did not fare well in the United States. Even during the Carter administration, Haitians were customarily denied asylum and sometimes deported.[1] Despite a highly visible and sometimes quite effective human rights policy, that administration was also very reluctant to grant asylum to those fleeing right-wing regimes in Central America.[2] A small exception occurred during 1979, when the President authorized "extended voluntary departure" status for Nicaraguans in the United States immediately before and immediately after the fall of the Somoza regime. At least 20,000 Nicaraguans were afforded relief from deportation. However, the program was short-lived, and not matched by any similar initiatives for Salvadorans, who began arriving at America's southern border with increasing frequency during the late 1970s. As a matter of foreign policy, the Executive Branch chose to characterize the political climate in El Salvador as an improving situation, and thus the State Department was reluctant to concede that Salvadoran asylum applicants risked persecution for fear of embarrassing and contradicting the Carter administration. The best available evidence indicates that in 1980, *no* Salvadorans were granted asylum, and that nearly 12,000 were deported.[3] This result was accomplished by giving most Salvadoran applicants only the most summary of interviews; it is explicable only in the context of an undeclared but nevertheless definitive State Department policy to keep "Salvadoran communist troublemakers" out of the United States.[4]

Carter took office in 1977 committed to criticizing regimes in this hemisphere which customarily engaged in serious human rights abuses.[5] He briefly considered advice that this policy be extended to refugees. Thus, in mid-1977, a major National Security Council Presidential review memorandum on human rights[6] urged President Carter to "demonstrate a generous humanitarian policy of providing refuge to victims of repression." The NSC recommended that humanitarian concern could best be demonstrated by increasing the number of "seventh preference" entrants and through a more liberal interpretation and use of the parole provision to admit individual refugees and groups of refugees who did not qualify under the Immigration and Naturalization Act. The policy memorandum continued:

> Specifically, we believe that the Attorney-General and the INS in considering applicants for parole into the United States should be more forthcoming with respect to innocent victims of authoritarian regimes. Such a change in policy would be a concrete demonstration of the sincerity of our commitment to human rights. . . . Dissidents in repressive countries, to the extent that they may be able to proceed to free countries, should generally be considered as refugees. Most such dissidents would qualify as refugees in the pending legislation that we support.[7]

The administration responded to this advice by establishing small parole programs for Chileans and Argentinians. However, ideological and *realpolitik* concerns, including a desire to refrain from being too visibly critical of pro-American, anti-Soviet regimes in Central America and the Caribbean, insured that no similar programs were established closer to home.

The starkest example of ideological discrimination in U.S. asylum policy during the late 1970s involved the Haitians. They were the first national group to come to American shores in substantial numbers for whom no special administrative or legislative policy had been put in place prior to their arrival. Arriving illegally and irregularly, the Haitian influx, which numbered between 30,000 to 50,000 between 1972 and 1980, was unique and unprecedented. Moreover, the mode of their arrival—in overcrowded homemade boats on Florida's coast—caused rising concern to community organizations, to state and local officials, and to Florida's Congressional delegation, led by Congressman Dante Fascell. In contrast to the Cuban flows, no federal resettlement programs were formulated and no special status outside of normal immigration patterns was awarded Haitians. The Carter White House responded by meeting with Gov. Robert Graham, his staff, and Haitian advocacy groups and putting together an ad hoc package of federal services and programs to augment local resources to respond to the Haitian influx.[8]

The United States had considered all but a handful of arriving Haitians as "economic migrants," and denied them any meaningful opportunity to present their asylum claims and to have them individually evaluated. The principal reason for this policy was the close political relationship between the U.S. government and the Duvalier regime. The shared anti-Communist objectives of both governments that dominated policy in the 1950s and 1960s continued to take priority in the 1970s.[9] The possibility of a shift in U.S. policy toward Haiti and its refugees occurred with the advent of the Carter administration. Initially the new administration took a number of important human rights initiatives in regard to Haiti. As part of an overall reduction of military aid to the region, Haiti was dropped from the list of foreign military sales recipients but kept its International Military Education and Training Program. On a visit to Haiti in August 1977, Andrew Young, the U.S. Ambassador to the United Nations, pressed the Haitian government to show greater concern for human rights. At a press conference in Port-au-Prince on August 15, Young expressed the Carter administration's desire to end support for regimes that violated human rights and favored the exploitation of the poor by the rich. Young signaled that improvement in the human rights situation would have a direct effect on the aid and cooperation Haiti received from the U.S. In a clear message to the Haitian government, Young said, "When people understand the way the winds are blowing and if they want to go with those winds, they trim their sails accordingly."[10]

Sensitive to this new dimension of American foreign policy and attempting to placate the Carter administration, the Haitian government took a series of steps to improve its human rights image in the U.S. Duvalier hired the American law firm of Peabody, Rivlin, Lambert and Meyers to influence US policy makers in the Department of State, AID, the Overseas Private Investment Corporation, the House Committee on International Relations, and the Senate Committee on Foreign Relations. He also contracted the public relations firm of Edelman International to enhance Haiti's image in the U.S.[11] At the same time, the Haitian government initiated a partial relaxation of official repression during 1977 and 1978, and Duvalier ordered the largest general amnesty of political prisoners in years. At the invitation of Haitian authorities, the Inter-American Human Rights Commission visited Haiti in July 1978 and issued a report a month later which acknowledged that some limited improvements had been made.

Although human rights conditions in Haiti improved somewhat during 1977 and 1978, deep systemic reform clearly did not take place, and structural barriers to human rights continued to exist.[12] According to the Department of State's human rights reports to Congress in 1977, brutality "verging on torture" had been employed "both as punishment for minor criminal infractions, to extract confessions, and to impose discipline in prison."[13] There continued to be a breakdown in the rule of law; there was no effective or independent judiciary; few legal safeguards existed to protect people who fell out of favor with the government. Practically nothing was done to develop institutional structures through which these basic violations could be ended.

Despite increasing recognition of human rights violations in Haiti, the Carter administration treated Haitian asylum applicants no better than had previous administrations, and the same sort of ideological discrimination continued to affect the processing of Haitian asylum claims. Moreover, concern grew in the U.S. government that Haitian migration was bringing to the U.S. large numbers of poor, black, and relatively unskilled people who were not assimilable to the domestic labor market. The flow of Haitians was seen to be less "manageable" than earlier refugee flows, particularly from Eastern Europe. It was an element in the growing fear among American policy makers and the public that instability and oppression in the Third World would give rise to a sustained, and possibly increased, flow of refugees in the future. These factors raised for U.S. officials the specter of opening the "floodgates" to mass migration from the Caribbean and Latin America. According to Edward T. Sweeney, the Miami INS District Director:

> We feel that any relaxation of the rules could produce a flood of economic refugees from all over the Caribbean, where virtually every government has serious socioeconomic and political problems. It could conceivably also apply to Mexicans who illegally cross the border.[14]

It was also feared that offers of easy asylum would send mixed messages to Haiti and could be interpreted as an unfriendly act and support for a Haitian exile movement. They would clearly encourage further migration from Haiti. Such motivations were behind the State Department's decision to return to Haiti ninety-seven refugees who had sailed into the U.S. naval base at Guantanamo Bay, Cuba, in August 1977. According to a State Department representative:

> To grant them political asylum . . . poses a problem of relations between the United States and the Haitian government, and to admit them as refugees from deteriorating economic conditions might encourage still more to flee.[15]

The INS also routinely detained all other arriving Haitian boat people and denied them a number of procedural rights, including easy access to lawyers.

Outraged by such U.S. government actions, a dedicated alliance of public interest lawyers and religious activists with the National Council of Churches began to publicize the Haitians' plight and to take legal actions on their behalf. These efforts were part of the emerging human rights movement in the United States during the late 1970s. In an attempt to counter the double standards and ideological bias of U.S. asylum policy, humanitarian organizations joined forces at times to champion the causes of refugees whose admission to the

United States served no clear foreign policy interest. Yet these humanitarian efforts to secure political asylum for more refugees from Haiti and other authoritarian regimes in the Western Hemisphere often proved futile, particularly when they ran into well-organized and obdurate governmental opposition.

Initially, humanitarian efforts on behalf of Haitians were successful. In November 1977, in reaction to the legal actions and after numerous protests and a broad public campaign, INS Commissioner Leonel F. Castillo acceded to the demands of the National Council of Churches that the INS release imprisoned Haitians without bond, authorize their employment, and changed INS regulations to allow "excludable" Haitians a hearing on their asylum claim before an immigration judge. The INS, however, did not adopt uniform procedures for exclusion and deportation proceedings until 1978, and since no Haitians who had been released in 1977 could be called in for hearings for more than a year, a backlog of 5,000 cases developed. In the meantime, the INS regional office in Florida mistakenly broadcast the message that all Haitians, rather than just those in the asylum process, were entitled to work authorizations. As a consequence, 3,000 additional Haitians suddenly appeared and registered, thus identifying themselves for the first time to INS officials.

This backlog was exacerbated by several additional developments that directly affected the flow of Haitians to the U.S. In 1978, the government of the Bahamas began to arrest and deport the Haitians illegally living in the country. Rather than risk deportation back to Haiti, Haitians began to flock in large numbers to Florida. The brief liberalized policies of the INS, and especially the availability of work authorizations, acted as a magnet for further migration. At the same time, Caribbean smugglers, with the aid of local Haitian officials, had stepped up their activities and were transporting large boatloads of Haitians to the U.S. It was inevitable that the heavy influx of Haitians in a few counties in southern Florida would begin to strain local social and health care service resources. This impact, combined with growing resentment over the work authorizations granted to Haitians, caused some backlash to erupt in Florida.

The dramatic increase in the number of Haitians arriving in south Florida and the backlog of asylum cases precipitated fear among government officials that a "black tide" was inundating the state. The INS responded by canceling the work authorizations, resuming the detention of Haitian males, and expediting deportation hearings. The INS launched its "Haitian Program," a well-coordinated operation in which INS and State Department officials collaborated to process and expel Haitians as quickly as possible.[16] The number of asylum hearings for Haitians in Miami increased from an average of five to fifteen per day in early 1978 to 100 to 150 a day by September 1978, with no more than five immigration judges hearing them. The few lawyers representing the Haitians often were scheduled to represent several clients whose hearings occurred simultaneously. Attorneys were not allowed to speak on behalf of their clients, and Haitians who attempted to speak for themselves were often provided with inadequate translations or none at all. Following the initiation of the expedited procedure, the percentage of asylum claim denials and the numbers of Haitians being deported increased substantially.[17]

While the Haitian Program was underway, several public interest groups filed lawsuits on behalf of the Haitians. In *Haitian Refugee Center v. Civiletti*,[18] a class action suit involving 4,000 Haitians challenging the INS mass deportation policies, two major complaints were voiced: (1) the government had denied Haitians meaningful hearings at the administrative level, and (2) it had singled out Haitians for disparate treatment, denied them equal protection, and subjected them to much harsher treatment than other aliens.

On July 25, 1979, Federal District Judge James Lawrence King issued an injunction temporarily blocking the deportation of Haitians by the INS. Later, in 1980, he issued his final opinion in *Haitian Refugee Center v. Civiletti*, which was a stinging criticism of U.S. policy toward Haitians. Judge King found:

> Those Haitians who came to the United States seeking freedom and justice did not find it. Instead, they were confronted with an Immigration and Naturalization Service determined to deport them. The decision was made among high INS officials to expel Haitians, despite whatever claims to asylum individual Haitians might have. A Program was set up to accomplish this goal. The Program resulted in wholesale violations of due process and only Haitians were affected.
>
> This Program, in its planning and executing, is offensive to every notion of constitutional due process and equal protection. The Haitians whose claims for asylum were rejected during the program shall not be deported until they are given a fair chance to present their claims for political asylum.[19]

Judge King's findings were based on abundant evidence submitted by the plaintiffs which demonstrated beyond doubt that the INS had sternly prejudiced every one of the several thousand Haitian cases involved in the class action.[20] INS memoranda had characterized all the arriving Haitians as illegal immigrants escaping poverty and not persecution and as posing a threat to local communities. Judge King also found that the Haitian Program made a mockery of due process guarantees, and that the Haitians were entitled to fair and unbiased consideration of their cases. Under the accelerated hearings for Haitian asylum claimants in Miami, Haitians were not given sufficient time to prepare their asylum applications, to obtain adequate assistance of counsel, or to state their case before an INS hearing officer. Thus, according to the court's opinion, the INS deliberately had not examined each case on its individual merits and had deprived Haitians of their due process rights.

It was also clear to the court that the Haitians alone had been singled out for harsh treatment. No other national group applying for political asylum had been routinely detained and denied work authorizations. Judge King drew attention to the continued existence of a "double standard" at work in U.S. asylum policy:

> The plaintiffs are part of the first substantial flight of black refugees from a repressive regime to this country. All the plaintiffs are black. Prior to the most recent Cuban exodus all of the Cubans who sought political asylum . . . were granted asylum routinely. None of the over 4000 Haitians processed during the INS program at issue in the lawsuit were granted asylum. No greater disparity can be imagined.[21]

Judge King went beyond conventional jurisprudence and used his opinion to refute the government's argument that all Haitians were economic migrants. He found that "much of Haiti's poverty is a result of Duvalier's efforts to maintain power," and that "the Haitians' economic situation is a political condition."[22] Human rights conditions in Haiti, Judge King concluded, were "stark, brutal and bloody."

Judge King ordered the INS to discontinue the deportation of these 4,000 Haitians until the government could prepare a plan whereby the plaintiffs would have their asylum applications reviewed in a nondiscriminatory and individualized manner. *Haitian Refugee Center v. Civiletti* was one of the first in a series of court interventions against government administrative practices regarding Haitians. In the years to come, refugee advocates would increasingly turn to the courts in order to curb U.S. government agencies which were intent on the speedy explusion of Haitians and other asylum applicants from the Western Hemisphere. There were political limits to humanitarian arguments, however, particularly when they were presented in a courtroom setting and ran headlong into stubborn governmental opposition. Although the courts would often temporarily halt deportations, governmental agencies made a number of regulatory changes that had the effect of frustrating refugee advocates by administratively negating those rulings. As a result, accelerated mass hearings, detention, denial of work authorization, and other deterrent measures to keep Haitians and others out of the U.S. were customarily reimposed.

Judge King's decision was handed down in July 1980, in the midst of a mass first asylum crisis for the U.S. during which some 130,000 Cubans and over 11,000 Haitians arrived in Florida. The flow of Haitians had increased dramatically in mid-1979 and reached its highest level in March and April 1980, just as Cuban mass asylum was getting underway. INS officials attributed this increase to the transmission of information to Haiti that the INS had been ordered to put a halt to the further deportation of Haitians.[23] Communication of this news may well have been a factor. Yet it was hardly the only one.

Simultaneous with this increased flow of Haitians to the U.S. there occurred a rapid deterioration in the human rights situation in Haiti. Following elections for the National Assembly which were held in February 1979, arbitrary detentions, torture, and harassment by the police were directed not only at political leaders, journalists, and human rights activists but at all sectors of the population. The rights of assembly, association, and expression were all severely repressed. The two opposition political parties founded in 1979 by Sylvio Claude and Gregoire Eugene, the Haitian Christian Democratic Party and the Social Christian Party, were both forced to suspend their activities, and their leaders were arrested. A meeting of the Haitian Human Rights League was broken up by men armed with clubs, and its president and some 200 visitors, including a representative from the U.S. Embassy, sustained injuries.[24] The militia, a group of armed forces loyal only to President Duvalier, assumed a more prominent and active role in government affairs, and a new cabinet, installed in November, 1979, contained a number of individuals identified as hard-liners and formerly associated with François Duvalier. A report on human rights in Haiti by the State Department released on February 5, 1980, stated:

> There were no institutional changes favoring political liberalization, . . . and if anything, the ability of Haitian citizens to express political views declined in 1979.[25]

Between October and December 1980, a new wave of arrests took place in which virtually all Haitian human rights activists, most independent journalists, and many lawyers active in the defense of political detainees and opposition leaders were arrested or expelled from the country, putting an end to the already limited rights to freedom of assembly and expression.[26]

Despite the extreme violation of human rights in Haiti, the INS and State Department continued to regard Haitians exclusively as economic migrants rather than as individuals threatened with persecution. They did so even though the adoption of a new Refugee Act in March 1980 clearly committed the United States to adhere to international legal standards and make asylum (or its statutory equivalent) available as a matter of right rather than discretion to any individual demonstrating that he or she was in fact a refugee. According to the INS Deputy District Director in Miami:

> What we're up against from our viewpoint is people who are fleeing an economic situation—poverty, low pay and lack of employment—coming here trying to better their way of life.
>
> Along the way their cause has been championed by attorneys, realizing that a claim to political asylum can delay things indeterminately.

We depend on the State Department to advise us if political persecution is going on. From what we have received from the State Department, there is no political persecution in Haiti.[27]

The State Department view, according to the report of the U.S. Coordinator of Refugee Affairs to Congress in April 1980, was that all Haitians entering the United States came as economic migrants rather than political refugees.[28] This view was further elaborated and modified somewhat by Stephen E. Palmer, Deputy Assistant Secretary for Human Rights and Humanitarian Affairs:

Determination of a particular asylum claim . . . is not a general referendum on human rights in the home country. . . . Instead, we must apply a narrow and clearly focused standard established by treaty and by U.S. statutes. The question in passing on an asylum application is this: Does this particular individual have a "well founded fear of persecution" based on race, religion, nationality, membership in a particular social group or political opinion if he or she were to return to the home country?[29]

Most of the applications we receive from Haitian nationals base the asylum claim solely on the fact that the applicants have departed from Haiti illegally. They assert that mere departure and the seeking of refuge in the United States will be treated as a political act by the government of Haiti and that that government will persecute them if they are returned. Most applications contain no allegation that the applicants or their families suffered persecution before they left or that other factors in their background would make them suspect politically in Haiti. We do not believe that such applications support a finding of a well-founded fear of persecution, and in such cases we recommend denial of the applications.[30]

Despite the official U.S. view of arriving Haitians, events transpired in the spring of 1980 to force a new Haitian admissions policy. The most important of these events was the sudden arrival of 130,000 Cuban emigrés on boats from Mariel harbor. The combined impact of the Cuban boat lift, peaking in May and June, and the increased flow of Haitians during the spring of 1980 created a difficult situation nationally and especially in Florida. A number of interest groups and humanitarian organizations, including the Congressional Black Caucus, complained bitterly about a system that rendered the asylum process a mere formality for Cubans, while using it as a barrier to exclude virtually every Haitian. The passage of the new Refugee Act in March, by removing all reference to Communism from the refugee definition, destroyed the legal argument for preferring the former group to the latter. The Cuban-Haitian comparison sharpened political pressure and gave added force to a campaign, underway for months, calling for executive action to allow all Haitian asylum applicants then present in the U.S. to remain.

While the humanitarian arguments for a fairer application of the refugee standard were gaining ground in the U.S., the chief concern of policy makers was the need to control and regulate admissions numbers. The 1980 Refugee Act has as one of its principal aims to impose a "more rational, stable and equitable Federal policy for the admission of refugees to this country and for assistance to them within the United States."[31] In the words of Secretary of State Cyrus Vance, such a policy was envisioned as "coherent and comprehensive," rather than "reactive" and "ad hoc."[32]

When Congress passed the new Refugee Act, it apparently believed that no more than 5,000 aliens per year would enter the United States with potentially valid asylum claims.[33] It was argued that this figure exceeded the number of applicants in any year under the old regulations in effect from 1974 to 1979. However, nearly 20,000 asylum claims were pending in November 1979, and at least as many potential claims were being administratively bypassed at the time the Refugee Act was enacted. In 1978 and 1979, for example, INS avoided processing most Nicaraguan and Ethiopian asylum claims by granting applicants "extended voluntary departure," which was still permitting them to remain in the United States without the immediate threat of deportation. A similar strategy was employed in 1979 and 1980 for Iranians, even though President Carter had proscribed granting them formal "extended voluntary departure" status.

Despite these indications that asylum claims were vastly increasing, U.S. legislators and policy makers were taken by surprise when the newly framed asylum machinery of the Refugee Act broke down with the large influx of Cubans to the U.S. in the spring of 1980. Within the space of a few months, the U.S. received nearly 140,000 Cubans and Haitians, and the smooth functioning of the asylum provisions of the Refugee Act which had been envisioned by its framers was effectively sabotaged. The boat exodus from Cuba coincided with the inflow of over 200,000 Indochinese and an indeterminate number of Ethiopians, Nicaraguans, Iranians, and Salvadorans seeking political asylum. In 1980 alone, 800,000 immigrants—more than those entering all the other countries in the world combined—entered the United States. The bureaucracies charged with regulating refugee flow were overwhelmed by this huge influx, and the American public believed that the nation was totally unable to control its borders. These developments strengthened the hands of restrictionists in the U.S. and threatened the right of asylum, which was an important component of the 1980 Refugee Act.

The Carter administration was particularly unprepared for the 1980 Cuban refugee crisis and reacted to it in an indecisive manner.[34] In order to fully understand this extraordinary episode in U.S. refugee policy, it is important to examine the principal events which preceded it. Under the Carter administration, the U.S. and Cuba had made progress toward normalizing relations. Of particular interest to the U.S. was Fidel Castro's announcement in November 1978 of a prisoner release program whereby some 3,000 political prisoners and 600 other Cubans imprisoned for minor crimes would be released for admission to the U.S. at the rate of 400 prisoners per month.[35] At the same time, Castro encouraged the Cuban exile community in America to visit Cuba in the hope of generating more sympathy for his regime from the group most vocally and violently opposed to it.

Both programs failed miserably to promote better Cuban-American relations. The political prisoner program was never enthusiastically embraced by the U.S. despite President Carter's pledge to do his "utmost to ease the plight . . . of released political prisoners" and his "hope that we will always stand ready to welcome more than our fair share of those who flee their homelands because of racial, economic, or religious oppression."[36] Significant bureaucratic opposition developed to sabotage the prisoner release program. In particular, Attorney General Griffin Bell did not trust Castro to release only *bona fide* political prisoners, and the admissions procedures slowed to a standstill as Bell personally reviewed each file, with the stated purpose of excluding "spies, terrorists, and common criminals."[37] Repeated efforts on the part of Castro to hold the Carter administration to its policy of providing refuge to anti-Communists failed, and political prisoners who were released and were awaiting resettlement in the U.S. provided a new source of opposition and dissension for the Communist regime in Havana.

The unprecedented visits of large numbers of Cuban-Americans to Havana in 1979 also backfired. The sudden arrival of wealthy friends and relatives highlighted for many Cubans who had never departed their homeland the attractiveness of the United States. It also highlighted the "sea of difficulties,"[38] economic and political, in which Cuba continued to swim. Plagued by its overdependence on an unsatisfactory and underpriced sugar crop, Cuba in 1979 and 1980 entered into a new era of hardships. For many Cubans, the visits of the exile community held out the hope of emigration as a way to escape these difficulties.

These pressures for mass emigration from Cuba were not adequately foreseen by the Carter administration.[39] To a certain extent this was understandable, since the White House and the State Department were preoccupied with other international crises.[40] After early November 1979, the overriding international issue confronting the government was the seizure and continued captivity of American hostages in Tehran. Almost every day after the start of the hostage crisis, the President and his advisers met to consider ways to end it but were thwarted by the maneuvering of the Ayatollah Khomeini regime. In April, the White House ordered a rescue attempt. The President and others worked intensively on the rescue mission, almost to the exclusion of other problems. In addition to the Iranian hostage crisis, in late 1979 the Soviet Union invaded Afghanistan, causing the administration to toughen its policy toward Russia and its allies. Economic problems also made considerable demands on the President's time. Inflation in the U.S. was reaching above 17 percent, and unemployment and interest rates were increasing. Senator Edward Kennedy was campaigning vigorously on these issues for the 1980 presidential nomination, and President Carter felt compelled to give greater attention to domestic economic issues.

Distracted as it was by these serious concerns, it is not surprising that the Carter administration was particularly unprepared for the influx of Cubans in the spring of 1980.[41] In March of that year, a busload of dissatisfied Cubans rammed into the gates of the Peruvian Embassy in Havana and were granted temporary asylum. Fidel Castro reopened the gates and another 10,000 Cubans, many of them seeking entry to the U.S., crowded into the grounds. The initial impulse of the Carter administration was to grant their request to come to the U.S. This was a predictable response, given the American government's tradition of hospitality toward anti-Castro Cubans for the past two decades. The U.S. decided, however, to try to internationalize the response and encouraged the start-up of an airlift of the 10,000 Cubans from Havana to Costa Rica, where, it was hoped, many of them would be resettled. At the same time, President Carter announced that America would designate 3,500 of the Cubans in the Peruvian Embassy as refugees admissible to the U.S. provided they met U.S. immigration requirements or entered under the political prisoner program. However, only 700 of those destined for Costa Rica were permitted to fly out by the Castro regime. Many of the remainder, as well as the 3,500 designated by President Carter, eventually entered the United States on the subsequent boatlift.

What began as a propaganda boost for the U.S. soon turned into a political triumph for Fidel Castro. On April 19, Castro announced that anyone who wished to leave Cuba could do so, and he opened Mariel harbor as their exit point. At the same time he encouraged Cuban-Americans to retrieve their relatives, and they responded with great speed, hiring a flotilla of assorted water craft to make the journey between Miami and Mariel.

Caught in a new and more complex calculus of response, the Carter administration found itself weighing a variety of reasons for welcoming Cubans warmly or discouraging their entry. President Carter's own rhetoric, his well-publicized human rights policy, his need to win the electoral support of the large Cuban-American community in Florida, and his need to respond to the attacks of candidate Ronald Reagan, who believed that the U.S. should move quickly to rescue those in the Peruvian embassy, and who "blasted Carter's efforts to bar refugees,"[42] required a generous response. Initially, Carter had the support of the news media. The great bulk of the early news coverage demonstrated a willingness to regard those fleeing in small boats as people suffering under Castro and deserving of special treatment. The press briefly labeled the boatlift a "freedom flotilla." Two weeks before the Mariel crisis began, the mayor of Miami indicated that he would welcome to the United States any Cuban refugees fleeing their homeland.[43] *Newsweek* described the Cuban influx as a "voyage to freedom,"[44] and scenes of families reuniting after years of separation appeared on television night after night.

The forces favoring restriction, however, were equally strong. The new Refugee Act permitted the admission of large numbers of refugees but required that they demonstrate fear of persecution as their motive for departure. It was clear almost from the beginning of the boat lift that a majority of the *Marielitos* would not meet the definitional requirements as outlined in the Refugee Act. Many were fleeing to join families or improve their economic livelihood in America. In addition, there was a strong sense that Castro was exploiting the migration fever to export Cubans deemed, not only by Cuba but also by the United States, as undesirable, the dregs of society. By forcing boat skippers to carry several thousand formerly institutionalized persons to the United States and by actively involving the Cuban government in the direction of traffic into and out of Mariel, Castro magnified this concern. Seething impotence and anger began to emerge in the American public, and national concern over uncontrolled immigration intensified. A public opinion poll in summer 1980 indicated that 80 percent of the U.S. public favored reducing the number of aliens entering the United States.[45]

Had Carter been able to exploit the 1980 flow and to argue forcefully, consistently, and often that the *Marielitos* were in fact voting with their feet, that their motivations were primarily political rather than economic, that the "dregs of Cuban society" made up only a small and manageable part of the 1980 refugee cohort, then the gap between generosity and restrictionism might have been bridged, and some of the negative effect of the flotilla's ungoverned arrival mitigated. However, despite a January 1980 State Department human rights report highly critical of the "totalitarian Marxist-Leninist system" in Cuba and its effect on the Cuban people,[46] despite remarks by President Carter just days before the boat lift comparing Cuba to East Berlin as a place desperate to keep its dissenters in,[47] and despite Vice President Mondale's early effort to make political capital out of the influx, no consistent effort to turn the 1980 exodus into a political and ideological asset rather than a liability occurred.

The administration alternated between viewing the boat lift as an embarrassment to Castro and a propaganda victory for the U.S. and expressing concern over the domestic impact of the threatened massive influx of Cubans.

Within a week of the April 21 start-up of the boat lift, over 1,500 boats manned by Cuban-Americans were standing off Mariel harbor waiting to take on Cuban emigrés. Federal officials attempted to enforce American immigration law and federal statutes against the smuggling in of aliens. They initiated proceedings against boat owners and captains who were sponsoring the boat lift, first by levying fines and later by seizing and impounding their vessels. But once the armada of boats had left Florida shores for Cuba, it was too late for enforcement of such laws. The Carter administration needed to take stronger steps at an earlier stage in the crisis to control the flow from Mariel. Negotiations with Castro for an orderly departure program were singularly ineffective.[48] Federal agencies, such as the Immigration and Naturalization Service and the Coast Guard, were slow in announcing their intention to enforce United States immigration law.[49]

Tough sanctions were also weakened when President Carter first stated his administration's position on the Mariel influx in a press conference on May 5. In response to a reporter's question, he indicated that over 10,000 Cubans had already arrived by sea, that "literally tens of thousands of others will be received in our country with understanding," and that "we'll continue to provide an open heart and open arms to refugees seeking freedom from Communist domination and from economic deprivation, brought about primarily by Fidel Castro and his government."[50] Such seeming encouragement to the Cuban emigrés stood in stark contrast to the tough words and actions of federal officials. Three days before Carter's "open heart and open arms" speech, the White House had issued a statement that the INS was concerned about criminals in the flotilla and would carefully screen each arrival.[51] A similar inconsistency was also evident in President Carter's use of the Coast Guard, first to safeguard the boat lift and then to stop the influx. According to one newspaper account, "As thousands of Cubans continue to express abhorrence of Fidel Castro's rule of their homeland by streaming away from it in anything that can float, the U.S. Coast Guard is laboring mightily to ensure their safe arrival on these shores in one of the biggest peacetime operations it has ever mounted."[52] A few weeks later, the Coast Guard was given orders to board vessels carrying Cubans to the United States, and began to play a key role in stopping unauthorized landings.

As the *Marielitos* continued to stream ashore, the public view of the boat lift and the official U.S. response shifted from a traditional, pro-Cuban attitude to one considerably more antagonistic toward Cuban migrants.[53] Approximately 130,000 Cubans arrived in south Florida in five months; 85,000 entered in May of 1980 alone.[54] Most arrived in Miami and its suburbs—an area badly torn by interethnic suspicions and strife, an area where the black communities had erupted into a bitter fight over bilingualism and the poor and uneducated of all races and nationalities were having an increasingly difficult time finding jobs and affordable shelter. The immensity of the flow quite simply overwhelmed the capacity of the community to cope. Difficulties were visible for all to see. The housing saga was perhaps the most dramatic and the most publicized. The spectacle of hundreds of refugees lodged in the Orange Bowl, lodged in tents under the interstate overpass, or lodged in resort hotels in Miami Beach illustrated for the American public President Carter's political miscalculation and his administration's impotence in the face of a mass influx of migrants. The concurrent spectacle of hundreds of Haitians incarcerated in an abandoned Nike missile site reinforced the point even more graphically. The resulting backlash might well have been expected.

Much of the backlash associated with the Cuban and Haitian influx was intensified by the view that those who arrived were "dysfunctional" people, i.e., not readily assimilable into the labor market or society generally. This view was strengthened by reports that some of the Cuban migrants were criminals and mental defectives hand-picked by Castro for expulsion, rather than relatives of Cuban-Americans voluntarily seeking freedom or family unification. When the media began reporting that Cuban officials were loading the boats at Mariel with criminals, mental patients, and toughs, the voluntary agencies began to find it increasingly difficult to find sponsors for the thousands of unattached single men in the camps. The temporary resettlement camps established in Florida, Arkansas, and Wisconsin quickly became unmanageable as the summer heat, idleness, and frustration there led to outbreaks of violence and well-publicized disorders which also reinforced the negative public image of the new arrivals.[55]

The bureaucracies charged with regulating refugee flow were overwhelmed by this massive influx, and the Carter administration made the decision that under such conditions it was impossible to invoke the asylum provisions of the 1980 Refugee Act. The INS lacked the personnel to interview expeditiously each person seeking asylum, much less to evaluate each applicant's claim properly. The Department of State, charged with issuing an "advisory opinion" as to the probable good faith of each applicant's "well-founded fear," was even more understaffed. At the height of the Cuban influx, only one State Department officer was assigned full time to handling asylum claims. By August 1980, this number had risen to three.[56] It soon became apparent that it was not possible to carry out individual screening of the Cubans' motives for departure. Instead, all the *Marielitos*, like most of the other Cubans entering since 1959, were treated as *de facto* refugees. President Carter also chose not to classify Cubans as statutory refugees under the new Refugee Act as had been suggested by Senator Kennedy,[57] because he believed that to confer refugee status would reward illegal entry and set a dangerous precedent.[58]

Facing rising public resentment against both Cubans and Haitians and acutely aware that 1980 was an election year, the Carter administration tried to neutralize the Cuban-Haitian entry dilemma. It sought to placate public opinion while not antagonizing the Cuban-American bloc or black Americans who were concerned that the government not treat Cubans better than black Haitians. A White House task force put in charge of handling both influxes temporized by giving both Cubans and Haitians the same provisional immigration status, which denied asylum but also prevented deportation. Even had the State Department or the INS intended to rubber-stamp automatic denials of asylum for Cuban applicants, litigation then pending before Judge King in the Southern District of Florida involving Haitians rendered it extremely likely that mass denials would be appealed to the courts. Unwilling to admit the Cubans as refugees under the Refugee Act without individual evaluations and both unable and unwilling to return them to Cuba, President Carter issued a declaration establishing the new status of "Cuban-Haitian entrant" on June 20, 1980.[59] This new classification allowed members of both groups who had arrived prior to June 20 to remain in the United States until their status was resolved. The Carter administration, in effect, granted parole to the Cuban-Haitian entrants. This was a particularly ironic development, as one of the major objectives of the Refugee Act of 1980 had been to eliminate the use of the parole provision.

By refusing to utilize the newly existing refugee legislation, Carter had to turn to traditional ad hoc expedients in responding to the crisis, and this affected the Carter administration's handling of both federal reimbursement of state and local expenses and federal funding of governmental agencies.[60] Initially, the government reimbursed the states for only 75 percent of certain social service and medical expenses and refused to fund the usual range of benefits made available to refugees in the U.S. In response to what was perceived as neglect of local impact on the part of the federal government, the Florida Congressional delegation pressed through the Fascell-Stone amendment to the Refugee Education Assistance Act, which forced the federal government to grant each entrant benefits equal to those of a refugee and to provide 100 percent reimbursement of state and local costs.[61] On October 10, 1980, the administration also extended the granting of Cuban-Haitian entrant status to those boat people who arrived after June 20.

The mass asylum crisis of 1980 raised fundamental questions about the ability of the United States to regulate the flow of refugees to its borders and about the principles that should govern the regulatory power it does possess. Coming during a time of deep economic and political malaise, the large-scale movements of boat people from the Caribbean generated unprecedented concern about U.S. refugee policy and about the ability of the 1980 act to regulate refugee flow and provide humane standards for admission in a "coherent and comprehensive" manner. The confused federal response to the mass asylum crisis engendered a widespread belief that the United States had no refugee policy, that refugee admissions were completely out of control, and that Congress lacked effective means of regulating administrative discretion. This belief was intensified by the relationship refugee admissions bore to overall immigration, and by growing public concern over large numbers of "illegal" or "undocumented" aliens entering the United States and its weakened job market. Tensions between the new arrivals and other groups in society arose in a number of places. Domestic backlash and the negative perception of the Carter administration's response to the Cuban-Haitian influx, coming at the same time as a record flow from Indochina, cast new doubts on America's willingness to admit refugees. President Reagan capitalized on those doubts after he assumed office, employing them to justify an asylum policy which continued to ignore the persecution claims of those fleeing authoritarian regimes in this hemisphere and which treated such asylum seekers with unprecedented harshness. Yet with respect to the Indochinese themselves, the Reagan administration's response was very different. Approaching refugees with a clear anti-Communist agenda in mind, it continued to welcome those whose departure from Communist countries promoted American "security interests." In so doing, it subordinated restrictionist concerns to familiar cold war goals.

Chapter 10

Reagan and the Closing Door

O N JULY 17, 1980, Ronald Reagan accepted the Republican nomination for President with a prayer:

> Can we doubt that only a Divine Providence placed this land, this island of freedom here as a refuge for all those people who yearn to breathe free? Jews and Christians enduring persecution behind the Iron Curtain; the boat people of Southeast Asia, Cuba, and of Haiti; the victims of drought and famine in Africa; the freedom fighters in Afghanistan.[1]

Yet slightly more than a year later he issued an executive order directing the United States Coast Guard to intercept boats laden with Haitians sailing in the general direction of the United States and to tow them back to Port-au-Prince.[2] "Interdiction" was the name given to the Coast Guard's work, and it proved remarkably successful. The migration of Haitian boat people to the United States, which had approached 12,000 during President Carter's last year in office, slowed to a trickle. Those who did reach the United States were either deported or "detained" in guarded camps which today also hold thousands of Central Americans who came here seeking refuge. For many "who yearn to breathe free," "this island of freedom" is unreachable; for others, it has become a prison.

However, the Reagan administration has continued to welcome some refugees. Responding to public clamor and Congressional pressures dating from President Carter's last days in office, when the size and character of the refugee flow interacted with a stagnant economy to produce significant backlash, its proposed refugee allocations have grown increasingly smaller, shrinking from 173,000 in 1981–1982[3] to 70,000 in 1985–1986.[4] Yet these figures, although low by the standards of 1979 and 1980, demonstrate a continuing willingness to respond favorably to many claims of hardship and persecution—provided they are lodged by refugees with the right ideological credentials. Under the allocation system established by the Refugee Act of 1980, tens of thousands of admission slots have been reserved each year for those fleeing Communist countries. A considerably smaller number have been reserved for those fleeing repression in other parts of the world. Of the 70,000 refugees slots available during the 1984–1985 fiscal year, as many as 64,000 were slotted for refugees from the Soviet Union, Eastern Europe, Communist Indochina, Cuba, and Afghanistan.[5] Thus, while the resurgence of restrictionist politics in the United States has played a major role in keeping overall refugee numbers down, it is ideology which has determined how the numbers that remain will be distributed. Under Ronald Reagan, a cold warrior of the old school, vague humanitarian pieties—and the ideologically neutral language of the 1980 law—have been subordinated to strident anti-Communism.

Caribbean and Central American refugees have borne the brunt of this ideological approach. With the exception of the Moskito Indians and some Ladinos in Nicaragua, many of whom have been driven from their lands by the leftist Sandinista government, and the few Cubans who still manage to reach the United States, almost all have fled authoritarian regimes supported by the United States. The hardships they have experienced and the fears they claim are at least as compelling as those of most recent Indochinese refugees. Haitians who opposed the Duvalier regime and were imprisoned for expressing their views fled, as did peasant farmers subjected to extortion and random violence by the *ton-ton macoutes*.[6] Salvadorans whose close relatives have "disappeared" have streamed northward toward the U.S. border, where they have been joined by others threatened by roaming "death squads," or terrified by the violence of the protracted civil war.[7] In Guatemala, where successive governments have systematically persecuted the large native American population, "pacifying" their villages and seizing their lands, as many as a million people have been driven from their homes.[8]

Common to virtually all of these refugees is the lack of any safe haven. Thus hundreds of Haitians reached France and were granted political asylum;[9] but thousands of others were unable to secure exit visas from Haiti or the papers and money which would have permitted them legally to enter some other land.

UNHCR has established camps for Salvadorans in Costa Rica and Honduras, but they are small, understaffed, and remote and capable of handling only a tiny fraction of the hundreds of thousands of people who have fled El Salvador since 1979.[10] The Guatemalan situation is even more desperate. During the early 1980s, refugees from Guatemala streamed into Mexico at a rate of 2,000 to 3,500 persons per week, until Mexico began vigorously policing its borders and discouraging new arrivals.[11] Thousands of Guatemalans were deported at that time.[12] Nevertheless, 100,000—perhaps as many as 150,000—Guatemalans managed to remain in Mexico or on the Mexican border. There, they became the target of periodic Guatemalan army attacks.[13]

Subjected to such misfortune, and uniquely able among the world's suffering people to reach the United States by road or by small boat, many of these refugees have entered America illegally since President Reagan took office. Thus, while Haitian immigration slowed dramatically, the illegal Salvadoran population continued to swell, reaching perhaps an estimated 300,000 to 500,000 by 1982.[14] The size of the illegal Guatemalan population in the United States, while much smaller, probably numbers in the tens of thousands. As has always been the case with refugee migrations to this country, some of those who have come have been able to demonstrate their fears with vivid evidence of persecution: scars inflicted through torture, pamphlets denouncing the trade unions or political parties where they once were active, photographs and letters memorializing those who have vanished while in government custody. Others, like those who escaped the Soviet Union in the early 1950s, have fled the generalized deprivation of political freedom, the threat of capricious interrogation or imprisonment, and the pervasive government of oversight which Edward R. Murrow once characterized as a "nameless terror"—and which, being "nameless," is difficult to explain to immigration officers who speak a foreign tongue. Still others—perhaps a majority—have left only with minor fears, but with the profound belief that life had become dangerous, unpleasant, and unmanageable at home, and could only be better in the peaceful and prosperous United States.

Distinguishing between such migrants when they seek asylum is a difficult task. There is no way of determining who is an "economic migrant," who a "political refugee" without carefully interviewing each applicant, testing credibility and evaluating each story for consistency with known facts. Yet the exercise of such care was precisely the obligation the United States assumed in 1980 when it adopted the new Refugee Act and committed itself to the standards prevailing under international law.[15] That obligation has been consistently ignored by Reagan's State Department and the Immigration and Naturalization Service in their handling of Caribbean and Central American asylum claims. Instead, the pre-1980 presumption that all—or virtually all—Haitians are "economic migrants" has been extended by the Reagan administration, so that now it reaches virtually all Western Hemisphere migrants, with the conspicuous exception of those fleeing Castro's Cuba.[16]

The unwillingness of the Reagan administration to regard any of those fleeing right-wing regimes as victims of persecution has been clear from the beginning, although government spokesmen have consistently denied that ideology has played any part in decisions concerning asylum, detention, or "interdiction." Thus the official justification for the decision to stop Haitian vessels was that such "interdiction" would deter "illegal migration by sea of large numbers of undocumented aliens into the southeastern United States."[17] That explanation was calculated to appeal to those who believed that too many illegal aliens were entering the United States. It complemented the politically popular efforts of Gov. Robert Graham of Florida to keep more Haitians from entering his state—efforts which included a personal "diplomatic" mission to Haiti to see if the flow could be cut off.[18] In a sense the Haitians were "illegal migrants," as are most asylum seekers. Yet the explanation exaggerated the impact of the Haitian migration by failing to note that at the peak of their flow, Haitian boat people probably constituted less than 1 percent of the undocumented population of the United States, and had considerably less effect on the local and national economy than the Cubans who entered in much greater numbers. By emphasizing the negative economic impact of Haitian flow, and by insisting—as it did in its annual reports to Congress on refugee admissions—that virtually all Haitians and Salvadoran asylum seekers had come to the United States to flee poverty rather than out of fear of persecution,[19] the Reagan administration was able to justify its slanted detention and asylum policies using traditional restrictionist arguments.

These arguments had the effect of characterizing asylum as a bad thing, justifiable only if "genuine" refugees were benefited. According to the official administration view, only those fleeing Communist countries ordinarily would be able to show the requisite "fear of persecution." The United States would be required to accept such refugees, not out of simple charity, but out of remorse for not having driven their oppressors from this hemisphere. Elliott Abrams, then serving as the Assistant Secretary of State for Human Rights, expressed the position of the Reagan administration in a June 1982 speech. Completely ignoring the fact that over a million people had already fled rightist regimes in Central America, he stated:

In fact, it is Communist rule that caused the greatest refugee flows of recent years. We can, therefore, have a very firm notion of what the expansion of

Communism to El Salvador and Guatemala would mean. It has the potential to create a Southeast Asia refugee crisis right here on our doorstep. Indeed, we have every reason to think the expansion of Communism in Central America would create this kind of incredible problem. I am always amazed when people come to me to voice their concern about refugees from El Salvador, yet who opposed the Administration's effort to avoid enlargement of that problem by giving El Salvador the aid it needs to defeat Communist led guerrillas."[20]

Abrams' views were representative. Rather than argue that more refugees from Cuba and other nations in the Caribbean basin provide a symbolic repudiation of Communism, Reagan policy makers have reversed the traditional rhetoric by implying that the spread of Communism poses a new immigration threat to the United States. In a speech to the National Governors' Association, Secretary of State Alexander Haig asked his audience to "just think what the level [of refugee flow] might be if the radicalization of this hemisphere continues, with the only alternative a totalitarian model in one state after another. . . . Why it would make the Cuban influx look like child's play."[21] The President himself adopted the same approach, demanding of Congress more U.S. support for El Salvador while asking, rhetorically:

> Must we wait while Central Americans are driven from their homes like the more than 4 million who have sought refuge out of Afghanistan or the 2.5 million who have fled Indochina or the more than 1 million Cubans who have fled Castro's Cuban utopia? Must we, by default, leave the people of El Salvador no choice but to flee their homes, creating another tragic human exodus?[22]

In June, 1983, Reagan stated that if the United States were to acquiesce in the establishment of a "string of anti-American Marxist dictatorships" in Central America, "the result could be a tidal wave of refugees—and this time they'd be feet people, not boat people—swarming into our country seeking a safe haven from communist repression to our south."[23] Although there was no basis to suppose that larger numbers of people would flee leftist governments than were fleeing the rightist regimes in El Salvador and Guatemala at the time, or that people fleeing leftist as opposed to rightist oppression had more meritorious claims to asylum status, the Reagan administration consistently attempted to gain domestic support for U.S. policies in El Salvador by eliciting fears of a "tidal wave" of refugees moving north should Central America "go Communist."

These official attitudes encountered little initial resistance either in the public at large or in Congress. Still numbed by the debacle of the 1980 mass asylum crisis from Cuba, few people were eager to extol the benefits of a generous asylum policy. The Reagan administration was therefore given a free hand to detain and deport those Haitians who did reach American shores and the thousands of Salvadorans and Guatemalans who entered by crossing the U.S.-Mexican border illegally. The detention policy established for these asylum seekers was not entirely unprecedented, since Haitians in Florida facing deportation during the middle and late 1970s had been subjected to imprisonment on a sporadic basis. In the last days of the Carter administration, those Haitians who did not qualify for "Cuban-Haitian entrant status" were customarily incarcerated when apprehended. However, the use of detention took a quantum leap forward during the Reagan years. New holding facilities were established in upper New York State and in the American Southwest, where most Salvadorans entered the United States. New programs were established which required that those arriving without adequate documentation be detained without bail.[24]

Until 1982, when legal actions taken on their behalf prompted the INS to announce a new, "non-discriminatory" detention policy[25] and to begin detaining other asylum seekers on a more regular basis,[26] Caribbean basin migrants were the exclusive targets of these programs. Detention in almost every instance was followed by deportation. INS officials attempted to coerce Salvadorans into leaving the country "voluntarily," and frequently succeeded in deporting them within hours after their arrival. Very few Haitians or Salvadorans were granted asylum. During fiscal year 1981, for example, 503 Haitians applied for asylum, and 5 claims were granted. During the same year, only 2 Salvadorans out of 5,510 applicants were granted asylum in the United States.[27] Since 1981, these figures have changed only slightly. Thus in 1983, 328 Salvadaran claims were approved, and 13,045 denied.[28] Meanwhile, the United States government has continued to deport Salvadorans to El Salvador at the rate of 300 to 500 per month.[29] Deportations to Haiti were more sporadic, in large measure because of unresolved lawsuits challenging government policies. But they also continued, as did the virtually automatic rejection of Haitian asylum claims. In 1983, only 23 Haitians out of 375 applicants were granted asylum.[30]

The harshness of the Reagan administration's treatment of Haitian and Salvadoran asylum applicants has inspired new attempts by the UNHCR, church leaders in the United States, liberal members of Congress, and political activists disenchanted by American policies in Central America and in the Caribbean to push harder for a more liberal asylum policy. To date, these efforts have had little practical effect, although the emerging "sanctuary movement" has lent moral urgency to the refugee issue. The limited effect of the UNHCR campaign to influence the Reagan administration illustrates, as few things can, how deeply entrenched current policy is.

Since 1981, the UNHCR, primarily through its offices in New York and Washington, has frequently expressed its concerns to the Reagan administration about the treatment being accorded Haitians and Salvadorans. After the announcement of plans to use the U.S. Coast Guard to return Haitians to Haiti, those concerns intensified. An internal UNHCR memorandum of October 29, 1981, noted:

> Whether or not the measures can be challenged from a legal point of view is not certain. The newly introduced interdiction measures, of course, deprive asylum seekers at sea of access to counsel and of the appeal possibilities which they would have had had they entered the USA. . . . The new interdiction measures could certainly constitute an undesireable precedent for other areas of the world (e.g. South East Asia) where UNHCR has sought to prevent asylum seekers being towed out to sea.[31]

However, UNHCR staff in the U.S. not only were incapable of changing the interdiction policy—they also had grave difficulty in getting initial support from the High Commissioner, Poul Hartling. On a mission to the U.S. in October and November 1981, Hartling failed to take up these matters forcefully with the United States government. Asked at a press conference about the Reagan Administration's claim that the Haitians and Salvadorans were "economic migrants," not refugees, he replied that a prospective host country was the one to make the decision. Moreover, he said, he was satisfied that the United States interviews of Haitians on the high seas "adhered to the absolutely fair and fine tradition to treat asylum seekers in a right and generous way."[32]

Hartling's remarks "provoked a storm of protest in the ranks of the UNHCR."[33] Hartling must have been aware at the time that U.S. treatment of Haitians was at variance with international standards and the asylum practice of other countries. France, for example, was much more willing to grant Haitians political asylum.[34] During 1981, of 550 Haitian applicants for asylum France recognized 60 percent as refugees, and during 1982, 90 percent of the 300 applicants were granted political asylum. Ultimately, more UNHCR pressure on the U.S. to change its policy was exerted at a higher level. During spring 1982, a UNHCR visit to the U.S. looked specifically at the Haitian interdiction program. According to sources in the UNHCR and the U.S. Immigration Service, the only concession made by the United States was a promise to afford Haitians intercepted on the high seas adequate shipboard asylum hearings. From September 1981 to March 1985, some 3,000 Haitians had been intercepted by the U.S. Coast Guard. Not one Haitian was found by U.S. authorities to have presented a valid claim to asylum,[35] and not one Haitian was taken to the U.S. to have his claim more carefully examined. Thus, although the U.S. was supposed to have changed INS guidelines governing the interdiction program, there was no evidence that actual asylum decisions were affected. Meanwhile, the interdiction program continued, as did the deportation of new Haitian arrivals. Official UNHCR efforts to halt these deportations were made selectively and with a minimum of publicity. Nevertheless, even in individual cases involving strong UNHCR support for particular applicants, the U.S. refused to alter its policies.

Somewhat greater resolve was demonstrated by UNHCR on issues involving Salvadorans, but the results were similar. The Washington liaison office of UNHCR supplemented its expressions of concern with a study mission in September 1981 to examine the detention centers where Salvadorans were being held. The report generated by this mission concluded that the physical conditions under which the Salvadorans were being held were generally "satisfactory." But it also stated, "Though in theory any Salvadoran illegal entrant may apply for asylum, there appears to be a systematic practice designed to secure the return of Salvadorans, irrespective of the merits of asylum claims. Hence, the overwhelming majority of those returning are doing so 'voluntarily' without apparently being freely advised of their asylum rights." [36]

After detailing how high bond, denial of work authorization, pressure to sign voluntary departure forms, summary hearings, and long detention all contributed to this systematic practice, the study team recommended that the INS use its discretionary powers to grant "extended voluntary departure" to the Salvadorans. In so doing, it explicitly noted the complete unwillingness of INS officials to grant asylum to any Salvadoran applicant, and implicitly recognized that not all such applicants would, under international legal standards, be entitled to "refugee" status. Its final recommendation was that

UNHCR continue to express its concern to the U.S. government that its apparent failure to grant asylum to any significant number of Salvadorans, coupled with continuing large-scale forcible and voluntary return to El Salvador, would appear to represent a negation of its responsibility assumed upon its adherence to the Protocol. [37]

These concerns continued to be voiced exclusively through private diplomatic channels until February 1982, when Senator Kennedy read the text of the UNHCR monitoring report into the *Congressional Record*. After the publication of that report, the asylum rejections rate fell, temporarily, from 99.9 percent to 94 percent. Yet the UNHCR continued to maintain its characteristic low profile, the State Department completely ignored UNHCR opinions regarding individual Salvadorans and Haitians, and the deportation of Salvadorans continued. The role of UNHCR in the United States remained severely limited. The UNHCR representative to the U.S. could review asylum files, could visit detention centers, and in early 1985 negotiated for a presence on the Coast Guard cutter which interdicted boatloads of Haitians, but in reality the UNHCR had no influence in asylum decision-making in the U.S.[38]

Its lack of influence was due partly to the UNHCR's special relationship to the United States. Dependent on the United States for a large percentage of its annual operating budget, it lacked the financial independence and institutional strength to challenge effectively its largest benefactor. Yet other institutions, ranging from the Congress of the United States to concerned churches, also discovered that their influence on the Reagan administration's asylum practices was minimal. The Congress, of course, possesses the power to change the law governing asylum. But since the early 1980s, its general concern has been that asylum be available only to people who are driven from their native lands by genuine fear of persecution, and that the INS conduct careful screening to insure that in each individual case such fear is present. Congress has considered amending the refugee definition to require clear proof of a threat to health or safety prior to a refugee's departure from home,[39] and has avoided any action which would authorize "blanket" asylum for Central American migrants. It also ignored the minimal due process afforded those intercepted off the Haitian coast and continued to appropriate money to the Coast Guard to conduct its "interdiction" campaign.[40] Nevertheless, the Congress has expressed some concern about the fairness of current asylum and detention practices. Since 1981, each house has approved its own version of legislation that would give immigration officers charged with hearing asylum claims additional education about human rights abuses in other nations and more training in the interviewing of asylum applicants.[41] Particularly in the version proposed by the House of Representatives, asylum adjudications would be granted more independence from the political offices of government.[42] However, the failure of Congress during the last several sessions to reach agreement on immigration reform legislation has consigned these measures to limbo.

But even when Congress has reached agreement and has urged the Executive Branch to be more generous, its recommendations have been ignored. "Extended voluntary departure" status, when granted to aliens the government might otherwise seek to deport, is less advantageous than asylum, since it is usually in effect only for a short period and can be withdrawn on short notice without a hearing. While it is in effect, however, it not only shields the alien from deportation but also permits him or her to avoid detention and to seek temporary employment. It is a humane alternative to penning people up in "holding centers" for months or years while their asylum claims are pending, and has frequently been granted by the Reagan administration to those entering the United States from countries with Marxist regimes such as Poland, Ethiopia, and Afghanistan.[43] However, it has not been used to benefit any recent Caribbean or Central American migrants. In 1983, both Houses of Congress, responding to the UNHCR report and published stories about the possible dangers Salvadoran returnees faced, and concerned about the treatment of Salvadoran "detainees," attached a nonbinding resolution to the Foreign Aid appropriations bill urging President Reagan to grant those Salvadorans who had entered the United States prior to January 1, 1983, "entended voluntary departure" status.[44] The President ignored that resolution, and his administration has continued to detain Salvadoran asylum seekers.

Faced with such intransigence, the main-line Protestant churches and many Roman Catholic dioceses have turned increasingly to nontraditional ways of influencing policy. In Florida and in the southwestern U.S., churches have pressed class action lawsuits challenging the government's treatment of Haitian and Central American refugees. To date, those lawsuits have had only limited success, although Haitian advocates won a significant victory in the summer of 1985 when the Supreme Court ruled that the regulations governing detention and the granting of parole do not permit overt discrimination on the basis of race or national origin.[45] Other church people, radically disaffected by the Reagan administration's Central American policies and its treatment of the region's refugees, have begun to pursue a public campaign of civil disobedience. Labeling their efforts the "sanctuary movement," they have helped Salvadorans and Guatemalans cross the Mexican-American border illegally, and have hidden illegal entrants in churches, monasteries, and parishioners' homes. When challenged by law enforcement personnel, they have argued that their actions were morally appropriate and entirely consistent with the mandates of American and international refugee law. Despite these claims, several have been arrested, tried, and convicted of criminal misconduct. However successful their efforts in raising public consciousness about the plight of Central American refugees, they have had no positive effect on the policies of the Reagan administration.

In keeping with its ideological impulses, the administration has been considerably more receptive to pressure to admit refugees from Communist countries. Some of that pressure has come from Poles and Ethiopians in the United States who have sought and ultimately obtained "extended voluntary departure" status for their compatriots facing possible deportation. But most pressure has come from the State Department, the private voluntary agencies, and a few Congressmen such as Senator Mark Hatfield who have continued to advocate generous refugee allocations for Indochina. Their efforts have been less dramatic than those employed during the crisis years from 1979 through 1980, and have encountered considerable resistance in the Congress and the Immigration Service. The concern first voiced by the INS District Director in Hong Kong, Joseph Sureck in February 1980—that American "benevolence in accepting [so many Indochinese] refugees" may have created a permanent "immigration problem"—has been reiterated frequently in the years since, and has found a responsive ear in the Congressional subcommittees most responsible for regulating immigration. Armed with the power to engage the President in "consultation" on refugee admissions levels, Congress has grown increasingly unwilling since 1981 to "rubber-stamp" executive admissions decisions, particularly when those decisions might permit more economically motivated migrants to enter the United States. Also eliciting strong positive responses—particularly from Representative Mazzoli's House Judiciary Subcommittee on Immigration, Refugees, and International Law—have been charges that some of the voluntary agencies advocating higher numbers for Indochina are self-seeking and financially irresponsible organizations whose principal objective is the promotion of "the refugee business"—or "Refugee, Inc.," as Representative Mazzoli has labeled it.[46]

These Congressional concerns have created special difficulties for those supporting the continuation of an Indochinese refugee admissions program. Adding to their difficulties have been continuing worries in Congress and in the individual states about the long-term costs of maintaining the most recent Indochinese migrants, many of whom have limited English language skills and little experience which would prepare them for working in the United States. Finally, the heavy burdens imposed on those willing to volunteer their time and efforts to help resettle so many Indochinese so quickly during President Carter's last years in office have led, perhaps inevitably, to sponsor "burnout" and "compassion fatigue." As the Vietnam war and the atrocities of the Pol Pot regime have faded into the past, it has become difficult to maintain broad public interest in the virtually static situation which persists today in Southeast Asia. Cambodians who remain in camps inside Thailand or continue to huddle along the Thai-Cambodian border, like the thousands of Laotians and Vietnamese who still desire to migrate to the United States, are less visible today than the victims of more recent disasters. Starving Ethiopians, Mexican earthquake survivors, and victims of other recent disasters have cornered much of the nation's generosity. Comparatively little grass-roots enthusiasm for a generous Indochinese program has manifested itself since 1980 or 1981. As a consequence, virtually all of the domestic forces influencing policy have demanded a radical reduction in Indochinese admission levels. Congress, fully aware of those forces, has responded by pressuring the Reagan administration into reducing the number of Indochinese permitted to enter the United States by 75 percent since 1980. This reduction, although very substantial, would have been even greater except for the persistent efforts of a small group of influential people inside and outside the Reagan administration, who have consistently argued that more generosity to the Indochinese is justified by cold war as well as humanitarian considerations.

The battle over the appropriate level of Indochinese admissions, which had begun in 1980 with conflict between the INS and the State Department over appropriate methods of screening individual migrants, resumed almost immediately after the November 1980 presidential election, when the INS again began to interview Indochinese individually. Again, the State Department resisted. Both sides mustered substantial support for their position. Predictably, the most persistent advocates of a "blanket" admissions policy included Ambassador Abramowitz and Lionel Rosenblatt, who continued to receive considerable support from Leo Cherne's remarkably effective lobby, the Citizens' Commission on Indochinese Refugees. They were joined by a number of "hard-liners" in the administration, including Secretary of State Alexander Haig and UN Ambassador Jeanne Kirkpatrick, who believed that a generous admissions policy was closely linked to U.S. support of Thailand and anti-Vietnamese efforts in Southeast Asia. Yet the influence of this coalition was almost exactly balanced by the political strength of those advocating a more restrictive policy. In addition to Sureck, the restrictionists included several members of Congress who launched a crusade for a more restrictive immigration policy, budget cutters in the Office of Management and Budget and in the Department of Health and Human Services, the Office of Legal Counsel of the Department of Justice, and, in a significant though peripheral role, the UNHCR.

Initially—although not immediately—the proponents of "blanket" admission were successful in reversing Sureck's decision to review on an individual basis refugee applications from Indochinese. Thus in the spring of 1981, after the INS had begun rejecting nearly all of the 31,000 Khmer refugees whom the State Department had identified as eligible under the United States admissions program and had also begun to defer the admission of a considerable number of Vietnamese, a major brouhaha erupted. Accusing the INS of disgraceful behavior, Ambassador Abramowitz cabled his superiors in Washington, "Presumably after World War II, INS would have rejected as refugees the remaining Jews from Germany on the grounds they could go back to Germany."[47]

Abramowitz' outburst achieved results largely because of the support from the strong pro-Indochinese program lobby and from Secretary of State Haig. Leo Cherne, the chairman of the Citizens' Commission on Indochinese Refugees, had close contacts with the Reagan administration. William Casey, the former vice chairman of the Citizens' Commission, was the new CIA Director, and Cherne was a prominent member of the President's Advisory Committee on Foreign Intelligence. In a letter to Haig, Cherne underscored the continuing importance of U.S. foreign policy interests in maintaining a large Indochinese admissions program. Cherne argued that the discussion about whether the Indochinese were "economic migrants" or "political refugees" arose

> both because the crisis nature of the problem has subsided somewhat and because, like all refugee flows, some Indochinese are impelled at least partly by economic motives. In addition, however, it seems clear to me that the swelling discussion of this subject is in part orchestrated by those, such as the UNHCR, OXFAM, the Friends society, some countries and others who, for philosophical reasons, wish to diminish the status of the refugees and their reasons for leaving with a view to refurbishing the reputation of Vietnam in the hope of speeding the process of reconciliation. It is clear that the continuing repression being applied in the process of communization of the societies of Indochina is entirely sufficient to create the flow of refugees which we are experiencing.[48]

Cherne argued, moreover, that a reduction in the number of Indochinese refugees to be admitted to the U.S. would discourage the countries in Southeast Asia from granting asylum, encourage repatriation and forced expulsions, and set a bad example for other Western nations with generous admissions policies. Further, Cherne argued, echoing his remarks of prior decades,

> It would give impetus to the increasingly popular rationalization that these refugees are, in fact, economic migrants, and that there is no sufficient political reason to flee the Communist nations of Indochina [and] would, above all, penalize victims of Communist repression and aggression with whom we have a special relationship.[49]

Secretary Haig, one of the vanquished American soldiers of Indochina, did not need to be convinced of the foreign policy importance and anti-Communist basis of continuing a large Indochinese admissions program. Following President Reagan's inauguration in 1981, it became U.S. policy to further isolate Vietnam for its occupation of Cambodia and to apply all possible forms of pressure on Hanoi to change its Cambodian policy. Regarding refugees, Haig told the ASEAN foreign ministers in Manila, "The time has come for a more concerted effort to deal with this long-standing and anguishing human problem at its source."[50] To get at the source, the Reagan administration tried to convince China, ASEAN, and the rest of the nonaligned world to cut off their aid programs to Vietnam and to support Chinese and American attempts to "bleed" Hanoi into submission by means of Chinese military pressure on the Sino-Vietnamese border and reinforcement of the Cambodian resistance on the Thai-Cambodian border. Haig was probably more concerned with maintaining the viability of the Cambodians as a guerrilla force on the Thai border than he was with moving them out of Thailand to the United States. Nevertheless, such movement was important to Thailand and thus contributed to general strategic goals. He therefore threw his weight behind the more liberal refugee admissions policy.

After strenuous lobbying by Abramowitz and Rosenblatt, Secretary Haig persuaded the Attorney General, William French Smith, to overrule the INS. State and INS reached agreement whereby those leaving Indochina for the remainder of the fiscal year, ending September 30, 1981 would continue to be considered automatically admissible to the U.S. as refugees and would not be subject to rigorous case-by-case interrogation. As a result, refugee processing started up again in spring 1981, and large numbers of refugees began to arrive in the U.S. during the spring and summer months. At the same time, the State Department sought approval from Congress and the Reagan administration to continue Indochinese admissions at nearly the same level that had prevailed since 1979.

These efforts met with considerable success in the White House. Thus, on September 21, 1981, President Reagan recommended that Congress approve a 1982 ceiling of 173,000 refugee slots and reserve 119,800 of those slots for Indochinese.[51] However, the three members of the House Judiciary Committee "consulted" by the President recommended that the overall allocation be reduced to 140,000,[52] and the fourth, Representative Mazzoli, recommended that the overall number be set no higher than 120,000, with a maximum of 84,000 slots reserved for Indochinese.[53] The lower levels recommended by the House of Representatives were based primarily on concerns about the domestic impact of larger refugee flows to the United States. Thus the McClory, Fish, and Rodino letter to President Reagan stated:

> we are concerned by your decision to maintain a high level of refugee admissions, because it is not accompanied by a request for adequate funding to meet their resettlement needs. At a time when we are sharply cutting social programs urgently needed by the disadvantaged and needy members of our society, it becomes more difficult to justify an annual Federal expenditure in excess of one billion dollars for refugees. Further, this growing competition for reduced Federal resources will undoubtedly produce increasing resentment toward refugees in general.[54]

In a separate letter to President Reagan, Representative Mazzoli endorsed the views of his colleagues but laid special emphasis on the impact that refugees had on state and local governments. Increased public health concerns, specifically noted by Representative Mazzoli in his letter to the President, were in many ways symbolic of misgivings which began to emerge in the early

1980s, particularly in those communities where refugees settled in large numbers. For example, 60,000 Indochinese settled in Orange County, California, between 1975 and 1982—approximately one-ninth of all the Indochinese then resettled in the United States. Drawn to California by good weather and favorable employment opportunities, by welfare and social services generous by national standards, and by a desire to rejoin family and friends, they quickly overloaded the public schools and medical facilities, and were blamed for a rise in the rate of tuberculosis and other diseases. Concern mounted over the increasing size of local refugee welfare budgets, inequities in the distribution system which allowed certain refugees to receive more benefits than other welfare recipients, the lengthening time many refugees appeared to spend on welfare, and the impact they had on housing, employment, education, and public health services. Particular concerns were voiced by Hispanics, who found it especially difficult to compete with the Indochinese in a very tight housing market.

Efforts were made at the state and local level to reform the welfare system, and Rep. Daniel Lungren, a Republican who represented the most heavily impacted area, sought unsuccessfully to obtain more federal aid. Orange County, unlike many with large refugee populations, had its own refugee coordinator, and took full advantage of the services of David Pierce, a Foreign Service officer with resettlement experience on temporary assignment to the county under a special federal program. It was also blessed with a large and dedicated cadre of volunteers who worked tirelessly to make refugees more self-sufficient, and to induce local businesses to open up more employment opportunities to refugees. Yet by the winter of 1981, Orange County's elected public officials were telling the Reagan administration what it had already been told by the governors of Florida and Colorado and by a significant number of Congressmen from other States: that local communities couldn't easily handle any more refugees and would prefer that the federal government take steps to keep them away.[55]

Similar messages came from other parts of the country that had been hit harder by the recession—St. Paul, Minnesota, for instance, which discovered that it had become, virtually overnight, the home of thousands of Hmong tribesmen from Laos, and Seattle, Washington, which struggled with a massive refugee problem at the same time that it sought to survive layoffs in the aircraft manufacturing industry. The federal government attempted to steer new arrivals away from heavily impacted areas but could do little to control secondary migration. Adding to the difficulties of these communities were the economic policies of the Reagan administration, with their emphasis on smaller federal programs and reduced spending. These policies tended to increase the local costs of being generous. Federal funding was reduced for social services, job

training, housing, education, food stamps, and public welfare. Policies restrict-
ing eligibility and limiting benefits were instituted. The refugee program was
not spared. Congress imposed a host of new restrictions on federal reimbursement to the states for refugee resettlement. New regulations, which became effective in April 1982, cut the maximum period entering refugees would be
eligible for special refugee aid from thirty-six months to eighteen months. As a
result, refugees were further encouraged to migrate to those states with liberal
welfare policies. Those states, in turn, were encouraged to seek more federal
funds, as well as a more direct acknowledgment that refugees, who had been
brought to the American mainland as a result of decisions made in Washington,
were primarily a matter of federal responsibility. When that gambit failed, state
governments mounted further pressures on the federal government to restrict
refugee admissions into the United States.

Even if Congress had been convinced that the majority of Indochinese seeking to enter the United States after mid-1981 were in fact genuine refugees
whose chief motive for flight was fear of persecution, it would have found it extremely difficult to resist restrictionist pressures. But in fact many in Congress,
taking their lead not only from the INS but also from the UNHCR and from
the Legal Counsel of the Department of Justice, shared Joseph Sureck's belief
that most of those seeking to enter the United States were economically
motivated. The UNHCR position, as expressed by the regional personnel in
Bangkok,[56] was the opposite of the one adopted by Leo Cherne. Pointing to
the continuing migration of more than a million people six years after the collapse of pro-American governments in Indochina, one UNHCR report suggested that many of those leaving the Indochinese states did so because of the
magnetic attraction offered by the large quotas announced by the United States
and not because of a specific fear of persecution. The U.S. program was increasingly perceived by the UNHCR as being unduly influenced by people who had
"a strong personal and emotional interest in maintaining high quotas," and
who believed "a continuing exodus from Indochina is a 'good thing'" because
"it helps to prevent the stabilization of the communist regimes in Indochina,
provides a useful source of intelligence information on the situation inside those
countries, and appears to demonstrate to the world that Indochinese continue
to vote with their feet."[57] In view of mounting evidence that many Indochinese
could not be classified as refugees according to international criteria and that the
program itself was working as a magnet, senior regional UNHCR personnel
argued that UNHCR was "in serious danger of being trapped into the continuing advocacy of resettlement programmes which were innovative—indeed,
revolutionary—only two years ago but are now increasingly out of phase with
the tenor of events. In particular, we need to revive our traditional emphasis on

the support of genuine refugees rather than to be identified as co-sponsors with resettlement countries of a migratory process which is not our legitimate concern."[58]

Similar sentiments were expressed in Congress, where Senator Huddleston submitted a resolution urging that

> the program for resettling Indochinese refugees shall be immediately and thoroughly investigated by the Executive and Congress to determine if the program is classifying as refugees large numbers of individuals who are migrating primarily for economic reasons, is encouraging the mass migration of individuals and is being administered in the strict manner Congress intended. Should the findings of this investigation so warrant, the program shall be phased out as soon as possible.
>
> The investigation shall give substantial weight to the testimony and professional opinions of Immigration and Naturalization Officers who have direct experience with the Indochinese resettlement program.[59]

These sentiments were given added support when the Office of the Legal Counsel of the Department of Justice issued a "Re-interpretation of the Refugee Act of 1980"[60] which sustained the position that the INS had the responsibility to determine, on a case-by-case basis, whether a person met the definition of refugee under that act. Bolstered by the findings of this report, Representative Mazzoli unequivocally took the side of the INS on the issue of the admissions eligibility of Indochinese and he encouraged the INS to actively defend its viewpoint:

> Let me encourage you to remember that the Department of Justice is, I believe, a co-equal department of Government, along with the State Department. I do not think they acted in a co-equal way in the spring. I think they got overwhelmed, run over, and stomped on by the State Department. I do not think they should have. I think that ought to be part of your feeling. If you as the legal experts in the country with statutory responsibilities in immigration and refugee matters firmly believe, and you have information to back you up, that people are not refugees then I think you ought to assert yourself and carry on.[61]

The disarray in the Reagan administration, which pitted a restrictive Justice Department against a State Department still seeking to fight Communism in Southeast Asia with a generous refugee admissions policy, permitted Congress to play down the entreaties of the State Department. Protestations by the State Department's Office of Refugee Programs that Indochinese admissions had "significant foreign policy implications"[62] were discounted, if not entirely ignored, as was a plea by UN Ambassador Jeanne Kirkpatrick, who asserted:

Thailand is our most exposed ally in Southeast Asia. The economic, as well as the political and military, security of Thailand is enormously important to the United States interests in that part of the world. And the destabilization of Thailand ranks high among the goals of our adversaries.

Our program to resettle the refugees in Thailand is as important to that country's stability as the economic and military aid we provide in more conventional ways. . . . We have said that we are with them for the long pull, that we can be counted upon to shoulder and to keep on shouldering our part of the joint burden.[63]

Congress continued to respond to domestic pressures, recommending each year from 1982 through 1985 that refugee allocations—including the sizable Indochinese numbers—be cut substantially from proposed Reagan administration figures. It also succeeded in pressuring the State Department to accept case-by-case processing of Indochinese refugees.

Recognizing the need to bring admissions levels down in order to maintain domestic support for the Indochinese refugee program, the State Department shifted emphasis in the fall of 1981 from resettlement to promoting repatriation and support for Thai "humane deterrence" measures to discourage further influx.[64] "Humane deterrence" meant putting new Indochinese refugee arrivals in substandard detention facilities with no hope of resettlement abroad in expectation that such action would deter further new arrivals. In testimony before Congress in October 1981,[65] Sheppard Lowman confirmed that it was U.S. policy to encourage Thailand in this initiative:

. . . the central goal in the implementation and management of the U.S. program will be to utilize only that admission authority required to maintain first asylum and to use the forthcoming months to develop a system of humane deterrence which could act to bring down the overall requirements of the Indochinese refugee program over time to much more manageable levels.[66]

Yet the continued presence of large numbers of Cambodians in Thailand, and the inability of the UNHCR to negotiate a deal with the Heng Samrin regime in Phnom Penh which would guarantee their safe return, inevitably spurred new efforts to promote more resettlement—and new conflicts between the State Department and the INS. Thus a serious breach between the Thai government and the United States emerged in April 1982, when the Immigration Service effectively vetoed a U.S. plan to accept 23,000 of the 85,000 Cambodian refugees remaining in holding centers in Thailand. All of those selected had close relatives in the United States, had worked for the U.S. government, or had been closely associated with the U.S.-supported Lon Nol regime. The plan, which had progressed to the point of informing the Cambodians selected that they would be soon traveling to the United States, was decimated when the INS subjected each selectee to a quick and often searing interview and rejected over half on the grounds that they did not meet the definitional criteria of the 1980 Refugee Act.

The situation was not confined to Cambodian refugees alone. The rejection rate of Vietnamese boat people in Hong Kong rose from 20 percent in late 1981 to over 65 percent in late 1982. INS opinions that these refugees had no "well-founded" fear of persecution if returned to Vietnam contradicted the State Department human rights report on Vietnam,[67] which indicated that would-be escapees had been executed or imprisoned for three to fifteen years at hard labor.

Tensions rose between State and voluntary agency personnel, on one hand, and INS officers, on the other. Complaints regarding INS behavior were so critical and forcefully expressed[68] that the INS had to send a special team of investigators to Thailand. Subsequently, new guidelines were sent to Sureck from Washington, but the high rates of INS rejections continued into 1983. Finally, John Gunther Dean, the new American Ambassador to Thailand, protested the conduct of INS officers. Dissatisfaction with the role of the INS grew not only in Thailand but, more importantly, within the United States, where the refugee bureaucracy, voluntary agencies, and their Congressional allies lobbied intensely for a change in Reagan administration policy. Responding in part to these pressures from the U.S. and also from UNHCR, in early 1983, Thailand eased its policy of "humane deterrence" and began a series of releases of Vietnamese and Laotians for resettlement. Finally, in mid-1983, the Reagan administration issued a National Security Council directive[69] which directed the Attorney General to issue further revised refugee processing guidelines and to establish certain categories for Indochinese refugees which would not require the presentation of "independent evidence regarding persecution." By July, such guidelines[70] were developed, and by fall 1983, the INS acceptance rates throughout Southeast Asia rose to 83 percent.

Since 1983, the Reagan administration has continued to support the State Department in its long battle with the INS over Indochinese acceptance rates. Despite a new skirmish which erupted in 1984, when the INS began questioning Cambodian claims on the grounds that many of those seeking to enter the United States had "collaborated" with the Pol Pot regime, those rates have remained high. As importantly, they have been backed up by continuing administration efforts to maintain Indochinese refugee allocations at or near current levels. The administration has been assisted in these efforts by periodic news stories of bloody clashes along the Thai-Cambodian border and the resulting devastation of the makeshift refugee camps that are still located there. Writers like Gail Sheehy have reported movingly of the fears that still haunt the survivors of Pol Pot's regime.[71] The Lawyers Committee for International

Human Rights, evaluating the current situation in Cambodia, has suggested that those fears may still be amply justified. In those areas still controlled by the Khmer Rouge, it has found overwhelming evidence of police state repression. Yet its image of life in the areas controlled by the Heng Samrin regime is hardly more favorable. There, it has found little respect for civil rights, and routine and brutal torture of political prisoners.[72] Reports such as these have reinforced the Reagan administration's view that Communist regimes are uniquely evil and that their victims are uniquely worthy of resettlement.

In the refugee allocations for 1985–1986 proposed by the Reagan administration, approximately 70 percent of the 70,000 refugee visas which the administration sought would have been given to the Indochinese, with virtually all of the remainder being given to people fleeing other Communist regimes in Eastern Europe, the Soviet Union, Cuba, and Afghanistan.[73] Explaining the administration's commitment to continuing Indochinese migration, James Purcell, the Director of the State Department's Bureau of Refugee Programs, explained:

> We should recognize . . . that for the foreseeable future, we will need to continue to admit a reasonable number of Indochinese refugees to the United States, both because it is our humanitarian duty to do so and because it is in our strategic interest to relieve the pressures that refugee populations place on friendly first-asylum states in the region.[74]

In fact, America's perceived "strategic interest" in Indochina is somewhat broader—and clearly more ideological. In February 1985, Secretary of State Schultz proclaimed it "America's moral duty" to "support the forces of freedom in Communist totalitarian states."[75] Pointing particularly to the situation in Cambodia, Schultz implied that continued U.S. support to "resistance forces" there would continue to keep the "Stalinist dictators of Hanoi"[76] from assuming complete control, and thus perpetuate the new "democratic revolution" which, according to Schultz, is "sweeping" Indochina—and the rest of the world.[77] As was the case thirty years earlier during the era of "liberation," U.S. support for those "risking their lives against Communist despotism"[78] involves arming those who remain behind to fight and sheltering those whose presence in friendly countries is "destabilizing" and whose resettlement in the West will help underline the failures of Communist rule.

The intensification of the cold war during the Reagan years has thus had the familiar effect of uniting strident anti-Communists and the private voluntary agencies in the common cause of preserving substantial refugee admissions. Those joint efforts have helped to preserve the Indochinese refugee program, although each year it continues to lose some ground to the increasingly restrictionist sentiment in Congress. In Fiscal Year 1986, for example, the President was compelled to trim 7,000 slots from his proposed refugee allocation after Senators Thurmond and Simpson and Representatives Rodino and Mazzoli all recommended that Indochinese numbers be trimmed by at least 12,000.[79] Senators Kennedy and Biden, who with Representatives Fish and Lungren advocated holding the line, lacked the clout to alter the recommendation of either the House or the Senate Immigration Subcommittee. And the principal voluntary agencies, which issued an unusual joint statement backing the original 70,000 figure and pledging to do all in their power to aid "those refugees from Indochina still awaiting a sign of welcome from the free world,"[80] were also unsuccessful. As a consequence, the Indochinese allocation continued to shrink.

Yet even that diminishing level of kindness appears generous when compared with the most recent choices made for those fleeing from countries such as Haiti, Guatemala, and El Salvador. Finding no similar "strategic interest" in moving any of the victims of authoritarian terror in this hemisphere to the United States, the administration has proposed no refugee allocation for them in Fiscal Year 1986. Instead, it is moving forward with a "contingency plan to transfer unused numbers from the Latin American admissions ceiling to other areas."[81] Thus, notwithstanding the Refugee Act of 1980 and the lobbying of humanitarian organizations to eliminate ideological considerations from refugee decision making, the Reagan administration continues to favor those fleeing left-wing or Marxist regimes and to rebuff those seeking to escape right-wing authoritarian regimes.

Chapter 11

Calculated Kindness

T HE UNITED STATES has traditionally proclaimed a generous and compassionate approach to refugee problems. Since 1945, more than 2 million aliens have entered the United States outside of regular immigration channels. Variously categorized as "displaced persons," "emergency migrants," or "refugees," they have come not only from Europe but also from Asia, Latin America and the Caribbean, and—in much smaller numbers—from the Middle East and Africa. Included have been more than 800,000 Cubans, 700,000 Indochinese, and at least a half-million Central and Eastern Europeans. Responsive to these numbers, politicians from Cleveland to Miami, from New York to San Diego, pay ritual homage to the "captive nations" and laud a dozen different sorts of "freedom fighters." President Reagan's nomination prayer, asking God's blessing on a nation generous enough to have accepted so many refugees, illustrates, as few remarks can, how firmly the tenet of welcome has reestablished itself, how much it has become again part of the official American creed.

Yet professions of faith are not always matched by deeds. For each statistic of welcome, there is another of exclusion, for each example of the open door, there is another of the door banging shut. The virulence of the government's campaign against Haitian and Salvadoran asylum seekers in recent years is unmatched. Since the late 1970s thousands of Haitians sought political asylum in the United States. Of these claims only a handful were granted. During the same period, tens of thousands of Salvadorans were "detained" in guarded camps, and tens of thousands more were shipped home against their will. Similar treatment has been accorded the nationals of many countries since the late 1940s, with Koreans, Filipinos, and Iranians particularly affected. Generosity has been real, but it has also been selective. It has extended no further than politics and the law have permitted.

Since the 1930s, when the United States first began to consider admitting refugees as a special class of immigrants, those politics and that law have changed greatly. The America that rejected all attempts to grant special visas to Jewish refugee children was a depression-wracked land, profoundly isolationist, and deeply committed to doctrines of racial superiority and ethnic prejudice. Its ingrained restrictionism probably owed as much to a fear of foreigners taking scarce American jobs as it did to maintaining—or reclaiming—Anglo-Saxon social hegemony. Yet the national origins quota system it maintained was specifically and intentionally discriminatory, and elevated concerns about race, language, and "assimilation" above any concerns about human suffering, or the desperate situation of particular refugees.

In the four decades since the end of World War II, American immigration politics have become notably less racist and more humane. The improvement in the general immigration environment has been matched by a greater federal awareness that refugees have special claims, and a greater willingness to ignore such factors as race or religion in fashioning special immigration opportunities for them. Jewish survivors of the holocaust, Eastern Europeans fleeing lands falling under Communist rule in the late 1940s, and the more recent refugees from Indochina have all benefitted from the more permissive attitude toward immigration which emerged when the United States put the Great Depression behind it. They have also been aided by the efforts of second- and third-generation Americans from Eastern and Southern Europe, who assumed greater political power after World War II, and spoke out strongly for a more generous and more equitable immigration law. Closely associated with the emergence of these more generally liberal sensibilities has been an increased public willingness to look beyond racial or ethnic stereotypes, and to see the desperation of those fleeing hardship or persecution. Thus, in the immediate aftermath of World War II, the nation—aided by the efforts of a more committed press, and more effective ethnic lobbying—began to recognize that Europe's few surviving Jews had experienced hell in Hitler's concentration camps, subsisted precariously in occupied Germany, and required resettlement opportunities if their future was to be assured. A generation later, similar awareness of the plight of Vietnamese "boat people" and of the Cambodian victims of Pol Pot made emigration to the United States seem not only acceptable, but morally imperative.

Yet the development of greater tolerance did not promote the abolition of all immigration limits, even for refugees. During the great immigration debate of the 1950s and 1960s, more "fairness" was frequently enunciated as a goal, but "open" borders were never seriously advocated. A new quota system was adopted in 1965, equalizing immigration opportunities for natives of every Eastern Hemisphere country. It substantially increased migration from many European countries and for the first time placed Asians and Africans on an equal immigration footing. But it established a limit on the number of visas which could be issued each year which was only slightly higher than the number established in 1924,[1] and reserved 94 percent of those visas for ordinary migrants rather than refugees.[2] Even as it "expanded" the immigration ceiling, it included within that ceiling migrants from the Western Hemisphere never before subject to any numerical limitations.[3] Thus, the new system went beyond the temporary displaced persons and refugee legislation passed in the late 1940s and 1950s because it recognized suffering and "fear of persecution" as perennial problems, and created an on-going authority to admit at least some refugees each year. But the number admissible when the 1965 immigration amendments took effect was limited to 10,200,[4] and never rose above 17,400.[5] Thus, the development of a more permanent commitment to the admission of refugees did not eliminate the need for selectivity; instead, the law demanded that the nation admit only those victims it regarded as most deserving—or best able to promote the "national interest."

Significantly, the 1965 immigration amendments, like all of the special refugee legislation enacted between 1948 and 1960, singled out those fleeing "Communist or Communist-dominated" lands[6] as the group for whom almost all resettlement slots would be reserved. Even in 1948, when memories of World War II and the Nazi Holocaust were still fresh, Congress made it clear when it passed the original Displaced Persons Act that it regarded the imposition of Communist rule in most of Eastern Europe as an important reason for welcoming DPs to the United States. As the cold war intensified during the 1950s and early 1960s, ideology became the principal determinant of merit, both positive and negative. Congress, obsessed with national security, made it virtually impossible for any refugee with significant Communist ties to enter the United States, however fearful of imprisonment, torture, or death they might be. On the other hand, it passed several bills permitting the entry of "selected anti-Communist defectors," and "escapees." As importantly, even when it was unwilling to initiate or enact legislation creating new statutory channels for the admission of anti-Communist refugees, it demonstrated a remarkable willingness to acquiesce in executive initiatives designed to bring them to the United States outside of the strict requirements of immigration law. Most of the Hungarian "freedom fighters" admitted to the United States in 1956 and 1957, for example, owed their admission to President Eisenhower's discovery that he possessed the authority to "temporarily" parole aliens into the country for pressing "humanitarian" reasons. Parole was subsequently used to bring over seven hundred thousand Cubans[7] to the United States, and continued to be employed long after the 1965 immigration amendments had been enacted. Until new refugee legislation was enacted in 1980, it served as the principal vehicle for bringing refugees—including virtually all of those arriving from Indochina between 1975 and 1980—to the United States.

The discovery of Presidential parole in 1956, and its subsequent use, substantially loosened the tie between refugee admissions and domestically-oriented immigration politics, though it did not entirely eliminate it. Thus, ethnic groups continued to lobby for more refugee admissions, but shifted more of their attention to winning friends in the Executive Branch. And Presidents remained indirectly accountable to Congress since they required Congressional authorization to transport the "parolees" to the United States, to provide them with aid after their arrival, or to regularize their immigration status after they had established residence. An informal practice of "consulting" with Congressional leaders before parole decisions were announced was established during the Hungarian uprising, and continued until 1980, when it was replaced by new, statutory "consultation" procedures.[8] Increasingly, however, the foreign policy objectives of the Executive Branch took priority over the persistent concerns of Congress about maintaining the integrity of the quota system, minimizing resettlement costs, and preserving its own institutional role in controlling immigration.[9]

Thus, the vehemence of the cold war was used as an implicit justification for paroling thousands of Hungarians and Cubans into the United States—just as it had been used explicitly by Presidents Truman and Eisenhower between 1948 and 1956 as justification for new and more generous refugee legislation. Ethnic groups, which had lobbied for that special legislation, were equally supportive of parole, since it promised not only increased immigration opportunities for their members, but also introduced new flexibility into immigration law and catered to popular anti-Communist sentiments. Congress, caught up in its own anti-Communist campaign, found it difficult to resist the executive's foreign policy arguments.

Even during the last days of World War II, many in Congress shared the State Department view that there was a connection between the large uprooted population of Eastern and Central Europe and future stability in the region. As

East-West tensions grew, a new understanding emerged: the people moving westward could be exploited as part of an ongoing propaganda campaign. Each defection, each crossing into Austria or West Berlin, was thus construed as a "ballot for freedom." In an era when Presidents spoke seriously of "liberation" and "roll-back," some of those who had "voted with their feet" were trained in the West to go back and vote with guns. Initiatives of this sort were frequently advocated in the halls of Congress, and in the popular press. For these and similar reasons, America encouraged the westward flow and, having encouraged it, adjusted its immigration law accordingly. It did so not only for the "escapees" of the early 1950s but also for the Hungarian and Cuban "freedom fighters." Until 1980, each revision of the law and every sizable refugee flow into the United States reflected the dominance of an anti-Communist ideology.

This is not to say that all special admissions since 1945 have been directly related to the cold war. Periodic "thaws," more localized foreign policy concerns, and genuine humanitarian motives contributed to a number of atypical immigration decisions, including the permanent admission of over 1,000 Ugandans in 1973 and the temporary stays of deportation granted Nicaraguans in 1978–1979 and Iranians in 1979–1981. At times, Congress has taken the lead, and paying considerable heed to humanitarian organizations like Amnesty International and lobbying groups like the American–Israel Public Affairs Committee (AIPAC), has resisted pressure from the White House and pushed through special programs for selected groups of refugees. During the 1970s, Soviet Jews and a few Chileans fleeing the Pinochet government have benefitted from such Congressional action. Nor is it to suggest that when State Department officials have played the principal role in securing the entry of putative refugees from Communist countries, they have been motivated solely by global political concerns. The history of the Indochinese migration to the United States provides but one example of the frequent symbiosis that obtains between humanitarian and political motives. When those motives are linked, concern over the fate of hundreds of thousands of people who are starving, or fearful of persecution on political grounds, or both, goes hand in hand with concerns over regional stability, overburdened countries of first asylum, and the positive political gains to be made by presenting a negative image of Communist rule. When no linkage exists, however, humanitarian motives have been almost always overwhelmed by political calculation. Thus it is not accidental that over 95 percent of all the special admissions permitted between 1948 and the present have involved individuals fleeing Marxist regimes. Nor is it accidental that many of those we have turned away—Chileans, Salvadorans, Korean dissidents—have been labeled as "left-wing" troublemakers. In 1980, however, Congress passed a new refugee act, and appeared to signal a fundamental shift in the nation's approach to refugees. Responding to pressures from refugee organizations, the United Nations High Commission for Refugees, and the domestic human rights lobby, it belatedly followed up on its 1968 approval of the UN Protocol Relating to the Status of Refugees, and changed the definition of refugee in the Immigration and Nationality Act to conform to international usage. Henceforward, persons fleeing *any* country—not just those behind the Iron Curtain—would be considered refugees, providing they could demonstrate a personal "well-founded fear of persecution." [10] The Refugee Act of 1980 also afforded a new statutory right to seek protection to any alien from any country who managed to reach America's borders and demonstrated the probability of such persecution.[11] Thus, Congress, acting in an era when human rights concerns were still fashionable, appeared to embrace new, more general humanitarian standards for determining refugee status.

The sources of that sentiment, both inside and outside of government, have been detailed in this book. Among them were new, more liberal Congressional leadership interested in the question of human rights and anxious to have American policy reflect national ideals; a greater acceptance of the United Nations as a normative force; activism in the refugee bureaucracy; the spread and growing sophistication of human rights organizations and public interest law firms; and the recognition by the churches of persecution and abject poverty in many parts of the world, including Chile, Haiti, Indochina, El Salvador, Guatemala, and the Sahel. Impelling that recognition and communicating it to a broader public was the press, and particularly television, which dramatized suffering in a manner that blurred fine political and legal distinctions. Thus the same medium that once generated sympathy for the youth of Hungary battling Soviet tanks armed only with stones and Molotov cocktails has, over the last fifteen years, tracked hundreds of foundering boats in the Caribbean and the South China Sea and brought the visual record of starvation on two continents nightly into millions of homes. The cataclysmic events that produced the heaviest flow of recent refugees, as well as the most significant modification of U.S. refugee law, occurred in Indochina. American willingness to accept so many "boat people"—and, a few months later, so many victims of Pol Pot's barbarous regime—was undoubtedly spurred by the East-West confrontation in the region. Yet the tremendous groundswell of sympathy that made their admission possible was prompted, not by ideology, but by fear of another holocaust. It was that type of fear that influenced Congress in its passage of the 1980 Refugee Act, and not a desire to impose "narrow and carefully-focused" limits on humanitarian entry.

Yet when it adopted the new "persecution" standard and established the special, flexible quota for refugees, Congress left essentially intact the existing executive discretion to determine immigration eligibility. In the words of one State Department official; "The Refugee Act established a set of new procedures, but instituted no new policy." Since it has gone into effect in 1980, the special, Presidentially determined refugee quota, designed to replace the old parole system and give Congress more say, has made token provision for admitting refugees from non-Communist countries. Asylum procedures have also been changed. New questions designed to elicit more information about possible persecution are asked, and the Immigration Service has been given more practical independence in its decision making. Yet the effects, particularly during the Reagan presidency, have been more cosmetic than real. Thus the refugee quota has continued to favor traditional, ideologically useful entrants. In recent years, about 1 million people have fled from El Salvador and Guatemala. Similar displacements have occurred in Afghanistan, Ethiopia, and the drought-stricken countries of the Sahel. Yet for 1986 the U.S. established quotas for no more than 3,000 refugees from Latin America and the Caribbean, 6,000 from the Middle East, and 3,000 from Africa—with the remaining 55,000 reserved for refugees from the Soviet Union, Eastern Europe, and Indochina.[12] The history of this allocation for Fiscal Year 1986 made it clear that many of the Middle Eastern slots would be reserved for Afghanis taking shelter from Soviet military attacks in Pakistan, and that most of the Latin American and Caribbean slots would be reserved for Cubans.[13] And practice, as distinguished from announced policy, is even more lopsided. In fiscal year 1982, only 579 of 3,000 slots allocated for Latin Americans were actually filled, and 577 of those 579 went to Cubans.[14] That pattern is typical. The refugee allocation has never been used to bring in Haitians or Guatemalans, and only a handful of Salvadorans and Africans have ever been brought into the U.S. as refugees.

Asylum practice has followed a similar pattern, "fairer" and less ideological in one respect only: the disfavor formerly extended to those fleeing right-wing military regimes has been universalized. During the Reagan years, for the first time, Poles have found it difficult to obtain formal asylum (though most have been granted "extended voluntary departure" status, and have not been subjected to detention or deportation). Some Afghans have been detained in Brooklyn, and even one Cuban has been deported. Yet, as always, the Haitians have been treated worse. Only relative newcomers from countries such as El Salvador and Guatemala can expect to be treated as badly. In 1984, only 3 of 761 Guatemalan applicants (less than 0.5 percent) and only 328 of 13,373 Salvadorans (less than 2.5 percent) were granted asylum. This contrasts sharply with the rates for Bulgarians (52 percent), Russians (51 percent), and Hungarians (28 percent).[15]

Commenting on the 1986 refugee allocation when it was first proposed, Representative Romano Mazzolli, the Chairman of the House Subcommittee on Immigration, Refugees and International Law complained:

> The Refugee Act of 1980 was intended to eliminate ideology and geography in our refugee admissions program. We seem not to have accomplished this most important objective. . . .[16]

His remarks, which were aimed primarily at the high percentage of Indochinese in the administration proposal, were echoed by others who objected to the almost total exclusion of Central Americans and Haitians from the refugee quota, and the continuing campaign to detain and deport asylum-seekers fleeing right-wing regimes. Other commentators, heavily involved with the resettlement of Indochinese, made no complaint about the distribution of numbers, but objected to the continuing tendency of the President, after consulting with Congress, to reduce the overall level of refugee admissions. Both sets of comments revealed a common understanding: the liberalization of American refugee policy which began immediately after World War II, and which had continued unabated for thirty-five years, had halted. Even during the Carter presidency, attempts to establish a genuinely humanitarian refugee policy had faltered. Despite a visible concern with human rights, the passage of the Refugee Act of 1980, and new initiatives to benefit Nicaraguan refugees and Chilean and Argentinian political prisoners, refugee allocations continued to reflect geopolitical priorities, and American asylum practice continued to favor those who claimed persecution at the hands of Communist governments. The intermittent campaign to incarcerate Haitians was resumed; the Salvadorans were routinely denied asylum. Under President Reagan, cold war politics have assumed an even more dominant—and certainly more open—role in America's approach to refugees. The annual allocation figures are skewed to favor refugees the United States regards as anti-Communist "freedom fighters." In a chorus of official statements, spokespersons for the administration characterize life under Communist rule as inherent persecution and dismiss stories of disappearances, torture, and imprisonment in countries like El Salvador as "exaggerations," or as accounts of localized abuse bearing no essential relationship to the governments in power. Meanwhile, American Coast Guard vessels ply the waters of Haiti seeking to "interdict" vessels bearing Haitian migrants, and each month hundreds of Salvadorans are taken from detention, denied asylum, and flown back to El Salvador.

Yet the intensity of recent measures against such asylum-seekers reveals more than the persistence of cold war politics. The overall reduction in refugee admissions since 1980, and the universally tougher approach to asylum taken by the INS both demonstrate that refugees *from every country* are less welcome than they were during the middle 1970s. The new rhetoric of the Reagan administration, which demands more aid for those combatting Communism in this hemisphere *lest* a "flood" of new refugees be created, reflects a similar perception. Even anti-Communists, although more welcome than their left-wing brethren, are no longer likely to be received with open arms. The new, anti-refugee trend, which first emerged in the late 1970s when Indochinese admissions began outstripping the capacity of the domestic resettlement system, took root with a vengeance in the summer of 1980. During the summer, some 125,000 Cuban boat people, recently embarked from the harbor of Mariel, arrived suddenly in south Florida. The disorders associated with their arrival awakened immigration fears and made intolerance respectable again.

The Mariel incident is important because it demonstrates how quickly welcome can wear out and how influential negative news stories, backed by vivid film clips, can be. In the beginning, the Mariel Cubans were greeted with a warmth approaching that accorded their predecessors, more than 700,000 of whom had entered the United States since 1959. The press labeled the *Marielitos* "the freedom flotilla." [17] President Carter welcomed them "with an open heart and open arms." [18] Within a period of weeks, as thousands streamed ashore each day in Florida, the welcome mat was snatched away. Coast Guard cutters, which had guided the first boats north to harborage in Key West, were used to divert others sailing south to pick up passengers at Mariel. The new arrivals, who at first had all been indiscriminately, but informally, characterized as refugees, were increasingly labeled as criminals, sociopaths, homosexuals, and "troublemakers."

The reversal of attitude can be traced to many factors, including an unfortunate early speech by President Carter which laid heavy emphasis on Castro's use of the boat lift as a means of exporting undesirables to the United States. Yet the chief cause was undoubtedly the drumbeat of publicity devoted to the riots that broke out in resettlement centers in Arkansas, Pennsylvania, and Wisconsin. In the weeks following these riots almost every rape, every robbery, every murder in the Greater Miami area was attributed to the *Marielitos*. However, the public image of the *Marielitos* is not only one of National Guardsmen bashing the heads of troublemakers at Fort Chaffee, although that image has the strongest emotional impact. Rather, it includes other graphic evidence of an overloaded system: people sleeping in the Orange Bowl because no beds were available in Dade County; tents pitched under the expressway in the heart of the city, filled with people waiting for sponsors; long lines at the immigration, welfare, and public health offices.

The image of refugees as difficult migrants, requiring special accommodation at a time when jobs and affordable housing for American citizens were becoming increasingly scarce and national welfare demands were rising, made it clear that admissions decisions had potential effects in the United States, as well as in the foreign policy arena. These effects became more pronounced during Ronald Reagan's first term as the recession deepened, and as cut-backs in federal spending put more pressure on local units of government to reduce social service expenditures. Increasingly often, those asserting probable persecution were subjected to the heightened scrutiny of a new restrictionism, which treated unproven fears as less significant than the competition for scarce commodities which those admitted as refugees, or claiming refugee status, seemed to embody. Thus, it was probably not accidental that as the nation moved deeper into the 1980s, less attention seemed to be paid in Congress and the press to the persecution and state-induced suffering that characterize genuine refugees, and more frequent comparisons were drawn between Indochinese and Caribbean Basin migrants seeking refugee status and the hundreds of thousands of illegal Mexican migrants crossing the Rio Grande in search of jobs.

Thus, despite the persistence of the rhetoric of welcome, a politics of limits has again assumed an important role in the American response to refugees and colored the Reagan response to new arrivals. Those politics, in conjunction with old ideological disputes, have also created new tensions between certain refugee advocates and the government. In 1984, the Justice Department initiated an undercover operation against a group of church workers in Arizona and Texas who had chosen as a matter of religious conscience to provide sanctuary to Central American migrants, primarily from El Salvador and Guatemala. Several people were subsequently tried and convicted of conspiracy to violate immigration laws, and others were indicted on charges of smuggling, transporting, and harboring illegal aliens. In conducting their investigation, U.S. agents posed as concerned Christians and infiltrated church meetings, bugged church phones with the aid of wiretapping equipment normally reserved for organized crime, and compiled some 40,000 pages of secretly taped conversations.[19] The government maintained that sanctuary workers were acting illegally when they smuggled Central Americans into the U.S. and shielded them from arrest in their churches, homes, and safehouses. Arguing that most Central Americans who came to the U.S. did so for economic rather than political reasons, the Justice department charged the sanctuary workers with publicly defying federal immigration authority. The sanctuary workers, on the other hand, claimed that those they sheltered had reason to fear persecution or death if deported. Thus they justified their actions on the grounds that they acted in accord with the UN Refugee Convention and Protocol, the 1980 Refugee Act, and the biblical imperative that obligated them to give aid to the stranger.

America has rendered such aid often in the last forty years and has called upon "divine providence" to witness its generosity. A tradition of generosity, sacrosanct and sanctimonious, has emerged which will not suddenly vanish. Embodied in law, in campaign rhetoric, and in a substantial public and private bureaucracy, and fueled by such factors as ideology, religious commitment, and a national heritage of guilt over old failures, like the refusal to grant asylum to Jewish refugees before World War II, and more recent ones, like the failure to offer promised protection to Indochinese allies, the commitment to some level of refugee resettlement is likely to continue into the distant future.

Yet what that level is likely to be and who will benefit will be conditioned by political considerations only marginally related to religious sentiment or the humanitarian efforts of nonbelieving men and women. Thus in late 1979, all of those Cambodians who sought to leave Thailand had a reasonable expectation of doing so, and could hope some day to enter the United States. Today, despite the advocacy of the Reagan administration and the Department of State, and despite their belief that a generous admissions policy will aid the United States in a continuing struggle with the forces of Communism, such hopes would be unwarranted. The Congressional and public reaction to the uncontrolled refugee migrations of the late 1970s and early 1980s has imposed new limits on generosity. When, early in 1985, Khmer refugee camps along the Thai-Cambodian border were razed and 230,000 Cambodians streamed into Thailand for protection, the American response was muted. The threat to Thailand's stability, as much as the threat to the refugees, prompted the administration to promote continued generosity, but no demand was made for bigger refugee allocations; instead, the sole concern of the State Department was "holding the line" on numbers available in the preceding fiscal year. In recent years, however, the line has not been held with equal tenacity on every front. When the United States has perceived that no vital interests will be served by welcoming refugees, or no propaganda points made, its generosity has been even more limited. Thus it has responded to famine in Africa with food and money, but no admission slots, and has completely ignored the desperate situation of thousands of refugees from East Timor, who have been driven from their homes by the Indonesian army's "scorched earth" policies there. Nowhere, however, has the calculation of America's refugee politics been more apparent than in this hemisphere. Pursuing policies forged in the crucible of the cold war, the United States has grown accustomed to regarding only the opponents of Communism as deserving of rescue. In the current restrictionist era, that belief has translated into an asylum policy totally at variance with the spirit of America's refugee law, and totally alien to the belief that refugees are desperate people, not pawns in a global game of chess with the Soviet Union.

Notes

NOTES FOR INTRODUCTION

1. According to the U.S. Committee for Refugees, the current number slightly exceeds 10 million. *World Refugee Survey, 1982* (U.S. Committee for Refugees, New York, 1982). A good 1981 estimate put the number at between 13 million and 16 million people. U.S. Congress, Senate, *Final Report of the Select Commission on Immigration and Refugee Policy*, joint hearings before the Subcommittee on Immigration and Refugee Policy, Senate Judiciary Committee, and the Subcommittee on Immigration. Refugees, and International Law, House Judiciary Committee (GPO, Washington, D.C., 97th Cong., 1st Sess. 1981), p. 7.

2. Exiles were common in Greek and Roman days. Aristide Zolberg traces the modern phenomenon to persecution which began in the fifteenth century when modern European nation-states were being formed. See Zolberg, "The Formation of New States as a Refugee-Generating Process," in G. Loescher and J. Scanlan (eds.), *The Global Refugee Problem: U.S. and World Response, Annals of the American Academy of Political and Social Science*, 467 (May 1983), pp. 24–38.

3. George Washington, "Address to the Members of the Volunteer Association and Other Inhabitants of the Kingdom of Ireland Who Have Lately Arrived in the City of New York," December 2, 1783, in *The Writings of George Washington*, XXVII (GPO, Washington, D.C., 1938), p. 254.

4. Emma Lazarus, "The New Colossus," *Poems of Emma Lazarus*, I (The Riverside Press, Cambridge, Mass., 1889), p. 202.

5. D. Wyman, *Paper Walls: America and the Refugee Crisis, 1938–41*, (University of Massachusetts Press, Amherst, 1968), pp. 96–97; also see D. Wyman, *The Abandonment of the Jews*, (Pantheon Press, New York, 1984), p. 107.

6. Senate Joint Resolution 64 and House Joint Resolution 168, 76th Cong., 1st Sess. (1939), reprinted in U.S. Congress, House Committee on Immigration, *Hearings: Admission of German Refugee Children* (GPO, Washington, D.C., 1939), p. 4.

7. Statement of Agnes Waters, House Committee on Immigration, *Hearings*, pp. 197–198.

8. Statement of Francis H. Kinnicutt, President, Allied Patriotic Societies Inc., ibid., p. 187.

9. Determining the total number of refugees who have entered the United States since 1945 is difficult because a variety of special classifications have been used by Congress and the Executive Branch over the last forty years to describe immigrants granted visas (or leave to remain in the United States) because of hardships ranging from physical persecution to wartime displacement to difficulties finding employment in postwar Europe. The 2 million–plus estimate includes "displaced persons," "refugees," "escapees," "parolees," "expellees," "conditional entrants," "asylees," and some of the "emergency migrants" admitted to the United States by special legislation. Not all of these immigrants meet the persecution-centered definition of refugee adopted by the United Nations in the 1951 Convention Relating to the Status of Refugees or the 1967 Protocol Relating to the Status of Refugees. Nor do all meet the current definition of refugee codified in American law, which is based on the 1951 and 1967 international definitions. That definition covers only individuals with a "well-founded fear of persecution" based on their race, religion, ethnic identity, or political views. See U.S. Code, Title 8, Section 101(a)(42). For the basis of the estimate, see Senate Report 256, 96th Cong., 1st Sess. (1979), p. 6 (Tables); Congressional Research Service, *U.S. Immigration Law and Policy, 1952–59* (GPO, Washington, D.C., 1979), pp. 15–25; A. Schwartz, *The Open Society* (William Warren & Co., Inc., New York, 1969), pp. 228–229 (Tables on Refugee Admission, 1946–1967); and the annual refugee allocation reports issued since 1979.

10. See E. Hull, *Without Justice for All* (Greenwood Press, Westport, Conn., 1985), p. 116; Congressional Research Service, *World Refugee Crisis: The International Community's Response* (Senate Judiciary Committee, Washington, D.C., 1979), p. xi.

11. Not counting over 120,000 Cubans who arrived in the United States in 1980, the authorized level of refugee admission for that year was 230,400. See *Congressional Record* 126 (April 21, 1980), p. 8410. The level of refugee admissions authorized for Fiscal Year 1985–86 is 63,000. See United States Catholic Conference, *Update: The Newsletter of Migration and Refugee Services*, Vol. 85, No. 10 (October 31, 1985), pp. 1–2.

12. For an example of President Reagan's refugee rhetoric, see his speech of July 17, 1980, *New York Times*, July 18, 1980, p. 8, accepting the Republican nomination for President. Also see Chapter 10.

13. Thus in 1980, Senator Walter Huddleston, working in close collaboration with the Federation for American Immigration Reform (FAIR), introduced legislation which would cap annual legal immigration to the United States, including that of refugees, at 650,000. See Senate Concurrent Resolution 94, 96th Cong., 2nd Sess. (1980), reprinted in *Congressional Record* 126 (May 14, 1980), p. 11267.

14. "Introduction," R. Garis, *Immigration Restriction* (The Free Press, New York, 1927), p. vii.

15. Gallup Poll April-May 1980, *The Gallup Opinion Index*, Report No. 177, pp. 6–8. (Of those polled, 56 percent indicated the U.S. should not permit Cubans to settle here; 34 percent approved more Cuban resettlement. Also, 66 percent of those polled believed immigration of political refugees should be halted until the U.S. unemployment rate dropped.

16. The argument that aliens who are likely to pose a welfare burden on the United States should be strictly limited in number has been advocated frequently by the Federation for American Immigration Reform (FAIR). Authors' interview with Roger Connor, Executive Director, FAIR, Washington, D.C., May 18, 1981. Also see Barry Chiswick, "The Economic Progress of Immigrants: Some Apparently Universal Patterns," in Barry Chiswick (ed.), *The Gateway: U.S. Immigration Issues and Policies* (American Enterprise Institute for Public Policy Research, Washington, D.C., and London, 1982), pp. 119–158. Chiswick uses economic data to argue that recent refugees are less likely to obtain employment than other recent migrants, pp. 128–129. However, he argues that inconclusive early evidence suggests that the first wave of Vietnamese are "making substantial progress" in finding work, pp. 144–145. For a critical account of welfare dependency statistics as applied to refugees, see Refugee Policy Group, "The Meaning of Welfare Dependency Rates," ICM *Migration News*, No. 3 (1983), pp. 25–35.

17. See "Table Series D 85-86—Unemployment: 1890–1970," in Bureau of the Census, *Historical Statistics of U.S.: Colonial Times to 1970* (U.S. Department of Commerce, Washington, D.C., 1975), p. 135.

18. Ibid. Estimates of civilian unemployment ranged from between 2 percent and 3 percent.

19. See testimony of Earl G. Harrison, U.S. Congress, House, Judiciary Committee, Subcommittee on Immigration and Naturalization, *Hearings on Permitting Admission of 400,000 Displaced Persons into the United States* (GPO, Washington, D.C., 1947), pp. 505–508.

20. Until the development of the Cuban Refugee Program in the early 1960s, discussed in Chapter 3, virtually no federal aid and very little state or local aid was available to refugees either on an individual or a group basis. Instead, the earliest legislation authorizing special admission slots for displaced persons and refugees required that they have sponsors who could provide "assurances" that they would find employment and housing when they reached the United States. See Section 7 of the Displaced Persons Act of 1948, United States Statutes-at-Large,

Vol. 62, p. 1009 (1948); Refugee Relief Act of 1953, United States Statutes-at-Large, Vol. 67, p. 400, (1953).

21. See L. Dinnerstein, *America and the Survivors of the Holocaust* (Columbia University Press, New York, 1982), pp. 122–123, 128–134.

22. W. Bernard, "Refugee Asylum in the United States: How the Law Was Changed to Admit Displaced Persons," *International Migration*, VIII, Nos. 1/2, p. 7.

23. Thus the 1965 amendments to the Immigration and Nationality Act, which for the first time set aside a portion of the annual immigration quota for refugees, were the culmination of a long legislative process which began in the early 1950s, when ethnic and other advocates of more immigration from Germany, Italy, and Eastern Europe sought unsuccessfully to reserve a percentage of the visas available each year for refugees, and to make them available without regard to the restrictive national origins quota system. See R. Divine, *American Immigration Policy, 1924–52* (Yale University Press, New Haven, Conn., 1957), p. 176; U.S. President's Commission on Immigration and Naturalization, *Whom We Shall Welcome* (GPO, Washington, D.C., 1953), pp. 118–119; E. Hutchinson, *Legislative History of U.S. Immigration Policy, 1798–1965* (University of Pennsylvania Press, Philadelphia, 1981), pp. 525–529. Such lobbying, however, played a relatively minor role between 1977 and 1980, when a new, nonideological refugee act was drafted, debated, and passed into law.

24. However, *after their arrival* legislative initiatives were undertaken on behalf of Cuban and Indochinese refugees to provide them with resettlement aid, and on behalf of all three groups to regularize their immigration status. See, e.g., the Migration and Refugee Assistance Act of 1962, United States Statutes-at-Large, Vol. 89, p. 87 (1975) (refugee aid).

25. In Fiscal Year 1985–86, for example, of 63,000 available refugee admission slots, at least 56,000 are allocated to refugees from Communist countries. Depending on how the remainder are distributed, virtually all could be distributed to people fleeing from countries which are run by Marxist governments. Thus slots are reserved for 45,500 refugees from Indochina, 9,500 from the Soviet Union and Eastern Europe, 6,000 from the Middle East and South Asia, 3,000 from Africa, and 3,000 from Latin America and the Caribbean. United States Catholic Conference, *Update: Newsletter of Refugee and Migration Services*, Vol. 85, No. 10 (October 31, 1985), pp. 1–2. In recent years virtually all Latin American and Caribbean refugee visas have gone to Cubans and all Middle Eastern refugee visas to Afghanis, and such African refugee visas as have been used have been directed toward Ethiopians.

26. The "sanctuary movement," perhaps the most visible—and most radical—evidence of that sympathy, is discussed in Chapters 10 and 11.

27. Department of State Authorization Act—FY 1984 and 85, Sec. 1012, United States Statutes-at-Large, Vol. 97, p. 1062 (1983). Proclaiming "the sense of Congress," the Secretary of State recommended that "extended voluntary departure status be granted" to Salvadorans in the United States as of January 1, 1983.

28. According to the sources cited in note 10, of the more than 2 million refugees admitted since World War II, approximately 730,000 have come from Indochina, 750,000 from Cuba, and at least 600,000 from the Soviet Union, Eastern Europe, and East Germany. At least 30,000 refugees from other Communist countries in Asia and the Middle East have also been admitted. Although hundreds of thousands of people have sought entry to the United States from right-wing regimes during the same period, the number of these people brought in as refugees or granted political asylum probably does not exceed 50,000.

29. R. McCollum, United States Department of State, ICMC *Migration News*, November-December 1958, p. 3, quoted in A. Bouscaren, *International Migrations since 1945* (Praeger, New York, 1963), pp. 15–16.

NOTES FOR CHAPTER ONE

1. J. P. Clark Carey, "Displaced Populations in Europe in 1944 with Partial Reference to Germany," *Department of State Bulletin* 12, No. 300 (March 25, 1945), p. 491.

2. Ibid.

3. Ibid.

4. L. Dinnerstein, *America and the Survivors of the Holocaust* (Columbia University Press, New York, 1982), p. 28 (20,000 of 60,000 dead within first week of freedom).

5. J. Vernant, *The Refugee in the Post-War World* (Yale University Press, New Haven, Conn., 1953), pp. 94–95.

6. Dinnerstein, *America,* pp. 111–112 (more than 100,000 Jewish arrivals from Poland in summer of 1946).

7. The national origins quota system, adopted as a permanent part of American immigration law in 1924, keyed the number of visas available to any national group to their percentage of the American population in 1890. The purpose and effect of this formula was to reduce Southern and Eastern European immigration. See M. Konvitz, *Civil Rights in Immigration* (Cornell University Press, Ithaca, N.Y., 1953), pp. 10–11 (quoting 1924 House report).

8. The exclusionary provisions of American immigration law disqualified for entry those "likely to be a public charge." This provision was used extensively during the 1930s and 1940s to keep refugees out of the United States. See Wyman, *Paper Walls.*

9. The Displaced Persons Act of 1948, as amended in 1950, permitted the entry of 415,744 special immigrants, of whom 349,000 were displaced persons or recent political refugees. See R. Divine, *American Immigration Policy, 1924–52* (Yale University Press, New Haven, Conn., 1957), p. 141 (Table 3).

10. E. Hutchinson, *Legislative History of American Immigration Policy, 1798–1965*

(University of Pennsylvania Press, Philadelphia, 1981), p. 270. Other bills introduced in 1945 and 1946 would have reduced, but not abolished, existing quotas.

11. Thus a survey taken by the American Institute of Public Opinion on January 14, 1946, revealed that only 5 percent of the American people favored increased Jewish immigration, and the majority favored either a reduction or a complete shut-off. A. Bouscaren, *International Migrations since 1945* (Praeger, New York, 1963), p. 7.

12. D. Wyman, *The Abandonment of the Jews* (Pantheon Books, New York, 1984), pp. 267–268, 275.

13. Steady pressure was exerted, however, by Interior Secretary Harold Ickes and others to permit the refugees "temporarily admitted" to the United States in 1944 to remain. Ibid., pp. 273–274.

14. UNRRA Council Resolution No. 1 (November 9, 1943) established the responsibility of providing "assistance in caring for . . . persons found in any areas under the control of the United Nations who by reason of war have been displaced from their homes and, in agreement with the appropriate governments, military authorities, or other agencies, in securing their repatriation or return." Quoted in Vernant, *The Refugee*, p. 30.

15. M. Proudfoot, *European Refugees, 1939–52* (Faber & Faber, London, 1957), p. 292.

16. Ibid. (Table 12, The Repatriation of Europeans: 1 March to 30 September, 1945). The 10 million returnees listed included Western Europeans returning from the east.

17. M. Elliot, *Pawns of Yalta* (University of Illinois Press, Champaign, 1982), p. 104. Proudfoot, *European Refugees*, p. 229, estimates that "at least 1½ million Poles, Hungarians, Bulgarians, Rumanians, Balts, [and] Central European Jews . . . had refused repatriation" by the beginning of October 1945.

18. Proudfoot, *European Refugees*, p. 229 (estimate of 2¾ million persons).

19. Ibid., p. 214; Elliot, *Pawns*, pp. 165–167.

20. Vernant, *The Refugee*, p. 31.

21. After World War II, the International Refugee Organization inherited several thousand White Russian refugees stranded in China who had fled the Soviet Union during the early 1920s; years after the expulsion of ethnic Chinese from Vietnam, thousands remained in refugee camps scattered throughout Asia. The phenomenon of refugees with no permanent haven is common; such migrants are usually referred to as "refugees in orbit."

22. The best account of the Roosevelt administration's 1944 rescue operations and of the subsequent transportation of 900 refugees to upstate New York, where they were interned until 1947, is contained in Wyman, *Abandonment*, pp. 265–276.

23. See Dinnerstein, *America*, p. 34.

24. Letter From President Harry S. Truman to General Dwight D. Eisenhower, August 30, 1945, reprinted in *Department of State Bulletin* 13, No. 327 (September 30, 1945), p. 455.

25. Report of Earl G. Harrison, reprinted in *Department of State Bulletin* 13, No. 327 (September 30, 1945), p. 455.

26. Ibid., p. 457.

27. Ibid., p. 461.

28. Ibid., p. 457.

29. Ibid., p. 460.

30. Letter from President Harry S. Truman to General Dwight D. Eisenhower, August 31, 1945, reprinted in *Department of State Bulletin* 13, No. 327 (September 30, 1945), pp. 455–456.

31. Directive by the President, December 22, 1945, reprinted in *Department of State Bulletin* 13, No. 339 (December 23, 1945), p. 983.

32. See statement by the President, "Immigration to the United States of Certain Displaced Persons and Refugees in Europe," December 22, 1945, reprinted in ibid., p. 981.

33. Ibid.

34. Ibid.

35. Ibid., p. 982.

36. Ibid.

37. The identical agreements of reciprocal procedures to be followed for Liberated Prisoners of War and Civilians dealt with the treatment that the Soviet Union, Great Britain, and the United States were to afford each others' citizens when they were freed or released from Nazi custody. Article 1 of the agreement, signed by the United States, Great Britain, and the Soviet Union on February 11, 1945, provided that "all . . . citizens . . . without delay . . . be separated from enemy prisoners of war and maintained separately from them . . . until they have been handed over." Proudfoot, *European Refugees*, p. 155, citing United States Department of State, Executive Agreement Series 505, Publication 2530 (1946). For a discussion of the intention of the parties to keep the agreement secret, see N. Bethell, *The Last Secret: Forcible Repatriation to Russia, 1944–47* (Andre Deutsch, London, 1974), p. 33.

38. Thus, in a memorandum for the President dated June 21, 1945, Joseph C. Grew, Acting Secretary of State, distinguished between two classes of "nonrepatriable" displaced persons: "Jewish surviors of Nazi persecutions and other groups such as Polish and Baltic nationals *whose return to their countries is delayed for political reasons*" (emphasis added). J. Grew, "Mr. Earl G. Harrison's Mission to Europe on Refugee Matters," Official Files, Box 555, Folder 127A. Intergovernmental Committee for Refugees, Harry S. Truman Library.

39. No serious opposition emerged from the Soviet Union and its allies to the resettlement of Jewish holocaust survivors, despite the fact that most were under

UNRRA jurisdiction. Thus both sides agreed that the Jews were genuinely "non-repatriable". See J. Stoessinger, *The Refugee and the World Community* (University of Minnesota Press: Minneapolis, 1956), p. 56. Also see Proudfoot, *European Refugees*, pp. 293–294.

40. For example, on the Jewish feast of Yom Kippur, in October of 1946, President Truman publicly announced continuing efforts to get Great Britain to admit an additional 100,000 Jews to Palestine. Harry S. Truman, *Public Papers of the Presidents, 1946* (GPO, Washington, D.C., 1963), pp. 442–444.

41. Dinnerstein, *America*, p. 263.

42. Presidential Proclamation No. 2283, "Immigration Quotas," April 28, 1938, in Code of Federal Regulations, Title 3, Compilation, 1936–38 (GPO, Washington, D.C., 1968), pp. 140–141.

43. In 1947–48, 100 percent of the visas available to the nationals of the Baltic countries—Austria, Czechoslovakia, Hungary, and Rumania—*were* issued, and the figures for Poland were nearly as high. Approximately 65 percent of the visas available for Germany were also issued during that period. "Immigration and Emigration, Fiscal Year 1947," *Immigration and Naturalization Service Monthly Review*, vol. VI, No. 4 (October 1948), pp. 46–48 (Chart III, Table II). However, during the two preceding years, immigration from the major DP-producing countries was considerably lower. *See Monthly Review, ibid.*, Vol. IV, No. 11 (May 1947), p. 143 (Table 9); and *Monthly Review, ibid.*, Vol. V, No. 7 (February 1948), p. 103.

44. According to Proudfoot, "Initially [the U.S.] intended to conform strictly to [the repatriation] requirement of the Yalta agreement, and, if necessary, to use force to transfer all persons to Soviet control who were designated as Soviet nationals." However, a directive from military headquarters on May 27, 1945, informed officers in the field that "the British and United States Governments had not recognized any territorial changes brought about by the war and that all persons from such areas will not be returned to their home districts nor treated as Soviet citizens unless they affirmatively claim Soviet citizenship." Proudfoot, *European Refugees*, pp. 214–215. For the screening procedures employed in August 1945, see ibid., pp. 215–217.

45. According to Proudfoot, ibid., p. 217, "Soviet claims were simply ignored except in the case of war criminals." According to Elliot, *Pawns*, pp. 84–89, those regarded as traitors to the Soviet Union because of their affiliation with the anti-Soviet Russian forces in Germany under the direction of General Vlasov were also returned quite automatically. Also see Bethell, *The Last Secret*, p. 188.

46. Proudfoot, *European Refugees*, pp. 292, 415–418. But see Elliot, *Pawns*, for view that "diminution," at least with respect to Soviet nationals, was merely a "dwindling" as the number of Soviets in American hands fell.

47. In Elliot's view, significant American reservations about continuing to cooperate with the Soviets had emerged by July 1947, but a trickle of Soviet nationals continued to depart until the end of 1949. Elliot, *Pawns*, pp. 122–123.

48. Dinnerstein, *America*, p. 112.

49. Vernant, *The Refugee*, p. 62.

50. Dinnerstein, *America*, pp. 111–112.

51. For a discussion of the repatriation provisions of the Potsdam agreement and their effect on European migration between 1945 and 1952, see Vernant, *The Refugee*, pp. 158–160.

52. Proudfoot, *European Refugees*, pp. 384–385.

53. Ibid., p. 380.

54. Ibid., pp. 380–382.

55. Ibid., p. 381.

56. "Closing of Displaced Persons Camps Considered," *Department of State Bulletin* 14, No. 351 (March 24, 1946), p. 498.

57. Acting Secretary of State Dean Acheson, "U.S. Zone in Germany Closed to Additional Displaced Persons," *Department of State Bulletin* 16, No. 408 (April 27, 1947), p. 766.

58. Authors' interview with John Thomas, Geneva, Switzerland, March 24, 1983.

59. Dean Acheson, *Present at the Creation* (Norton, New York, 1969), pp. 170–173.

60. Dinnerstein, *America*, p. 107.

61. Ibid., p. 117.

62. Ibid., pp. 6, 114–115.

63. Ibid., p. 115.

64. Ibid., p. 122.

65. According to William Bernard, "The Board was of flexible size, to allow for the inclusion of both individuals and representatives of as wide a variety of organizations as possible. Bernard, "Refugee Asylum in the United States: How the Law was Changed to Admit Displaced Persons," *International Migration*, VIII, Nos. 1/2, p. 7.

66. Quoted in Dinnerstein, *America*, p. 129.

67. Ibid., pp. 131–132.

68. U.S. Congress, House, Judiciary Committee, Subcommittee on Immigration and Naturalization, *Hearings on Permitting Admission of 400,000 Displaced Persons into the United States* (GPO, Washington, D.C., 1947), p. 2.

69. Ibid., p. 3.

70. Ibid., pp. 3–4.

71. Ibid., p. 3.

72. Ibid.

73. According to one source, "it became increasingly obvious that the 1948 [DP] Act turned out to be a vehicle for bringing to the United States former Nazi collaborators." M. Wischnitzer, *To Dwell in Safety: The Story of Jewish Migration since 1800* (Jewish Publication Society of America, Philadelphia, 1948), p. 272,

citing Abraham Duker, "On the Need for Screening Displaced Persons Applying for Entry into the United States," *Congressional Record* 94 (August 2, 5, and 6, 1948), pp. A4762, A4891, A4944.

74. Bernard, "Refugee Asylum," p. 7.

75. Ibid., p. 8.

76. Ibid., p. 9.

77. *Hearings on Permitting Admission* (1947), p. 508.

78. Ibid., pp. 509–512.

79. Ibid., p. 512.

80. See "Table Series D 85–86—Unemployment: 1890–1970," in Bureau of the Census, *Historical Statistics of U.S.: Colonial Times to 1970* (U.S. Department of Commerce, Washington, D.C., 1975), p. 135.

81. Bernard, "Refugee Asylum," p. 9.

82. Dinnerstein, *America*, p. 159, quoting Goldthwaite H. Dorr, the State Department consultant hired to help achieve passage of the DP act.

83. Bernard, "Refugee Asylum," p. 9.

84. Dinnerstein, *America*, pp. 149–150.

85. See "Immigration Policy in Party Platforms and Composition of Congress, 1848–1964," Hutchinson, *Legislative History*, Appendix A, pp. 624–636.

86. *Congressional Record* 94 (June 1, 1948), p. 6806. Also see pp. 6805, 6807.

87. See Remarks of Representative Gossett, "A New Fifth Column or the Refugee Racket," *Congressional Record* 93 (July 2, 1947), pp. 8173–8176 (indicating that there were "many subversives among refugees" and that "Trojan horses are offered us on every hand").

88. *Hearings on Permitting Admission* (1947), p. 560 (exchange with Secretary of State Marshall), pp. 6, 89 (exchanges with Representative Stratton).

89. See, e.g., Dinnerstein, *America*, pp. 263–264, subscribing to the view of Susan Hartmann that Truman was a "weak and inconsistent legislative leader." S. Hartmann, *Truman and the 80th Congress* (University of Missouri Press, Columbia, 1971), pp. 7, 42, 100, 211, 213.

90. Harry S. Truman, State of the Union Address, Jan. 6, 1947, in *Public Papers of the Presidents—Harry S. Truman* (GPO, Washington, D.C., 1963), p. 10.

91. Harry S. Truman, "Special Message to Congress on the Admission of Displaced Persons," July 7, 1947, in ibid., pp. 327–329.

92. Acheson, *Present at the Creation*, p. 201.

93. Ibid., pp. 78–79.

94. Stoessinger, *Refugee and World Community*, p. 51; Proudfoot, *European Refugees*, p. 401.

95. Stoessinger, *Refugee and World Community*, p. 51.

96. Ibid., pp. 41–42.

97. According to one scholarly source, between 1946 and 1953, 440,000 nationals of the Baltic states were arrested or deported by Soviet officials, and 90,000 others died in guerrilla warfare. R. Misiunas and R. Taagepera, *The Baltic States: Years of Dependence* (University of California Press, Berkeley, 1983), p. 279 (Table 5). Elliot, *Pawns*, p. 207, estimates that half of the estimated 2.5 million Soviet citizens repatriated from Europe died in gulags after the war. Hundreds of thousands of others were forcibly recruited into the Soviet army or placed in internal exile. Ibid., pp. 208–210. For a less than dispassionate account, written at the height of the cold war, see A. Kalme, *Total Terror: An Exposé of Genocide in the Baltics* (Appleton-Century-Crofts, New York, 1951). News of Soviet deportations to Siberia reached the West sometime in 1945. See Proudfoot, *European Refugees*, p. 276.

98. A period of "selective UNRRA repatriation" extended from October 1945 to June 1947. Ibid. More than a million people returned to Eastern Europe, the great majority voluntarily.

99. According to Dean Acheson, the decision to wind up UNRRA operations at the end of 1946 was taken by the U.S. despite pressure from its Allies to keep the organization going to meet continuing relief needs. Wind-up operations continued into 1947. Acheson, *Present at the Creation*, p. 201.

100. Annex to the Constitution of the International Refugee Organization, Part I, Sec. C., Part 1(a), reprinted as Appendix to Senate Report 950, 80th Cong., 2nd Sess. (1948).

101. IRO Constitution, Art. 2; Annex, Art. 1(c). Also see Annex, Part II.

102. Proudfoot, *European Refugees*, p. 401.

103. For the IRO to become operational, fifteen states had to join and commit themselves, in total, to meeting at least 75 percent of the IRO budget. See testimony of Gen. John Hilldring, U.S. Congress, Senate, Foreign Relations Committee, *Hearings: Providing for Membership and Participation by the United States in the International Refugee Organization* (GPO, Washington, D.C., 1947), p. 47. Until August 28, 1948, when those figures were met, the IRO existed and acted as a "provisional" organization.

104. Statement by Under Secretary of State Dean Acheson, Senate Committee on Foreign Relations, March 1, 1947, reprinted in *Department of State Bulletin* 16, No. 401 (March 9, 1947), p. 426.

105. Dinnerstein, *America*, pp. 141–142.

106. Remarks of Senators Revercomb and Ellender, *Congressional Record* 93, (March 25, 1947), pp. 2485, 2487; remarks of Representative Gossett, *Congressional Record* 93 (June 25, 1947), p. 7671.

107. Joint Resolution Providing for Membership and Participation by the United States in the International Refugee Organization, United States Statutes-at-Large, Vol. 62, pp. 214–215 (July 1, 1947) ("acceptance of membership . . . is given upon condition [that no] person shall be admitted or settled or resettled in the United States . . . without prior approval by Congress, and this joint resolu-

tion shall not be construed as such prior approval [and will not] have the effect of abrogating, suspending, modifying, adding to, or superseding any of the immigration laws . . . of the United States").

108. *Congressional Record* 93 (June 25, 1947), p. 76711.

109. Ibid.

110. Senator Revercomb, joined by Senator Dworshak, attempted to raise this question on the floor of the Senate, asking if America's financial contribution to the IRO would entail a similar resettlement commitment. They received no satisfactory response. Ibid. (March 25, 1947), pp. 2494–2498.

111. U.S. Congress, House, Committee on Foreign Affairs, *International Refugee Organization: Hearings on H.J. Res. 207*, 80th Cong., 1st Sess (1947), pp. 36–37. In later testimony on the DP Act, General John Hilldring was blunter. He indicated that the United States should not "use the German police and our own soldiers to round up all of the displaced persons at point of bayonet, load them into trucks or boxcars, and transport them to Eastern Europe." *Hearings on Permitting Admission* (1947), p. 129.

112. *Hearings on Permitting Admission* (1947), p. 505.

113. Ibid.

114. *Department of State Bulletin* 16, No. 415 (June 15, 1947), p. 1165. Also see remarks of Senator Vandenberg, *Congressional Record* 93 (March 25, 1947), p. 2485.

115. *Congressional Record* 93 (June 25, 1947), p. 7671.

116. Ibid. (March 25, 1947), p. 2492.

117. Ibid. (June 26, 1947), p. 7749.

118. Ibid.

119. *Congressional Record* 94 (June 10, 1948), p. 7760.

120. Remarks of Representative Henshaw, ibid., p. 7765.

121. Remarks of Representative Fogarty, ibid. (June 11, 1948), p. 7872.

122. Hutchinson, *Legislative History*, p. 280, citing Displaced Persons Act of 1948, Sec. 3(a), United States Statutes-at-Large, Vol. 62, p. 1009 (June 25, 1948).

123. Ibid., Sec. 3(b).

124. It did, however, establish 3,000 special nonquota immigration slots for "eligible displaced orphans." Ibid.

125. Remarks of Representative Keating, *Congressional Record* 94 (June 10, 1948), p. 7745.

126. Displaced Persons Act of 1948, Sec. 2.

127. Ibid., Sec. 5(a).

128. Ibid., Sec. 3(a).

129. Ibid., Sec. 6

130. *Hearings on Permitting Admission*, p. 396.

131. Ibid., p. 399.

132. Ibid.

133. Misiunas and Taagepera, *The Baltic States*, p. 279 (Table 5).

134. Displaced Persons Act of 1948, Sec. 12.

135. See Dinnerstein, *America*, pp. 138, 174–175. Also see Divine, *American Immigration Policy*, pp. 124–125.

136. Statement of the President, "Signing of the Displaced Persons Act of 1948," June 25, 1948, *Department of State Bulletin* 19, No. 470 (July 4, 1948), p. 21.

137. Ibid., p. 22.

138. An Act to Amend the Displaced Persons Act of 1948, United States Statutes-at-Large, Vol. 64, pp. 219–222 (June 16, 1950). See particularly Secs. 1, 4, and 6.

139. U.S. Congress, House, *Report No. 581—Amending the Displaced Persons Act of 1948*, House report, 81st Cong., 1st Sess. (Committee Print, 1949), p. 15.

140. Ibid., p. 16.

141. "President's Budget Message for 1951," *Department of State Bulletin* 22, No. 551 (January 23, 1950), p. 137 (Table—"International Affairs and Finance").

142. Edward R. Murrow, Transcript of CBS Radio Broadcast, October 17, 1949, pp. 3–4, Harry N. Rosenfield Papers, Box 22, File, Alphabetical—Speech Material, Harry S. Truman Library.

143. John Foster Dulles, "A Policy of Boldness," *Life*, 32 (May 19, 1952), p. 154.

144. Alexander Wiley, in U.S. Congress, House, Committee on the Judiciary, *Hearings on Amending the Displaced Persons Act of 1948* (GPO, Washington, D.C., 1949), quoted in Divine, *American Immigration Policy*, p. 33.

145. According to the Conference report on the 1950 DP act amendments, the Department of State made "urgent representations" on behalf of the 15,000 figure. See U.S. Congress, House, *Report No. 2187—Amending the Displaced Persons Act of 1948*, Conference report, 81st Cong., 2nd Sess. (Committee Print, 1950), p. 12.

146. Ibid.

147. Central Intelligence Act of 1949, Sec. 8, United States Statutes-at-Large, Vol. 63, p. 212 (1949).

148. *Report, No. 2187*, p. 12.

149. Ibid.

NOTES FOR CHAPTER 2

1. *United States Statutes-at-Large*, Vol. 64, p. 987 (1950).

2. Ibid., Internal Security Act of 1950, Sec. 2(1).

3. Ibid., Sec. 22.

4. "Internal Security Act of 1950—Veto Message of the President of the United States," *Congressional Record* (September 22, 1950), p. 15631.

5. U.S. Displaced Persons Commission, *The DP Story: the Final Report of the United States Displaced Persons Commission* (GPO, Washington, D.C., 1952), pp. 70–71.

6. Thus the House and Senate originally intended to give exemptions only to those who had belonged "involuntarily" to Nazi or Fascist organizations. See House of Representatives Report 118, 82nd Cong., 1st Sess. (1952).

7. Act of March 28, 1951, United States Statutes-at-Large, Vol. 65, p. 28 (1951).

8. Section 212(a) (28)(I), Immigration and Nationality Act of 1952, United States Statutes-at-Large, Vol. 66, p. 163 (1952). The act required evidence of opposition to the program of the subversive party or organization for at least five years.

9. With the exception of the two modifications discussed in the previous paragraph, it also retained the exclusionary provisions of the Internal Security Act. See Sec. 212(a) (28) of the Immigration and Nationality Act of 1952.

10. In 1951, eight bills were proposed in Congress to increase Italian and Greek Immigration. E. Hutchinson, *Legislative History of American Immigration Policy, 1798–1965* (University of Pennsylvania Press, Philadelphia, 1981), p. 299.

11. *Congressional Record* 98 (June 25, 1952), p. 8033.

12. The original expiration date of June 30, 1951, was extended for six months by the Act of June 21, 1951, United States Statutes-at-Large, Vol. 65, p. 96 (1951).

13. The commission held eleven hearings between September 1 and October 30, 1952. It heard testimony from 400 witnesses and accepted written statements from 232 others. Summarizing and extrapolating from this massive body of opinion, it issued its final report to the President on January 1, 1953. In that report it laid heavy emphasis on the link between immigration and foreign policy, on the reception of escapees as "a most vital aspect of the cold war," and on the connection between "excess population" in Europe and the strength of European Communist parties. The President's Commission on Immigration and Naturalization, *Whom We Shall Welcome: Report of the President's Commission* (GPO, Washington, D.C., 1953), pp. 47, 61–63.

14. According to Hutchinson, *Legislative History*, p. 310, several bills were introduced after the passage of the McCarran-Walter Act seeking additional refugee visas. None proposed abolition of the national origins system.

15. United States Statutes-at-Large, Vol. 67, p. 400 (1953).

16. Ibid., Sec. 2(b), Sec. 4(a)(2),(3).

17. Such suspicions persisted throughout the early 1950s. For an example of an immigration study dominated by such suspicions, see M. Bennett, *American Immigration Policies* (Public Affairs Press, Washington, D.C., 1963).

18. For a discussion of the continuing but unacknowledged importance of Anglo-Saxon hegemony to the restrictionists, see R. Divine, *American Immigration Policy, 1924–1952* (Yale University Press, New Haven, Conn., 1957), pp. 166–167.

19. Harry S. Truman, "Special Message to Congress," March 24, 1952, *Public Papers of the Presidents, Harry S. Truman, 1952* (GPO, Washington, D.C., 1966), p. 211.

20. D. Wyman, *Paper Walls: America and the Refugee Crisis, 1938–41* (University of Massachusetts Press, Amherst, 1968), pp. 156–171.

21. *New York Times*, January 7, 1950, p. 8.

22. Ibid., October 16, 1949, p. 39.

23. Ibid., September 17, 1953, p. 10.

24. M. Bennett, *American Immigration Policies*, p. 314 (note 128).

25. Ibid., pp. 203–204.

26. See, e.g., *Shaughnessy v. United States ex rel. Mezei*, United States Supreme Court Reports, Vol. 345, p. 206 (1953) (ordering alien suspected of subversion detained indefinitely on Ellis Island without a hearing of any kind); and *Harisiades v. Shaughnessy*, United States Supreme Court Reports, Vol. 342, p. 580 (1952) (permanent resident aliens formerly members of Communist Party ordered deported without a showing they presented any clear or present danger to the United States).

27. United States Congress, Senate, *Report No. 1515*, 81st Cong., 2nd Sess. (GPO, Washington, D.C., 1950), p. 782.

28. Ibid.

29. Ibid.

30. See United States Displaced Persons Commission, *Fifth Semi-annual Report to the President and the Congress*, January 1, 1951 (GPO, Washington, D.C., 1951).

31. Not all of those affected were former Communists. As initially written, the Internal Security Act of 1950 also barred the entry of former Nazis and Fascists. Perhaps as many as half of those with entry problems could trace them to former right-wing associations.

32. Edward R. Murrow's October 17, 1949, CBS radio broadcast, quoted in Chapter 1, on page 23, was one of the many attacks on McCarran during the period. His continuing resistance to Jewish immigration also generated considerable criticism. See Leonard Dinnerstein, *America and the Survivors of the Holocaust* (Columbia University Press, New York, 1982), pp. 226–234.

33. Senate Bill No. 728, 82d Cong., 1st Sess. (1951), introduced by Senator McCarran.

34. Internal Security Act Amendments (1951).

35. Act of June 21, 1951, United States Statutes-at-Large, Vol. 65, p. 96 (1951).

36. See J. Loftus, *The Belarus Secret* (Knopf, New York, 1982), pp. 87–90; 93–94, for a full account of anti-Nazi intelligence operations after World War II.

37. Romuald Misiunas and Rein Taagepera, *The Baltic States: Years of Dependence* (University of California Press, Berkeley, California, 1983), p. 86.

38. D. Wise and T. Ross, *The Invisible Government* (Random House, New York, 1964), p. 96, quoting Allen Dulles memo in United States Congress, Senate, Armed Services Committee, *Hearings: National Defense Establishment*, 80th Cong., First Sess. (1947), pp. 525–528.

39. NSC 4/A (Official Meeting Minutes, 6th Meeting, Table B), Box RG273, National Security Council Policy Paper Files, National Archives.

40. NSC Memo 10/A, "Report on Office of Special Projects," July 18, 1948, Box RG273, National Security Council Policy Paper Files, National Archives.

41. Ibid.

42. Wise and Ross, *The Invisible Government,* pp. 96–97.

43. A. Karalekas, *History of the Central Intelligence Agency* (Aegean Park Press, Laguna Hills, Calif., 1977), p. 31.

44. Ibid., quoting NSC 68.

45. Ibid., p. 36.

46. Thomas Powers, *The Man Who Kept the Secrets: Richard Helms and the CIA* (Knopf, New York, 1979), p. 40.

47. Ibid.

48. Psychological Strategy Board, Policy Guidance No. D-18/a, "Psychological Operations Plan for Soviet Orbit Escapees, Phase A," December 20, 1951, p. 5, David D. Lloyd Collection, Box 3, File: Immigration-Memo No. 4, Harry S. Truman Library.

49. Ibid., pp. 3 (note 2), 7–8.

50. Ibid., p. 7.

51. A general account of Radio Free Europe broadcasting, summarizing types of programs usually aired, is contained in Business Research Staff, General Motors Corp., "Report on Radio Free Europe," December 15, 1952, C. D. Jackson Papers, Box 45, File: Free Europe Committee Correspondence (2), Dwight D. Eisenhower Library. Sample program schedules are also in A. Michie, *Voices Through the Iron Curtain: The Radio Free Europe Story* (Dodd, Mead, New York, 1963), pp. 48–54. The Michie book devotes heavy emphasis to the broadcasting of stories of successful escape.

52. Examples of fabricated messages are given in a publication of the Soviet Information Bureau, *Caught in the Act* (1960), p. 153, Allen Dulles Papers, Box 90, Seeley Mudd Library, Princeton University.

53. E. Barrett, *Truth Is Our Weapon* (Funk & Wagnalls, New York, 1953), p. 73.

54. R. Holt, *Radio Free Europe* (University of Minnesota Press, Minneapolis, 1956), p. 323 (quoting Polish Desk, Radio Free Europe, "Fireside Chat No. 117," June 7, 1953).

55. Testimony of Foy Kohler, Assistant Administrator of Broadcasting Service, International Information Administration, "Hearing on International Information Programs," February 20, 1952, in U.S. Congress, House, Committee on Foreign Affairs, *United States Foreign Policy and the East-West Confrontation,* selected executive session hearings of the Committee, 1951–1956, Vol. XIV, p. 320.

56. Under Secretary of State David Bruce, "Report on the U.S. Foreign Information Program and Psychological Warfare Planning," July 3, 1952 (pursuant to

NSC Memorandum 59/1, March 10, 1950), Box R6 273, National Security Council Policy Paper Files, National Archives.

57. S. Steven, *Operation Splinter Factor* (J. P. Lippincott, New York, 1974), pp. 207–210.

58. C. D. Jackson–Allen Dulles, Letter of October 6, 1954, C. D. Jackson Papers, Box 40, Allen Dulles File, Dwight D. Eisenhower Library.

59. Michie, *Voices Through the Iron Curtain*, pp. 73–74.

60. Holt, *Radio Free Europe*, p. 285.

61. Ibid., quoting Czechoslovak Guidance No. 10, June 30, 1953, p. 10.

62. James B. Conant–A. E. Dulles, Telegram of August 13, 1953, C. D. Jackson Papers, NLE 83–535, # 1–2, Dwight D. Eisenhower Library.

63. Institute for Public Opinion Research, Inc. (IPOR) "Program Opinions of Satellite Refugees," Report A95, July, 1951, p. 49, Charles Hulten Collection, Box 17, File: VOA, 1951, Harry S. Truman Library.

64. Ibid., "Reactions of Young Listeners," p. 10, "Indications of Voice of America Penetration," p. 11, Charles Hulten Collection, Box 15, File: VOA, 1950— Program Evaluation: Jamming, Harry S. Truman Library.

65. Richard C. Sheldon and John Dutkowski, "Are Soviet Satellite Refugee Interviews Projectable?" *Public Opinion Quarterly*, Vol. 16, No. 4 (Winter 1952–1953), p. 582.

66. Ibid., p. 581.

67. IPOR, Report A95, p. 217, Charles Hulten Collection, Box 18, File: Communications Media and Hungarian Refugees, Harry S. Truman Library.

68. That screening was conducted not only under the terms of the Internal Security Act of 1950 but also under the terms of the DP act of 1948, which barred the entry of former Nazis and others regarded as security risks.

69. Loftus, *The Belarus Secret*, pp. 84–87, 105.

70. Ibid., p. 104.

71. Ibid., p. 84.

72. Henry N. Rosenfield, "Speech Before Bethesda Park Club Jewish Community Group," February 1, 1952, Henry N. Rosenfield Papers, Box 23, Alphabetical File—Speeches, 1952, Harry S. Truman Library.

73. Ibid.

74. Memo from Harry N. Rosenfield to John W. Gibson and Edward M. O'Connor [December 1951], David D. Lloyd Collection, Box 3, File: Immigration, Memoranda # 4, Harry S. Truman Library.

75. Ibid., pp. 2–4.

76. Telegram from Ellis Briggs, U.S. Ambassador to Switzerland, to Secretary of State, December 6, 1951, David D. Lloyd Collection, Box 3, File: Immigration, Memoranda # 4, Harry S. Truman Library.

77. Ibid.
78. International Rescue Committee, *Saving Freedom's Seed Corn* (pamphlet) (1958), p. 10.
79. Ibid.
80. David D. Lloyd Collection, Harry S. Truman Library.
81. Ibid., pp. 8–9.
82. Ibid., p. 13.
83. Ibid.
84. A. Levenstein, *Escape to Freedom: The Story of the International Rescue Committee* (Greenwood Press, Westport, Conn., 1983), p. 44.
85. President Harry S. Truman, "Special Message to Congress," March 24, 1952, in *Public Papers of the Presidents, Harry S. Truman, 1952* (GPO, Washington, D.C., 1963), pp. 211–212.
86. In secret testimony before the House Committee on Foreign Affairs, Edward W. Barrett, Assistant Secretary of State for Public Affairs, detailed an incident in which the Voice of America dispatched an army officer to interview refugees from a Communist Chinese village. His account was subsequently printed in *Reader's Digest.* U.S. Congress, United States Foreign Policy and the East-West Confrontation, p. 270.
87. Mutual Security Act of 1951, Sec. 101(a) United States Statutes-at-Large, Vol. 65, p. 373 (1951).
88. Ibid., Sec. 101(a)(I).
89. United States Congress, Senate, Committee on Foreign Relations, *Hearings: Mutual Security Act of 1952* (GPO, Washington, D.C., 1952), p. 373.
90. Immigration and Nationality Act, Sec. 212(a) (28) (I) (ii), (1952).
91. Joint hearings of the Senate and House Immigration Subcommittees were held in 1950, and much of the testimony consisted of criticism of the McCarran-Walter bill. See R. Divine, *American Immigration Policy,* pp. 171–172, quoting *Revision of Immigration, Naturalization, and Nationality Laws,* Joint Hearings before the Subcommittees of the Committees on the Judiciary, 82nd Cong., 1st Sess. (Washington, D.C., 1951). Requests for additional hearings by the antirestrictionists over the next two years were routinely denied.
92. Thus the House Report claimed that the McCarran-Walter bill's "basic changes" in the immigration statute:
    "1. Eliminate race as a bar to immigration and naturalization."
    "2. Eliminate discrimination between sexes."
    "3. Introduce a system of selective immigration by giving a special preference to skilled aliens urgently needed in this country."
    U.S. Congress, House, *Report No. 1365,* 82d Cong., 2nd Sess. (1952), reprinted in *U.S. Code Congressional and Administrative News,* Vol. 2 (1952) (West Publishing Co., St. Paul, Minn., 1952), p. 1679.

93. Ibid., pp. 1691–1692.

94. Ibid., p. 1689 ("This bill strengthens the provisions relating to excludable classes to provide added assurance that undesirable aliens will not gain admission to the United States.")

95. Ibid.

96. Hutchinson, *Legislative History*, pp. 298–299, provides an account of Judd's efforts to introduce legislation removing the anti-Asian bias from American law. See also note 98, below.

97. Ibid., pp. 1689–1690 (100 minimum for any Asian quota area, but 2,000 maximum for *all* quota areas in the "Asia-Pacific triangle").

98. Divine, *American Immigration Policy*, pp. 173–174. Also see "An Oriental Quota for the Refugee Act of 1953," *Washington Evening Star*, July 27, 1953, reprinted in W. Moquin (ed.), *Refugees and Victims*, "Makers of America" Series, Vol. 9 (Encyclopaedia Britannica Educational Corp., n.p., n.d.), pp. 34–35 (quoting Judd to the effect that omission of Asians "will serve notice" to "those with yellow skin that you cannot join the white man's club. Where will these people look in such an event? The answer is obvious: to the club organized by Uncle Joe Stalin").

99. Ibid., Divine, *American Immigration Policy* (quoting Senator Lehman as saying that the McCarran bill would lead to "the blackening of the name of America all over the world").

100. J. Stoessinger. *The Refugee and the World Community* (University of Minnesota Press, Minneapolis, Minn., 1956), p. 154 (noting "steadfast" refusal of George Warren, U.S. delegate to the IRO General Council, to commit additional U.S. funds).

101. George Warren, Sr., "The Development of United States Participation in Intergovernmental Efforts to Solve Refugee Problems" (unpublished manuscript prepared for the Department of State, n.d.), pp. 109–112.

102. Stoessinger, *Refugee and World Community*, p. 167; Ronald S. Scheinman, "The Office of the United Nations High Commissioner for Refugees and the Contemporary International System" (unpublished doctoral dissertation, University of California, Santa Barbara, 1974), p. 145. Scheinman attributes the refusal of the United States to grant the UNHCR any relief funding until 1955 to a preoccupation with its own cold war objectives and the U.S.-controlled economic and military aid programs which furthered them, pp. 140–161.

103. Convention Relating to the Status of Refugees, July 28, 1951, United Nations Treaty Series, No. 2545, Vol. 189, p. 137, Art, IB (events giving rise to protection had to occur in Europe prior to January 1, 1951, unless signatory nation agreed to broader geographical scope).

104. Ibid., Art. 33 ("No contracting state shall expel or return [*refouler*] a refugee in any manner whatsoever to the frontiers of territories where his life or freedom would be threatened on account of his race, religion, nationality, or membership of a particular social group or political opinion").

105. GAOR Fourth Session, Third Committee, 262nd meeting, November 14, 1949. Quoted in Scheinman, "Office of the United Nations High Commissioner," p. 95.

106. E. Buehrig, *The UN and the Palestine Refugees* (Indiana University Press, Bloomington, 1971). Also see David P. Forsythe, "The Palestine Question: Dealing with a Long-Term Refugee Situation," in G. D. Loescher and J. Scanlan (eds.), *The Global Refugee Problem: U.S. and World Response, Annals of the American Academy of Political and Social Science*, Vol. 467 (May 1983), pp. 89–94.

107. According to Scheinman, "Office of the United Nations High Commissioner," p. 161, UNRRA was created in 1951 at the behest of the United States and received 65 to 75 percent of its annual budget from the United States.

108. U.S. Congress, House, *Report No. 1841—Expellees and Refugees of German Ethnic Origin*, 81st Cong., 2nd Sess. (1950), p. 87 (recommending that even if maximum assimilation was achieved in West Germany, "slightly in excess of 1,000,000 German expellees and refugees should be offered emigration opportunities"). This conclusion was consistent with that reached by other contemporary observers. See, e.g., P. J. Bouman, G. Beijer, and S. J. Oudegeest, *The Refugee Problem in Western Germany* (Martinus Nijhoff, The Hague, 1950), p. 23 ("Every day that the distress among the refugees is continued will make it more difficult to find a solution to all their problems. [T]heir unrest is growing and their sense of inferiority is great").

109. Truman, "Special Message to Congress," March 24, 1952, p. 209.

110. Ibid., pp. 209–211.

111. Ibid., pp. 214–215.

112. Memorandum from Jack K. McFall, Assistant Secretary of State, to David P. Lloyd, "Comments of the Department of State on Draft Presidential Message to Congress Calling for a Special New Immigration Program and Aids to Iron Curtain Refugees," Paragraph 8, March 7, 1952, David D. Lloyd Collection, Box 2, File: H—Immigration, Harry S. Truman Library.

113. Ibid., Paragraph 2.

114. Ibid., Paragraph 8.

115. Mutual Security Act of 1951, Sec. 101 (a), United States Statutes-at-Large, Vol. 65, pp. 353–354 (1951).

116. Telegram from John W. Gibson, Chairman, U.S. Displaced Persons Commission, to Richard E. Neustadt, Special Assistant in the White House, n.d., David D. Lloyd Collection, Box 2, File: H—Immigration, Harry S. Truman Library.

117. L. Gerson, *The Hyphenate in Recent American Politics and Diplomacy* (University of Kansas Press, Lawrence, 1964), pp. 178–189.

118. Typical was a speech before the American Legion, delivered on August 25, 1952, in which Eisenhower said, "We must tell the Kremlin that never shall we desist in our aid to every man and woman of those shackled lands who seeks refuge with us."

119. Gen. Walter Bedell Smith, Acting Secretary of State, "President's Proposal for Admission of European Migrants," *Department of State Bulletin* 28, No. 729 (June 15, 1953), pp. 857–859.

120. Statement of Gen. Walter Bedell Smith, Acting Secretary of State, in U.S. Congress, House, Committee on the Judiciary, *Hearings: Emergency Immigration Program* (GPO, Washington, D.C., 1953), pp. 5–6.

121. Refugee Relief Act of 1953, Sec. 4, United States Statutes-at-Large, Vol. 67, pp. 401–402 (1953).

122. Ibid., Sec. 2, p. 400.

123. Rep. Walter was principal author of the House minority report opposing the Refugee Relief Act of 1953. With six of his colleagues, he argued that

[t]o superimpose this special scheme of assisted immigration upon our regular quota and non-quota immigration system means actually to destroy the principle of national origins upon which our immigration system is based.

H. Rep. No. 974, 83rd Cong., 1st Sess. (1953) ("Minority Views"), reprinted in *U.S. Code Congressional and Administrative News,* Vol. 2 (1953), p. 2121.

124. Refugee Relief Act of 1953, Sec. 11, p. 405.

125. Testimony of Scott McLeod before the Immigration Subcommittee of the Senate Committee on the Judiciary, in U.S. Congress, Senate, Committee on the Judiciary, *Hearings: Investigation into the Administration of the Refugee Relief Act* (April 13–May 27, 1955) (GPO, Washington, D.C., 1955), pp. 23–25.

126. Ibid., pp. 1–355.

127. Gerson, *The Hyphenate,* p. 219.

128. Allen Dulles, Director, CIA, March 5, 1952 in U.S. Congress, House, Committee on Foreign Affairs, *United States Foreign Policy and the East–West Confrontation,* selected executive session hearings of the Committee, 1951–1956, Vol. XIV (GPO, Washington, D.C., 1980), p. 333.

129. International Rescue Committee, *Saving Freedom's Seed Corn,* p. 24.

130. Ibid.

NOTES FOR CHAPTER 3

1. W. Corson, *The Armies of Ignorance: The Rise of the American Intelligence Empire* (Dial Press, New York, 1977), p. 347.

2. Ibid.

3. NSC 5412/1, quoted in ibid., p. 343.

4. Ibid.

5. S. Ambrose, *Ike's Spies: Eisenhower and the Espionage Establishment* (Doubleday, New York, 1981), pp. 236–37 ("liberation" rhetoric was exclusively for domestic consumption; conditions were not regarded as propitious for an uprising in Europe).

6. Immigration and Nationality Act, Sec. 212(d) (5); United States Code, Title 8, Sec. 1182(d) (5).

7. See *New York Times*, February 11, 1956, p. 6.

8. *New York Times*, January 2, 1958, p. 2, January 28, 1958, p. 5.

9. Paul Tabori, *The Anatomy of Exile* (George C. Harrap and Co., London, 1972), p. 254.

10. James A. Michener, *The Bridge at Andau* (Random House, New York, 1957), p. 288, quoting (with obvious approval) an unnamed "Hungarian sociologist."

11. Ibid., pp. 229–230.

12. Ibid., p. 230.

13. Ibid.

14. It cannot be concluded that everyone who fled Hungary in 1956 or 1957 *by that fact alone* converted themselves retroactively into refugees with a "well-founded fear of persecution." More than 6,000 Hungarians in Yugoslavia and a smaller but still significant number in Austria chose to return voluntarily to Hungary. The UNHCR played a key role in supervising this "voluntary repatriation," which, to the best of the authors' knowledge, resulted in no reprisals. Author's interview with Georges Koulischer, UNHCR, Geneva, Switzerland, March 28, 1982.

15. *New York Times*, November 24, 1956, p. 1, November 25, 1956, p. 36.

16. Anthony T. Bouscaren, *International Migrations since 1945* (Praeger, New York, 1963), p. 52.

17. Ibid.

18. *New York Times*, November 14, 1956, p. 17, November 15, 1956, p. 28, November 23, 1956, p. 3.

19. J. V. Taft, D. S. North, and D. A. Ford, *Refugee Resettlement in the U.S.: Time for a New Focus* (New TransCentury Foundation, Washington, D.C., 1979), p. 51.

20. Ibid., p. 62.

21. Ambrose, *Ike's Spies*, p. 237.

22. Ibid.

23. Ibid., p. 230.

24. Ferent Kobol, quoted in J. Michener, *The Bridge at Andau*, p. 250.

25. Ferenc Kobol, quoted in ibid., p. 251.

26. *The Nation*, June 24, 1961, p. 553.

27. Ibid., p. 554.

28. Ambrose, *Ike's Spies*, p. 240.

29. See Personal Letter, Dwight David Eisenhower—C. D. Jackson, November 19, 1956, Eisenhower Papers/DDE/Nov. '56 Misc(2), Dwight D. Eisenhower Library.

30. International Rescue Committee, *That Freedom May Not Perish* . . . (IRC) pamphlet) (1957).

31. Aaron Levenstein, *Escape to Freedom: The Story of the International Rescue Committee* (Greenwood Press, Westport, Conn., 1981), p. 54.

32. Ibid., p. 51.

33. "Hungarians to Hold Rally in Garden," *New York Times*, November 6, 1956, p. 28.

34. Levenstein, *Escape to Freedom*, p. 55.

35. Arthur A. Markowitz, "Humanitarianism v. Restrictionism: The United States and the Hungarian Refugees," *International Migration Review*, Vol. 7, No. 1 (Spring 1973), pp. 46–47, paraphrasing a White House release, November 2, 1956, reprinted in *Department of State Bulletin* 35 (November 2, 1956), p. 64.

36. Martin Bursten, *Escape from Fear* (Syracuse University Press, Syracuse, N.Y., 1958), p. 53.

37. Ibid., p. 52.

38. White House press release, *Department of State Bulletin* 35 (November 19, 1956), p. 808.

39. White House press release, ibid. (December 10, 1956), p. 913.

40. See Bursten, *Escape from Fear*, p. 54. However, Sec. 1182(d)(3) of Title 8 of the United States Code, by its explicit terms, applies only to *nonimmigrants*, not to those seeking permanent residence in the United States.

41. Section 1182(d)(5), Title 8, United States Code.

42. House Report No. 1365, 82d Cong., 2nd Sess. (1952) reprinted in 1952 *U.S. Code Congressional and Administrative News* (West Publishing Co., St. Paul, Minn., 1952), Vol. 2, p. 1706.

43. Bursten, *Escape from Fear*, p. 200.

44. Ibid., pp. 199–200.

45. "Refugee Aid Urged," *New York Times*, November 15, 1956, p. 10.

46. Ibid., November 29, 1956, p. 20.

47. Ibid., December 1, 1956, p. 10.

48. Ibid., December 3, 1956, p. 3.

49. Markowitz, "Humanitarianism," p. 50.

50. "Providing for the Needs of the Hungarian Refugees: Report to President Eisenhower by Vice-President Nixon, January 1, 1957," *Department of State Bulletin* 36 (January 21, 1957), p. 94.

51. Ibid.

52. Ibid., p. 95.

53. Markowitz, "Humanitarianism," p. 54, citing Elmo Roper, "The Americans and the Hungarian Story," *Saturday Review* 40 (May 11, 1957).

54. Markowitz, "Humanitarianism," p. 52, note 27.

55. Bursten, *Escape from Fear*, p. 200.

56. The Judiciary Committee vote is noted in ibid. at p. 201. The Nixon report,

"Providing for the Needs of the Hungarian Refugees," at p. 96, recommended the provision of "flexible authority to grant admission to this country of additional numbers of Hungarian and other refugees from communist persecution, through the use of non-quota visas within the annual ceiling." President Eisenhower, in a message to the Congress on the recommended revision of the Immigration and Nationality Act, January 31, 1957, recommended that Congress enact legislation specifically authorizing the grant of temporary parole to "escapees, selected by the Secretary of State, who have fled or in the future flee from communist persecution and tyranny." He also proposed that the number of such parole admissions be limited to "the average number of aliens who, over the past eight years, have been permitted to enter the United States outside the basic immigration system." *Department of State Bulletin* 36 (February 18, 1957), p. 248.

57. Taft, North, and Ford, *Refugee Resettlement*, p. 55.

58. Markowitz, p. 49.

59. Ibid., p. 23.

60. Ibid., p. 20 (Table 3).

61. Ibid., p. 16 (Table 1).

62. Ibid., p. 61 (Table 6).

63. Ibid., p. 23.

64. Ibid., p. 54.

65. Bursten, *Escape from Fear*, pp. 169–173.

66. Ambrose, *Ike's Spies*, p. 239.

67. William Colby and Peter Forbath, *Honorable Man: My Life in the CIA* (Simon & Schuster, New York, 1978), pp. 134–35, quoted in Ambrose, *Ike's Spies*, p. 239.

68. Roy S. Cline, *The CIA under Reagan, Bush and Casey* (Acropolis Books, Washington, D.C., 1981), pp. 205–207.

69. Steve Weissman, "Last Tangle in Tibet," *Pacific Research and World Empire Telegram*, IV, 5 (July-August 1973), pp. 5–7.

70. All figures on Cuban migration from 1959 through 1980 are estimates, compiled from a variety of sources, including Immigration and Naturalization Service *Annual Reports*, 1960–1978; Max Azicri, "The Politics of Exile: Trends and Dynamics of Political Change among Cuban-Americans," *Cuban Studies/Estudios Cubanos*, 11(2)/12(1) (July 1981–January 1982), pp. 55–73; U.S. Congress, Senate, *Report on the Refugee Act of 1980*, Senate Report No. 256, 96th Cong., 2nd Sess. (1980); and various documents of the Cuban Refugee Assistance Program, included in Carlos E. Cortes (ed.), *Cuban Refugee Programs* (Arno Press, New York, 1980).

71. Authors' interview with Wayne Smith, Washington, D.C. (May, 1983).

72. According to one source, "U.S. authorities have taken unusual steps to facilitate the entry of disaffected Cubans, even going so far as to allow the majority to enter without visas. No other potential exile group in the hemisphere has been so advantaged. If Castro's politics created the potential for mass exodus, U.S. policies

made the exodus possible." R. F. Fagen, R. A. Brody, and T. J. O'Leary, *Cubans in Exile: Disaffection and the Revolution* (Stanford University Press, Stanford, Calif., 1968), p. 102.

73. The ad hoc responses of consular and immigration officials were largely due to the lack of any formal refugee definition and special admissions bureaucracy applicable to arriving Cubans. Indicative of the government's undiscriminating approach to the Cuban migrants was the working definition of "Cuban refugee" employed by the Cuban Refugee Program when it became operational in February 1961. Under that definition, any Cuban registered at the Cuban Refugee Emergency Center in Miami who left Cuba after January 1, 1959, bearing proper identification from the Immigration and Naturalization Service and holding the status of parolee, permanent resident, or student, or granted indefinite voluntary departure, was deemed a refugee. John F. Thomas, "Cuban Refugees in the United States," *International Migration Review*, 1, 2 (1967), reprinted in Cortes (ed.), *Cuban Refugee Programs.*

74. Sources for the historical materials in this chapter on U.S.-Cuban relations include, inter alia, Hugh Thomas, *Cuba: The Pursuit of Freedom* (Harper & Row, New York, 1971); Philip W. Bonsal, *Cuba, Castro, and the United States* (University of Pittsburgh Press, Pittsburgh, 1971); John Barlow Martin, *U.S. Policy in the Caribbean: A Twentieth Century Fund Essay* (Westview Press, Boulder, Colo., 1978); Virginia Dominguez, *The Dilemma of the Caribbean Peoples in the United States* (Yale University Press, New Haven, Conn., 1975); Jorge I. Dominguez, *Cuba, Order and Revolution* (Harvard University Press, Cambridge, Mass., 1978); Lynn Darrell Bender, *The Politics of Hostility* (InterAmerican University Press, Hato Rey, Puerto Rico, 1975); Lester A. Sobel (ed.), *Castro's Cuba in the 1970's* (Facts on File, New York, 1978); and *New York Times Index*, 1959–1980.

75. Fagen, Brody, and O'Leary, *Cubans in Exile*, p. 75. Much of Cuba's professional class left Cuba in the spring of 1959, and during the first six months of 1960, ibid., p. 65 (Table 5.2). Most fitted the definition of "self-imposed political exiles" coined by Fagen, Brody, and O'Leary, since their departure was usually not attributable to direct persecution, but to the radical changes in the political, economic, and social environment of Castro's Cuba.

76. "Exile" and "Cuban refugee" have been used interchangeably from 1959 on. During the early 1960s, however, the former term predominated in newspaper accounts and was frequently linked—as it has been consistently since—with attempts to overthrow the Castro regime.

77. H. Thomas, *Cuba*, p. 1271.

78. Ibid., p. 1243.

79. Kennedy apparently arrived at this view independently of the Eisenhower administration, since prior to learning of its CIA initiatives in Cuba, he had commenced urging the arming of exiles in the United States as part of his presidential campaign.

80. The official civilian unemployment rate for the City of Miami in 1960 was 7.3 percent. U.S. Department of Commerce, *County and City Data Book, 1962*

(GPO, Washington, D.C., 1962), p. 498 (Table 6—Cities "Civilian Labor Force, 1960"). Miami newspapers indicate that the level may have approached 10% during 1961.

81. T. Voorhees, *Report to the President of the United States on the Cuban Refugee Problem* (GPO, Washington, D.C., 1961), p. 5, reprinted in Cortes (ed.), *Cuban Refugee Programs.*

82. Ibid., p. 1.

83. Resettlement and registration figures are drawn from J. Thomas, "Cuban Refugees in the United States," p. 14, Table 2. The flow estimate is a projection based on INS annual figures and estimated rates of flow.

84. A. Schlesinger, Jr., *A Thousand Days: Kennedy in the White House* (Houghton Mifflin, Boston, 1965), p. 242.

85. *Washington Post,* April 18, 1960, p. 14.

86. Speech before the American Society of Newspaper Editors, April 20, 1961, *Department of State Bulletin* 44, No. 1141 (May 8, 1961), p. 660.

87. Ibid.

88. Ibid.

89. Ibid.

90. Ibid., p. 659.

91. It was alleged by former Defense Department consultant Lowell Ponte that in 1969–1970, the CIA attempted to damage Cuba's sugar crop by means of a cloud-seeding program. *New York Times,* June 27, 1976, p. 7. In 1977, it was reported by *Newsday* that "anti-Castro terrorists had introduced African swine flu into Cuba in 1971" with at least tacit CIA approval. Sobel (ed.), *Castro's Cuba in the 1970's,* p. 131.

92. U.S. Congress, Senate, Select Committee to Study Governmental Operations with respect to Intelligence Committees, *Alleged Assassination Plots Involving Foreign Leaders: Senate Report, No. 465,* 94th Cong., 1st Sess. (1975), pp. 289–290.

93. *New York Times,* May 1, 1963, p. 11. Also see *New York Times,* April 17, 1963, p. 1.

94. The terms of that agreement, which included withdrawal of the Soviet missiles from Cuba, the termination of the American naval blockade, and U.S. "assurances against the invasion of Cuba" are contained in an exchange of letters between Chairman Nikita Khrushchev and President John. F. Kennedy on October 26 and 27, 1962. See *Department of State Bulletin,* Vol. XLVII, No. 1220 (November 12, 1962), pp. 741–743. Both letters are reprinted in D. Larson, *The Cuban Crisis of 1962* (Houghton Mifflin, Boston, 1963), pp. 155–58 and pp. 159–60.

95. George Ball, "Principles of Our Policy Toward Cuba," speech before a convention of the Omicron Delta Kappa Society, April 23, 1964, *Department of State Bulletin* 50 (May 11, 1964), p. 741.

96. See Act of August 21, 1958 (Public Law No. 700), 85th Cong., 2nd Sess., United

States Statutes-at-Large, Vol. 72; p. 699 (Hungarian adjustment of status); Act of November 2, 1966 (Public Law No. 732), 89th Cong., 2nd Sess., United States Statutes-at-Large, Vol. 80, p. 1161 (Cuban adjustment of status).

97. United States Congress, Subcommittee to Investigate Problems Connected with Refugees and Escapees, *Hearings: Cuban Refugee Problems* (GPO, Washington, D.C., 1962), p. 73, reprinted in Cortes (ed.), *Cuban Refugee Programs.*

98. Ibid.

99. Ibid.

NOTES FOR CHAPTER 4

1. Abba Schwartz, *The Open Society* (Morrow, New York, 1968), p. 170.

2. Article 33, 1951 Convention Relating to the Status of Refugees, incorporated by the 1967 Protocol Relating to the Status of Refugees.

3. For background see John Scanlan and Gilburt Loescher, "U.S. Foreign Policy, 1959–80: Impact on Refugee Flow from Cuba," *Annals of the American Academy of Political and Social Science* 467 (May 1983), pp. 116–137.

4. Schwartz, *The Open Society*, p. 170.

5. U.S. Senate, Subcommittee to Investigate Problems Connected with Refugees and Escapees of the Committee on the Judiciary, *Refugee Problem in Hong Kong and Macao*, 87th Cong., 2nd Sess. (May 29, June 7, 8, 28, and July 10, 1962).

6. See, for example, an address by Abba P. Schwartz, Administrator of the Bureau of Security and Consumer Affairs, delivered on April 3, 1964, which included the generous reception of Cubans as part of a more general, ongoing pattern of refugee resettlement promoting U.S. foreign policy and humanitarian interests. "Foreign and Domestic Implications of U.S. Immigration," *Department of State Bulletin* 36 (January 27, 1957), p. 96.

7. Law of June 28, 1962 (Public Law No. 510), 87th Cong., 2nd Sess., United States Statutes-at-Large, Vol. 76, p. 21, reprinted in [1962] *U.S. Code Congressional and Administrative News* (West Publishing Co., St. Paul, Minn., 1962), Vol. 1, pp. 153–156.

8. Senate Report No. 989, 87th Cong., 1st Sess. (1962) reprinted in ibid., p. 1792.

9. Ibid., p. 1793.

10. Ibid.

11. Ibid.

12. "Message to Congress on the Recommended Revision of the Immigration and Naturalization Act," January 31, 1957, *Department of State Bulletin* 36 (February 18, 1957), p. 248.

13. Schwartz, *The Open Society*, pp. 138–139, quoting Senator Kennedy, remarks on introduction of Senate Joint Resolution 110, *Congressional Record* 105 (June 17, 1959), p. 11014.

14. Schwartz, *The Open Society,* pp. 138–139.

15. Special message to Congress with proposals concerning changes in our immigration and nationality laws, February 8, 1956, *Public Papers of the Presidents, Dwight D. Eisenhower 1956* (GPO, Washington, D. C., 1958), pp. 240–248.

16. Ibid.

17. Ibid.

18. "Providing for the Needs of the Hungarian Refugees: Report to President Eisenhower by Vice-President Nixon, January 1, 1957," *Department of State Bulletin* 36 (January 21, 1957), p. 94.

19. Schwartz, *The Open Society,* p. 114.

20. John F. Kennedy, immigration message to Congress, July 23, 1963, *Congressional Record* 109 (July 31, 1963), p. 13769.

21. Section 1153(a)(7), Title 8, United States Code (repealed by the Refugee Act of 1980).

22. Senate Report No. 748, 89th Cong., 1st Sess. (1965), p. 17, reported in [1965] *U.S. Code Congressional and Administrative News,* Vol. 2, p. 3335. Also see House of Representatives Report No. 745, 89th Cong., 1st Sess. (1965), pp. 15–16.

23. Schwartz, *The Open Society,* p. 127.

24. Lyndon B. Johnson, "Remarks at the Signing of the Immigration Bill," Liberty Island, New York, October 3, 1965 *Public Papers of the Presidents, Lyndon B. Johnson, 1965,* Vol. II (GPO, Washington, D.C., 1966), p. 1039.

25. Authors' interview with Wayne Smith, Washington, D.C., December 1983.

26. "Memorandum of Understanding Concerning the Movement to the United States of Cubans Wishing to Live in the United States," "Third Separate Note on Political Prisoners," November 6, 1965, reprinted in House Committee on Foreign Affairs, *Hearings: Cuba and the Caribbean* (GPO, Washington, D.C., 1970), pp. 5–9.

27. Testimony of Virginia Dominguez, House Judiciary Committee, Subcommittee on Immigration, Refugees, and International Law, May 24, 1979, *Hearings on the Refugee Act of 1979,* House Report 2816 (GPO, Washington, D.C., 1979).

28. For an excellent treatment of the symbolic function of political migrations to the United States, see Silvia Pedraza-Bailey, "Cubans and Mexicans in the United States: The Functions of Political and Economic Migration," *Cuban Studies/Estudios Cubanos,* 11(2)/12(1) (July 1981–January 1982), pp. 79–97.

29. Statement of Robert A. Hurwitch, Deputy Assistant Secretary of State for Inter-American Affairs, July 8, 1970, House Committee on Foreign Affairs, *Hearings: Cuba and the Caribbean,* p. 5.

30. Arthur Goldberg, Statement before the General Assembly, December 21, 1965, *Department of State Bulletin* 50, No. 1387 (January 24, 1966), p. 128.

31. Ibid., pp. 128–129.

32. At issue was a $1 million appropriation by the UN Special Fund and the Food

and Agricultural Organization for an agricultural research station in Cuba. The United States objected continually to the grant of such technical assistance from 1961 through the spring of 1963. See Secretary of State Rusk, "U.S. Position on Special Food Project in Cuba," February 13, 1963, *Department of State Bulletin* 48, No. 1237 (March 11, 1963), p. 357.

33. For more than a year before the end of the freedom flights, it had been reported that Cuba might end them because of the economic effects of losing its professional class. See *New York Times*, December 6, 1971, p. 25.

34. Until November 2, 1966, no mechanism existed in the law "to adjust the status" of Cubans paroled into the United States to that of lawful permanent resident aliens. This situation was remedied by the passage of the Act of November 2, 1966, United States Statutes-at-Large, Vol. 80, p. 1161 (1966).

35. The legislation providing for Cuban adjustment of status required physical presence in the United States for at least two years before permanent resident status could be obtained. Ibid., Act of November 2, 1966, Sec. 1. Five years after a Cuban alien's entry into the United States, he became eligible for U.S. citizenship. See House Report No. 1978, 89th Cong., 2nd Sess. (1966), reprinted in [1966] *U.S. Code Congressional and Administrative News* (West Publishing Co., St. Paul, Minn., 1966), p. 3800.

36. See coverage of Cuban admissions issues in the *Miami Herald* for the period 1970 to 1972.

37. *New York Times*, June 26, 1971.

38. Ibid., July 10, 1970, p. 4.

39. Protocol Relating to the Status of Refugees (January 31, 1967), United Nations Treaty Series Vol. 606, p. 267.

40. The authors argue this point in greater detail in Gilburt Loescher and John Scanlan, "Human Rights, U.S. Foreign Policy, and Haitian Refugees," *Journal of InterAmerican Studies and World Affairs*, Vol. 26, No. 3 (August 1984), pp. 313–356.

41. The characteristics of the Duvalier regime have been analyzed and described in several studies. These include Matts Lundahl, *Peasants and Poverty: A Study of Haiti* (Croom-Helm, London, 1979); Robert Rotberg, *Haiti: The Politics of Squalor* (Houghton Mifflin, Boston, 1971); Robert and Nancy Heinl, *Written in Blood: The Story of the Haitian People* (Houghton Mifflin, Boston, 1978); Bernard Diederich and Al Burt, *Papa Doc: The Truth about Haiti Today* (McGraw-Hill, New York, 1969); and Leslie Manigat, *Haiti of the Sixties* (Center of Foreign Policy Research, Washington, D.C., 1964).

42. *New York Times*, February 28, 1959.

43. Heinl and Heinl, *Written in Blood*, p. 622.

44. *New York Times*, March 10 and November 21, 1975.

45. A report in 1973 by Amnesty International noted, "Haiti's prisons are still filled with people who have spent many years in detention without ever being charged

or brought to trial. Amnesty International remains seriously concerned with the continued repression of dissent in Haiti and the denial of human and legal rights. . . . The variety of torture to which the detainee is subjected is incredible. . . . In fact, those prisons are death traps . . . [and] find a parallel with the Nazi concentration camps of the past but have no present-day equivalent." *Amnesty International Report* (Amnesty International, London, 1973). In 1975, Amnesty International saw little or no improvement in the Haitian government's treatment of its citizens: "Arrests are carried out without warrants and often take the form of disappearances or kidnapping. . . . Prisones are not allowed lawyers, nor contact with their families on arrest nor—with few exceptions—are they charged or brought to trial." *Amnesty International Annual Report, 1975–1976* (Amnesty International, London, 1976).

46. This estimate is based on newspaper reprints and Congressional testimony. No comprehensive record of asylum applications, approvals, and denials existed prior to 1980, and accounts of asylum granted to Haitians by State Department personnel frequently failed to distinguish a recent record of almost universal denial from the record prior to 1973. The general accuracy of the estimate had been confirmed in authors' interviews with the INS Central Office personnel in May 1983.

47. Christopher Hanson, "Behind the Paper Curtain: Asylum Policy Versus Asylum Practice," *NYU Review of Law and Social Change,* Vol. VII, No. 107, (Winter 1978).

48. Senator Edward W. Brooke, *U.S. Foreign Assistance for Haiti,* report to the Senate Committee on Appropriations, April 1974, pp. 13–14, reprinted in U.S. House, Subcommittee on International Organizations, *Human Rights in Haiti,* 94th Cong., 1st Sess., November 18, 1975, pp. 89–90.

49. *Human Rights in Haiti,* and U.S. House, Subcommittee on Immigration, Citizenship, and International Law, *Haitian Emigration,* 94th Cong., 2nd Sess., July 1976.

50. *Haitian Emigration.*

51. Ibid., p. 1.

52. *Human Rights in Haiti,* pp. 11–12.

53. Ira Gollobin testimony, in ibid., p. 36.

54. See Dean Rusk, "Letter of Submittal to the President," July 25, 1968, reprinted in *Congressional Record* 114, (September 20, 1968), p. 27758.

55. Testimony of Larry Dawson, U.S. Congress, Senate Committee on Foreign Relations, Senate Executive Report No. 14, 90th Cong., 2nd Sess., 1968, p. 6.

56. 1951 Convention Relating to the Status of Refugees, Art. 33(1).

57. Ibid., Art. 1A(2).

58. *Human Rights in Haiti,* p. 36, referring to "The President's Message to the Senate Recommending Its Advice and Consent to the Protocol, August 5, 1968," *Weekly Compilation of Presidential Documents,* Monday, August 5, 1968, p. 1167.

59. Testimony of Leonard F. Chapman, Commissioner of the INS, *Human Rights in Haiti*, p. 17.

NOTES FOR CHAPTER 5

1. Congressional Research Service, *Human Rights and U.S. Foreign Assistance*, a report prepared for the Committee on Foreign Relations, U.S. Senate, November 1979, pp. 16–29.
2. Congressional Research Service, *U.S. Immigration Law and Policy: 1952–1979*, a report prepared for the Committee on the Judiciary, U.S. Senate, May 1979, pp. 71–78.
3. Senate Report No. 256, 96th Cong. 1st Sess. (1979), p. 6, (Table I).
4. See Sec. 1153(a)(7), Title 8, United States Code (repealed by the Refugee Act of 1980).
5. Louise Holborn, *Refugees: A Problem of Our Time: The Work of the United Nations High Commissioner for Refugees, 1951–1972* (Scarecrow Press, Metuchen, N.J., 1975), Vol. 1, pp. 516–517.
6. Ibid., p. 518.
7. The story of the British response to the Ugandans is told in Derek Humphrey and Michael Ward, *Passports and Politics* (Penguin Books, Harmondsworth, England, 1974). See pp. 40–42, 44.
8. *International Protection of Human Rights: The Work of International Organizations and the Role of U.S. Foreign Policy*, hearings before the Subcommittee on International Organizations and Movements, Committee on Foreign Affairs, House of Representatives, 93rd Cong., 1st Sess. (GPO, Washington, D.C., 1973).
9. *Human Rights in the World Community: A Call for U.S. Leadership*, report of the Subcommittee on International Organizations and Movements, Committee on Foreign Affairs, House of Representatives, 93rd Cong., 2nd Sess. (GPO, Washington, D.C., 1974).
10. Donald Fraser, "Congress's Role in the Making of International Human Rights Policy," in Donald P. Kommers and Gilburt D. Loescher (eds.), *Human Rights and American Foreign Policy* (University of Notre Dame Press, Notre Dame, Ind., 1979), pp. 247–255; and David Weissbrodt, "Human Rights Legislation and U.S. Foreign Policy," *Georgia Journal of International and Comparative Law*, 7 (1977), pp. 231–287.
11. See U.S. House, Committee on Foreign Affairs, Subcommittee on Europe, *Denial of Human Rights to Jews in the Soviet Union*, 92nd Cong., 1st Sess., May 17, 1971, pp. 34–35, 37–39, 42–45.
12. Ibid., p. 42.
13. U.S. House, Committee on Foreign Affairs, Subcommittee on Europe, *Soviet Jewry*, 92nd Cong., 1st Sess., November 9 and 10, 1971, pp. 21–22.

14. U.S. House, *Denial of Human Rights to Jews in the Soviet Union*, p. 2.

15. Statement of Rep. Edward Koch on the floor of the Congress, March 4, 1971.

16. U.S. House, *Soviet Jewry*, p. 44.

17. See Robert O. Freedman (ed.), *Soviet Jewry in the Decisive Decade: 1971–1980* (Duke University Press, Durham, N.C., 1984).

18. For background see Paula Stern, *Water's Edge: Domestic Politics and the Making of American Foreign Policy* (Greenwood Press, Westport, Conn., 1979), and William Korey, "Jackson-Vanik and Soviet Jewry," *Washington Quarterly*, Winter 1984, pp. 116–128.

19. U.S. House, *Soviet Jewry*, pp. 295–300.

20. Ibid.

21. Ibid., pp. 34–35.

22. U.S. House, Committee on Foreign Affairs, Subcommittee on State Department Organization and Foreign Operations, *Department of State Authorization for Fiscal Year 1973*, 92nd Cong., 2nd Sess., March 1972; Comptroller General of the United States, *U.S. Assistance Provided for Resettling Soviet Refugees*, June 20, 1977.

23. *American Jewish Yearbook 1973* (American Jewish Committee, New York, 1974), p. 218.

24. William Safire, *Before the Fall* (Doubleday, New York, 1975), p. 575.

25. Ibid., p. 451.

26. For background to the Jackson amendment and the U.S. and Soviet response to this legislation see Stern, *Water's Edge*; Korey, "Jackson-Vanik"; Freedman (ed.), *Soviet Jewry*; Henry Kissinger, *White House Years* (Little, Brown, Boston, 1979); and Richard Nixon, *RN: The Memoirs of Richard Nixon* (Grosset & Dunlap, New York, 1978).

27. See Stern, *Water's Edge*, and Russell Warren Howe and Sarah Hays Trott, *The Power Peddlers* (Doubleday, New York, 1977), pp. 225–270.

28. For background, see the Amnesty International report *Chile* (AI Publications, London, 1974). See generally the record of a hearing before the Senate Judiciary Committee's Subcommittee to Investigate Problems Connected with Refugees and Escapees entitled *Refugee and Humanitarian Problems in Chile, Part 2*, 93rd Cong., 2nd Sess., July 23, 1974, and hearings before the House Committee on Foreign Affairs Subcommittees on Inter-American Affairs and on International Organizations and Movements entitled *Human Rights in Chile*, 93rd Cong., 2nd Sess., December 7, 1973, and May 7, 23, and June 11, 12, and 18, 1974. The United Nations Commission on Human Rights and the Inter-American Commission on Human Rights also visited Chile on fact-finding missions and found gross violations of human rights.

29. *General Policy for Dealing with Requests for Asylum by Foreign Nationals*, hearings before the Subcommittee on Immigration, Citizenship, and International Law of the House Committee on the Judiciary, 93rd Cong., 1st Sess., (1973), p. 295.

30. Seymour Hersh *The Price of Power* (Summit Books, New York, 1983).

31. U.S. Senate, Judiciary Committee, Subcommittee to Investigate Problems Connected with Refugees and Escapees, *Refugee and Humanitarian Problems in Chile, Part 1*, 93rd Cong., 1st Sess. (1973), p. 24.

32. See T. Farer, "The Inter-American Commission: A Personal Assessment," *Center Magazine*, May/June 1984, pp. 39–40.

33. See *Congressional Record* 119 (September 25, 1973), pp. 31444–31445.

34. C. Hanson, "Behind the Paper Curtain: Asylum Policy Versus Asylum Practice," *NYU Review of Law and Social Change*, Vol. VII, No. 107 (Winter 1978), p. 111.

35. The following account of the activity of the international agencies and the U.S. response to the Chilean refugee crisis is based on the authors' interviews with James Carlin, Director, Office of Refugee and Migration Affairs, Department of State, 1975–1978, and Director of ICEM, 1978 to the present, Geneva, June 1983; Roberto Kojak, ICEM Chief of Mission, Chile, Geneva, June 1983; Lissen Schou, ICEM, Chile, Geneva, June 1983; R. Jerrell, ICEM, Geneva, June 1983; Gretchen Brainard, ICEM, Washington, D.C., March 1983; Oleg Haselman, UNHCR, Latin America, Geneva, March and June 1983; Jose Zalaquett, Amnesty International, London, July 1983; and Judy Chavchavdze, Bureau of Refugee Programs, Department of State, Washington, D.C., March 1983).

36. Authors' interview with Jerrell.

37. Authors' interview with Kojak.

38. U.S. Senate, Judiciary Committee, Subcommittee to Investigate Problems Connected with Refugees and Escapees, *Refugees and Humanitarian Problems in Chile, Part 3*, 94th Cong., 1st Sess., October 2, 1975, pp. 24–27.

39. Authors' interview with Kojak.

40. Hanson, "Behind the Paper Curtain," p. 113.

41. U.S. Senate, *Refugee and Humanitarian Problems in Chile, Part 3*," pp. 38–39.

42. Ibid., pp. 28–29.

43. Authors' interview with Chavchavdze.

44. Public Law 93–189, December 17, 1973, Sec. 35.

45. Public Law 94–559, December 30, 1974, Sec. 25.

NOTES FOR CHAPTER 6

1. Authors' interview with Louis Weisner, former Director of Office of Refugee and Migration Affairs (1973–1975), Washington, D.C., November 1983.

2. Authors' interview with Ambassador John Gunther Dean, Bangkok, Thailand, January 1984.

3. Letter referred to in ibid. and quoted in William Shawcross, *Sideshow: Kissinger, Nixon and the Destruction of Cambodia* (Simon & Schuster, New York, 1979), p. 362.

4. See "La Guerre Est Finie," *Newsweek,* May 5, 1975, pp. 22–29.

5. The only systematic survey conducted on the causes and characteristics of the massive movement of refugees out of the central and northern regions of South Vietnam that were overrun by the Communist forces in late March and early April 1975 is Le Thi Que, A. Terry Rambo, and Gary D. Murfin, "Why They Fled: Refugee Movement During the Spring 1975 Communist Offensive in South Vietnam," *Asian Survey,* 16, No. 9 (September 1976), pp. 855–863.

6. For an account of the collapse of military resistance in the highlands and the chaotic evacuation from Da Nang, see Arnold Isaacs, *Without Honor: Defeat in Vietnam and Cambodia* (Johns Hopkins University Press, Baltimore, 1983), pp. 342–379.

7. The following account of the U.S. evacuation is based on *Refugees from Indochina,* hearings before the Subcommittee on Immigration, Citizenship, and International Law of the Committee on the Judiciary, U.S. House of Representatives, 94th Cong., 1st and 2nd Sess., April 8, 9, 14, May 22, July 17, 22, October 8, December 8, 1975, and *Aftermath of War: Humanitarian Problems of Southeast Asia,* staff report prepared for the Subcommittee to Investigate Problems Connected with Refugees and Escapees, Committee on the Judiciary, U.S. Senate, 94th Cong., 2nd Sess., May 17, 1976 (GPO, Washington, D.C., 1975 and 1976, respectively). Related General Accounting Office reports include *Review of Preliminary Estimates of Evacuation Costs, Temporary Care, and Resettlement Costs of Vietnamese and Cambodian Refugees,* May 1975; *U.S. Provides Safe Haven for Indochinese Refugees,* June 1975; and *Evacuation and Temporary Care Afforded Indochinese Refugees: Operation New Life,* June 1976. See also the accounts given in Frank Snepp, *Decent Interval* (Random House, New York, 1979); Gail Paradise Kelly, *From Vietnam to America* (Westview Press, Boulder, Colo., 1977); Arnold Isaacs, *Without Honor;* and authors' interviews with Lionel Rosenblatt, Sheppard Lowman, and Hank Cushing, Washington, D.C., December 1982 and November 1983.

8. See the President's Address Delivered Before a Joint Session of the Congress, April 10, 1975, *Weekly Compilation of Presidential Documents,* Vol. 11, No. 15, pp. 359–364.

9. The Interagency Task Force had representation from the Departments of State and Defense, the CIA, and the Joint Chiefs of Staff.

10. The President's News Conference of April 3, 1975, *Weekly Compilation of Presidential Documents,* Vol. 11, No. 14, p. 328.

11. Ibid., p. 328.

12. House Committee on the Judiciary, *Refugees from Indochina,* 94th Cong., 1st Sess., April 8, 1975, pp. 1–66.

13. The first planeload of 243 Vietnamese orphans and 62 adults crashed shortly after takeoff and everyone was killed.

14. Letter quoted in Tizano Terzani, *Giai Phong! The Fall and Liberation of Saigon* (St. Martin's Press, New York, 1976), p. 43.

15. Snepp, *Decent Interval*, p. 274.

16. See the President's News Conference of April 3, 1975, *Weekly Compilation of Presidential Documents*, Vol. 11, No. 14, pp. 327–330, and the President's Address Delivered Before a Joint Session of Congress, April 10, 1975, *Weekly Compilation of Presidential Documents*, Vol. 11, No. 15, pp. 359–364.

17. Senate Judiciary Committee, Subcommittee to Investigate Problems Connected with Refugees and Escapees; *Hearings: Indochina Evacuation and Refugee Problems: Part II, The Evacuation*, 94th Cong., 1st Sess., April 15, 25, and 30, 1975, and *Indochina Evacuation and Refugee Problems: Part IV, Staff Reports Prepared for the Use of the Subcommittee*, 94th Cong., 1st Sess., June 9 and July 8, 1975, pp. 1–2; House Committee on the Judiciary, *Refugees from Indochina*, April 14, 1975, pp. 139–186.

18. Snepp, *Decent Interval*, p. 293.

19. Authors' interviews with Gilbert Jaeger, January 1985, and UNHCR officials in New York, Geneva, and Bangkok, 1983 and 1984.

20. House Committee on the Judiciary, *Refugees from Indochina*, April 14, 1975, pp. 148, 149, 175, 177–185.

21. Testimony of Secretary of State Henry Kissinger, Appropriations Committee, House of Representatives, April 1975.

22. Nguyen Van Thieu, Saigon Radio broadcast announcing his resignation as President of South Vietnam, April 21, 1975.

23. CBS News Interview, April 21, 1975, *Weekly Compilation of Presidential Documents,* Vol. 11, No. 17, pp. 415–417.

24. *New York Times*, April 24, 1975, p. 34.

25. As a result, the Senate Judiciary Committee's Subcommittee to Investigate Problems Connected with Refugees and Escapees was later to report, "The record is clear that there has been little relationship between the categories of Vietnamese targeted for evacuation and parole into the U.S. and the refugees now under U.S. control." See *Indochina Evacuation and Refugee Problems: Part IV*, p. 2.

26. Authors' interviews with Sheppard Lowman and Hank Cushing. See also Snepp, *Decent Interval.*

27. Senate Committee on the Judiciary, *Indochina Evacuation and Refugee Problems*, June 9 and July 8, 1975, p. 5.

28. Snepp, *Decent Interval*, pp. 473–474.

29. The first of four U.S. refugee camps to open was Camp Pendleton, California, on April 29, 1975. Fort Chaffee, Arkansas, quickly followed, opening May 2. Then came Eglin Air Force Base, Florida, May 4, and Fort Indiantown Gap, Pennsylvania, May 28.

30. See Kelly, *From Vietnam to America*, p. 40.

31. Vietnam Humanitarian Assistance and Evacuation Bill, May 1, 1975, *Weekly Compilation of Presidential Documents*, Vol. 11, No. 18, p. 474.

32. Remarks of the President upon Signing Executive Order 11860 Establishing the

Committee on Refugees from Southeast Asia, May 19, 1975, ibid., No. 21, pp. 531–532.

33. Cited in David Binder, "House, 246 to 162, Bars $327 Million for Refugee Aid," *New York Times*, May 25, 1975, p. 17.

34. President's Advisory Committee on Indochina Refugees, Executive Order 11860, May 19, 1975, *Weekly Compilation of Presidential Documents*, Vol. 11, No. 21, p. 532.

35. Indochina Migration and Refugee Assistance Act of 1975, United States Code, Title 22, Section 2601.

36. House Committee on the Judiciary, *Refugees from Indochina*, May 22, 1975, pp. 205–216.

37. Ibid.

38. "The New Americans, Are They Welcome? A Refugee Referendum," *Gallup Opinion Index*, Report No. 119 (May 1975), pp. 2–5.

39. "Vietnamese Refugees Find Starting Anew Is a Frustrating Ordeal," *Wall Street Journal*, May 22, 1975, p. 1.

40. Douglas E. Kreeland, "Wide Hostility Found as First Exiles Arrive," *New York Times*, May 2, 1975.

41. Drummond Ayres, Jr., "Official Assures Arkansas over Impact of Refugees," *New York Times*, May 2, 1975.

42. See, for example, the remarks of Representatives Eilberg, Cohen, and Russo in House Committee on the Judiciary, *Refugees from Indochina*, May 22, 1975, pp. 205–216.

43. Julia Taft, David North, and David Ford, *Refugee Resettlement in the U.S.: Time for a New Focus* (New TransCentury Foundation, Washington, D.C., 1979), p. 107.

44. See testimony of Julia Taft in House Committee on the Judiciary, *Refugees from Indochina*, July 17, 1975, pp. 228–247.

45. Authors' interview with Julia Taft, Washington, D.C., April 1983.

46. See the testimony of voluntary agency officials in House Committee on the Judiciary, *Refugees from Indochina*, July 22, 1975, pp. 313–406. Also see authors' interview with Wells Klein, New York, April 1983.

47. Taft, North, and Ford, *Refugee Resettlement in the U.S.*, p. 109.

48. Darrel Montero, *Vietnamese-Americans: Patterns of Resettlement and Socio-Economic Adaptation in the United States* (Westview Press, Boulder, Colo., 1979); Darrel Montero and Judith McDowall, "Refugees: Making It," *New York Times*, March 12, 1979; Senate Committee on the Judiciary, *Humanitarian Problems of Southeast Asia, 1977–78*, 95th Cong., 2nd Sess., March 1978, pp. 20–38; Robert and Jennifer Bach, "An Employment Profile of Southeast Asian Refugees in the United States," *Monthly Labor Review*, October 1980; Comptroller General of the United States, *Domestic Resettlement of the Indochinese Refugees: Struggle for Self-Reliance* (GAO, Washington, D.C., May 10, 1977).

49. Authors' interviews with UNHCR officials in Geneva, June 1983 and 1984.

50. Authors' interview with M. Bijleveld, UNHCR Resettlement Officer in Thailand 1975–1977, Geneva, June 1983.

51. Authors' interview with Julia Taft, Washington, D.C., April 1983, and authors' interview with George Gordon-Lennox, UNHCR Representative on Guam, Washington, D.C., December 1982. See also Interagency Task Force for Indochinese Refugees, *Report to the Congress*, December 15, 1975, pp. 13–15.

NOTES FOR CHAPTER 7

1. See Jean and Simone Lacouture, *Vietnam voyage a travers une victoire* (Seuil, Paris, 1976), and Theodore Jacqueney, "Vietnam's Gulag Archipelago," *New York Times*, September 17, 1976.

2. Interviews with David McAree, Amnesty International, London, August 1983; William Shawcross, London, July 1983; and Vietnam Desk Officer, U.S. Department of State, Washington, D.C., March 1979. See also Nguyen Long with Harry H. Kendall, *After Saigon Fell: Daily Life under the Communists* (Institute of East Asian Studies, University of California at Berkeley, 1981), and *Report of an Amnesty International Mission to the Socialist Republic of Vietnam*, June 1981.

3. The description of events in Laos is based on authors' interviews with Martin Barber, UNHCR official in Laos and Thailand from 1973–1981, London, July and August 1983, and on Martin Stuart-Fox (ed.), *Contemporary Laos* (University of Queensland Press, London, 1983).

4. This account of U.S. policy during 1976–1978 is based on authors' interviews with Sheppard Lowman, Hank Cushing, and Lionel Rosenblatt, Washington D.C., December 1982 and November 1983.

5. *Refugees from Indochina*, hearings before Subcommittee on Immigration, Citizenship, and International Law of the Committee on the Judiciary, House of Representatives, 94th Cong., 2nd Sess., February 5, 1976, pp. 507–570.

6. See U.S. Congress, Joint Economic Committee, *Indochinese Refugees: The Impact on First Asylum Countries and Implications for American Policy* (GPO, Washington, D.C., 1980).

7. See for example, Henry Kamm, "Thais Returning Refugees to Laos, Sometimes to Official Mistreatment," *New York Times*, February 18, 1978.

8. For a Malaysian view of the Vietnamese boat people see Zakaria Haji Ahmad, "Vietnamese Refugees and ASEAN," *Contemporary Southeast Asia*, Vol. 1 (May 1979), pp. 66–74.

9. *The Indochinese Exodus: A Humanitarian Dilemma*, a GAO report (GAO, Washington, D.C., April 24, 1979); *Refugees from Indochina: Current Problems and Prospects*, a report submitted by a Congressional delegation to Southeast Asia, December 28, 1978, to January 13, 1979, under the auspices of the Subcommittee on Asian and Pacific Affairs, Committee on Foreign Affairs, U.S. House of Representatives, 96th Cong., 1st Sess., April 30, 1979. Also see authors' interviews with UNHCR officials in Geneva, New York, and Bangkok, 1983 and 1984.

10. Authors' interviews with Gilbert Jaeger, former Director, UNHCR Division of Protection, January 1985, and with UNHCR officials in Geneva, New York, and Bangkok, 1983 and 1984.

11. Authors' interviews with George Warren, Jr., of ICEM, former official in the Office of Refugee and Migration Affairs, Department of State, Geneva, April and June 1983.

12. Authors' interviews with Martin Barber, former UNHCR official in Laos and Thailand, London, July and August 1983; Jacques Cuenod, former UNHCR representative in Laos, Geneva, June 1983; Zia Rizvi, former UNHCR Regional Coordinator, Thailand, New York, January 1983; M. Biljeveld, former UNHCR resettlement officer, Thailand, Geneva, June 1983; Nick Morris, former UNHCR official in Thailand, Geneva, June 1983.

13. Authors' interview with Sheppard Lowman, Washington, D.C., November 1983.

14. Authors' interview with John Crowley, Bangkok, January 1984.

15. Robert DeVecchi, *Indochinese Parole Program Situation Report* (International Rescue Committee, New York, November 25, 1977).

16. This effort resulted in a new parole on July 15, 1977, for 15,000 Indochinese, including 7,000 "boat cases."

17. Authors' interview with Sheppard Lowman, Washington, D.C., November 1983.

18. Ibid.

19. Authors' interview with Leo Cherne, New York, March 1983.

20. Leo Cherne, *A Personal Recollection* (International Rescue Committee, New York, undated).

21. The Citizens' Commission on Indochinese Refugees was composed of Cherne; William Casey, former Under Secretary of State for Economic Affairs; Monsignor John Ahearn, Catholic Archdiocese of New York; Rabbi Marc Tanenbaum, American Jewish Committee; John Richardson, President, Freedom House; Mrs. Thelma Richardson; Bayard Rustin, President, Philip Randolph Institute; James Michener, author; Professor Kenneth Caulten, Colgate Rochester Divinity School; Cecil Lyon, former Ambassador to Chile and Sri Lanka; Stephen Young, law professor; and Robert DeVecchi and Louis Weisner of the International Rescue Committee.

22. Cherne, *A Personal Recollection.*

23. Testimony of John Ahearn and Bayard Rustin before Subcommittee on Immigration, Citizenship, and International Law of the Committee on the Judiciary, U.S. House of Representatives, March 1, 1978.

24. There was some resentment on the part of blacks to the admission of Indochinese, who were perceived as competitors for jobs, housing, and social services, especially in the New Orleans area. See, in particular, "Vietnamese Take Jobs from Blacks is Charge," *Times-Picayune,* April 14, 1978; "Jobs, Housing Taken by

Viets, Blacks Charge," *States-Item,* April 14, 1978; and "Vietnamese in Middle of Job, Relocation Dispute," *Louisiana Weekly,* April 15, 1978.

25. "Black Americans Urge Admission of the Indochinese Refugees," *New York Times,* March 19, 1978.

26. Authors' interview with John Crowley, Bangkok, January 1984.

27. Bernard Gwertzman, "New Policy Approved to Admit Indochinese—25,000 Are Expected to Enter U.S. in Year under Interim Rules," *New York Times,* March 31, 1978.

28. Unpublished letter from Leo Cherne to members of Citizens' Commission on Indochinese Refugees, July 12, 1978, p. 5, in authors' files.

29. See Amnesty International, *Submission to the Government of the Socialist Republic of Vietnam on Amnesty International's Current Concerns,* April 1983, p. 6.

30. Those fears quickly reached Washington. See unpublished State Department cable, Morton Abramowitz, "Socialist Transformation in South Vietnam," August 1978, in authors' files.

31. B. Wain, *The Refused: The Agony of the Indochinese Refugees* (Simon & Schuster, New York, 1981), gives a good account of this activity.

32. See *Refugees from Indochina: Current Problems and Prospects,* April 30, 1979.

33. *Washington Star,* January 2, 1979.

34. *Wall Street Journal,* December 30, 1978.

35. Authors' interview with Ambassador Morton Abramowitz, Washington, D.C., December 1982.

36. A typical effort to portray Vietnam in this light was made by Deputy Assistant Secretary of State for East Asian and Pacific Affairs Robert Oakley in testimony before Congress: "The people who are leaving Vietnam today are not victims of the war. They are victims of an ideology and a society that these people no longer want to remain within." House Committee on Foreign Affairs, Subcommittee on Asian and Pacific Affairs, *Indochinese Refugees,* 96th Cong., 1st Sess., May 22, 1979, p. 25.

37. See, for example, *Refugees from Indochina: Current Problems and Prospects,* April 30, 1979; *The Indochinese Refugee Situation, August 1979,* 96th Cong., 1st Sess., September 16, 1979.

38. See a letter in authors' files from Senators Byrd and Bayh and sixteen others to President Carter, September 14, 1978. The U.S. had voted no on several World Bank loans to Vietnam in 1978, including loans for irrigation projects which would have assisted "needy people" in Vietnam.

39. See Assistant Secretary Richard Holbrooke's testimony in House Committee on Foreign Affairs, Subcommittee on Asian and Pacific Affairs, *Indochinese Refugees,* June 13, 1979.

40. See G. J. L. Coles, UNHCR "Background Paper for the Asian Working Group on the International Protection of Refugees and Displaced Persons," December 1982, p. 21, in authors' files.

41. Ibid., p. 22.

42. *New York Times*, June 25, 1979.

43. Ibid., July 2, 1979.

44. House Committee on Foreign Affairs, Subcommittee on Asian and Pacific Affairs, *Indochinese Refugees*, May 22, 1979.

45. Authors' interview with Sheppard Lowman, November 1983.

46. Cited in *New York Times*, May 24, 1979.

47. House Committee on Foreign Affairs, Subcommittee on Asian and Pacific Affairs, *Indochinese Refugees*, May 22, 1979.

48. *Time*, July 9, 1979, pp. 28–32.

49. Cited in Wain, *The Refused*, p. 262.

50. Coles, "Background Paper," pp. 30–31.

51. Bruce Grant, *The Boat People* (Penguin Books, London, 1979) and Wain, *The Refused*.

NOTES FOR CHAPTER 8

1. Unclassified telegram from Joseph Sureck, INS District Director, Hong Kong, to INS Washington, D.C., April 7, 1981, pp. 10–13, in authors' files.

2. Anthony Paul and John Barron, *Murder of a Gentle Land* (Reader's Digest Press, Pleasantville, N.Y., 1977); Francois Ponchaud, *Cambodge Année Zero*, (Julliard, Paris, 1977).

3. See William Shawcross, *The Quality of Mercy* (Simon & Schuster, New York, 1984), pp. 65–67.

4. Ibid.

5. Joel Brinkley, "Living the Cambodian Nightmare," *Louisville Courier-Journal*, December 2, 1979, pp. 1–4.

6. Leo Cherne, "Into a Dark Bottomless Hole," appeal to the Board of Trustees of Freedom House, June 17, 1975.

7. See Shawcross, *The Quality of Mercy*, for a discussion of the lack of response to the mass murder in Cambodia.

8. Authors' interviews with William Shawcross, London, July 1983.

9. Authors' interviews with Leo Cherne and Robert DeVecchi, New York, January and April 1983.

10. Ibid.

11. See "Secretary Schultz's Proposed Refugee Admissions for FY 1986," statement before the Subcommittee on Immigration and Refugee Policy of the Senate Judiciary Committee, September 17, 1985, reprinted in *Current Policy* 738, U.S. Department of State, Washington, D.C., p. 4.

12. See for example, Eilberg's comments in *Admission of Refugees into the United States*, Subcommittee on Immigration, Citizenship, and International Law of the House Judiciary Committee, 95th Cong., 1st Sess., February 24, March 3, April 22, 1977. Elizabeth Holtzman, Chairman of the House Subcommittee on Immigra-

tion, Refugees, and International Law at the time of the passage of the 1980 Refugee Act, argued that the use of parole limited the capacity of Congress to oversee refugee admissions and believed that "any new legislation should clearly define what part Congress will play in refugee decision-making, and that role should not be a pro forma one." U.S. Congress, House of Representatives, *Hearings Before the Subcommittee on Immigration, Refugees, and International Law of the Committee on the Judiciary, House of Representatives, Ninety-sixth Congress, First Session, on H.R. 2816, Refugee Act of 1979*, p. 2. Attorney General Griffin Bell agreed, acknowledging that the use of the parole authority "has the practical effect of giving the Attorney General more power than the Congress in determining the limits on the entry of refugees into the country." U.S. Library of Congress, Congressional Research Service, *Review of U.S. Refugee Resettlement Programs and Policies* (GPO, Washington, D.C., 1980), p. 42.

13. Senator Kennedy, *Congressional Record*, Vol. 125, No. 30 (March 13, 1979), p. 52633, fn. 1.

14. On March 22, 1979, President Carter announced the formation of the Select Commission as required by the legislation that created it (Public Law 94–412).

15. Wiliam Korey, "Jackson-Vanik and Soviet Jewry," *Washington Quarterly*, Winter 1984, pp. 116–128.

16. Foreign Assistance and Related Programs Appropriations Act, 1979 (Public Law 95–481).

17. Norman L. Zucker, "Refugee Resettlement in the United States: Policy and Problems," *Annals of the American Academy of Political and Social Science*, Vol. 467 (May 1983), pp. 172–186.

18. Authors' interview with Dick Clark, Washington, D.C., March 1983. Clark also lobbied for a more comprehensive and orderly refugee program. *Hearings . . . on H.R. 2816, Refugee Act of 1979*, p. 42.

19. Refugee Act of 1980, March 17, 1980, (Public Law 96–212).

20. Authors' interviews with Lionel Rosenblatt, Washington, D.C., December 1982. See also Shawcross, *The Quality of Mercy*, and Linda Mason and Roger Brown, *Rice, Rivalry, and Politics* (University of Notre Dame Press, Notre Dame, Ind., 1983).

21. Authors' interview with Martin Barber, former UNHCR official in Thailand, London, July 1983.

22. The archives of the Cambodia Crisis Center were made available to the authors at the Center for Civil and Human Rights at the University of Notre Dame.

23. Authors' interviews with Morton Abramowitz, Washington, D.C., December 1982, and Sheppard Lowman, Washington, D.C., November 1983.

24. Authors' interviews with Morton Abramowitz and Lionel Rosenblatt.

25. Letter to Prime Minister Kriangsak Chamanand, from Stephen Solarz and other Congressmen, June 5, 1979.

26. Authors' interviews with Morton Abramowitz and Lionel Rosenblatt.

27. Authors' interviews with Martin Barber, Morton Abramowitz, William Shawcross, and Lionel Rosenblatt, December 1982; Mark Malloch-Brown, UNHCR, Geneva, June 1983; and numerous UNHCR and volag staff in Geneva and Bangkok, June 1983 and January and June 1984. See also Shawcross, *The Quality of Mercy.*

28. Authors' interview with Morton Abramowitz.

29. Authors' interviews with Lionel Rosenblatt, Martin Barber, and John Crowley.

30. The activities of the Khmer Emergency Group are described in Shawcross, *The Quality of Mercy*, and Mason and Brown, *Rice, Rivalry, and Politics.*

31. Shawcross, *The Quality of Mercy.*

32. KEG internal document, November 6, 1979 as cited in Mason and Brown, *Rice, Rivalry, and Politics*, p. 101.

33. "What to Do?" Abramowitz cable to Department of State, Washington, D.C., November 26, 1979.

34. Authors' interview with Morton Abramowitz.

35. Authors' interviews with Morton Abramowitz, Lionel Rosenblatt, Hank Cushing, and Sheppard Lowman.

36. Authors' interview with John Crowley.

37. *The Indochinese Refugee Situation: August 1979*, report of a Study Mission of the U.S. House of Representatives, September 16, 1979, pp. 15–16.

38. Unpublished document in authors' files.

39. October 1, 1979, letter reproduced in *Congressional Record*, October 18, 1979, p. E5146.

40. "Deathwatch: Cambodia," *Time*, November 12, 1979, pp. 42–48.

41. Authors' interviews with Morton Abramowitz, Lionel Rosenblatt, Martin Barber, Zia Rizvi, John Crowley, and Sheppard Lowman.

42. Ibid.

43. Authors' interview with Lionel Rosenblatt.

44. Authors' interview with Zia Rizvi.

45. Authors' interviews with Lionel Rosenblatt, Morton Abramowitz, and Sheppard Lowman.

46. Authors' interview with John Crowley.

47. Authors' interviews with Morton Abramowitz and Lionel Rosenblatt.

48. Authors' interviews with Frank Loy, Washington, D.C., March 1983, and Victor Palmieri, San Francisco, Calif., Feburary 1983.

49. Authors' interviews with Zia Rizvi, Martin Barber, and Mark Malloch-Brown.

50. Unpublished letter to the Citizens' Commission from Leo Cherne, "Re: Cambodian Developments II," October 13, 1980, p. 2, in authors' files.

51. Authors' interview with Richard Smyser, Geneva, June 1984.

52. Cited in Shawcross, *The Quality of Mercy.*

53. See, in particular, Joint Economic Committee, *Indochinese Refugees;* Milton Osborne, "The Indochinese Refugee Situation: A Kampuchean Case Study," in Charles A. Price (ed.), *Refugees: The Challenge of the Future,* Academy of the Social Sciences in Australia, Fourth Academy Symposium, November 3–4, 1980, pp. 31–75; and Martin Barber, "Resettlement of Indochinese in 1981–82," UNHCR internal memorandum, Bangkok, April 22, 1981.

54. Barber, "Resettlement of Indochinese," cover note by A. J. F. Simmance, UNHCR Regional Representative for Western South Asia, to R. Sampatkumar, Chief, South and Southeast Asia Regional Section, UNHCR Headquarters, Geneva.

55. Sureck's letter is quoted in an unclassified telegram cited above from Sureck to INS Washington, D.C., April 7, 1981, pp. 10–13.

56. Ibid., pp. 4–5.

57. Don Bonker, "New U.S. Refugee Policy Needed Badly," *Washington State Teamster's Magazine* (n.d.), reprinted in *Congressional Record* 126 (June 12, 1980), pp. 14578–14579.

NOTES FOR CHAPTER 9

1. See Gilburt Loescher and John Scanlan, "Human Rights, U.S. Foreign Policy, and Haitian Refugees," *Journal of InterAmerican Studies and World Affairs,* Vol. 26, No. 3 (August 1984), pp. 313–356, and Naomi Zucker, "The Haitians Versus the United States: The Courts as Last Resort," *Annals of the American Academy of Political and Social Science,* Vol. 467 (May 1983), pp. 151–162.

2. This is dealt with in detail in Gilburt Loescher and John Scanlan, *Human Rights, Power Politics, and the International Refugee Regime: The Case of U.S. Treatment of Caribbean Basin Refugees,* World Order Studies Occasional Papers Series, No. 14, Princeton University, 1985.

3. See Golden Neary, "Refugees Denied Asylum," *In These Times,* February 17–23, 1982. This statistic is borne out in estimates for later periods supplied by Senator Kennedy's office and the INS.

4. Authors' interview with asylum officer in the State Department, Washington, D.C., May 18, 1980.

5. Lars Schoultz, *Human Rights and U.S. Policy Toward Latin America* (Princeton University Press, Princeton, N.J., 1981).

6. Presidential Review Memorandum/NSC 28: Human Rights, August 15, 1977, pp. 27–28, in authors' files.

7. Ibid., p. 28.

8. Authors' interview with Eugene Eidenberg, Deputy Assistant to President Carter for Intergovernmental Affairs, Washington, D.C., March 14, 1983.

9. See G. D. Loescher and John A. Scanlan, *U.S. Foreign Policy and Its Impact on Refugee Flow from Haiti*, N.Y.U. Center for Latin American and Caribbean Studies Occasional Papers, No. 42, April 1984.

10. *Washington Post*, August 16, 1977, pp. A1, A12.

11. Schoultz, *Human Rights*, p. 64.

12. Sen. Edward Brooke, U.S. Senate, Committee on Appropriations, *Review of Factors Affecting U.S. Diplomatic and Assistance Relations with Haiti*, 95th Cong. 2nd Sess., November 15, 1977.

13. U.S. Congress, House Committee on International Relations and Senate Committee on Foreign Relations, *Country Reports on Human Rights Practices*, submitted by the Department of State, February 3, 1978, pp. 172–176.

14. "Haitians Who Fled to U.S. Suing for Asylum as Political Refugees," *New York Times*, October 17, 1976.

15. "101 Haitian Refugees Pose Painful Problem for U.S.," *New York Times*, September 1, 1977.

16. *The Haitians in Miami: Current Immigration Practices in the United States* (Lawyers Committee for International Human Rights, New York, 1978), and Ronald Copeland and Patricia Weiss Fagen, *Political Asylum: A Background Paper on Concepts, Procedures and Problems*, Refugee Policy Group paper, Washington, D.C., December 1982.

17. Ibid.

18. *Haitian Refugee Center v. Civiletti*, Vol. 503, p. 442, Federal Supplement (Southern District Florida 1980). (Affirmed Vol. 676, p. 1023, Federal Reporter, 2nd Series [11th Circuit Court of Appeals 1982].)

19. Ibid.

20. Ibid., pp. 513–514.

21. Ibid., p. 451.

22. Ibid., p. 508.

23. Raymond Morris, INS District Director for Miami, believed that the halting of deportation acted as a "magnet." See U.S. Congress, Joint Select Commission on Immigration and Refugee Policy, *Miami Regional Hearing*, 1980, p. 18, unpublished, on file at Center for Civil and Human Rights, University of Notre Dame, Notre Dame, Indiana.

24. For a detailed account of this incident see Michael Hooper, *Violations of Human Rights in Haiti* (Lawyers Committee for International Human Rights, New York, 1980), pp. 29–32. Also see *Amnesty International Annual Report 1980;* "Haitian Migration to the U.S.," *Department of State Bulletin*, August 1980, pp. 77–78; and Alex Stepick, *Haitian Refugees in the U.S.*, Minority Rights Group Report No. 52, London, January 1982. Apparently the Haitian government has never conducted an inquiry into this incident, and no one has been charged with any crimes in connection with the violent actions of these security forces.

25. U.S. Congress House Committee on International Relations and Senate Committee on Foreign Relations, *Country Reports on Human Rights Practices,* submitted by the Department of State, February 5, 1980, p. 341.

26. *Violations of Human Rights in Haiti, June 1981–September 1982: A Report to the Organization of American States* (Lawyers Committee for International Human Rights, New York, November 1982).

27. Cited in Michael Leapman, "Haiti Boat People Are America's Newest Problem," *The Times* (London), March 12, 1980.

28. See *Congressional Record,* Vol. 126 (daily edition, April 21, 1980), p. 53961. In January 1980, the U.S. had refused to accept as refugees a number of Haitian journalists expelled from Haiti for clearly political reasons.

29. As cited in Mario A. Rivera, "The Cuban and Haitian Influxes of 1980 and the American Response: Retrospect and Prospect," in *Caribbean Migration,* House Subcommittee on Immigration, Refugees, and International Law, 96th Cong., 2nd Sess., June 17, 1980, p. 300.

30. *Caribbean Migration,* p. 210.

31. House Report No. 608, 96th Cong., 1st Sess. (1979), p. 1.

32. Senate Rep. No. 256; 96th Cong., 1st Sess. (1979).

33. Actually no limit is placed on the admission of "asylees" under the act, although a limit of 5,000 is placed on the number of asylees permitted to adjust their status to that of "permanent resident" in any given year.

34. Authors' interviews with Victor Palmieri, San Francisco, February 1983, and Ronald Copeland, Washington, D.C., May 1981. Victor Palmieri also shared with us the prologue to his unpublished manuscript on U.S. refugee policy during his tenure as U.S. Coordinator for Refugee Affairs.

35. "Castro Would Free 3000," *New York Times,* November 23, 1978, p. 7.

36. "Remarks by President Carter at Commemoration of Universal Declaration of Human Rights," December 6, 1978, *Weekly Compilation of Presidential Documents,* Vol. 14, No. 49 (December 11, 1978), p. 2163.

37. *New York Times,* November 25, 1978, p. 25. The reluctance of Attorney General Bell to move quickly on the processing of Cuban political prisoners was confirmed in authors' interview with Doris Meisner, INS, Washington, D.C., May 16, 1983.

38. The phrase is from a speech made by Fidel Castro in December 1979. The speech is quoted and analyzed in Rivera, "The Cuban and Haitian Influxes of 1980," p. 291.

39. Authors' interviews with Victor Palmieri, San Francisco, February 1983, Ronald Copeland, Washington, D.C., May 1981, and Eugene Eidenberg, Washington, D.C., March 14. 1983.

40. Ibid.

41. Authors' interviews with Wayne Smith, Washington, D.C., November 1982,

Miles Ferchette, Washington, D.C., May 1981, and Phil Chicola, Washington, D.C., March 1983.

42. *New York Times*, April 6, 1980, p. 4.

43. "Commissioners Join Cry for U.S. to Accept Cubans," *Miami Herald*, April 7, 1980, p. 8A (quoting the mayor as saying, "Either we admit [the Cubans] or we take down the Statue of Liberty").

44. "Sea Lift from Cuba to Key West," *Newsweek*, May 5, 1980, p. 59.

45. Cited in Elizabeth Hull, *Without Justice for All: The Constitutional Rights of Aliens* (Greenwood Press, Westport, Conn., 1985), p. 4.

46. U.S. Congress, *Country Reports on Human Rights Practices*, February 5, 1980, pp. 291–297.

47. Speech before the American Society of Newspaper Editors, April 10, 1980, in *Public Papers of the Presidents: Jimmy Carter, 1980* (GPO, Washington, D.C., 1981), Vol. 1, p. 642.

48. Authors' interviews with Wayne Smith, Miles Ferchette, Phil Chicola, and Victor Palmieri.

49. Ronald Copeland, "The Cuban Boatlift of 1980: Strategies in Federal Crisis Management," *Annals of the American Academy of Political and Social Science*, May 1983, pp. 138–150.

50. "League of Women Voters—Remarks and a Question-and-Answer Session," *Compilation of Presidential Documents*, Vol. 16 (May 5, 1980), pp. 828, 835.

51. "Cuban Refugees: White House Announcement of Federal Actions in Response to the Emergency," May 2, 1980, ibid., Vol. 1, p. 819.

52. "Coast Guard Shepherding Cubans from Danger to Succor: Small Boat Armada Depends on 'Mothering' by Cutters," *Christian Science Monitor*, May 8, 1980.

53. "The Cuban Tide Is a Flood," *Newsweek*, May 19, 1980, p. 29, and "Open Heart, Open Arms," *Time*, May 19, 1980, p. 14.

54. Copeland, *The Cuban Boatlift of 1980*, pp. 138–150.

55. Ibid. and authors' interview with Eugene Eidenberg.

56. Authors' interviews with State Department and INS officials, Washington, D.C., May 18–19 and August 12–13, 1980.

57. Authors' interviews with officials of the Department of Health and Rehabilitative Services of Florida, in Tallahassee and Miami, Florida, June 1982.

58. Authors' interviews with Victor Palmieri and Eugene Eidenberg.

59. Announcement of Victor H. Palmieri, U.S. Coordinator of Refugee Affairs, June 20, 1980.

60. Letter from Senator Kennedy, May 20, 1980, to President Carter, reprinted in *Congressional Record* 126 (June 26, 1980), pp. 26436–26437.

61. Refugee Education Assistance Act of 1980 (Public Law 96–422), 94 Stat. 1799, 1809.

NOTES FOR CHAPTER 10

1. Ronald W. Reagan "Acceptance Speech," Detroit, Michigan, July 17, 1980, reported in *New York Times*, July 18, 1980, p. 8.

2. President Ronald W. Reagan, "High Seas Interdiction of Illegal Aliens," Executive Order No. 12324, September 29, 1981, *Federal Register*, Vol. 46, p. 48109 (1981).

3. "Congress Grapples with Immigration Issues," *Congressional Quarterly Almanac*, Vol. XXXVII (1981), Congressional Quarterly, Inc., Washington, D.C., 1982, pp. 423–424.

4. Secertary of State George Schultz, "Proposed Refugee Admissions for FY 1986," September 17, 1985, reprinted in United States Department of State, *Current Policy 738*, Washington, D.C., 1985, p. 1.

5. See Nadine Cohodas, "Refugee Entries Up in 1984; Same Level Expected in 1985," *Congressional Quarterly Weekly Report*, Vol. 42 (December 8, 1984), p. 3077 (Table—"United States Refugee Admissions, Fiscal Year 1981–85").

6. Motives for Haitian flight are treated in Lawyers Committee for International Human Rights, *A Report to the OAS Organization of American States: Violations of Human Rights in Haiti, June, 1981–September, 1982* (Lawyers Committee for International Human Rights, New York, 1982). Additional details were provided in authors' interview with Michael H. Hooper and Mark Murphy, February 1982.

7. Motives for Salvadoran departure are treated in Sid L. Mohn, "Central American Refugees: The Search for Appropriate Responses," in U.S. Committee for Refugees, *1983 World Refugee Survey* (United States Committee for Refugees, New York, 1983), pp. 42–47. A fuller account will appear in Patricia Weiss Fagen and Sergio Aguayo, *Fleeing the Maelstrom: Central American Refugees* (Westview Press, Boulder, Colo., forthcoming).

8. Motives for Guatemalan departure are treated in United Nations, Economic and Social Council, *Situation of Human Rights in Guatemala, with Note by the Secretary General*, General Assembly A/38/485, November 4, 1983. Also see Mohn, "Central American Refugees," pp. 43–44.

9. Authors' interviews with O. Hasselman, Director of Europe and the Americas Division, UNHCR, Geneva, Switzerland, June 1983, and H. Taviani, UNHCR representative to France, Paris, July 1984.

10. See Heritage Foundation, "Are United Nations Camps Cheating Refugees in Honduras?" *Backgrounder No. 368*, Washington, D.C., July 23,1984; also see International Council of Voluntary Agencies (ICVA), "Consultations on Central American refugees and Mexico," series of mimeographed reports on ICVA–UNHCR discussions of Central American refugee situation, Geneva, Switzerland, 1982–1984.

11. For a description of Mexican border police practices, see Elizabeth Ferris, "The Politics of Asylum: Mexico and the Central American Refugees," *Journal of In-*

terAmerican Studies and World Affairs, Vol. 26, No. 3 (August 1984), pp. 368–370.

12. Ibid., p. 368.

13. Ibid., p. 373 (estimating sixty-eight incursions into camps on Mexican territory by 1983).

14. See "Murder by Deportation," *Washington Monthly*, February 1984, p. A-12 (estimating Salvadoran population in U.S. at 300,000). Also see estimate of 250,000 to 400,000 Salvadorans in U.S. as of August 1982, in Mohn, "Central American Refugees," p. 43.

15. When the Congress enacted the Refugee Act of 1980, it explicitly announced its intention of bringing United States practice in line with prevailing international practice. See House Report No. 781, 96th Cong., 2nd Sess. (1981), p. 20; and Senate Report No. 256, 96th Cong., 1st Sess. (1979), p. 4.

16. See Schultz, "Proposed Refugee Admissions," p. 4 (reserving refugee admission slots for 1,800 Cuban political prisoners and their families).

17. President Ronald W. Reagan, "High Seas Interdiction of Illegal Aliens," Proclamation No. 4865, September 29, 1981, *Federal Register*, Vol. 46, p. 48107 (1981).

18. Art Harris, "Boatlift Bloat Sends Angry Florida Officials into Tropical Politics," *Washington Post*, December 22, 1981, p. A-7 (reporting "State Visits" to President François Duvalier of Governor Graham and Lieutenant Governor Hixon in September 1981, demanding cessation of Haitian emigration).

19. See United States Department of State, "Country Reports on the World Refugee Situation," Mimeographed reports sent to Congress with proposed refugee allocations in 1980, 1981, 1982, and 1983. Also see United States Congress, House Committee on International Relations and Senate Committee on Foreign Relations, *Country Reports on Human Rights Practices*, submitted by the Department of State and published annually.

20. Speech, June 2, 1982, reprinted in *Department of State Bulletin*, Vol. 82, No. 2066 (September 1982), p. 44.

21. "Haig Fears Exiles from Latin America May Flood the U.S.," *New York Times*, February 23, 1982, p. A1.

22. "Central America: Defending our Vital Interests," address before a joint session of Congress, April 27, 1983, reprinted in *Department of State Bulletin*, Vol. 83, No. 2075 (June 1983), p. 4.

23. Speech before a Republican fund-raising dinner, Jackson, Mississippi, June 20, 1983.

24. For a discussion of the new detention policy and the litigation surrounding it, see Thomas Aleinikoff and David Martin, *Immigration: Process and Policy* (West Publishing Co., St. Paul, Minn., 1985), pp. 302–314.

25. Ibid.

26. Ibid.

27. *INS Report: Asylum Applications for Fiscal Year 1982*, cited in I. Kurzban, "A Critical Analysis of Refugee Law," *University of Miami Law Review*, Vol. 36 (September 1982), p. 873, n. 45.

28. Authors' interviews with UNHCR officials, Washington, D.C., and Geneva, Switzerland, November 1983 and January and March 1985.

29. Authors' interview with Joachim Henkel, UNHCR, Washington, D.C., 1985.

30. Authors' interviews with UNHCR officials, Washington, D.C., March 1985.

31. Cited in William Shawcross, *The Quality of Mercy: Cambodia, the Holocaust and Modern Conscience* (Simon & Schuster, New York, 1984), pp. 326–327.

32. Ibid., pp. 326–327.

33. "Refugee Law Violated," *The Guardian* (Manchester, England), December 10, 1981.

34. Authors' interviews with UNHCR officials in Geneva, June 1983 and January 1985, and in Washington, D.C., March 1985.

35. Ibid.

36. "Report of United Nations High Commissioner for Refugees Mission to Monitor INS Asylum Processing of Salvadoran Illegal Entrants—September 13–18, 1981," reprinted in *Congressional Record*, February 11, 1982, pp. S827–S831.

37. Ibid., p. S831.

38. Authors' interviews with UNHCR staff in Geneva, January 1985, and Washington, D.C., March 1985.

39. Authors' conversations with Senator Allen Simpson, Chairman, Subcommittee on Immigration and Refugee Policy, Senate Judiciary Committee, and with Arnold Leibowitz, Special Counsel to the Subcommittee, October 1981.

40. See House Report No. 783, 97th Cong., 2nd Sess. (1982), p. 12 (House directs the Coast Guard to examine "the cost and effectiveness of the Coast Guard's Haitian refugee interdiction program," makes no recommendation that program be discontinued, and imposes no special restrictions on expenditure of "interdiction" funds).

41. The principal legislation considered since 1982 has been the "Immigration Reform and Control Act," otherwise known as the "Simpson-Mazzoli bill." The Senate passed an early version of the bill, S. 2222, on August 17, 1982, but the House failed to follow suit. On May 18, 1983, the Senate passed a slightly amended version of the bill, S. 529. The House failed to act during 1983 but passed its own version of the bill, H.R. 1510, on June 20, 1984, by a five-vote margin. Attempts to reconcile substantial differences between the two measures in conference failed. See "Immigration Reform Dies at Session's End," *Congressional Quarterly Almanac*, Vol. XL (1984), Congressional Quarterly, Inc., Washington, D.C., 1985, pp. 229–238. New legislation, sponsored by Senator Simpson and Representative Rodino, Chairman of the House Judiciary Committee, was introduced early in 1985.

42. Several provisions in the House bill expanding on the procedural rights of asylum seekers, including the right of aliens apprehended at the border to obtain legal counsel and an administrative hearing when claiming asylum and the right of rejected asylum seekers to bring "class action" lawsuits challenging a pattern or practice of due process violations in asylum processing, were deleted in June 1984. Ibid., p. 232. In their final 1984 forms, both the House and Senate versions of the bill limited the availability of judicial review to asylum seekers, but gave those immigration officers adjudicating asylum claims greater independence from the Department of State.

43. According to Alienikoff and Martin, *Immigration,* p. 469, "extended voluntary departure" status has been granted at one time or another to aliens from Cuba, Chile, Vietnam, Lebanon, Ethiopia, Uganda, Nicaragua, Iran, Afghanistan, and Poland. At present, Ugandans are the only nationality not under Communist domination who are granted extended voluntary departure status.

44. Act of November 22, 1983 (Department of State Authorization), United States Statutes-at-Large, Vol. 97, p. 1062 (1983) (declaring "sense of the Congress" that Salvadorans in the United States since January 1, 1983, be granted "extended voluntary departure" status).

45. *Jean* v. *Nelson,* Supreme Court Reporter, Vol. 472 (1985).

46. Authors' interviews with voluntary agency personnel, New York and Washington, D.C., April–June 1983.

47. Authors' interviews with Wells Klein, American Council for Nationalities Service, May 1983 and William Shawcross, July 1983.

48. Memorandum from Leo Cherne, Chairman, Citizens' Commission on Indochinese Refugees, to Alexander Haig, Secretary of State, February 9, 1981.

49. Ibid., p. 2.

50. Secretary of State Alexander Haig, "Statement to ASEAN Ministers," Manila, June 20, 1981, *Department of State Bulletin,* Vol. 81 (August 1981), p. 40.

51. Letter of President Reagan to Rep. Peter Rodino, "Proposed Refugee Admissions, Fiscal Year 1982," September 21, 1981, reprinted in *Congressional Record* 127 (daily edition November 18, 1981), p. 48543.

52. Letter of Representatives McClory, Fish, and Rodino to President Reagan, September 30, 1981, reprinted in ibid., p. 48545.

53. Letter of Representative Mazzoli to President Reagan, September 30, 1981, reprinted in ibid., p. 48545.

54. McClory, Fish, and Rodino letter.

55. Authors' interviews with refugee resettlement officials, voluntary agency personnel, and members of the local press, Orange County, Calif., February 1983.

56. Martin Barber, "Resettlement of Indochinese in 1981–82," UNHCR internal memorandum, Bangkok, April 22, 1981.

57. Ibid., p. 10.

58. Ibid., cover note by A. J. F. Simmance, UNHCR Regional Representative for

Western South Asia, to R. Sampatkumar, Chief, South and Southeast Asia Regional Section, UNHCR Headquarters, Geneva.

59. *Congressional Record*, 127, July 22, 1981, p. S8194.

60. United States Department of Justice, Office of Legal Counsel, memorandum "Re-Interpretation of the Refugee Act of 1980," reprinted in U.S. House of Representatives Judiciary Committee, Subcommittee on Immigration, Refugees, and International Law, *Oversight Hearings*, 97th Cong., 1st Sess., September 16, 17, and 23, 1981, pp. 24–31.

61. *Oversight Hearings*, p. 68.

62. Ibid., p. 54.

63. Statement by Ambassador Jeanne J. Kirkpatrick, U.S. Permanent Representative to the United Nations, on September 29, 1981 in ibid., p. 67. These arguments closely paralleled those being made by the Citizens' Commission on Indochinese Refugees.

64. Authors' interview with Sheppard Lowman, Washington, D.C., November 1983.

65. U.S. House, Committee on Foreign Affairs, Subcommittee on Asian and Pacific Affairs, *United States Policy Toward Indochina since Vietnam's Occupation of Kampuchea*, 97th Cong., 1st Sess., October 15, 21, and 22, 1981, pp. 201–221.

66. Ibid., p. 221. Also authors' interview with Sheppard Lowman, Washington, D.C., November 1983.

67. U.S. Congress, *Country Reports on Human Rights Practices*, February 1982.

68. See, for example, Gail Sheehy, "Cambodian Refugees: America's Double Cross," *Washington Post*, February 6, 1983, p. 85; *Refugee Reports*, Vol. 4, No. 2 (January 28, 1983).

69. National Security Council, Directive No. 93, "Refugee Policy and Processing Refugees from Indochina," May 13, 1983, in authors' files.

70. U.S. Department of Justice, INS, "Worldwide Guidelines for Overseas Refugee Processing," July 1983.

71. *New York Times*, September 23, 1984, Sec. VI, p. 44.

72. Ibid., December 13, 1984, Sec. I., p. 6.

73. Schultz, "Proposed Refugee Admissions," p. 1.

74. Testimony of James N. Purcell, Director of Bureau of Refugee Programs, before the Subcommittee on Immigration, Refugees, and International Law of the House Judiciary Committee, April 17, 1985, reprinted in "Refugee Assistance: Overseas and Domestic," United States Department of State, *Current Policy 693*, Washington, D.C., 1985.

75. Secretary of State George Schultz, "America and the Struggle for Freedom," address before the Commonwealth Club of California, February 22, 1985, United States Department of State, *Current Policy 659*, Washington, D.C., 1985, pp. 4, 5.

76. Ibid., p. 2.
77. Ibid., p. 1.
78. Ibid., p. 2.
79. U.S. Catholic Conference *UPDATE: Newsletter of Migration and Refugee Services,* Vol. 85, No. 10 (October 31, 1985), pp. 1–2.
80. Joint statement of voluntary agencies, "Indochinese Refugees: A Burden or an Opportunity?" in ibid., pp. 12–14.
81. Schultz, "Proposed Refugee Admissions," p. 4.

NOTES FOR CHAPTER 11

1. As established in 1965, the annual immigration quota—which was initially applicable only to the Eastern Hemisphere—was 170,000. See Section 115(a) of Title 8 of the *United States Code* (1965–1968 Supplement No. IV). This figure was not all-inclusive, since thousands of "immediate relatives" of American citizens were admissible each year as "non-quota" immigrants. The much more inclusive Eastern Hemisphere quota under the old National Origins Quota System was determined on a country-by-country basis, and totalled approximately 155,000. See Presidential Proclamation No. 2980, July 2, 1952 in *Federal Register,* vol. 17, p. 6019 (July, 1952).

2. Prior to its repeal in 1980, Section 1153(a)(7) of Title 8 of the *United States Code* (1965–1968 Supplement No. IV)—the so-called "seventh preference"—reserved 6 percent of the annual immigration quota for refugees who met its definitional criteria. See note 6, below.

3. Section 21 of the 1965 Immigration Amendments established a commission to examine the merits of bringing Western Hemisphere migrants within the quota system for the first time in American history. Act of October 3, 1965, *United States Statutes-at-Large,* vol. 79, pp. 920–21 (1965). Following the affirmative recommendation of that Commission, a separate Western Hemisphere Quota of 120,000 was created in 1968.

4. See notes 1 and 2, above.

5. Eastern and Western Hemisphere Quotas were amalgamated in 1978 and the visa-preference system (including the "seventh preference") was made applicable to the entire world. See Public Law No. 412, 95th Cong., 2d Sess., *United States Statutes-at-Large,* vol. 92, p. 907 (1978).

6. Prior to its repeal in 1980, Section 1153(a)(7) of Title 8 of the *United States Code* (1965–1968 Supplement no. IV) made refugee admission slots available to individuals who

> because of persecution or fear of persecution on account of race, religion or political opinion . . . have fled (I) from any Communist or Communist-dominated country or area, or (II) from any country in the general area of the Middle East.

Another provision of Section 1153(a)(7) permitted the issuance of refugee visas to "persons uprooted by catastrophic natural calamity as defined by the President." The Middle Eastern provision was never used to bring significant members of refugees to the United States, and the "catastrophic natural calamity" provision was never used at all.

7. According to Senate Report No. 256, 96th Cong., 1st Sess. (1979), p. 6 (Table 1—"Historical Summary of Refugee Parole Actions"), 692,219 Cubans had been paroled into the United States prior to July, 1979.

8. See INA Section 207(d) and (e), codified in Title 8, Section 1157(d) and (e), *United States Code* (1982 ed.)

9. Institutional concerns about preserving Congressional Immigration authority held much of the debate in 1965 about the possible restriction of the President's parole authority. See Chapter 4, supra, pp. 72–74. Also see Senate Report No. 748, 89th Cong., 1st Sess. (1965), p. 17 and House of Representatives Report No. 745, 89th Cong., 1st Sess. (1965), pp. 15–16.

10. INA Section 101 (a)(42), codified in Title 8, Section 1101 (a)(42), *United States Code* (1982 ed.).

11. See INA Section 208 and 243(h), codified in Title 8, Sections 1158 and 1253(h), *United States Code* (1982 ed.) (defining the process of granting "asylum" or "withholding of deportation" to aliens who reach American territory and demonstrate that they meet the refugee definition or produce convincing evidence that their "life or freedom would be threatened" if returned).

12. For the final Fiscal Year 1986 allocation figures, see Presidential Determination No. 85–21, October 16, 1985, reprinted in *Congressional Record*, 131 (October 29, 1985 daily ed.), pp. H9308–H9309.

13. See Secretary of State George Schultz, "Proposed Refugee Admissions for FY 1986", Department of State, Bureau of Public Affairs, *Current Policy* No. 738 (1985), pp. 1, 4.

14. Statement of Michael Posner, Executive Director, Lawyers Committee for International Human Rights in Peter I. Rose (ed.), *Working with Refugees* (Proceedings of the Simon S. Shargo Memorial Conference) (Center for Migration Studies, New York, 1985), p. 36.

15. Arthur C. Helton, "Second Class Refugees," *New York Times*, April 2, 1985, Section 1, p. 27.

16. Letter of Romano L. Mazzolli to President Ronald Reagan, September 27, 1985, in *Congressional Record*, 131 (October 29, 1985 daily ed.), p. H9308.

17. See, e.g., "Flight to Freedom," *Newsweek*, April 28, 1980, pp. 1, 38–40.

18. "League of Women Voters, Remarks and a Question-and-Answer Session," May 5, 1980, in *Public Papers of the Presidents, Jimmy Carter, 1980–81*, Washington, D.C., GPO, vol. I, p. 642.

19. *New York Times*, January 23, 1985, p. 24; January 24, 1985, p. 10; March 29, 1985, p. 6; June 16, 1985, p. 35.

Bibliography

ARCHIVAL MATERIALS

Cambodia Crisis Center. University of Notre Dame. Notre Dame, Ind.
   Collected Papers
Citizens' Commission for Indochinese Refugees. New York.
   Collected Papers
John F. Kennedy Library. Boston, Mass.
   President's Office Files
   National Security Files
Dwight D. Eisenhower Library. Abilene, Kans.
   ACW Diary Collection
   Cabinet Collection
   DDE Collection
   International Collection
   C. D. Jackson Papers
Harry S. Truman Library. Independence, Mo.
   David D. Lloyd Collection
   Charles Hulten Collection
   Official Files
   Harry N. Rosenfield Papers
   George Warren Papers

Seeley Mudd Library. Princeton, N.J.
  Allen Dulles Papers
  John Foster Dulles Papers
National Security Council Policy Paper Files. National Archives. Washington, D.C.
  Record Group 273

INTERVIEWS

Morton Abramowitz (formerly U.S. Ambassador to Thailand), Washington, D.C., December 1982.

M. Acosta (INS Inspector, Refugee Processing Center, Miami, Fla.), Miami, Fla., August 1980.

Ada Adler (Department of State, Office of U.S. Coordinator for Refugee Affairs), Washington, D.C., January 1983.

Jim Anderson (formerly Joint Voluntary Agency staff, Ban Thai Samart), Ban Thai Samart, Thailand, January 1983.

Ross Anderson (formerly Joint Voluntary Agency, Hong Kong), Hong Kong, January 1983.

J. Anvar (UNHCR, Geneva, Switzerland), Geneva, Switzerland, June 1983.

Larry Arthur (State Department, Bureau of Human Rights and Humanitarian Affairs, Asylum Officer), Washington, D.C., May 1980.

Diego Ascencio (Consular Affairs, Department of State), South Bend, Ind., May 1984.

Christopher Avery (Amnesty International Legal Department), London, England, June 1983.

Martin Barber (British Refugee Council, formerly UNHCR, Bangkok, Thailand, and Vientiane, Laos), London, England, July and August 1983.

Michel Barton (UNHCR, Geneva), Geneva, June 1983.

Robert Beckham (Department of State, Haiti desk officer), Washington, D.C., May 1980.

Peter Bell (Carnegie Endowment, formerly assistant to Joseph Califano, Department of Health, Education, and Welfare), Washington, D.C., January 1983.

Linda Berkowitz (Department of Health and Human Services), Miami, Fla., June 1982.

A. W. Bijleveld (formerly UNHCR, Thailand), Geneva, Switzerland, June 1983.

Gretchen Brainard (Intergovernmental Committee on Migration, Washington Office), Washington, D.C., January, 1983.

Stan Breen (American Refugee Committee, Minneapolis), Washington, D.C., December 1982.

Richard Brown (Department of State, Central American Affairs, Deputy Director), Washington, D.C., May 1980.

Jessie Bunch (Indochinese Refugee Action Center), Washington, D.C., March 1983.

Robert Burrows (UNHCR, Bangkok, Thailand), Bangkok, Thailand, January 1983.

James Carlin (Director, Intergovernmental Committee for Migration, Geneva, Switzerland, and formerly Department of State, Director, Office of Refugees and Migration Affairs, Washington, D.C.), Geneva, Switzerland, March and June 1983.

David Carliner (attorney), Washington, D.C., August 1980.

Margaret Carpenter (Department of State, Office of U.S. Coordinator for Refugee Affairs), Washington, D.C., May 1980.

Tom Casey (Federal Emergency Management Agency), Washington, D.C., May 1981.

Judy Chavchavdze (State Department, Bureau of Refugee Programs), Washington, D.C., March 1983.

Leo Cherne (Chairman, International Rescue Committee and Citizens' Commission for Indochinese Refugees), New York, April 1983.

Philip Chicola (Department of State, Bureau of Refugee Programs), Washington, D.C., January and March 1983.

Dick Clark (formerly U.S. Coordinator for Refugee Affairs), Washington, D.C., March 1983.

Joseph Coleman (Department of State, Office of U.S. Coordinator for Refugee Affairs), Washington, D.C., January 1983.

G. D. L. Coles (UNHCR, Legal Protection Division), Geneva, Switzerland, January 1985.

Roger Conner (Federation for American Immigration Reform), Washington, D.C.

Alexander Cook (formerly Minority Counsel, Senate Subcommittee on Immigration and Refugee Policy), Washington, D.C., August 1980.

Alicia Cooper (International Rescue Committee, Orange County, Calif.,), Santa Ana, Calif., February 1983.

Ronald Copeland (formerly Office of the U.S. Coordinator for Refugee Affairs), Washington, D.C., May 1981.

Simon Cornwall (formerly Commission for Coordination of Services to Displaced Persons in Thailand), Bangkok, Thailand, January 1983.

John Crowley (Joint Voluntary Agency, Refugee Program, U.S. Embassy, Bangkok, Thailand), Bangkok, Thailand, January 1984.

J. Cuenod (formerly UNHCR, Laos), Geneva, Switzerland, June 1983.

John Cullen (Director, Orderly Departure Program, Bangkok, Thailand), Bangkok, Thailand, January 1984.

Susan Cuming (formerly UNHCR Resettlement Officer, Bangkok, Thailand), Bangkok, Thailand, January 1984.

Hank Cushing (Department of State, Bureau of Refugee Programs), Washington, D.C., January 1983, and Geneva, Switzerland, April 1983.

G. Da Cunha (UNHCR, Geneva, Switzerland), Geneva, Switzerland, June 1984.

Martin Danziger (INS Central Office, Washington, D.C.), Washington, D.C., June 1980.

Fletcher Davis (Pastor, St. Anselm's Episcopal Church, Garden Grove, Calif.), Garden Grove, Calif., February 1983.

Larry Dawson (formerly Department of State, Office of Refugees and Migration Affairs), Washington, D.C., June 1980. (Interview by Gracia Berg.)

John Gunther Dean (formerly U.S. Ambassador to Thailand and Cambodia), Bangkok, Thailand, January 1983.

Dale Dehaan (Immigration and Refugee Program, Church World Service, formerly Deputy High Commissioner for Refugees, UNHCR, Geneva, and aide to Sen. Edward Kennedy), New York, December 1982.

Robert DeVecchi (International Rescue Committee, Indochina desk), New York, January and November, 1983.

Josh DeWind (formerly Center for Migration Studies, Columbia University), New York, November 1982.

Joan Edwards (UNHCR staff at Phanat Nikhom Processing Center), Phanat Nikhom, Thailand, January 1984.

Eugene Eidenberg (Carter White House staff for domestic affairs), Washington, D.C., March 1983.

Michael Eiland (INS Central Office, Washington, D.C.), Washington, D.C., May 1983.

Phyllis Eisen (Zero Population Growth), Washington, D.C., December 1982.

Arthur P. Enders (Counsel House Subcommittee on Immigration, Refugees, and International Law), Washington, D.C., May 1983.

Tom Farer (formerly InterAmerican Commission on Human Rights), Princeton, N.J., November 1982.

Klaus Feldman (formerly UNHCR, New York and Chief, Resettlement Section, Geneva), South Bend, Ind., September 1980, and Geneva, Switzerland, June 1984.

Jack Fortner (formerly, INS Director, Bangkok, Thailand), Hong Kong, January 1983.

Mark Franken (U.S. Catholic Conference), Washington, D.C., May 1983.

Myles Frechette (formerly Department of State, Cuban desk officer), Washington, D.C., May 1981.

Dennis Gallagher (Refugee Policy Group), Washington, D.C., November 1982.

Pierce Gerrety, Jr. (UNHCR, Geneva, Switzerland), Geneva, Switzerland, March 1983.

Guy Goodwin-Gill (UNHCR, Americas desk), Geneva, Switzerland, June 1984 and January 1985.

George Gordon-Lennox (UNHCR Liaison Office, Washington, D.C.), Washington, D.C., December 1982.

Mark Graham (International Refugee Integration Resource Center), Geneva, Switzerland, March and June 1983.

Mary Jo Groterrath (formerly Select Commission on Immigration and Refugee Policy), Washington, D.C., May 1980.

Thomas Hammar (Swedish Commission on Immigration Research), Stockholm, Sweden, April 1983.

Malcom Harper (OXFAM), Oxford, England, July 1983.

Peter Harris (Far Eastern Service, BBC, formerly OXFAM Regional Director for Kampuchea), London, England, August 1983.

Oleg Haselman (formerly UNHCR, Latin America Regional Representative and head Americas and Europe Division, Geneva, Switzerland), Geneva, Switzerland, March and June 1983.

Michael Heilman (Assistant General Counsel, Immigration and Naturalization Service), Washington, D.C., May 1983.

Joachim Henkel (UNHCR, Washington, D.C., formerly UNHCR, North America desk, Geneva, Switzerland), Geneva, Switzerland, March and June 1983, Washington, D.C., November 1983 and March 1985.

Nguyen Van Hiep (Vietnamese refugee, Phanat Nikhom Processing Center), Phanat Nikhom, Thailand, January 1983.

Donald Hohl (Migration and Refugee Services, U.S. Catholic Conference), Washington, D.C., April 1980.

Michael Hooper (National Emergency Coalition for Haitian Refugees), New York, April 1983.

James Howell (State of Florida, Department of Health and Rehabilitative Services), Tallahassee, Fla., June 1982.

D. Eric Hultman (U.S. Senate, Judiciary Committee, minority staff), Washington, D.C., August 1980.

Beverly Hunter-Curtis (Refugee Coordinator, Orange County, Calif.), Santa Ana, Calif., February 1983.

Dolores Irwin (journalist, *Santa Ana Register*), Santa Ana, Calif., February 1983.

Ivor Jackson (UNHCR, Legal Protection Division), Geneva, Switzerland, January 1985.

Gilbert Jaeger (formerly UNHCR Director of Protection and Assistance), Brussels, Belgium, August 1984, and Zeist, Netherlands, January 1985.

R. Jerrell (Intergovernmental Committee for Migration, Geneva, Switzerland), Geneva, Switzerland, March and June 1983.

Doug Johnson (formerly Ethnic Affairs Officer, Ban Thai Samart), Ban Thai Samart, Thailand, January 1983.

J. Wilson Kaan (World Relief, Hong Kong), Hong Kong, January 1984.

C. K. Kalumiya (UNHCR Legal Protection Division and formerly UNHCR Liaison Office, Washington, D.C.), Geneva, Switzerland, January 1985.

John R. Kelly (formerly UNHCR, New York), New York, March 1980.

Mirza Hussein Khan (formerly, UNHCR representative, Khao-I-Dang refugee camp), Khao-I-Dang, Thailand, January 1983.

James King (INS Inspector, Refugee Processing Center, Miami, Fla.), Miami, Fla., August 1980.

Harry Klajbor (INS Central Office, Washington, D.C.), Washington, D.C., June 1980.

Wells Klein (American Council for Nationalities Service), New York, May 1983.

Roberto Kojak (Intergovernmental Committee on Migration, Chile), Geneva, Switzerland, June 1983.

David Kornbluth (formerly Department of State, Refugee Officer, Hong Kong), Hong Kong, January 1983.

G. Koulischer (UNHCR, Geneva, Switzerland), Geneva, Switzerland, March and June 1983.

F. Krenz (UNHCR Legal Protection Division), Geneva, Switzerland, June 1983.

R. Krug (State Department, Bureau of Refugee Programs), Washington, D.C., December 1982.

Dan Larson (Joint Voluntary Agency staff, Lutheran Immigration and Refugee Service, Hong Kong), Hong Kong, January 1983.

Arnold Leibowitz (U.S. Senate Judiciary Committee, staff aide) Washington, D.C., February 1983.

Robert Lombardo (State of Florida, Department of Health and Rehabilitative Services), Tallahassee, Fla., June 1982.

Ellen Lutz (Amnesty International USA), Washington, D.C., May 1980.

K. Lyonette (UNHCR, Geneva, Switzerland), Geneva, Switzerland, June 1983.

Michael Malloy (Canadian Mission, Geneva, Switzerland) Geneva, Switzerland, March 1983 and June 1984.

Richard Marshall (U.S. Attorney's Office, Civil Division, Miami, Fla.), Miami, Fla., August 1980.

David Martin (formerly Department of State, Bureau of Human Rights and Humanitarian Affairs), Washington, D.C., May 1980.

Olen Martin (formerly INS, Bangkok, Thailand), Bangkok, Thailand, January 1983.

Chong Mona-Lee (Hmong leader, Ban Vinai refugee camp), Ban Vinai, Thailand, January 1984.

Michael Leifer (Southeast Asia specialist, London School of Economics and Political Science), London, England, July 1983.

Sheppard Lowman (formerly Department of State, Office of Refugee and Migration Affairs, Bureau of Refugee Programs, and U.S. Embassy, Saigon), Washington, D.C., November 1983.

Frank Loy (formerly Office of U.S. Coordinator for Refugee Affairs and Bureau of Refugee Programs, Department of State), Washington, D.C., March 1983.

Wendy Turnbull Luers (formerly Amnesty International USA), Princeton, N.J., September 1982.

Jean Lujan (INS, Office of General Counsel, Washington, D.C.), Washington, D.C., June 1980. (Interview by Gracia Berg.)

David McAree (Amnesty International, researcher for Vietnam), London, England, August 1983.

John McCarthy, (U.S. Catholic Conference), Washington, D.C., May 1983.

Gail McGee (formerly Refugee Coordinator, Orange County, Calif.), Santa Ana, Calif., February 1983.

D. McNamara (UNHCR, East Asia, Geneva, Switzerland), Geneva, Switzerland, March and June 1983.

Mark Malloch-Brown (formerly UNHCR, Thailand), Geneva, March and June 1983.

Evan Maxwell (journalist, *Los Angeles Times*), Orange County, California, February 1983.

Doris Meisner (Immigration and Naturalization Service, Director's Office), Washington, D.C., May 1983.

Peter Mejer (UNHCR, Hong Kong), Hong Kong, January 1983.

Nick Morris (UNHCR, Geneva, Switzerland), Geneva, Switzerland, June 1983.

Raymond Morris (formerly INS District Director, Miami, Fla.), Miami, Fla., August 1980.

P. M. Mousalli (UNHCR, Director of Protection), Geneva, Switzerland, January 1985.

Michael Muller (UNHCR, New York), New York, January 1983.

Mark Murphy (National Emergency Coalition for Haitian Refugees), New York, April and November 1983.

Peter O'Donnell (State of Florida, Refugee Program Administrator), Tallahassee, Fla., June 1982.

Victor Palmieri (formerly U.S. Coordinator for Refugee Affairs), San Francisco, Calif., February 1983.

David Pasquarelli (State of Florida, Department of Health and Rehabilitative Services), Tallahassee, Fla., June 1982.

Robert Pastor (formerly National Security Council staff, Western Hemisphere), Washington, D.C., January 1983.

David Pierce (U.S. State Department officer on assignment to Orange County, Calif.), Santa Ana, Calif., February 1983.

Paul Pilkauskas (U.S. Mission, Geneva, Switzerland), Geneva, March 1983.

Mike Posner (Director, Lawyers Committee for International Human Rights), New York, May 1980.

David Pringree (State of Florida, Department of Health and Rehabilitative Services), Tallahassee, Fla., June 1982.

Col. Kitti Puthiporn (formerly Task Force 80, commander Khao-I-Dang refugee camp), Khao-I-Dang, Thailand, January 1983.

Nguyen Van Quan (Vietnamese refugee, Phanat Nikhom Processing Center), Phanat Nikhom, Thailand, January 1983.

Donald Ranard (Center for International Policy), Washington, D.C., May 1980.

Pat Rengel (Amnesty International USA), Washington, D.C., May 1980.

Zia Risvi (formerly UNHCR Regional Representative to Southeast Asia), New York, January, 1983.

Nigel Rodley (Amnesty International Legal Department head), London, England, June 1983.

Lionel Rosenblatt (formerly head of Khmer Emergency Group and Refugee Program, U.S. Embassy, Bangkok, Thailand), Washington, D.C., December 1982.

Gary Rubin (American Jewish Committee, formerly U.S. Committee for Refugees), New York, January 1983.

Robert Saaf (formerly UNHCR, Bangkok, Thailand), Zirndorf, Federal Republic of Germany, August 1984.

Ronald S. Scheinman (formerly Select Commission on Immigration and Refugee Policy), Washington, D.C., May 1980.

Derrick Schoen (HHS, Office of Refugee Resettlement), Washington, D.C., August 1980.

Lissen Schou (formerly Intergovernmental Committee on Migration, Chile), Geneva, Switzerland, June 1983.

John Schroeder (formerly Director INS, Bangkok, Thailand), Bangkok, Thailand, January 1983.

Susan Sharpe (State of Florida, Department of Health and Rehabilitative Services), Tallahassee, Fla., June 1982.

William Shawcross (journalist), London, England, August 1983.

Frank Sievarts (State Department, Bureau of Refugee Programs), New York, April 1983.

A. Simmance (UNHCR, Assistance Division, formerly UNHCR, Bangkok, Thailand), Geneva, Switzerland, January 1985.

M. Sloss (INS Supervisor, Refugee Processing Center, Miami, Fla.), Miami, Fla., August 1980.

James Smith (INS, Assistant Officer-in-Charge, Refugee Processing Center, Miami, Fla.), Miami, Fla., August 1980.

Wayne Smith (Carnegie Endowment, formerly U.S. Liaison Office, Havana, Cuba), Washington, D.C., January 1983.

W. Richard Smyser (Deputy UNHCR High Commissioner and formerly Acting U.S. Coordinator for Refugee Affairs, Department of State), Geneva, Switzerland, June 1984.

Nina Solarz (U.S. Committee for Refugees, Washington, D.C.), Washington, D.C., May 1983.

Barry Stein (Michigan State University), South Bend, Ind., June 1983.

Carel Sternberg (International Rescue Committee), New York, November 1983.

Judy Stowe (Far Eastern Service, BBC), London, England, July 1983.

William Stubbs (formerly, Department of State, Refugee Officer, Thailand), Bangkok, Thailand, January 1983.

Sue Ann Sullivan (Haitian Refugee Project), Washington, D.C., May 1980.

Joseph Sureck (formerly INS Regional Director, Asia), Hong Kong, January 1983.

Dick Frederick Swartz (attorney for Haitian plaintiffs in *Haitian Refugee Center v. Civiletti* and President, National Immigration, Refugee and Citizenship Forum), South Bend, Ind., April 1981.

Julia Taft (formerly Director Interagency Task Force, and Acting U.S. Coordinator for Refugee Affairs, Department of State), Washington, D.C., July 1982 and March 1983.

Jacques Terlin (formerly UNHCR representative to Thailand), Bangkok, Thailand, January 1983.

John Thomas (International Refugee Organization, Department of State, Cuban Refugee Program, Intergovernmental Committee for European Migration), Geneva, Switzerland, March and April 1983.

Ralph Thomas (Select Commission on Immigration and Refugee Policy), Washington, D.C., May 1980.

Jerry Tinker (U.S. Senate, Judiciary Committee, staff aide), Washington, D.C., May 1983.

Michael Trominski (INS, Officer-in-Charge, Refugee Processing Center, Miami, Fla.), Miami, Fla., August 1980.

Nick Van Praag (formerly UNHCR, Washington, D.C.), Washington, D.C., March 1985.

Jose Vargas (Hispanic Affairs Officer, Santa Ana, Calif.), Santa Ana, Calif., February 1983.

Msgr. Bryan Walsh (Director, Catholic Charities, Archdiocese of Miami), Miami, Fla., August 1980.

George Warren, Jr. (Intergovernmental Committee for Migration, Geneva, Switzerland, formerly Department of State Office of Refugee and Migration Affairs, Washington, D.C.), Geneva, Switzerland, March and June 1983.

Harriet Weider (Commissioner, Orange County, Calif.), Santa Ana, Calif., February 1983.

Louis Weisner (International Rescue Committee, formerly Director, Office of Refugee and Migration Affairs, Department of State), Washington, D.C., November 1983.

Dennis White (Immigration and Refugee Planning Center, Orange County, Calif.), Santa Ana, Calif., February 1983.

Nanda Wijaytilke (UNHCR, Bangkok, Thailand), Bangkok, Thailand, January 1983.

Michael Williams (Amnesty International Asia head, researcher for Vietnam), London, England, August 1983.

Roger Winter (U.S. Committee for Refugees), Washington, D.C., December 1982.

Jim Woods (formerly INS Supervisor, Ban Thai Samart), Ban Thai Samart, Thailand, January 1983.

Jose Zalaquett (Amnesty International deputy head), London, England, July 1983.

ORAL HISTORIES

George V. Allen (Director, USIA). Dwight D. Eisenhower Library.

Richard M. Bissell (CIA). Columbia University Library.

Charles Bohlen (U.S. Ambassador to the USSR). Columbia University Library.

Ellis Briggs (U.S. Ambassador to Czechoslovakia), Columbia University Library.

Walter H. Judd (Republican Congressman from Minnesota). Dwight D. Eisenhower Library.

Mary Pillsbury Lord (U.S. Representative to UN Human Rights Commission). Dwight D. Eisenhower Library.

John J. McCloy (U.S. High Commissioner for Germany). Columbia University Library.

Thomas Mann (U.S. Department of State). Dwight D. Eisenhower Library.

Livingston Merchant (U.S. Department of State). Columbia University Library.

Joseph Swing (U.S. Commissioner of Immigration and Naturalization). Columbia University Library.

Earl Streibert (Director, USIA). Dwight D. Eisenhower Library.

George L. Warren, Jr. (U.S. Representative to the International Refugee Organization and U.S. Department of State). Harry S. Truman Library.

SERIAL PUBLICATIONS

American Jewish Yearbook. 1973.

American Journal of International Law. Various dates.

Amnesty International Report. 1975–1985.

Bangkok Post. 1979–1985.

British Yearbook of International Law. Various dates.

Bulletin of Concerned Asian Scholars. Various dates.

Bulletin. Lawyers Committee for International Human Rights. New York. Various dates.

Cambodian Action Update. 1979–1981.

Chicago Tribune. Various dates.

Christian Science Monitor. Various dates.

Congressional Record. 1946–1985.

Congressional Quarterly Weekly. Various dates.

Cuban Studies/Estudios Cubanos. Various dates.

Economic and Social Progress in Latin America. Inter-American Development Bank (IDB). 1958–1980.

Far Eastern Economic Review. 1975–1985.

Freedom at Issue. New York. Various dates.

GIST. U.S. Department of State. Various dates.

Human Rights Bulletin. International League for Human Rights. New York. Various dates.

Human Rights Internet. Washington, D.C. Various dates.

Indochina Issues. Various dates.

Indochinese Refugee Reports. Various dates.

International Migration Review. Center for Migration Studies. New York. Various dates.

International Migration. Various dates.

Interpreter Releases. American Council for Nationality Services. Various dates.

Los Angeles Times. Various dates.

Matchbox. Amnesty International USA. New York. Various dates.

Miami Herald. 1959–1982.

Migration Today. World Council of Churches. Geneva, Switzerland. Various dates.

Migration News. Geneva, Switzerland. Various dates.

Migration Today. Various dates.

Monthly Dispatch. Intergovernmental Committee for Migration. Geneva, Switzerland. Various dates.

New York Times. 1945–1985.

New York Times Index. 1945–1985.

New York Times Magazine. Various dates.

News from the Committee. American Jewish Committee. 1984–1985.

Newsweek. Various dates.

People Magazine.

Philadelphia Inquirer. Various dates.

Reader's Digest. Various dates.

Refugee Bulletin. UNHCR. Bangkok, Thailand. 1983–1985.

Refugee Abstracts. International Refugee Integration Research Center. Geneva, Switzerland. 1982–1985.

Refugee Reports. 1979–1985.

Refugee. Refugee Documentation Project, York University. Various dates.

Refugees and Human Rights Newsletter. Church World Service. Various dates.

Refugees. Geneva, Switzerland. Various dates.

Refugees. World Council of Churches. Geneva, Switzerland. Various dates.

Santa Ana Register. 1975–1983.

Southeast Asia Chronicle. Various dates.

The Guardian. Manchester, England. Various dates.

The Gallup Opinion Index. Various dates.

The New Republic. Various dates.

The Progressive. Various dates.

The Bulletin. International Commission of Jurists. Geneva, Switzerland. Various dates.

The Washington Magazine. Various dates.

The Times. London. Various dates.

The Economist. London. Various dates.

Time Magazine. Various dates.

U.S. News and World Report. Various dates.

U.S. Code Congressional and Administrative News. 1947–1985.

United States Immigration and Naturalization Service Monthly Review. 1946–1950.

UPDATE. United States Catholic Conference. Washington, D.C. Various dates.

Update: Latin America. Washington Office on Latin America. Various dates.

Washington Post. Various dates.

Weekly Compilation of Presidential Documents. 1980–1985.

World Refugee Survey. American Council for Nationalities Service. New York. 1965–1984.

BOOKS AND MONOGRAPHS

Acheson, Dean. *Present at the Creation.* New York: Norton, 1966.

Aga Khan, Sadruddin. *Legal Problems Related to Refugees and Displaced Persons.* The Hague: Academy of International Law, 1976.

Aleinikoff, Thomas A., and Martin, David. *Immigration: Process and Policy.* St. Paul, Minn.: West Publishing Co., 1985.

Ambrose, Stephen E. *Eisenhower: 1948–52.* New York: Simon & Schuster, 1983.

——. *Ike's Spies: Eisenhower and the Espionage Establishment.* New York: Doubleday & Co., 1981.

Americas Watch and the American Civil Liberties Union, *Report on Human Rights in El Salvador.* New York: Vintage Books, 1982.

Baldwin, C. Beth. *Capturing the Change: The Impact of Indo-Chinese Refugees in Orange County.* Santa Ana, Calif.: Immigrant and Refugee Planning Center, 1982.

Barrett, Edward W. *Truth Is Our Weapon.* New York: Funk & Wagnalls, 1953.

Bauer, Raymond A., Inkeles, Alex, and Kluckhohn, Clyde. *How the Soviet System Works: Cultural, Psychological and Social Themes.* New York: Vintage Books, 1956.

Bender, Lynn. *The Politics of Hostility.* Hato Rey, Puerto Rico: InterAmerican University Press, 1975.

Bennett, Marion T. *American Immigration Policies.* Washington: Public Affairs Press, 1963.

Bentz, Thomas. *New Immigrants: Portraits in Passage.* New York: Pilgrim Press, 1981.

Bernard, William (ed.). *American Immigration Policy: A Reappraisal.* New York: Harper, 1950.

Bethell, Nicholas. *The Last Secret: Forcible Repatriation to Russia, 1944–47.* London: Andre Deutsch, 1974.

Bonsall, Philip W. *Cuba, Castro, and the United States.* Pittsburgh, Pa.: University of Pittsburgh Press, 1971.

Bouman, P. J., Bejer, G., and Oudegeest, S. J. *The Refugee Problem in Western Germany.* The Hague: Martinus Nijhoff, 1950.

Bouscaren, Anthony T. *International Migrations since 1945.* New York: Frederick A. Praeger, 1963.

——. *The Security Aspects of Immigration Work.* Milwaukee: Marquette University Press, 1959.

Brown, Francis J. (ed.). *Refugees.* Special Issue of Annals of the American Academy of Political and Social Science, 203 (1939).

Bryce–La Porte, Roy Simon (ed.). *A Sourcebook on the New Immigration: Implications for the United States and the International Community.* New Brunswick, N.J.: Transaction Books, 1980.

Brzezinski, Zbigniew. *Power and Principle: Memoirs of a National Security Adviser.* New York: Farrar, Straus, & Giroux, 1983.

Buehrig, E. *The U.N. and Palestinian Refugees: A Study in Non-Territorial Administration.* Bloomington: Indiana University Press, 1971.

Bursten, Martin. *Escape from Fear.* Syracuse, N.Y.: Syracuse University Press, 1958.

Butlinger, Joseph. *Vietnam: A Dragon Embattled.* Vol. 2. New York: Frederick A. Praeger, 1967.

Cafferty, Pastora San Juan, Chiswick, Barry, R., Greely, Andrew M., and Sullivan,

Teresa A. *The Dilemma of American Immigration: Beyond the Golden Door.* New Brunswick, N.J.: Transaction Books, 1983.

Carter, Jimmy. *Keeping Faith: Memoirs of a President.* New York: Bantam Books, 1982.

Caute, David. *The Great Fear.* New York: Simon & Schuster, 1978.

Chandler, Edgar H. S. *The High Tower of Refuge: The Inspiring Story of Refugee Relief Throughout the World.* New York: Frederick A. Praeger, 1959.

Chiswick, Barry (ed.). *The Gateway: U.S. Immigration Issues and Policies.* Washington, D.C., and London: American Enterprise Institute for Public Policy Research, 1982.

Chomsky, Noam. *Towards a New Cold War.* New York: Pantheon Books, 1982.

Clay, Lucius D. *Decision in Germany.* New York: Doubleday, 1950.

————. *Germany and the Fight for Freedom.* Cambridge, Mass.: Harvard University Press, 1950.

Cline, Roy. *The CIA under Reagan, Bush, and Casey.* Washington, D.C.: Acropolis Books, 1981.

Colby, William and Forbath, Peter. *Honorable Men: My Life in the CIA.* New York: Simon & Schuster, 1978.

Corson, William R. *The Armies of Ignorance.* New York: Dial Press/James Wade, 1977.

Cortes, Carlos E. (ed.). *Cuban Refugee Programs.* New York: Arno Press, 1980.

Crewdson, John. *The Tarnished Door: The New Immigrants and the Transformation of America.* New York: Times Books, 1983.

Davidowicz, Lucy S. *The War Against the Jews, 1933–45.* New York: Bantam Books, 1976.

Davie, Maurice R. *Refugees in America.* New York: Harper & Brothers, 1947.

Diederich, B. and Burt, A. *Papa Doc: The Truth About Haiti Today.* New York: McGraw-Hill, 1969.

Dinnerstein, Leonard. *America and the Survivors of the Holocaust.* New York: Columbia University Press, 1982.

Divine, Robert A. *American Immigration Policy.* New Haven, Conn.: Yale University Press, 1957.

Dominguez, Jorge I. *Cuba, Order and Revolution.* Cambridge, Mass.: Harvard University Press, 1978.

Dominquez, Virginia. *From Neighbor to Stranger: The Dilemma of the Caribbean Peoples in the United States.* New Haven, Conn.: Yale University Press, 1975.

Dornberg, John. *The Other Germany.* New York: Doubleday & Co., 1968.

Douge, Daniel. *Caribbean Pilgrims: The Plight of the Haitian Refugees.* Hicksville, N.Y.: Exposition Press, 1982.

Dunkerly, James. *The Long War: Dictatorship and Revolution in El Salvador.* London: Junction Books, 1985.

Eliar, Ariel. *Between Hammer and Sickle.* New York: New American Library, 1969.

Elliot, Mark. *Pawns of Yalta.* Champaign: University of Illinois Press, 1982.

Evans, Rowland, and Novak, Robert. *The Reagan Revolution.* New York: E. P. Dutton, 1981.

Fagen, Richard F., Brody, Richard A., and O'Leary, Thomas J. *Cubans in Exile: Disaffection and the Revolution.* Stanford, Calif.: Stanford University Press, 1968.

Fagen, Patricia Weiss, and Aguayo, Serjio. *Fleeing the Maelstrom: Central American Refugees.* Boulder, Colo.: Westview Press, forthcoming.

Feingold, Henry L. *The Politics of Rescue: The Roosevelt Administration and the Holocaust, 1938-45.* New Brunswick, N.J.: Rutgers University Press, 1970.

Fitzpatrick, John C. (ed.). *The Writings of George Washington.* XXVII. Washington, D.C.: Government Printing Office, 1938.

Flannerly, Harry W., and Sager, Gerhart H. *Which Way Germany?* New York: Hawthorne Books, 1968.

Ford, Gerald R. *A Time to Heal: The Autobiography of Gerald R. Ford.* New York: Harper & Row, 1979.

Freedman, Robert D. (ed.). *Soviet Jewry in the Decisive Decade, 1971-1980.* Durham, N.C.: Duke University Press, 1984.

Friedman, Saul. *No Haven for the Oppressed: United States Policy Toward Jewish Refugees, 1938-1945.* Detroit: Wayne State University Press, 1973.

Garis, Roy L. *Immigration Restriction.* New York: The Free Press, 1927.

Gastil, R. (ed.). *Freedom in the World, 1982.* Westport, Conn.: Greenwood Press, 1982.

Gerson, Lewis L. *The Hyphenate in Recent American Politics and Diplomacy.* Lawrence: University of Kansas, 1964.

Glazer, Nathan (ed.). *Clamor at the Gates: The New American Immigration.* San Francisco: Institute for Contemporary Studies, 1985.

Goodwin-Gill, Guy. *The Refugee in International Law.* Oxford and London: Clarendon Press, 1983.

Grahl-Madsen, Atle. *The Status of Refugees in International Law.* I and II. Leiden: A. W. Sijthoff, 1966, 1972.

———. *Territorial Asylum.* Dobbs Ferry, N.Y.: Oceana Publications, 1980.

Grant, Bruce. *The Boat People.* London: Penguin Books, 1979.

Grothe, Peter. *To Win the Minds of Men: The Story of the Communist Propaganda War in East Germany.* Palo Alto, Calif.: Pacific Books, 1958.

Halperin, Morton H. *Bureaucratic Politics and Foreign Policy.* Washington, D.C.: Brookings Institute, 1974.

Hartmann, Susan. *Truman and the 80th Congress.* Columbia: University of Missouri Press, 1971.

Hawthorne, Lesleyanne (ed.). *Refugee: The Vietnamese Experience.* New York: Oxford University Press, 1982.

Heinl, R., and Heinl, N. *Written in Blood: The Story of the Haitian People.* Boston: Houghton Mifflin, 1978.

Hersh, Seymour. *The Price of Power.* New York: Summit Books, 1983.

Hirschman, Albert O. *Exit, Voice and Loyalty: Responses to Decline in Firms, Organizations, and States.* Cambridge, Mass.: Harvard University Press, 1970.

Hofstetter, Richard (ed.). *U.S. Immigration Policy.* Durham, N.C.: Duke University Press, 1984.

Holborn, Louise. *International Refugee Organization.* London: Oxford University Press, 1956.

————. *Refugees: A Problem of Our Time: The Work of the United Nations High Commissioner for Refugees.* I and II. Metuchen, N.J.: Scarecrow Press, 1975.

Holt, Robert T. *Radio Free Europe.* Minneapolis: University of Minnesota Press, 1956.

Howe, Russell Warren, and Trott, Sarah Hays. *The Power Peddlers.* New York: Doubleday, 1977.

Howell, David (ed.). *Southeast Asian Refugees in the USA: Case Studies of Adjustment and Policy Implications.* Special issue of *Anthropological Quarterly,* 55 (July 1982).

Hull, Elizabeth. *Without Justice for All.* Westport, Conn.: Greenwood Press, 1985.

Humphrey, Derek, and Ward, Michael. *Passports and Politics.* London: Penguin Books, 1974.

Hutchinson, Edward P. *Legislative History of U.S. Immigration Policy, 1798–1965.* Philadelphia: University of Pennsylvania Press, 1981.

Hutchinson, P. (ed.). *The New Immigration.* Special issue of *Annals of the American Academy of Political and Social Science,* 36 (September, 1966).

International Bibliography of Refugee Literature (working edition). Geneva: International Refugee Integration Resource Centre, 1985.

Isaacs, Arnold. *Without Honor: Defeat in Vietnam and Cambodia.* Baltimore: John Hopkins University Press, 1983.

Jacobs, Dan N., and Paul, Ellen Frankel (eds.). *Studies of the Third Wave: Recent Migration of Soviet Jews to the U.S.* Boulder, Colo.: Westview Press, 1981.

Kalme, Albert. *Total Terror: An Expose of Genocide in the Baltics.* New York: Appleton-Century-Crofts, 1951.

Karalekas, Anne. *History of the Central Intelligence Agency.* Laguna Hills, Calif.: Aegean Park Press, 1977.

Karnow, Stanley. *Vietnam: A History.* New York: Viking Press, 1983.

Kee, Robert. *Refugee World.* London: Oxford University Press, 1961.

Keely, Charles B. *Global Refugee Policy: The Case for a Development Oriented Strategy.* New York: The Population Council, Inc., 1981.

Kelly, Gail Paradise. *From Vietnam to America.* Boulder, Colo.: Westview Press, 1977.

Kissinger, Henry. *White House Years.* Boston: Little, Brown and Company, 1979.

Kommers, Donald, and Loescher, Gilburt (eds.). *Human Rights and American Foreign Policy.* Notre Dame, Ind.: University of Notre Dame Press, 1979.

Konvitz, Milton R. *Civil Rights in Immigration.* Ithaca, N.Y.: Cornell University Press, 1953.

Kritz, Mary, Keely, Charles B., and Tomasi, S. M. (eds.). *Global Trends in Migration: Theory and Research in International Population Movements.* Staten Island, N.Y.: Center for Migration Studies, 1981.

Kritz, Mary M. (ed.). *U.S. Immigration and Refugee Policy: Global and Domestic Issues.* Lexington, Mass.: D. C. Heath, 1982.

Kubat, Daniel (ed.). *The Politics of Migration Policies.* Staten Island, N.Y.: Center for Migration Studies, 1979.

Kulischer, Eugene M. *Europe on the Move: War and Population Changes, 1917–1947.* New York: Columbia University Press, 1948.

Kuper, Leo. *Genocide: Its Political Uses in the 20th Century.* New Haven, Conn.: Yale University Press, 1981.

Lacouture, Jean and Simone. *Vietnam: Voyage a travers une victoire.* Paris: Seuil, 1976.

Langley, Lester D. *The Cuban Policy of the U.S.* New York: John Wiley & Sons, 1968.

——. *U.S. and the Caribbean, 1900–70.* Athens, Ga.: University of Georgia Press, 1980.

Lowenthal, Abraham F. *The Dominican Intervention.* Cambridge, Mass.: Harvard University Press, 1972.

Lejburn, James G. *The Haitian People.* New Haven, Conn.: Yale University Press, 1966.

Lernoux, Penny. *Cry of the People.* New York: Doubleday & Co., 1980.

Levenstein, Aaron. *Escape to Freedom: The Story of the International Rescue Committee.* Westport, Conn.: Greenwood Press, 1983.

Levering, Ralph B. *The Public and American Foreign Policy 1918–1978.* New York: William Morrow & Co., 1978.

Levy, Deborah M. *Transnational Legal Problems of Refugees: 1982 Michigan Yearbook of International Legal Studies.* New York: Clark Boardman, 1982.

Lichtenberg, Judith. "Moral Boundaries and National Boundaries: A Cosmopolitan View." Working Paper NB-4, University of Maryland Center for Philosophy and Public Policy, August 13, 1980.

Lillich, Richard B. *The Human Rights of Aliens in Contemporary International Law.* Manchester, England: Manchester University Press, 1984.

Liu, William T., Lamanna, M., and Murata, A. *Transition to Nowhere: Vietnamese Refugees in America.* Nashville, Tenn.: Charter House Publishers, 1979.

Loescher, Gilburt D., and Loescher, Ann. *The World's Refugees: A Test of Humanity.* New York: Harcourt Brace Jovanovich, 1982.

Loescher, G. D., and Scanlan, John. *Human Rights, Power Politics, and the International Refugee Regime: The Case of U.S. Treatment of Caribbean Basin Refugees.* Princeton University Center for International Studies, World Order Studies Occasional Papers Series, No. 14. Princeton, N.J., 1985.

———. *U.S. Foreign Policy and Its Impact on Refugee Flow from Cuba.* New York University Center for Latin American and Caribbean Studies Occasional Paper No. 42. New York, 1984.

Loescher, G. D., and Scanlan, John A. (eds.). *The Global Refugee Problem: U.S. and World Response. Special Issue of Annals of the American Academy of Political and Social Science,* 467 (May 1983).

Loftus, John. *The Belarus Secret.* New York: Alfred A. Knopf, 1982.

Long, Nguyen, with Kendall, Harry H. *After Saigon Fell: Daily Life under the Communists.* Berkeley: Institute of East Asian Studies, University of California, 1981.

Louis, John B. *Basic Documents of the United Nations.* Brooklyn, N.Y.: Foundation Press, 1968.

Lundahl, M. *Peasants and Poverty: A Study of Haiti.* London: Croom-Helm, 1979.

Macallister-Smith, Peter. *International Humanitarian Assistance: Disaster Relief Actions in International Law and Organization.* Dordrecht: Martinus Nijhoff, 1985.

MacEoin, G., and Riley, N. *No Promised Land: American Refugee Policies and the Rule of Law.* Boston, Mass.: OXFAM America, 1982.

Maguire, R. *Bottom-up Development in Haiti.* Rosslyn, Va.: Inter-American Foundation, 1981.

Manigat, L. *Haiti of the Sixties.* Washington, D.C.: Center of Foreign Policy Research, 1964.

Marchetti, Victor, and Marks, John D. *The CIA and the Cult of Intelligence.* New York: Alfred A. Knopf, 1974.

Marrus, Michael R. *The Unwanted: European Refugees in the Twentieth Century.* New York: Oxford University Press, 1985.

Marrus, Michael, and Paxton, Robert. *Vichy France and the Jews.* New York: Basic Books, 1981.

Marshall, Dawn I. *The Haitian Problem: Illegal Migration to the Bahamas.* Mona, Puerto Rico: Institute of Social and Economic Research, 1979.

Martin, John Barlow. *U.S. Policy in the Caribbean: A Twentieth Century Fund Essay.* Boulder, Colo.: Westview Press, 1978.

Mason, Linda, and Brown, Roger. *Rice, Rivalry, and Politics.* Notre Dame, Ind.: University of Notre Dame Press, 1983.

Mayne, Richard. *The Recovery of Europe.* New York: Harper & Row, 1970.

McGowan, James. *Wrapped in Wind's Shawl: The Refugees of South East Asia and the Western World.* New York: Presidio Press, 1980.

McNeill, William, and Adams, Ruth. *Human Migrations: Patterns and Policies.* Bloomington: Indiana University Press, 1978.

Melander, Goran. *Refugees in Orbit.* Geneva: International University Exchange Fund, 1978.

Mesa-Lago, Carmelo (ed.). *Revolutionary Change in Cuba.* Pittsburgh, Pa.: University of Pittsburgh Press, 1971.

Michener, James A. *The Bridge at Andau.* New York: Random House, 1957.

Michie, Allen. *Voices Through the Iron Curtain: The Radio Free Europe Story.* New York: Dodd, Mead, & Company, 1963.

Millet, Richard. *Guardians of the Dynasty.* New York: Orbis Press, 1977.

Ministry for Foreign Affairs of the Hungarian People's Republic, *Documents on the Hostile Activity of the United States Government Against the Hungarian People's Republic.* Budapest: Hungarian State Publishing House, 1951.

Misiunas, Romuald, and Taagepera Rein. *The Baltic States: Years of Dependence.* Berkeley: University of California Press, 1983.

Montero, Daniel. *Vietnamese Americans: Patterns of Resettlement and Socioeconomic Adaptation in the United States.* Boulder, Colo.: Westview Press, 1979.

Montgomery, Tommie Sue. *Revolution in El Salvador.* Boulder, Colo.: Westview Press, 1982.

Moquin, Wayne (ed.). *Refugees and Victims.* "Makers of America" Series, Vol. 9. [Chicago:] Encyclopedia Britannica Educational Corp., n.d.

Morris, Milton D. *Immigration: The Beleaguered Bureaucracy.* Washington, D.C.: Brookings Institute, 1985.

Morris, Roger. *Uncertain Greatness: Henry Kissinger and American Foreign Policy.* New York: Harper & Row, 1977.

Morse, Arthur O. *While Six Million Died: A Chronicle of American Apathy.* New York: Random House, 1967.

Murphey, H. B. M. *Flight and Settlement.* Lucerne, Switzerland: UNESCO, 1955.

Nicholls, David. *From Desalines to Duvalier: Haiti: Race, Color and National Independence.* New York: Cambridge University Press, 1980.

Nickle, James W. "Human Rights and the Rights of Aliens." Working Paper NB-3, University of Maryland Center for Philosophy and Public Policy, July 30, 1980.

Nixon, Richard. *RN: The Memoirs of Richard Nixon.* New York: Grosset & Dunlap, 1978.

North, David S., Lewin, Lawrence S., and Wagner, Jennifer R. *Kaleidoscope: The Resettlement of Refugees in the United States by the Voluntary Agencies.* Washington, D.C.: New TransCentury Foundation, Levin and Associates, and National Opinion Research Center, 1982.

Norwood, Frederick A. *Strangers and Exiles: A History of Religious Relief.* I and II. New York: Abingdon Press, 1969.

Office of the United Nations High Commissioner for Refugees. *Collection of International Instruments Concerning Refugees.* Geneva, Switzerland: UNHCR, 1979.

Olson, James Stewart. *The Ethnic Dimension in American History.* New York: St. Martin's Press, 1977.

Orbach, William. *The American Movement to Aid Soviet Jews.* Amherst: University of Massachusetts, 1979.

Osborne, Milton, Male, Beverly, Lawrie, Gordon, and O'Malley, W. J. *Refugees: Four Political Case Studies.* Canberra Studies in World Affairs, No. 3. Canberra: Australian National University, 1981.

Panish, Paul. *Exit Visa: The Emigration of Soviet Jews.* New York: Coward, McCann & Geoghegan, 1981.

Papademetriou, Demetrios G., and Miller, Mark J. (eds.). *The Unavoidable Issue: U.S. Immigration Policy in the 1980's.* Philadelphia, Pa.: Institute for the Study of Human Issues, 1983.

Paul, Anthony, and Barron, John. *Murder of a Gentle Land.* Pleasantville, N.Y.: Reader's Digest Press, 1977.

Pedraza-Bailey, Silvia. *Political and Economic Migrants in America: Cubans and Mexicans.* Austin: University of Texas Press, 1984.

Philipson, Larrin, and Llerena, Rafael. *Freedom Flights: Cuban Refugees Talk about Life under Castro and How They Fled His Regime.* New York: Random House, 1980.

Ponchaud, François. *Cambodge Année Zero.* Paris: Juilliard, 1977.

Poole, Peter A. *The Vietnamese in Thailand.* Ithaca, N.Y.: Cornell University Press, 1970.

Portes, Alejandro, and Bach, Robert L. *Latin Journey: Cuban and Mexican Immigrants in the United States.* Berkeley: University of California Press, 1985.

Powers, Thomas. *The Man Who Kept the Secrets: Richard Helms and the CIA.* New York: Alfred A. Knopf, 1979.

Prielo, Yolando. *Cuban Migration of the 1960's in Perspective.* New York University Center for Latin American and Caribbean Studies Occasional Paper No. 46. New York, 1984.

Prohias, Rafael J., and Casal, Lourdes. *The Cuban Minority in the U.S.: Preliminary Report on Need Identification and Program Evaluation.* Boca Raton, Fla.: Florida Atlantic University, 1973.

Proudfoot, Malcolm J. *European Refugees: 1939–1952: A Study in Forced Population Movement.* London: Faber & Faber, 1957.

Rees, Elfan. *We Strangers and Afraid: The Refugee Story Today.* New York: Carnegie Endowment, 1960.

Rogg, Eleanor Meyer. *Assimilation of Cuban Exiles: The Role of Community and Class.* New York: Aberdeen Press, 1974.

Rose, Peter I. (ed.). *Working with Refugees: Proceedings of the Simon S. Shargo Memorial Conference.* Staten Island, N.Y.: Center for Migration Studies, forthcoming.

Rotberg, Robert I., and Clague, Christopher K. *Haiti: The Politics of Squalor.* Boston, Mass.: Houghton Mifflin, 1971.

Safire, William. *Before the Fall.* New York: Doubleday, 1975.

Schechtman, Joseph B. *The Arab Refugee Problem.* New York: Philosophical Library, 1952.

———. *European Population Transfers.* New York: Oxford University Press, 1946.

——. *Population Transfers in Asia.* New York: Hallsby Press, 1949.

——. *Postwar Population Transfers in Europe 1945–55.* Philadelphia: University of Pennsylvania Press, 1962.

——. *The Refugee in the World: Development and Integration.* New York: A. S. Barnes & Co., 1963.

——. *The United States and the Jewish State Movement.* New York: Hertzl Press, Thomas Yoseloff, 1966.

Schlesinger, Arthur M., Jr. *A Thousand Days: Kennedy in the White House.* Boston: Houghton Mifflin, 1965.

Schmidt, H. *The United States Occupation of Haiti, 1916–1934.* New Brunswick, N.J.: Rutgers University Press, 1971.

Schoultz, Lars. *Human Rights and United States Policy Toward Latin America.* Princeton, N.J.: Princeton University Press, 1981.

Schwartz, Abba P. *The Open Society.* New York: William Morrow & Co., 1968.

Segal, Aaron Lee. *Population Policy in the Caribbean.* Lexington, Mass.: Lexington Books, 1975.

Shawcross, William. *The Quality of Mercy: Cambodia, the Holocaust and Modern Conscience.* New York: Simon & Schuster, 1984.

——. *Sideshow: Kissinger, Nixon and the Destruction of Cambodia.* New York: Simon & Schuster, 1979.

Shea, Susan, and Vencill, Mary. *The Administration of the Refugee Resettlement Program in the State of California.* Berkeley, Calif.: Berkeley Planning Associates, 1982.

Simpson, John Hope. *The Refugee Problem.* London: Oxford University Press, 1939.

Snepp, Frank. *Decent Interval.* New York: Random House, 1977.

Sobel, Lester A. (ed.). *Castro's Cuba in the 1970's.* New York: Facts on File, 1978.

——. *Refugees: A World Report, 1979.* New York: Facts on File, 1980.

Sorensen, Theodore. *Kennedy.* New York: Harper & Row, 1965.

Stein, Barry N., and Tomasi, Silvano M. (eds.). *Refugees Today.* Special issue of *International Migration Review,* 15 (Spring-Summer 1981).

Stern, Paula. *Water's Edge: Domestic Politics and the Making of American Foreign Policy.* Westport, Conn.: Greenwood Press, 1979.

Steven, Stewart. *Operation Splinter Factor.* New York: J. P. Lippincott, 1974.

Stewart, Barbara McDonald. *United States Government Policy on Refugees from Nazism, 1933–1940.* New York: Garland Publishing, 1982.

Stoessinger, John. *The Refugee and the World Community.* Minneapolis: University of Minnesota Press, 1956.

Stone, I. F. *The Truman Era.* New York: Random House, 1953.

Stuart-Fox, Martin. *Contemporary Laos.* London: University of Queensland Press, 1983.

Tabori, Paul. *The Anatomy of Exile.* London: George C. Harrap and Co., 1972.

Taft, J. V., North, D. S., and Ford, D. A. *Refugee Resettlement in the U.S.: Time for a New Focus.* Washington, D.C.: New Transcentury Foundation, 1979.

Tata, Robert J. *Haiti: Land of Poverty.* New York: University Press of America, 1982.

Terzani, Tiziano. *Giai Phong!: The Fall and Liberation of Saigon.* New York: St. Martin's Press, 1976.

Thomas, Hugh. *Cuba: The Pursuit of Freedom.* New York: Harper & Row, 1971.

Tokes, Rudolf (ed.). *Dissent in the U.S.S.R.* Baltimore, Md.: Johns Hopkins University Press, 1975.

Tomasi, Lydio F. (ed.). *In Defense of the Alien.* V. Proceedings of the 1982 Annual Legal Conference on Refugees and Territorial Asylum. New York: Center for Migration Studies, 1983.

Tomasi, Silvano M., and Keely, Charles B. *Whom Have We Welcomed? The Adequacy and Quality of United States Immigration Data for Policy Analysis and Evaluation.* Staten Island, N.Y.: Center for Migration Studies, 1975.

University of Miami, Center for Advanced International Studies. *The Cuban Immigration, 1959–1966, and Its Impact in Miami, Dade County, Fla.* Coral Gables, Fla.: University of Miami, 1967.

——. *Psycho-Socio Dynamics in Miami.* Coral Gables, Fla.: University of Miami, 1969.

Vance, Cyrus. *Hard Choices: Critical Years in America's Foreign Policy.* New York: Simon & Schuster, 1983.

Vernant, Jacques. *The Refugee in the Post-War World.* New Haven, Conn.: Yale University Press, 1953.

Vogelgessang, Sandy. *American Dream, Global Nightmare: The Dilemma of U.S. Human Rights Policy.* New York: W. W. Norton, 1980.

Wain, Barry. *The Refused: The Agony of the Indochina Refugees.* New York: Simon & Schuster, 1981.

Weil, T. *Area Handbook for Haiti.* Washington, D.C.: Government Printing Office, 1973.

White, Theodore H. *Fire in the Ashes: Europe in Mid-Century.* New York: William Sloane Associates, 1959.

Wiesel, Elie. *The Jews of Silence: A Personal Report on Soviet Jewry.* New York: New American Library, 1967.

Wischnitzer, Mark. *To Dwell in Safety: The Story of Jewish Migration since 1980.* Philadelphia, Pa.: Jewish Publication Society of America, 1948.

Wise, David, and Ross, Thomas. *The Invisible Government.* New York: Random House, 1964.

Woodbridge, George. *UNRRA.* 3 vols. New York: Columbia University Press, 1950.

Wyman, David. *The Abandonment of the Jews: America and the Holocaust, 1941–1945.* New York: Pantheon Books, 1984.

——. *Paper Walls: America and the Refugee Crisis, 1938–41.* Amherst: University of Massachusetts Press, 1968.

Zucker, Naomi Flink, and Zucker, Norman L. *The Guarded Gate: The Dilemma of Contemporary American Refugee Policy.* New York and London: Harcourt Brace Jovanovich, forthcoming.

ARTICLES AND SPEECHES

"Congress Grapples with Refugee Issues," *Congressional Quarterly Almanac,* 37 (1983): 423–424.

"Deathwatch Cambodia," *Time,* November 12, 1979: 42–48.

"Haig Fears Exiles from Latin America May Flood the United States," *New York Times,* February 23, 1982: A1.

"Immigration Reform Dies at Session's End," *Congressional Quarterly Almanac,* 40 (1985): 229–238.

"Lifeline—Salvadoran Refugees," *People Magazine,* 18 (August 9, 1982): 18.

"Murder by Deportation," *Washington Monthly,* February, 1984: 12–22.

"Refugee Law Violated," *The Guardian* (England, December 10, 1981: 7.

"Refugees: A Cool and Wary Reception," *Time,* May 12, 1975: 24–26.

"Yearning to Breathe Free," *Time,* May 14, 1979: 14–15.

Abrams, Elliott, "Human Rights and the Refugee Crisis," *U.S. State Department Bulletin,* September 1982: 43–45.

Acheson, Dean, statement before the Senate Committee on Foreign Relations, March 1, 1981, reprinted in *Department of State Bulletin,* 16 (March 9, 1947): 424–429.

Aga Khan, Sadruddin, "Human Rights and Mass Exodus: Developing An International Conscience," 11th Annual Minority Rights Group Lecture, Royal Institute for International Affairs, London, February 10, 1983.

——, "Mass Exodus," in Lydio F. Thomasi (ed.), *In Defense of the Alien,* V (New York: Center for Migration Studies, 1983): 10–18.

——, "Towards a Humanitarian World Order," *Third World Affairs,* 1985: 105–123.

Ahmad, Zakaria Haj, "Vietnamese Refugees and Asean," *Contemporary Southeast Asia,* 1 (May 1979): 66–74.

Alienikoff, T. Alexander, "Political Asylum in the Federal Republic of Germany and Republic of France: Lessons for the United States," *University of Michigan Journal of Law Reform,* 17 (Winter 1984): 183–241.

Anker, Deborah, "The Development of U.S. Refugee Legislation," in Lydio F. Tomasi (ed.), *In Defense of the Alien,* VI (New York: Center for Migration Studies 1983): 154–166.

——, "The Forty-Year Crisis: A Legislative History of the Refugee Act of 1980," *San Diego Law Review,* 19 (Winter 1981): 9–89.

——, "The Refugee Act of 1980: An Historical Perspective," in Lydio F. Tomasi (ed.), *In Defense of the Alien*, V (New York: Center for Migration Studies, 1983): 89–94.

Avery, Christopher L., "Refugee Status Decision-Making in Ten Countries," *Stanford Journal of International Law*, 19 (Summer 1983): 235–356.

Azciri, Max, "The Politics of Exile: Trends and Dynamics of Political Change among Cuban-Americans," *Cuban Studies/Estudios Cubanos*, 11/12 (July 1981–January 1982): 55–73.

Bach, Robert L., "Cuba in Crisis," *Migration Today* 8 (1980): 15–18.

——, "The New Cuban Immigrants: Their Background and Prospects," *Monthly Labor Review*, October 1980: 39–46.

Bach, Robert L., and Bach, Jennifer B., "Employment Patterns of Southeast Asian Refugees," *Monthly Labor Review*, October 1980: 31–38.

Ball, Under Secretary of State George, "Principles of Our Policy Toward Cuba," speech before a convention of the Omicron Delta Kappa Society, April 23, 1964, *Department of State Bulletin*, 50 (May 11, 1964): 738–744.

Bayer, Gunther, "The Political Refugee 35 Years Later," *International Migration Review*, 15 (Spring 1981): 26–34.

Bender, Lynn Darrell, "The Cuban Exiles: An Analytical Sketch," *Journal of Latin American Studies*, 5 (1973): 271–278.

Bernard, William S., "How to Influence the Public for a Better Understanding of the Problems of Immigrant Families and Social Welfare Measures Needed in Order to Facilitate a Better Integration of the Newcomers," *International Migration*, 14 (1976): 84–90.

——, "Refugee Asylum in the United States: How the Law Was Changed to Admit Displaced Persons," *International Migration*, 8 (1975): 3–20.

Blodgett, Nancy, "Sanctuary: Church Workers Face Trial," *American Bar Association Journal*, 71 (April 1985): 19.

Bonker, Donald, "New U.S. Refugee Policy Needed Badly," *Washington State Teamster's Magazine*, reprinted in *Congressional Record*, 126 (June 12, 1980): 14578–14579.

Boswell, T., "In the Eye of the Storm: The Context of Haitian Migration to Miami, Florida," *Southeastern Geographer*, 23 (November 1983): 53–57.

——, "The New Haitian Diaspora," *Caribbean Review*, 11 (Winter 1982): 18.

Brinkley, Joel, "Living the Cambodian Nightmare," *Louisville Courier-Journal*, December 2, 1979: 1–4.

Brown, MacAlister, "Laos: Bottoming Out," *Current History*, 82 (April 1983): 154–157, 180–182.

Carey, Joan Clark, "Displaced Populations in Europe in 1944 with Special Reference to Germany," *Department of State Bulletin*, 12 (March 25, 1945): 491–500.

Carlin, James L., "The Development of U.S. Refugee and Migration Policies: An

International Context," *Journal of Refugee Resettlement*, 1 (August 1981): 9–14.

——, "The International Context of U.S. Immigration Policy," lecture at Georgetown University, January 28, 1981.

——, "Significant Refugee Crises since World War II and the Response of the International Community," *Michigan Yearbook of International Legal Studies*, New York: Clark Boardman, 1982: 3–25.

Carliner, David, "Asylum Procedures: Proposed Immigration Reform and Control Act of 1982," in Lydio F. Tomasi (ed.), *In Defense of the Alien*, V (New York: Center for Migration Studies, 1983): 98–102.

Casal, Lourdes, and Hermandes, Andres R. "Cubans in the U.S.: A Survey of the Literature," *Cuban Studies*, 5 (July 1975): 25–51.

Cherne, Leo, "Into a Dark Bottomless Hole," Appeal to the Board of Trustees, Freedom House. New York, Citizens' Commission for Indochinese Refugees Papers, June 17, 1975.

Chisholm, Shirley, "The United States, Latin American Relations, and the Reagan Administration's Immigration Proposals," speech, New York, March 4, 1982.

Chiswick, Barry, "The Economic Progress of Immigrants: Some Apparently Universal Patterns," in Barry Chiswick, (ed.), *The Gateway: U.S. Immigration Issues and Policies* (Washington, D.C., and London: American Enterprise Institute for Public Policy, 1982).

Christopher, Warren, "Refugees: A Global Issue," *Current Policy*, No. 201 (Washington, D.C.: Department of State, Bureau of Public Affairs, July 23, 1980).

Clark, William P., "Personal Liberties and National Security," *Department of State Bulletin*, 82 (December 1982): 25–37.

Cohodas, Nadine, "Refugee Entries Up in 1984; Same Level Expected in 1985," *Congressional Quarterly Weekly Report*, 42 (December 8, 1984): 3077.

Coles, G. J. L., "Background Paper for the Asian Working Group on the International Protection of Refugees and Displaced Persons." San Remo, Italy: International Institute of Humanitarian Law, 1982.

——, "The Problem of Mass Expulsion." San Remo, Italy: International Institute of Humanitarian Law, April 16–18, 1983.

Conde, D., "Guatemalan Refugees in Mexico," *Cultural Survival Quarterly*, 7 (1983): 49–53.

Conner, Roger, and Grant, Lindsay, "The Proposed Immigration Model: A Response from Interested Groups," in Lydio F. Tomasi, Austin T. Fragomen, Jr., and Rosemarie Rogers (eds.), *In Defense of the Alien*, IV (New York: Center for Migration Studies, 1981): 73–82.

Copeland, Ronald, "The Cuban Boatlift of 1980: Strategies in Federal Crisis Management," *Annals of the American Academy of Political and Social Science*, 467 (May 1983): 138–150.

——, "The 1980 Cuban Crisis: Some Observations," *Journal of Refugee Resettlement*, 1 (August 1981): 22–33.

Coste, Brutus, "Propaganda to Eastern Europe," *Public Opinion Quarterly*, 14 (Winter 1950–51): 639–666.

Cowan, Paul, "America Denied: The Plight of People Seeking Political Asylum," *Village Voice*, November 13, 1984: 13–20.

Davidowicz, Lucy S., "American Jews and the Holocaust," *New York Times Magazine*, April 18, 1982: 46–48.

Davies, Derele, "Caught in History's Vice," *Far Eastern Economic Review*, December 25, 1981: 17–21.

——, "The U.S. and the Refugees: From Charity to Cynicism," *Far Eastern Economic Review*, July 17, 1981: 29–31.

DeVecchi, Robert P., "Politics and Policies of First Asylum in Thailand," *World Refugee Survey*, 1982: 20–24.

Douglas, Eugene, "The Problem of Refugees in a Strategic Perspective," *Strategic Review*, Fall 1982: 11–20.

——, "Refugee Policy Through the Looking Glass: A View from a Washington Office," speech before Hanns Seidel Siftung. Washington, D.C.: Office of the U.S. Coordinator for Refugee Affairs, February 21, 1985.

Eisenhower, President Dwight D., "Message to Congress on Revising the Immigration and Nationality Act," *Department of State Bulletin*, 36 (February 18, 1957): 247–250.

——, "Special Message to Congress with Proposals Concerning Changes in Our Immigration and Nationality Laws," *Public Papers of the Presidents, Dwight D. Eisenhower, February 8, 1956.* (Washington, D.C.: Government Printing Office, 1958): 240–248.

——, "Speech Before the American Legion," August 25,1952, New York, quoted in part in Stephen Ambrose, *Eisenhower: 1948–1952* (New York: Simon and Schuster, 1983): 547.

Enders, Thomas O., "Certification of Progress in El Salvador," *Department of State Bulletin*, March 1983.

Etzioni, Amitai, "Refugee Resettlement: The Infighting in Washington," *The Public Interest*, 65 (Fall 1981): 15–29.

Evans, Alona E., "Political Refugees and the United States Immigration Laws," *American Journal of International Law*, 66 (1972): 571.

——, "Political Refugees and U.S. Immigration Laws: A Case Note," *American Journal of International Law*, 62 (October 1968): 921–926.

Fagen, Patricia Weiss, "Applying for Asylum in New York: Law, Policy, and Administrative Practice," New York: New York University Research Program in Inter-American Affairs, April 1984.

Fairchild, Harry Pratt. "Should the Jews Come In?" *The New Republic*, 97 (January 25, 1939): 344.

Fallows, James, "Immigration: How It's Affecting New York," *The Atlantic*, 252 (November 1983): 45–106.

Far Eastern Economic Review, "Asia's Refugees," *Asia 1979 Yearbook*: 126–128.

——, "Asia's Refugees," *Asia 1980 Yearbook:* 110–115.

Farer, Tom, "The Inter-American Commission: A Personal Assessment," *Center Magazine,* May-June 1984: 39–40.

Ferris, Elizabeth G., "The Politics of Asylum: Mexico and the Central American Refugees," *Journal of InterAmerican Studies and World Affairs,* 26 (August 1984): 357–384.

Fascell, Dante, "U.S. Immigration Policy: Federal-State Coordination." Washington, D.C.: Georgetown University, December 5, 1980.

Ford, President Gerald P., "CBS Interview," *Weekly Compilation of Presidential Documents,* 11 (April 21, 1975): 415–417.

——, "The President's Address Delivered Before a Joint Session of the Congress," *Weekly Compilation of Presidential Decuments,* 11 (April 10, 1975): 359–364.

——, "President's Advisory Committee on Refugees. Executive Order 11860," *Weekly Compilation of Presidential Documents,* 11 (May 19, 1975): 532.

——, "The President's News Conference," *Weekly Compilation of Presidential Documents,* 11 (April 3, 1975): 327–330.

——, "Remarks of the President upon Signing Executive Order 11860 Establishing the Committee on Refugees from Southeast Asia," *Weekly Compilation of Presidential Documents,* 11 (May 19, 1975): 531–532.

——, "Vietnam Humanitarian Assistance and Evacuation Bill," *Weekly Compilation of Presidential Documents,* 11 (May 1, 1975): 474.

Forsythe, David P., "The Palestine Question: Dealing with a Long-Term Refugee Situation," *Annals of the American Academy of Political and Social Science,* 467 (May 1983): 89–101.

Fragomen, Austin T., "The Final Report and Recommendations of the Select Commission on Immigration and Refugee Policy: A Summary," *International Migration Review,* 15 (1981): 758–768.

Fragomen, A., Jr., and Tomasi, Lydio F. (eds.), *In Defense of the Alien,* II (New York: Center for Migration Studies, 1980): 117–126.

Fraser, Donald. "Congress' Role in the Making of International Human Rights Policy," in Kommers, Donald and Loescher, Gilburt (eds.), *Human Rights and American Foreign Policy* (Notre Dame, Ind.: University of Notre Dame Press, 1979).

Frost, Frank, "Vietnam, Asean, and the Indochina Refugee Crisis," *Southeast Asian Affairs,* 1980: 347–367.

Gallup Poll Index, "The New Americans, Are They Welcome? A Refugee Referendum," *Gallup Poll Index,* Report No. 119 (May 1975): 2–5.

Gerlach, Allen, "El Salvador: Background to the Violence," *Contemporary Review,* 239 (July 1981).

Ghoshal, Animesh, and Crowley, Thomas M., "Refugees and Immigrants: A Human Rights Dilemma," *Human Rights Quarterly,* 5 (August 1983): 327–347.

Gitelman, Zvi, "Exiting from the Soviet Union: Emigres or Refugees?," *Michigan Yearbook of Transnational Legal Studies,* 1982: 43–61.

Goldberg, Arthur, "Statement Before the General Assembly," *Department of State Bulletin*, 50 (January 24, 1966): 128–129.

Gomey, Lionel, and Comerson, Bruce, "El Salvador: The Current Danger," *Foreign Policy*, Summer 1981.

Goodstadt, Leo, "Race, Refugees and Rice: China and the Indochina Triangle," *Round Table*, July 1978.

Gordenker, Leon, "Global Trends in Refugee Movements," in Lydio F. Tomasi (ed.), *In Defense of the Alien*, V (New York: Center for Migration Studies, 1983): 4–9.

———, "The International Setting of American Refugee Policy," in D. Papademetriou and M. Miller (eds.), *The Unavoidable Issue* (Philadelphia: Institute for the Study of Human Issues, 1983).

———, "Organizational Expansion and Limits in International Services for Refugees," *International Migration Review*, 15 (Spring 1981): 74–87.

———, "Refugees in Developing Countries and Transnational Organization," *Annals of the American Academy of Political and Social Science*, 467 (May 1983): 62–77.

Gordon, Charles, "Rights of Aliens to Claim Asylum," in Austin Fragomen, Jr., and Lydio F. Tomasi (eds.), *In Defense of the Alien*, II (New York: Center for Migration Studies, 1980): 117–126.

Gordon, Dennis R., and Munro, Margaret M., "The External Dimension of Civil Insurrection: International Organizations and the Nicaraguan Revolution," *Journal of Interamerican Studies and World Affairs*, 25 (February 1983): 59–81.

Grahl-Madsen, Atle, "The Boat People: Our Concern," *AWR Bulletin*, 17 (1979): 97–100.

———, "Identifying the World's Refugees," *Annals of the American Academy of Political and Social Science*, 467 (May 1983): 11–23.

———, "International Solidarity and the Protection of Refugees," *AWR Bulletin*, 1 (1981): 19–47.

———, "Regulating the Refugees: U.N. Convention/Protocol on Territorial Asylum and Legal Developments in Various Countries," in Lydio F. Tomasi (ed.), *In Defense of the Alien*, V (New York: Center for Migration Studies, 1983): 64–70.

Haig, Secretary of State Alexander, "Statement to ASEAN Ministers," June 20, 1981, *Department of State Bulletin*, 81 (August 1981): 40.

Haines, David, Rutherford, Dorothy, and Thomas, Patrick, "Southeast Asian Refugees in the United States," *Migration Today*, 11 (1982): 9–39.

Hanson, Christopher T., "Behind the Paper Curtain: Asylum Policy v. Asylum Practice," *New York University Review of Law and Social Change*, 7 (Winter 1978): 107–141.

Harris, Art, "Boatlift Sends Angry Florida Officials into Tropical Politics," *Washington Post*, December 22, 1981: A-7.

Hawke, David, "The Killing of Cambodia," *The New Republic*, November 15, 1982: 17–21.

Hecklinger, Carol P., "The Basic Reception and Placement Grant," in Lydio F. Tomasi (ed.), *In Defense of the Alien*, V (New York: Center for Migration Studies, 1983): 116–119.

Helton, Arthur, "Political Asylum under the 1980 Refugee Act: An Unfulfilled Promise," *University of Michigan Journal of Law Reform*, 17 (1984): 243.

Henkel, Joachim, "International Protection of Refugees," in Lydio F. Tomasi (ed.), *In Defense of the Alien*, V (New York: Center for Migration Studies, 1983): 53–63.

Hewlett, Sylvia Ann. "Coping with Illegal Immigrants," *Foreign Affairs*, 60 (Winter 1981–1982): 358–378.

Hiebert, Murray, "Famine in Kampuchea: Politics of a Tragedy," *Indochina Issues*, 4 (December 1979): 1–6.

Hohl, Donald W., "The Indochinese Refugee: The Evolution of United States Policy," *International Migration Review*, 12 (Spring 1978): 128–132.

———, "The United States Refugee Act of 1980," *Migration News*, 29 (July-December 1980): 10–15.

Holborn, Louise. "The League of Nations and the Refugee Problem," *Annals of the American Academy of Political and Social Science*, 203 (May, 1939): 124–135.

Holbrooke, Richard C., "Admission of 15,000 Indochinese," Department of State statement. Washington, D.C.: Department of State, Bureau of Public Affairs, August 4, 1977.

Huyck, Earl E., and Bouvier, Leon F., "The Demography of Refugees," *Annals of the American Academy of Political and Social Science*, 467 (May 1983): 39–61.

International Commission of Jurists, *Bulletin*, 17 (1963): 19–25.

———, *Bulletin*, 25 (1966): 1–5.

———, *Bulletin*, 31 (1967): 28–33.

International Institute for Strategic Studies, "Indochina and ASEAN," *Strategic Survey 1982–1983*, 1983: 95–99.

Jacqueney, Theodore, "Vietnam's Gulag Archipelago," *New York Times*, September 17, 1976.

Jaeger, Gilbert, "Refugee Asylum: Policy and Legislative Developments," *International Migration Review*, 15 (Spring 1981): 52–68.

Johnson, President Lyndon B., "Remarks at the Signing of the Immigration Bill," October 3, 1965, *Public Papers of the Presidents, Lyndon B. Johnson, 1965*, Vol. II (Washington, D.C.: Government Printing Office, 1966): 1038–1040.

Kennedy, Edward M., "Refugee Act of 1981," *International Migration Review*, 15 (May 1981): 141–156.

Kennedy, President John F., "Immigration Message to Congress," *Congressional Record*, 109 (July 31, 1963): 13769.

———, "Speech Before the American Society of Newspaper Editors," April 20, 1961, *Department of State Bulletin*, 44 (May 8, 1961): 659–661.

Kiljunen, Kimmo, "The Tragedy of Kampuchea," *Alternatives*, 9 (1983): 251–270.

Klein, Wells C., "Mass Asylum," in Lydio F. Tomasi (ed.), *In Defense of the Alien*, V (New York: Center for Migration Studies, 1983): 19–22.

Korey, William, "The Future of Soviet Jewry: Emigration and Assimilation," *Foreign Affairs*, Fall 1979: 67–82.

Kurth, James, "Refugees: America Must Do More," *Foreign Policy*, 36 (Fall 1979): 12–19.

Kurzban, Ira G., "A Critical Analysis of Refugee Law," *University of Miami Law Review*, 36 (September 1983): 865–882.

Lacouture, J., "Cambodge: La Revolution suicidée," *Nouvel Observator*, October 1978: 110–126.

Landstreet, Barent, "Cuba," in Segal, Aaron Lee (ed.), *Population Process in the Caribbean* (Lexington, Mass.: D. C. Heath, 1975).

Leapman, Michael, "Haiti Boat People Are America's Newest Problem," *The Times* (London), March 12, 1980.

Leifer, Michael, "Conflict and Regional Order in Southeast Asia," *Adelphi Papers*, 162. London: International Institute for Strategic Studies, 1980.

Leibowitz, Arnold H. "The Refugee Act of 1980: Problems and Congressional Concerns," *Annals of the American Academy of Political and Social Science*, 467 (May 1983): 163–172.

Leimsidor, Bruce, "The Matching Grant Program," in Lydio F. Tomasi (ed.), *In Defense of the Alien*, V (New York: Center for Migration Studies, 1983): 108–111.

LeMaster, Roger J., and Zall, Barnaby, "Compassion Fatigue: The Expansion of Refugee Admissions to the U.S.," *Boston College International and Comparative Law Review*, 6 (Spring 1983): 447–474.

Leo Grande, Leo, "Cuba Policy Recycled," *Foreign Policy*, 46 (Spring 1982): 105–119.

———, "The Revolution in Nicaragua: Another Cuba?" *Foreign Affairs*, 58 (Fall 1979): 28–50.

Leo Grande, Leo, and Robbins, Carla A., "Oligarchs and Officers: The Crisis in El Salvador," *Foreign Affairs*, 58 (Summer 1980): 1084–1103.

Loescher, G. D., "Power Politics in Indochina," *The Year Book of World Affairs*, 1983: 129–148.

Loescher, Gilburt, and Scanlan, John, "Human Rights, U.S. Foreign Policy and Haitian Refugees," *Journal of Inter-American Studies and World Affairs*, 26 (August 1984): 313–356.

———, "Mass Asylum and U.S. Policy in the Caribbean," *World Today*, 37 (October 1981): 387–395.

MacEoin, Gary, "Playing Politics with Refugees," *The Progressive*, 44 (July 1980).

McCarthy, K., and Ronfledt, D., "Immigration as an Intrusive Global Flow," in M. Kritz (ed.), *United States Immigration and Refugee Policy* (Lexington, Mass.: D. C. Heath, 1983).

McDougal, Myles S., Lasswell, Harold D., and Chen, Lung-chu, "The Protection of Aliens from Discrimination and World Public Order: Responsibility of States Conjoined with Human Rights," *American Journal of International Law,* 70 (1976): 434.

Mahoney, Larry, "Welcome to Camp Krome," *Tropic,* January 10, 1982.

Mancorz, Paul, "A Model of Professional Adaptation of Refugees: The Cuban Case in the U.S. 1959–1970," *International Immigration,* 11 (1973): 171–183.

Markowitz, Arthur A., "Humanitarianism v. Restrictionism: The United States and the Hungarian Refugees," *International Migration Review,* 7 (Spring 1973): 46.

Martin, David A., "The Refugee Act of 1980: Its Past and Future," *University of Michigan Yearbook of Transnational Law,* 1982: 91–123.

Maselli, G., "World Population Movements," *International Immigration,* 9 (1971): 117–125.

Maynard, P. C. "The Legal Competence of the UNHCR," *The International and Comparative Law Quarterly,* 31 (July 1983): 415–425.

Mitchell, William L., "The Cuban Refugee Program," *Social Security Bulletin,* Washington, 25 (March 1962): 3–8.

Mohn, Sid L. "Central American Refugees: The Search for Appropriate Responses," in *1983 World Refugee Survey* (New York: U.S. Committee for Refugees, 1983: 42–47.

Montgomery, Tommie Sue, "El Salvador: The Descent into Violence," *International Policy Report,* March 1982: 1–11.

Morris, Stephen J., "Human Rights in Vietnam under Two Regimes," in R. D. Gastil, (ed.), *Freedom in the World, 1982* (Westport, Conn.: Greenwood Press, 1982): 219–253.

Mullen, Chris, "The CIA: Tibetan Conspiracy," *Far Eastern Economic Review,* 89 (September 5, 1975): 30–34.

Muskie, Secretary of State Edmund, "The United States and World Refugees," *Current Policy,* No. 231. Washington, D.C.: Department of State, Bureau of Public Affairs, October 6, 1980.

Neary, Golden, "Refugees Denied Asylum," *In These Times,* February 17–23, 1982.

Neehaus, Marjorie, "Vietnam 1978: The Elusive Peace," *Asian Survey,* 19 (January 1979): 85–94.

Nichols, Nick, "Castro's Revenge," *Washington Monthly,* 14 (March 1982): 38–42.

Nixon, Vice President Richard M., "Providing for the Needs of the Hungarian Refugees: Report to President Eisenhower by Vice President Nixon," January 21, 1957, *Department of State Bulletin,* 36 (January 21, 1957): 94–99.

Nocosa, Joseph, "Tales of the Vienna Airport," *Harper's Magazine* 264 (May 1982): 58.

Nordland, Rod, "Cambodia's Holocaust," *Philadelphia Inquirer* June 1980.

——, "Khmer Refugees: Reaching for Oscars," *Indochinese Issues,* 30 (Fall 1982): 1–6.

Novak, Michael, and Schiflee, Richard, "Speeches by the U.S. Delegation Before the United Nations Commission on Human Rights," *World Affairs,* 1981: 226–263.

Osborne, Milton, "The Indochinese Refugee Situation: A Kampuchean Case Study," in Charles A. Price (ed.), *Refugees: The Challenge of the Future* (Canberra: Academy of the Social Sciences in Australia November 1980): 31–75.

——, "The Indochinese Refugees: Cause and Effects," *International Affairs,* 56 (January 1980): 37–53.

Palmieri, U.S. Coordinator for Refugee Affairs Victor, "Global Refugee Problems," *Current Policy,* No. 178. Washington, D.C.: Department of State, Bureau of Public Affairs, April 30, 1980.

——, "Humanitarian Relief in Southeast Asia," *Current Policy,* No. 150. Washington, D.C.: Department of State, Bureau of Public Affairs, March 24, 1980.

Pedraza-Bailey, Silvia. "Cubans and Mexicans in the United States: The Functions of Political and Economic Migration," *Cuban Studies/Estudios Cubanos,* 11 and 12 (July 1981 and January 1982): 80–96.

Peter, Arnold, and Novian, Farhad, "The Numbers Game: The Politics of U.S. Refugee Policy Toward Central America," *LaRaza Law Journal,* 1 (Spring 1984): 168–193.

Pilger, John, "America'a Second War in Indochina," *New Statesmen,* 100 (August 1, 1980): 10–15.

Pingree, David H., "U.S. Domestic Resettlement: A State Perspective," in Lydio F. Tomasi (ed.), *In Defense of the Alien,* V (New York: Center for Migration Studies, 1983): 103–107.

Porter, Gareth, "Vietnam's Ethnic Chinese and the Sino-Vietnamese Conflict," *Bulletin of Concerned Asian Scholars,* 12 (November 4, 1980): 55–60.

Portes, Alejandro, and Bach, Robert L., "Immigrant Earnings: Cuban and Mexican Immigrants in the United States," *International Migration Review,* 14 (1980): 315–341.

Portes, Alejandro, Clark, Juan M., and Bach, Robert L., "The New Wave: A Statistical Profile of Recent Cuban Exiles in the United States," *Cuban Studies/Estudios Cubanos,* 7 (January 1977): 3–32.

Portes, Alejandro, Clark, Juan M., and Lopez, Manuel M., "Six Years Later: The Process of Incorporation of Cuban Exiles in the United States," *Cuban Studies/Estudios Cubanos,* 11–12 (July 1981 and January 1982): 1–24.

Posner, Michael H., "Asylum Adjudication Process," in Lydio F. Tomasi (ed.), *In Defense of the Alien,* V (New York: Center for Migration Studies, 1983): 95–97.

Purcell, James N., testimony before the Subcommittee on Immigration, Refugees, and International Law, House Judiciary Committee, April 17, 1985, reprinted in "U.S. Department of State Refugee Assistance: Overseas and Domestic," *Current*

Policy, No. 693. Washington, D.C.: Department of State, Bureau of Public Affairs, 1985.

Que, Le Thi, Rambo, A. Terry, and Murfin, Gary. "Why They Fled: Refugee Movement During the Spring 1975 Communist Offensive in South Vietnam," *Asian Survey,* 16 (September 1976): 855–863.

Reagan, Ronald W., "Acceptance Speech," July 17, 1980. Reported in *New York Times,* July 18, 1980: 8.

———, "Central America: Defending Our Vital Interests," address before a joint session of Congress, April 27, 1983, reprinted in *Department of State Bulletin,* 83 (June 1983): 1–5.

Refugee Policy Group, "The Meaning of Welfare Dependency Rates," ICMC *Migration News,* 3 (1983): 25–35.

Reny, Anselme, "The Duvalier Phenomenon," *Caribbean Studies,* 14 (July 1974): 38–65.

Rivera, Mario A., "The Cuban and Haitian Influxes of 1980 and the American Response: Retrospect and Prospect," in U.S. Congress, House, Committee on the Judiciary, *Oversight Hearings: Caribbean Migration,* 96th Congress, 2nd Session, 1980.

Rogg, Eleanor Meyer, and Holmberg, Joan J., "The Assimilation of Cubans in the United States," *Migration Today,* 11 (1983): 8–48.

Rose, Peter I., "The Business of Caring: Refugee Workers and Voluntary Agencies," *Refugee Reports,* 4 (1981): 1–6.

———, "Links in a Chain: Observations of the American Refugee Program in Southeast Asia," *Migration Today,* 9 (1981): 22–33.

———, "The Politics and Morality of U.S. Refugee Policy," *Center Magazine,* September-October 1985: 2–14.

———, "Some Reflections on Refugee Policy," *Dissent,* Fall 1984: 484–486.

———, "Some Thoughts about Refugees and the Descendants of Theseus," *International Migration Review,* 15 (Spring-Summer 1981): 8–15.

Rusk, Secretary of State Dean, "Letter of Submittal to the President," *Congressional Record,* September 20, 1968: 27758.

———, "U.S. Position on Special Food Project in Cuba," *Department of State Bulletin,* 48 (March 11, 1963): 357.

Salomone, Frank A., "The Role of the Voluntary Agencies in the Resettlement of Ugandan Asians in the U.S.A.," *International Migration,* XIII (1975): 75–91.

Salter, Paul S., and Mings, Robert C., "The Projected Impact of Cuban Settlement on Voting Patterns in Metropolitan Miami, Florida," *Professional Geographer,* 24 (1972): 123–131.

Scanlan, John, "Asylum Adjudication: Some Due Process Implications," *University of Pittsburgh Law Review,* 44 (Winter 1983): 261–286.

———, "Regulating Refugee Flow: Legal Alternative and Obligation under the Refugee Act of 1980," *Notre Dame Lawyer,* 56 (April 1981): 618–646.

——, "Who Is a Refugee? Procedures and Burden of Proof under the Refugee Act of 1980," in Lydio F. Tomasi (ed.), *In Defense of the Alien*, V (New York: Center for Migration Studies, 1983): 23–37.

Scanlan, John A., and Loescher, G. D., "Mass Asylum and Human Rights in American Foreign Policy," *Political Science Quarterly*, 97 (Spring 1982): 39–56.

——, "U.S. Foreign Policy, 1959–80: Impact on Refugee Flow from Cuba," *Annals of the American Academy of Political and Social Science*, 467 (May 1983): 116–137.

Schaefer, Richard I., and Schaefer, Sandra T., "Reluctant Welcome: U.S. Response to South Vietnamese Refugees," *New Community*, 4 (Autumn 1975): 366–370.

Scheinman, Ronald S., "Refugees: Goodby to the Good Old Days," *Annals of the American Academy of Political and Social Science*, 467 (May 1983): 78–88.

Schroeder, Richard C., "Refugee Policy," *Educational Research Reports*, 1 (May 30, 1980): 387–404.

Schultz, Secretary of State George, "America and the Struggle for Freedom," address Before the Commonwealth Club of San Francisco, February 22, 1985, reprinted in *Current Policy*, No. 659. Washington, D.C.: Department of State, Bureau of Public Affairs, 1985.

——, "Proposed Refugee Admissions for FY 1986," September 17, 1985, in *Current Policy*, No. 738. Washington, D.C.: Department of State, Bureau of Public Affairs, 1985.

Schwartz, Abba, "Foreign and Domestic Implications of U.S. Immigration," *Department of State Bulletin*, 36 (January 27, 1957): 96.

Segal, A., "Haiti," in A. Segal (ed.), *Population Patterns in the Caribbean* (Lexington, Mass.: D. C. Heath, 1975): 197–204.

Shawcross, William, "Cambodia: A Decade of Destruction," *Washington Post*, March 16–21, 1980.

——, "Cambodia's Burial," *New York Review of Books* 31 (May 10, 1984): 16.

——, "In a Grim Country," *New York Review of Books*, 28 (September 24, 1981): 62.

——, "The Destruction of Cambodia: Millions Die in Cockpit of International Rivalry," *Roundtable*, January 1980: 33–38.

——, "The Khmer Rouge's Iron Grip on Cambodia," *Far Eastern Economic Review*, January 2, 1976: 9–10.

——, "Refugees and Rhetoric," *Foreign Policy*, 36 (Fall 1979).

Sheehy, Gail, "Cambodian Refugees: America's Double Cross," *Washington Post*, February 6, 1983: 85.

Sheldon, Richard C., and Dutkowski, John, "Are Soviet Satellite Refugee Interviews Projectable?" *Public Opinion Quarterly*, 16 (Winter 1952–1953): 579–594.

Simpson, Alan K., "A Difficult Balance," in Lydio F. Tomasi (ed.), *In Defense of the Alien*, V (New York: Center for Migration Studies, 1983): 120–124.

Smith, Patrick, "Pull Factor Gets the Push," *Far Eastern Economic Review*, July 17, 1981: 26–28.

Smith, Wayne, "Dateline Havana: Myopic Policy," *Foreign Policy*, 48 (Fall 1982): 157–174.

Smyser, W. R., "Refugees: A Never Ending Story," *Foreign Affairs*, 64 (Fall 1985): 154–168.

Soskiss, Philip, "The Adjustment of Hungarian Refugees in New York," *International Migration Review*, Fall 1967: 40–46.

Stein, Barry N., "The Commitment to Refugee Resettlement," *Annals of the American Academy of Political and Social Science*, 467 (May 1983): 187–201.

——, "Indochinese Refugees: The 'New' Boat People," *Migration Today*, 6 (December 1978).

——, "Legislative and Judicial Developments: The Geneva Conference and the Indochinese Refugee Crisis," *International Migration Review*, 13 (Winter 1979): 716–723.

——, "The Refugee Experience: An Overview of Refugee Research," paper presented at a conference on the refugee experience sponsored by Minority Rights Group and the Royal Anthropological Institute, London, February 22, 1980.

Stelf, William, "Hopeless in Haiti," *The Progressive*, 43 (October 1979): 34.

Stepan, Alfred, "The United States and Latin America: Vital Interests and the Instruments of Power," *Foreign Affairs, American and the World-1979*, 58 (1979): 659–692.

Stepick, Alex, "Haitian Boat People: A Study in the Conflicting Forces Shaping U.S. Immigration Policy," *Law and Contemporary Problems*, 45 (Spring 1982): 163–196.

Stern, Lewis M., "Response to Vietnamese Refugees: Surveys of Public Opinion," *Social Work*, July 1981: 306–311.

Suhrke, Astri, "Global Refugee Movements and Strategies of Response," in Mary M. Kritz (ed.), *U.S. Immigration: Global and Domestic Issues* (Lexington, Mass.: D. C. Heath, 1982).

——, "Indochinese Refugees and American Policy," *World Today*, February 1981: 54–62.

——, "Indochinese Refugees: The Law and Politics of First Asylum," *Annals of the American Academy of Political and Social Science*, 467 (May 1983): 102–115.

——, "A New Look at America's Refugee Policy," *Indochina Issues*, 10 (September 1980): 1–8.

Swartz, Dale F., "First Asylum and Governance: Thoughts on a Framework for Making Hard Choices," in Lydio F. Tomasi (ed.), *In Defense of the Alien*, V (New York: Center for Migration Studies, 1983): 71–78.

Tang, Truong Nhu, "The Myth of a Liberation," *New York Review of Books*, 16 (October 21, 1982).

Tawardros, Jerri Blaney, "A Comparative Overview of the Vietnamese and Cuban Refugee Crises: Did the Refugee Act of 1980 Change Anything?" *Suffolk Transnational Law Journal*, 6 (Spring 1982): 25–57.

Teitlebaum, Michael S., "Immigration, Refugees, and Foreign Policy," *International Organization*, 38 (Summer 1984): 429–450.

———, "Right vs. Right: Immigration and Refugee Policy in the United States," *Foreign Affairs*, Fall 1980: 21–59.

Thomas, John F., "Cuban Refugees in the United States," *International Migration Review*, 1 (1967), reprinted in Carlos E. Cortes (ed.), *Cuban Refugee Programs* (New York: Arno Press, 1980): 46–57.

———, "The U.S.A. as a Country of First Asylum," *International Migration*, 3 (1965): 5–14.

Togi, Doan Uan, and Chanoff, David, "Learning from Vietnam," *Encounter*, 59 (October 1982).

Truman, Harry S., "International Affairs and Finance," excerpts from "President's Budget Message for 1951," reprinted in *Department of State Bulletin*, 22 (January 23, 1950): 136–139.

———, "Special Message to Congress," March 24, 1952, in *Public Papers of the Presidents, Harry S. Truman 1952* (Washington, D.C.: Government Printing Office, 1965): 209–215.

———, "Special Message to the Congress on the Admission of Displaced Persons," July 7, 1947 in *Public Papers of the Presidents, Harry S. Truman 1947* (Washington, D.C.: Government Printing Office, 1963): 327–329.

———, "State of the Union Address," in *Public Papers of the Presidents, Harry S. Truman 1947* (Washington, D.C.: Government Printing Office, 1963): 1–6.

Tsamenyi, B. Martin, "The Boat People: Are They Refugees?" *Human Rights Quarterly*, 5 (August 1983): 348–373.

Valenta, Jiri, "The Soviet-Cuban Alliance in Africa and the Caribbean," *World Today*, February 1981: 45–53.

———, "The USSR, Cuba, and the Crisis in Central America," *Orbis*. 25 (Fall 1981): 715–747.

Weis, Paul, "The International Protection of Refugees," *American Journal of International Law*, 48 (1954): 193.

———, "Legal Aspects of the Convention of 28 July 1951 Relating to the Status of Refugees," *British Yearbook of International Law*, 30 (1953): 478.

———, "The 1967 Protocol Relating to the Status of Refugees and Some Questions of the Law or Treaties," in *British Yearbook of International Law*, 42 (1967): 36–70.

Weissbrodt, David, "Human Rights Legislation and U.S. Foreign Policy," *Georgia Journal of International and Comparative Law*, 7 (1977): 231–287.

Weissman, Steve, "Last Tangle in Tibet," *Pacific Research and World Empire Telegram*, 4 (July-August 1973).

Willday, Diana, "Resettlement of Indochinese Refugees and Displaced Persons," speech at University of Freiburg, Switzerland, May 2, 1980.

Wilson, Larman, "The Dominican Republic and Haiti," in Harold E. Davis and

Larman Wilson (eds.), *Latin American Foreign Policies: An Analysis* (Baltimore: Johns Hopkins Press, 1975): 198–218.

Wright, Robert, "Cuban/Haitian Contracts Granted by HHS," in Lydio F. Tomasi (ed.), *In Defense of the Alien*, V (New York: Center for Migration Studies, 1983): 112–115.

Young, Stephen, "Who Is a Refugee? A Theory of Persecution," in Lydio F. Tomasi (ed.), *In Defense of the Alien*, V (New York: Center for Migration Studies, 1983): 38–52.

Zinner, P., "Revolution in Hungary: Reflections on the Vicissitudes of a Totalitarian System," *Journal of Politics*, 21 (February 1959): 3–36.

Zolberg, Aristide, "Contemporary Transnational Migrations in Historical Perspective: Patterns and Dilemmas," in Mary M. Kritz (ed.), *U.S. Immigration and Refugee Policy* (Lexington, Mass.: D. C. Heath, 1983): 15–51.

———, "The Formation of New States as a Refugee-Generating Process," *Annals of the American Academy of Political and Social Science*, 467 (May 1983): 24–38.

———, "International Migration Politics in a Changing World System," in William McNeill and Ruth Adams (eds.), *Human Migrations: Patterns and Policies* (Bloomington: Indiana University Press, 1978).

Zucker, Naomi Flink, "The Haitians Versus the United States: The Courts as Last Resort," *Annals of the American Academy of Political and Social Science*, 467 (May 1938): 151–162.

———, "Huddled Masses Department: Some People Are More Equal than Others," *The Progressive*, 46 (March 1982): 39–42.

Zucker, Norman, "Refugee Resettlement in the United States: Policy and Problems," *Annals of the American Academy of Political and Social Science*, 467 (May 1983): 172–186.

———, "Refugee Resettlement in the United States: The Role of the Voluntary Agencies," in Deborah M. Levy. *Transnational Legal Problems of Refugees: 1982 Michigan Yearbook of International Legal Studies* (New York: Clark Boardman, 1982): 155–179.

PAMPHLETS AND REPORTS

Adamic, Louis. *America and the Refugees*, Public Affairs Pamphlet No. 29. New York: Public Affairs Committee, Inc., 1939.

American Civil Liberties Union, National Immigration and Alien Rights Project. *Salvadorans in the United States: The Case for Extended Voluntary Departure.* Washington, D.C.: American Civil Liberties Union, December 1983.

Americas Watch Committee. *Guatemalan Refugees in Mexico 1980–1984.* New York: Americas Watch Committee, September 1984.

Americas Watch Committee and American Civil Liberties Union. *Report on Human Rights in El Salvador.* New York: Vintage Books, 1982.

Americas Watch, Helsinki Watch, and Lawyers' Committee for International Human Rights. *A Critique of the Department of State's Country Reports on Human Rights for 1981.* New York, April 1982.

——, ——, and ——. *Review of the Department of State's Country Reports on Human Rights Practices for 1982.* New York, February 1983.

——, ——, and ——. *". . . In the Face of Cruelty": The Reagan Administration's Human Rights Record in 1984.* New York, 1985.

Americas Watch and Lawyers' Committee for International Human Rights. *Free Fire: a Report on Human Rights in El Salvador.* Fifth supplement. New York, 1984.

Amnesty International. *Allegations of Human Rights Violations in Democratic Kampuchea,* statement submitted by AI to UN Sub-Commission on Prevention of Discrimination and Protection of Minorities. August 1978.

——. *Amnesty International Appeals Against Forcible Repatriation of Kampuchean Refugees.* London: Amnesty International, May 29, 1980.

——. *Amnesty International Reports 1977–1985.* London: Amnesty International, 1977–1985.

——. *Amesty International Reports Massacres in New Guatamalan Security Drive.* London: Amnesty International, October 11, 1982.

——. *Chile.* London: Amnesty International, 1974.

——. *Guatemala: A Government Program of Political Murder.* London: Amnesty International, 1981.

——. *Guatemala: Massive Extrajudicial Executions in Rural Areas under the Government of General Efrain Rios Montt.* London: Amnesty International, July 1982.

——. *Haiti Briefing.* London: Amnesty International, March 13, 1985.

——. *Haiti: Human Rights Violations: October 1980-October 1981.* London: Amnesty International, November 1981.

——. *Political Prisoners in the People's Democratic Republic of Laos.* London: Amnesty International, March 1980.

——. *Report,* London: Amnesty International, March 1, 1973.

——. *Report of an Amnesty International Mission to the Socialist Republic of Vietnam 10–21 December 1979.* London: Amnesty International, 1981.

——. *Submission to the Government of the Socialist Republic of Vietnam on Amnesty International's Current Concerns.* London, Amnesty International, April 1983.

Archer, Robert. *Vietnam: The Habit of War.* London: Catholic Institute for International Relations, 1983.

Bar of the City of New York, Committee on Immigration and Nationality Law. *The Future of Political Asylum in the United States.* April 1984.

Brandel, Sarah K. *Refugees: New Dimensions to an Old Problem.* Washington, D.C.: Overseas Development Council, 1980.

Bull, David. *The Poverty of Diplomacy: Kampuchea and the Outside World.* Oxford: OXFAM, 1983.

Campbell, John C. *United States Policy Toward Communist Eastern Europe,* background paper for Seventh Midwest Seminar on U.S. Foreign Policy. Minnesota World Affairs Center, 1964.

Cerquone, Joseph. *Vietnamese Boat People.* New York: U.S. Committee for Refugees, February 1984.

Cherne, Leo. *A Personal Recollection.* New York: International Rescue Committee, 1979.

Christian Legal Aid Service. *Human Rights in El Salvador: Report for the Period January-December 1983.* Geneva: World Council of Churches, 1984.

Committee for the Defense of Human Rights in Honduras, *Report on Human Rights in Honduras in 1983.* Geneva: World Council of Churches, 1984.

Copeland, Ronald, and Fagen, Patricia Weiss. *Political Asylum: A Background Paper on Concepts, Procedures and Problems.* Washington, D.C.: Refugee Policy Group, December 1982.

DeVecchi, Robert. *Indochinese Parole Program Situation Report.* New York: International Rescue Committee, November 25, 1977.

D'Souza, Frances, and Crisp, Jeff. *The Refugee Dilemma,* Minority Rights Group Report No. 43. London: Minority Rights Group, February 1985.

Fagen, Patricia Weiss. *Refugee and Asylum Issues in Inter-American Relations.* Washington, D.C.: Refugee Policy Group, February 1983.

———. *Refugees and Displaced Persons in Central America.* Washington, D.C.: Refugee Policy Group, March 1984.

———. *Resource Paper on Political Asylum and Refugee Status in the United States.* Washington, D.C.: Refugee Policy Group, 1985.

———. *Well-Founded Fears and the Burden of Proof in Political Asylum: The Stevie Case.* Washington, D.C.: Refugee Policy Group, July 1983.

Forbes, Susan. *Adaptation and Integration of Recent Refugees to the United States.* Washington, D.C.: Refugee Policy Group, 1985.

———. *The Geographic Distribution of Indochinese Refugees.* Washington, D.C.: Refugee Policy Group, January 1983.

———. *Meaning of Welfare Dependency Rates.* Washington, D.C.: Refugee Policy Group, 1982.

Ford Foundation. *Refugees and Migrants: Problems and Program Responses.* New York, 1983.

Frankel, Robert. *The Resettlement of Indochinese Refugees in the United States: A Selected Bibliography.* Washington, D.C.: Indochina Refugee Action Center, 1980.

Gallagher, Dennis. *United States Refugee Policy in Latin America.* Washington, D.C.: Refugee Policy Group, February 1983.

Gallagher, Dennis, Forbes, Susan, and Fagen, Patricia Weiss. *Of Special Humanitarian Concern: U.S. Refugee Admissions since Passage of the Refugee Act.* Washington, D.C.: Refugee Policy Group, 1985.

Hamilton, J. Patrick. *Cambodian Refugees in Thailand: The Limits of Asylum.* New York: U.S. Committee for Refugees, 1982.

Heritage Foundation, "Are United Nations Camps Cheating Refugees in Honduras?" *Backgrounder,* No. 368. Washington, D.C., July 23, 1984.

Hooper, M., and Murphy, M. *Violations of Human Rights in Haiti,* New York: Lawyers' Committee for International Human Rights, 1980.

International Rescue Committee. *A Chronology of the International Rescue Committee's Special Studies, Commissions and Specific Rescue Projects,* New York: IRC, n.d.

——. *Resettling Hungarian Refugees: A Report on the Resettlement Activities of the International Rescue Committee, Inc., 1957–1959.* (Mimeo.) New York, 1960.

——. *Saving Freedom's Seed Corn.* New York: IRC, 1958.

Jones, Allen K. *Iranian Refugees: The Many Faces of Persecution.* New York: U.S. Committee for Refugees, December 1984.

Kuper, Leo. *International Action Against Genocide,* Minority Rights Group Report No. 53. London: Minority Rights Group, 1984.

Lawyers' Committee for International Human Rights. *The Haitians in Miami: Current Immigration Practices in the United States.* New York: Lawyers' Committee for International Human Rights, 1978.

——. *Honduras: A Crisis on the Border,* a report on Salvadoran refugees in Honduras. New York, 1985.

——. *A Report to the OAS: Violations of Human Rights in Haiti, June, 1981–September, 1982.* New York: Lawyers' Committee for International Human Rights, 1982.

Lawyers' Committee for International Human Rights and Americas Watch. *El Salvador's Other Victims: The War on the Displaced.* New York, April 1984.

Lawyers' Committee for International Human Rights, Americas Watch Committee, and International League for Human Rights. *Haiti: Report of Human Rights Mission, June 26–29, 1983.* New York: Lawyers' Committee for International Human Rights, August 1983.

Lichtenberg, J. *Persecution vs. Poverty: Are the Haitians Refugees?* College Park, Md.: Center for Philosophy and Public Policy, Spring 1982.

Lutheran Council in the U.S.A. *Fact-finding Tour of Southeast Asia Refugee Situation, January 19–23, 1983.* New York: Religious Advisory Committee, January 31, 1983.

Mullen, Chris. *The Tibetans,* Minority Rights Group Report No. 49. London: Minority Rights Group, 1981.

Newland, Kathleen. *Refugees: The New International Politics of Displacement,* Worldwatch Paper 43. Washington, D.C.: Worldwatch Institute, March 1981.

Refugee Policy Group. *The U.S.-Based Refugee Field: An Organizational Analysis.* Washington, D.C.: Refugee Policy Group, April 1982.

——. *Refugee Issues: Current Status and Directions for the Future.* Washington, D.C.: Refugee Policy Group, 1983.

Rubin, Gary. *The Asylum Challenge to Western Nations.* New York: U.S. Committee for Refugees, December 1984.

———. *Refugee Protection: An Analysis and Action Proposal.* New York: U.S. Committee for Refugees, March 1983.

Spillane, Mary. *Flight to Uncertainty: Poles Outside Poland.* New York: U.S. Committee for Refugees, 1982.

Stepick, Alex. *Haitian Refugees in the U.S.,* Minority Rights Group Report No. 52. London: Minority Rights Group, January 1982.

Tripp, Rosemary E. (ed.). *1980 World Refugee Survey.* New York: U.S. Committee for Refugees, 1980.

———. *1981 World Refugee Survey.* New York: U.S. Committee for Refugees, 1981.

———. *1982 World Refugee Survey.* New York: U.S. Committee for Refugees, 1982.

———. *1983 World Refugee Survey.* New York: U.S. Committee for Refugees, 1983.

———. *1984 World Refugee Survey.* New York: U.S. Committee for Refugees, 1984.

Zellerbach Commission. *Report on the European Refugee Situation,* sponsored by the International Refugee Rescue Committee. N.p.: International Rescue Committee, 1957.

CONGRESSIONAL MATERIALS

U.S. Congress, House. *Message from the President of the United States Authorizing Additional 300,000 Immigrants into United States to Alleviate Problems Created by Communist Tyranny in Europe.* House Document No. 400. 82nd Congress, 2nd Session, 1952.

U.S. Congress, House, Committee on Appropriations. *Department of Transportation and Related Agency Appropriation Bill: House Report No. 783.* 97th Congress, 2nd Session, 1982.

———. *Supplemental Appropriation bill, 1978.* Hearings, 95th Congress, 1st Session, 1977.

———. *Supplemental Appropriation bill, 1978: Report with Additional Views to accompany H.R. 9375.* 95th Congress, 1st Session, 1977.

U.S. Congress, House, Committee on Appropriations, Subcommittee on Foreign Operations and Related Agencies. *Foreign Assistance and Related Agencies Appropriations for 1978.* Hearings, 95th Congress, 1st Session, 1977.

———. *Foreign Assistance and Related Agencies Appropriations for 1979.* Hearings, 95th Congress, 2nd Session, 1978.

U.S. Congress, House, Committee on Appropriations, Subcommittee on the Departments of Labor and Health, Education, and Welfare. *Departments of Labor, and Health, Education, and Welfare Appropriations for 1979.* Hearings, 95th Congress, 2d Session, 1978.

——. *Indochina Refugee Assistance.* Hearing, 95th Congress, 1st session, 1977.

U.S. Congress, House, Committee of Conference. *Amending the Displaced Persons Act of 1948: House Report No. 2187.* 81st Congress, 2nd Session, 1950.

——. *Displaced Persons Act of 1948: House Report No. 2410.* 80th Congress, 2nd Session, 1948.

——. *Immigration and Nationality Act: House Conference Report No. 1101 on H.R. 2589.* 89th Congress, 1st Session, 1965.

——. *Internal Security Act of 1950: House Conference Report No. 3112 on H.R. 9490.* 81st Congress, 2nd Session, 1950.

——. *Refugee Act of 1980: House Conference Report No. 781,* 96th Congress, 2nd Session, 1982.

——. *Refugee Relief Bill of 1953: House Report No. 1069.* 83rd Congress, 1st Session, 1953.

——. *Status of Cuban Refugees: House Conference Report No. 2332 on H.R. 15183.* 89th Congress, 2nd Session, 1966.

U.S. Congress, House and Senate, Joint Economic Committee. *Indochinese Refugees: The Impact on First Asylum Countries and Implications for American Policy.* Washington, D.C.: Government Printing Office, 1980.

U.S. Congress, House, Committee on Foreign Affairs. *Cuba and the Caribbean.* Hearings. 91st Congress, 2nd Session, 1970.

——. *Emergency Security Assistance Act of 1973.* Hearings, 93rd Congress, 1st Session, 1973.

——. *The Indochinese Refugee Situation August 1979.* Report of a study mission. 96th Congress, 1st Session, 1979.

——. *International Refugee Organization: Hearings on H.S. Res. No. 207.* 80th Congress, 1st Session, 1947.

——. *Mutual Security Program, Part 1.* Selected Executive Session Hearings of the Committee, 1951–1956: Historical Series, Vol. IX. Washington: Government Printing Office, 1980.

——. *Situation in Indochina.* Hearings, 93rd Congress, 1st Session, 1973.

——. *To Amend the Foreign Assistance Act of 1961.* Hearings, 91st Congress, 2nd Session, 1970.

——. *United States Foreign Policy and the East-West Confrontation.* Selected Executive Session Hearings of the Committee, 1951–1956: Historical Series, Vol. XIV. Washington: Government Printing Office, 1980.

U.S. Congress, House Committee on Foreign Affairs, Subcommittee on East Asia and the Pacific. *International Commission for Supervision and Control in Laos.* Hearings, 88th Congress, 1st Session, 1963.

——. *U.S. Policy and Programs in Cambodia.* Hearings, 93rd Congress, 1st Session, 1973.

U.S. Congress, House, Committee on Foreign Affairs, Subcommittee on Europe.

Denial of Human Rights to Jews in the Soviet Union. Hearings, 92nd Congress, 1st Session, 1971.

——. *Soviet Jewry.* Hearings, 92nd Congress, 1st Session, 1971.

U.S. Congress, House, Committee on Foreign Affairs, Subcommittee on Europe, Subcommittee on International Organizations and Movements. *Tension and Detente: Congressional Perspectives on Soviet American Relations Report.* 93rd Congress, 1st Session, 1973.

U.S. Congress, House, Committee on Foreign Affairs, Subcommittees on Inter-American Affairs and on International Organizations and Movements. *Human Rights in Chile.* Joint Hearings, 93rd Congress, 2nd Session, 1973–1974.

U.S. Congress, House, Committee on Foreign Affairs, Subcommittee on International Operations. *The Refugee Act of 1979.* Hearing, 96th Congress, 1st Session, 1979.

——. *U.S. Refugee Policy.* Hearing, 96th Congress, 1st Session, 1979.

U.S. Congress, House, Committee on Foreign Affairs, Subcommittee on International Organizations. *Briefing on the Growing Refugee Problem: Implications for International Organizations.* Hearing, 96th Congress, 1st Session, 1979.

U.S. Congress, House, Committee on Foreign Affairs, Subcommittee on State Department Organization and Foreign Operations. *Department of State Authorization for Fiscal Year 1973.* Hearings, 92nd Congress, 2nd Session, 1972.

U.S. Congress, House Committee on Immigration and Naturalization. *Admission of German Refugee Children: Hearings on H.J. Res. 165 and H.J. Res. 168.* 76th Congress, 1st Session, 1939.

U.S. Congress, House and Senate, Committees on Immigration and Naturalization, and on Immigration. *Admission of German Refugee Children: Joint Hearings on S.J. Res. 64 and H.J. Res. 168.* 76th Congress, 1st Session, 1939.

U.S. Congress, House, Committee on Intelligence, Subcommittee on Oversight. *The Cuban Emigres: Was There a U.S. Intelligence Failure?* Staff report. 96th Congress, 2nd Session, 1980.

U.S. Congress, House, Committee on International Relations, *Human Rights and U.S. Policy: Argentina, Haiti, Indonesia, Iran, Peru, and the Philippines.* Reports. 94th Congress, 2nd Session, 1976.

——. *The Vietnam-Cambodia Emergency, 1975: Part I. Vietnam Evacuation and Humanitarian Assistance.* Hearings. 94th Congress, 1st Session, 1975.

——. *War Powers: A Test of Compliance Relative to the Danang Sealift, the Evacuation of Phnom Penh, the Evacuation of Saigon, and the Mayaguez Incident.* Hearings, 94th Congress, 1st Session, 1975.

——. *Worldwide Ruling on Immigration: Report to Accompany H.R. 12443.* 95th Congress, 2nd Session, 1978.

U.S. Congress, House, Committee on International Relations, Subcommittee on Asian and Pacific Affairs. *Human Rights in Asia: Communist Countries.* Hearing, 96th Congress, 2nd Session, 1980.

——. *The Indochinese Refugee Situation*. Report. 96th Congress, 1st Session, 1979.

——. *Indochinese Refugees*. Hearings, 96th Congress, 1st Session, 1979.

——. *1979—Tragedy In Indochina: War Refugees, and Famine*. Hearings, 96th Congress, 1st Session, 1979.

——. *1980—the Tragedy in Indochina Continues: War, Refugees, and Famine*. Hearings, 96th Congress, 2nd Session, 1980.

——. *Prospects for Regional Stability: Asia and the Pacific*. Report. 95th Congress, 2nd Session, 1978.

——. *Refugee Developments in Vietnam, Cambodia, and Laos, and United States Policy Regarding Indochinese Refugees*. Hearings, 95th Congress, 2nd Session, 1978.

——. *Refugees from Indochina: Current Problems and Prospects*. Report. 96th Congress, 1st Session, 1979.

——. *Security and Stability in Asia*. Report. 96th Congress, 1st Session, 1979.

——. *U.S. Policy Toward Indochina since Vietnam's Occupation of Kampuchea*. Hearings, 97th Congress, 1st Session, 1981.

U.S. Congress, House, Committee on International Relations, Subcommittee on International Organizations. *Anti-Semitism and Reprisals Against Jewish Emigration in the Soviet Union*. Hearing, 94th Congress, 2nd Session, 1976.

——. *Human Rights and United States Foreign Policy: A Review of the Administration's Record*. Hearing, 95th Congress, 1st Session, 1977.

——. *Human Rights in Cambodia*. Hearing, 95th Congress, 1st Session, 1977.

——. *Human Rights in Chile*. Hearing, 94th Congress, 1st Session, 1975.

——. *Human Rights in Haiti*. Hearing, 94th Congress, 1st Session, 1975.

——. *Human Rights in the International Community and in U.S. Foreign Policy, 1945–75*. 95th Congress, 1st Session, 1977. Study prepared by the Library of Congress, Congressional Research Service.

——. *Human Rights in Iran*. Hearings, 94th Congress, 2nd Session, 1976.

——. *Human Rights in Iran*. Hearings, 95th Congress, 1st Session, 1977.

——. *Human Rights in the Philippines: Recent Developments*. Hearings, 95th Congress, 2nd Session, 1978.

——. *Human Rights in Thailand*. Hearings, 95th Congress, 1st Session, 1977.

——. *Human Rights: The Work of International Organizations and the Role of U.S. Foreign Policy*. Hearings, 93rd Congress, 1st Session, 1973.

——. *Human Rights in the World Community: A Call for U.S. Leadership*. Report. 93rd Congress, 2nd Session, 1974.

——. *Religious Persecution in El Salvador*. Hearings, 95th Congress, 1st Session, 1977.

U.S. Congress, House, Committee on International Relations, Subcommittee on International Security and Scientific Affairs. *War Powers: A Test of Compliance Relative to the Danang Sealift, the Evacuation of Phnom Penh, the Evacuation of Saigon, and the Mayaguez Incident*. Hearings, 94th Congress, 1st Session, 1975.

U.S. Congress, House, Committee on International Relations, Subcommittee on Investigations. *The Vietnam-Cambodia Emergency, 1975: Part II. The Cambodia-Vietnam Debate.* Hearings, 94th Congress, 1st Session, 1975.

———. *The Vietnam-Cambodia Emergency, 1975: Part III. Vietnam Evacuation: Testimony of Ambassador Graham A. Martin.* Hearing, 94th Congress, 2nd Session, 1976.

U.S. Congress, House and Senate, Committee on International Relations and Committee on Foreign Relations. *Country Reports on Human Rights Practices, 1978–1984.* Washington, D.C.: Government Printing Office, 1978–1984.

U.S. Congress, House, Committee on the Judiciary. *Adjusting Status of Cuban Refugees to that of Lawful Permanent Residents: House Report No. 1978 on H.R. 15183.* 89th Congress, 2nd Session, 1966.

———. *Adjustment of Status for Indochina Refugees: Report Together with Additional Views to Accompany H.R. 7769.* 95th Congress, 1st Session, 1977.

———. *Amending the Displaced Persons Act of 1948: House Report No. 581.* 81st Congress, 1st Session, 1949.

———. *Amending Immigration and Nationality Act, and for Other Purposes: House Report No. 745 on H.R. 2580.* 89th Congress, 1st Session, 1965.

———. *Clarifying Immigration Status of Illegal Aliens: House Report No. 118.* 82nd Congress, 1st Session, 1951.

———. *Displaced Persons Act of 1948: House Report No. 1854.* 80th Congress, 2nd Session, 1948.

———. *Displaced Persons Analytical Bibliography: House Report No. 1687.* 81st Congress, 2nd Session, 1950.

———. *Displaced Persons in Europe and Their Resettlement in the United States: House Report No. 1507.* 81st Congress, 2nd Session, 1950.

———. *Emergency Immigration Program: House Report No. 974.* 83rd Congress, 1st Session, 1953.

———. *Migration and Refugee Assistance: Hearing on H.R. 8291.* 87th Congress, 1st Session, 1961.

———. *Refugee Admissions and Resettlement Program—Fiscal Year 1981.* Hearing, 96th Congress, 2nd Session, 1980.

———. *Refugee Admission Proposal for Fiscal Year 1982.* Hearing, 97th Congress, 1st Session, 1981.

———. *Revision of Laws Relative to Immigration, Naturalization and Nationality: House Report No. 1365.* 82nd Congress, 2nd Session, 1952.

U.S. Congress, House, Committee on the Judiciary, Subcommittee No. 1. *Admission of 300,000 Immigrants: Hearings on H.R. 7376.* 82nd Congress, 2nd Session, 1952.

———. *Emergency Immigration Program: Hearings on H.R. 361.* 83rd Congress, 1st Session, 1953.

———. *Migration and Refugee Assistance.* Hearing, 87th Congress, 1st Session, 1961.

U.S. Congress, House, Committee on the Judiciary, Special Subcommittee on Current Immigration and Naturalization Problems. *Expellees and Refugees of German Ethnic Origin: House Report No. 1841.* 81st Congress, 2nd Session, 1950.

U.S. Congress, House, Judiciary Committee, Subcommittee on Immigration and Naturalization. *Permitting Admission of 400,000 Displaced Persons into the United States: Hearings on H.R. 2910.* 80th Congress, 1st Session 1947.

———. *U.S. Refugee Program: Oversight Hearings.* 97th Congress, 1st Session, 1981.

U.S. Congress, House, Committee on the Judiciary, Subcommittee on Immigration, Citizenship, and International Law. *General Policy for Dealing with Requests for Asylum by Foreign Nationals.* Hearings, 93rd Congress, 1st Session, 1973.

———. *Haitian Emigration.* Report. 94th Congress, 2nd Session, 1976.

———. *Hearings on the Refugee Act of 1979: House Report 2816.* 96th Congress, 1st Session, 1979.

———. *Immigration and Refugee Issues in Southern California: An Investigative Trip.* Report. 97th Congress, 1st Session, 1981.

———. *Immigration Reform.* Hearings, 97th Congress, 1st Session, 1981.

———. *Indochina Refugees.* Hearings, 94th Congress, 1st Session, 1975.

———. *Indochina Refugees—Adjustment of Status.* Hearings, 95th Congress, 1st Session, 1977.

———. *Indochinese Refugees: An Update.* Staff report. 95th Congress, 2nd Session, 1978.

———. *Refugee Act of 1979.* Hearings, 96th Congress, 1st Session, 1979.

———. *Refugees from Indochina.* Hearings, 94th Congress, 1st and 2nd Sessions, 1975–1976.

U.S. Congress, House, Committee on the Judiciary, Subcommittee on Immigration, Refugees, and International Law. *Administration's Proposals on Immigration and Refugee Policy.* Joint hearing, 97th Congress, 1st Session, 1981.

———. *Admission of Refugees into the United States.* Hearings, 95th Congress, 1st Session, 1977.

———. *Admission of Refugees into the United States, Part II.* Hearings, 95th Congress, 1st and 2d Sessions, 1978.

———. *Caribbean Migration: Oversight Hearings.* 96th Congress, 2nd Session, 1980.

———. *Consultation Session on Refugee Parole Programs.* Hearing, 95th Congress, 2nd Session, 1978.

———. *Emigration of Soviet Jews.* Report. 94th Congress, 2nd Session, 1975.

———. *Extension of Indochina Refugee Assistance Program: Hearings on H.R. 9133, H.R. 9134, and H.R. 9110,* 95th Congress, 1st Session, 1977.

———. *Immigration Reform: Part 1: Hearings on Omnibus Immigration Control Act.* 97th Congress, 1st Session, 1981.

———. *Indochinese Refugee Problem.* Hearings, 96th Congress, 1st Session, 1979.

———. *Indochinese Refugees and U.S. Refugee Policy.* Hearings, 95th Congress, 1st and 2nd Sessions, 1978.

——. *Reauthorization of Refugee Act of 1980*. Hearings, 97th Congress, 2nd Session, 1982.

——. *Reauthorization of the Refugee Act of 1980*. Hearings, 98th Congress, 1st Session, 1983.

——. *Refugee Act of 1979: Hearings on H.R. 2816*. 96th Congress, 1st Session, 1979.

——. *Refugee Act of 1980 Amendments*. Hearings, 97th Congress, 1st Session, 1981.

——. *U.S. Refugee Program: Oversight Hearings*. 97th Congress, 1st Session, 1981.

U.S. Congress, House, Committee on the Judiciary, Subcommittee on Its Trip to the Soviet Union. *Emigration of Soviet Jews*. Report of special study. 94th Congress, 2nd Session, 1976.

U.S. Congress, House and Senate, Committees on the Judiciary, Subcommittees on Immigration and Naturalization. *Revision of Immigration, Naturalization, and Nationality Laws: Joint Hearings on S. 716, H.R. 2379, and H.R. 2816*. 82nd Congress, 1st Session, 1951.

U.S. Congress, House and Senate. Committees on the Judiciary, Subcommittees on Immigration, Refugees, and International Law, and on Immigration and Refugee Policy. *Immigration Reform and Control Act of 1982: Joint Hearings on H.R. 5872 and S. 2222*. 97th Congress, 2nd Session, 1982.

U.S. Congress, House, Committee on Population. *Immigration to the United States*. Hearings, 95th Congress, 2nd Session, 1978.

U.S. Congress, House, Committee on Un-American Activities. *Protection of United States Against Un-Americans and Subversive Activities: House Report No. 2980 on H.R. 9490*. 81st Congress, 2nd Session, 1950.

U.S. Congress, House, Select Commission on Immigration Policy. *U.S. Immigration Policy and the National Interest*. Report, Washington, D.C.: Select Commission, February 1981.

U.S. Congress, Senate, Committee on Agriculture, Nutrition, and Forestry, Subcommittee on Foreign Agricultural Policy. *Food Aid to Cambodia*. Hearing, 96th Congress, 1st Session, 1979.

U.S. Congress, Senate, Committee on Appropriations. *Departments of Labor and Health, Education, and Welfare and Related Agencies Appropriations for Fiscal Year 1978*. Hearings, 95th Congress, 2nd Session, 1977.

——. *Foreign Assistance and Related Programs Appropriations for Fiscal Year 1979: Hearings, on H.R. 12931*, 95th Congress, 2nd Session, 1978.

——. *Review of Factors Affecting U.S. Diplomatic and Assistance Relations with Haiti*. Special Report by Senator Brooke, 95th Congress, 2nd Session, 1977.

——. *U.S. Foreign Assistance for Haiti: Report No. 620*. 93rd Congress, 2nd Session, 1974.

U.S. Congress, Senate, Armed Services Committee. *National Defense Establishment: Hearings on S. 758*. 80th Congress, 1st Session, 1947.

U.S. Congress, Senate, Committee on Finance, Subcommittee on International

Trade. *Continuing Presidential Authority to Waive Freedom of Emigration Provisions.* Hearing, 98th Congress, 2nd Session, 1984.

U.S. Congress, Senate, Committee on Foreign Relations. *Human Rights and U.S. Foreign Assistance.* Report. 96th Congress, 1st Session, 1979.

——. *International Refugee Organization: Senate Report No. 51.* 80th Congress, 1st Session, 1947.

——. *Migration and Refugee Assistance Act of 1961.* Hearing, 87th Congress, 1st Session, 1961.

——. *Mutual Security Act Extension: Hearings on H.R. 7005*, 82nd Congress, 2nd Session, 1952.

——. *Providing for Membership and Participation by the United States in the International Refugee Organization: Hearings on S. J. Res. 77.* 80th Congress, 1st Session, 1947.

——. *United States Protection of Khmer Refugees.* Staff report. 98th Congress, 2nd Session, 1984.

U.S. Congress, Senate, Committee on Foreign Relations, Subcommittee on Arms Control, Oceans, International Operations, and Environment. *Cambodian Famine and U.S. Contingency Relief Plans.* Hearing, 96th Congress, 1st Session, 1979.

U.S. Congress, Senate, Committee on Foreign Relations, Subcommittee on East Asian and Pacific Affairs. *Indochina.* Hearing, 95th Congress, 2nd Session, 1978.

——. *Southeast Asia.* Hearings, 96th Congress, 2nd Session, 1980.

——. *Southeast Asia Refugee Crisis.* Hearing, 96th Congress, 1st Session, 1979.

——. *U.S. Policy in East Asia.* Hearing, 96th Congress, 1st Session, 1979.

U.S. Congress, Senate, Committee on Foreign Relations, Select Committee to Study Governmental Operations. *Covert Action In Chile 1963–1973.* Report. 94th Congress, 1st Session, 1975.

U.S. Congress, Senate, Committee on Foreign Relations, House, Committee on Foreign Affairs. *Country Reports on Human Rights Practices.* 95th Congress, 1st Session, 1977.

——. *Country Reports on Human Rights Practices.* 95th Congress, 2nd Session, 1978.

——. *Country Reports on Human Rights Practices.* 96th Congress, 1st Session, 1979.

——. *Country Reports on Human Rights Practices,* 96th Congress, 2nd Session, 1980.

——. *Country Reports on Human Rights Practices,* 97th Congress, 1st Session, 1981.

——. *Country Reports on Human Rights Practices,* 97th Congress, 2nd Session, 1982.

——. *Country Reports on Human Rights Practices,* 98th Congress, 1st Session, 1983.

——. *Country Reports on Human Rights Practices,* 98th Congress, 2nd Session, 1984.

——. *Country Reports on Human Rights Practices,* 99th Congress, 1st Session, 1985.

U.S. Congress, Senate, Committee on Human Resources. *Indochina Migration and Refugee Assistance Amendments of 1978: Hearing on S. 3309.* 95th Congress, 2nd Session, 1978.

——. *Indochina Refugee Children's Assistance Act Amendments of 1977: Hearing on S. 2108.* 95th Congress, 1st Session, 1977.

U.S. Congress, Senate, Committee on the Judiciary. *Adjusting Status of Cuban Refugees to That of Lawful Permanent Residents: Senate Report No. 1675.* 89th Congress, 2nd Session, 1966.

——. *Amending the Displaced Persons Act of 1948: Senate Report No. 1237.* 81st Congress, 2nd Session, 1950.

——. *Amending Immigration and Nationality Act, and for Other Purposes: Senate Report No. 748.* 89th Congress, 1st Session, 1965.

——. *Caribbean Refugee Crisis: Cubans and Haitians.* Hearing, 96th Congress, 2nd Session, 1980.

——. *Displaced Persons Act of 1948: Senate Report No. 950.* 80th Congress, 2nd Session, 1948.

——. *Emergency Migration Act of 1953: Senate Report No. 629.* 83rd Congress, 1st Session 1953.

——. *Escapees and Refugees in Western Europe: Senate Report No. 552.* 83rd Congress, 1st Session, 1953.

——. *Immigration and Nationality Act, with Amendments and Notes on Related Laws,* 7th ed. Washington, D.C.: Government Printing Office, 1980.

——. *The Immigration and Naturalization Systems of the United States: Senate Report No. 1515.* 81st Congress, 2nd Session, 1950.

——. *Indochina Refugee Children's Assistance Act Amendments of 1977: Hearing on S. 2108.* 95th Congress, 1st Session, 1977.

——. *Investigation into the Administration of the Refugee Relief Act.* Hearings, 84th Congress, 1st Session, 1955.

——. *Protecting Internal Security of the United States: Senate Report No. 2369 on S. 4027.* 81st Congress, 2nd Session, 1950.

——. *Protection of the United States Against Un-American and Subversive Activities, Parts. 1 and 2: Senate Report No. 1358 on S. 2311.* 81st Congress, 2nd Session, 1950.

——. *Readings on U.S. Immigration Policy and Law.* 96th Congress, 2nd Session, 1980. Compendium prepared by the Congressional Research Service, Library of Congress, for the Select Commission on Immigration and Refugee Policy.

——. *The Refugee Act of 1979, S. 643.* Hearing, 96th Congress, 1st Session, 1979.

——. *The Refugee Act of 1979: Senate Report No. 256 on S. 643.* 96th Congress, 1st Session, 1979.

——. *Refugee Laws: Hearing on S. 643:* 96th Congress, 1st Session, 1979.

——. *Review of U.S. Refugee Resettlement Programs and Policies.* Report. 96th Congress, 1st Session, 1979.

——. *Review of U.S. Refugee Resettlement Programs and Policies.* Report. 96th Congress, 2nd Session, 1980.

——. *U.S. Refugee Programs.* Hearing, 96th Congress, 2nd Session, 1980.

——. *U.S. Refugee Program, 1981.* Hearings, 96th Congress, 2nd Session, 1980.

——. *World Refugee Crisis: The International Community's Response.* 96th Congress,

1st Session, 1979. Report prepared by the Congressional Research Service, Library of Congress.

U.S. Congress, Senate, Committee on the Judiciary, Subcommittee on Immigration and Refugee Policy. *Annual Refugee Consultation for 1985: Hearing on Consultation Between the Executive Branch and the Judiciary Committee of the Congress.* 98th Congress, 1st Session 1983.

———. *Asylum Adjudication: Hearings on How We Determine Who Is Entitled to Asylum and Who Is Not?* 97th Congress, 1st Session, 1981.

———. *The Authorization of the Refugee Act of 1980.* 98th Congress, 1st Session, 1983.

———. *Emergency Migration of Escapees, Expellees, and Refugees: Hearings on S. 1917.* 83rd Congress, 1st Session, 1953.

———. *Immigration Emergency Legislation: Hearing on S. 1725 and S. 1983.* 98th Congress, 1st Session, 1983.

———. *Reauthorization of the Refugee Act of 1980.* Hearings, 98th Congress, 1st Session, 1983.

———. *Refugee Act of 1979: Hearings on H.R. 2816.* 96th Congress, 1st Session, 1979.

———. *Refugee Problems in Central America.* Report. 98th Congress, 1st Session, 1983.

———. *Refugee Problems in Southeast Asia: 1981.* Staff report. 97th Congress, 2nd Session, 1982.

———. *U.S. Immigration Law and Policy: 1952–1979.* Report. 96th Congress, 1st Session, 1979.

U.S. Congress, Senate, Committee on the Judiciary, Subcommittee to Investigate Problems Connected with Refugees and Escapees. *African Refugee Problems.* Hearing, 89th Congress, 1st Session, 1965.

———. *Aftermath of War: Humanitarian Problems of Southeast Asia.* Staff report. 94th Congress, 2nd Session, 1976.

———. *Civilian Casualty and Refugee Problems in South Vietnam.* Findings and recommendations. 90th Congress, 2nd Session, 1968.

———. *Civilian Casualty, Social Welfare, and Refugee Problems in South Vietnam.* Hearings, 90th Congress, 1st Session, 1967.

———. *Civilian Casualty, Social Welfare, and Refugee Problems in South Vietnam.* Hearings, 90th Congress, 2nd Session, 1968.

———. *Civilian Casualty, Social Welfare, and Refugee Problems in South Vietnam.* Hearings, 91st Congress, 1st Session, 1969.

———. *Cuban Refugee Problem.* Hearings, 89th Congress, 2nd Session, 1966.

———. *Cuban Refugee Problem: Senate Report No. 1328 on S. Res. 50.* 87th Congress, 1st Session, 1962.

———. *Cuban Refugee Problems.* Hearings, 87th Congress, 1st Session, 1961.

———. *Cuban Refugee Problems.* Hearings, Part 2. 87th Congress, 2nd Session, 1963. Reprinted in Carlos E. Cortes (ed.), *Cuban Refugee Programs* (New York: Arno Press, 1980).

———. *Humanitarian Problems in Indochina.* Hearings, 93rd Congress, 2nd Session, 1974.

———. *Humanitarian Problems in Lebanon, Part II.* Hearing, 94th Congress, 2nd Session, 1976.

———. *Humanitarian Problems In South Vietnam and Cambodia: Two Years after the Cease-Fire.* Study mission report. 94th Congress, 1st Session, 1975.

———. *Humanitarian Problems of Southeast Asia, 1977–78.* Report. 95th Congress, 2nd Session, 1978.

———. *Indochina and Refugee Problems: Part V. Conditions in Indochina and Refugees in the U.S.* Hearing, 94th Congress, 1st Session, 1975.

———. *Indochina Evacuation and Refugee Problems Part I: Operation Babylift and Humanitarian Needs.* Hearing, 94th Congress, 1st Session, 1975.

———. *Indochina Evacuation and Refugee Problems Part II: The Evacuation.* Hearings, 94th Congress, 1st Session, 1975.

———. *Indochina Evacuation and Refugee Problems Part IV: Staff Reports.* 94th Congress, 1st Session, 1975.

———. *Problems of War Victims in Indochina Part I: Vietnam.* Hearing, 92nd Congress, 2nd Session, 1972.

———. *Problems of War Victims In Indochina Part II: Cambodia and Laos.* Hearing, 92nd Congress, 2nd Session, 1972.

———. *Problems of War Victims In Indochina Part III: North Vietnam.* Hearings. 92nd Congress, 2nd Session, 1972.

———. *Problems of War Victims in Indochina Part IV: North Vietnam.* Hearing, 92nd Congress, 2nd Session, 1972.

———. *Refugee and Humanitarian Problems in Chile, Part I.* Hearing, 93rd Congress, 2nd Session, 1974.

———. *Refugee and Humanitarian Problems In Chile, Part II.* Hearings, 93rd Congress, 2nd Session, 1974.

———. *Refugee and Humanitarian Problems in Chile, Part III.* Hearings, 94th Congress, 1st Session, 1975.

———. *Refugee and Humanitarian Problems In Vietnam.* Hearings, 95th Congress, 2nd Session, 1978.

———. *Refugee Consultation.* Hearing, 96th Congress, 1st Session, 1979.

———. *Refugee Crisis in Cambodia.* Hearing, 96th Congress, 1st Session, 1979.

———. *Refugee Crisis In Southeast Asia: Results of the Geneva Conference.* Hearing, 96th Congress, 1st Session, 1979.

———. *Refugee Problem in Hong Kong and Macao.* Hearings, 87th Congress, 2nd Session, 1962.

———. *Refugee Problems in South Vietnam and Laos.* Hearings, 89th Congress, 1st Session, 1965.

———. *Refugee Problems in South Vietnam.* 89th Congress, 2nd Session, 1966.

——. *Refugees and Civilian War Casualty Problems in Indochina.* Staff Report 91st Congress, 2nd Session, 1970.

——. *Relief and Rehabilitation of War Victims in Indochina Part I: Crisis in Cambodia.* Hearing, 93rd Congress, 1st Session, 1973.

——. *Relief and Rehabilitation Of War Victims in Indochina Part II: Orphans and Child Welfare.* Hearings, 93rd Congress, 1st Session, 1973.

——. *Relief and Rehabilitation of War Victims in Indochina Part III: North Vietnam and Laos.* Hearing, 93rd Congress, 1st Session, 1973.

——. *Relief and Rehabilitation of War Victims in Indochina Part IV: South Vietnam and Regional Problems.* Hearing, 93rd Congress, 1st Session, 1973.

——. *Relief and Rehabilitation of War Victims in Indochina: One Year after the Cease-fire.* Study mission report. 93rd Congress, 2nd Session, 1974.

——. *U.S. Apparatus of Assistance for Refugees Throughout the World.* Hearings, 89th Congress, 2nd Session, 1966.

——. *U.S. Assistance to Refugees Throughout the World.* Findings and recommendations. 91st Congress, 1st Session, 1969.

——. *War-Related Civilian Problems in Indochina Part I: Vietnam.* Hearings, 92nd Congress, 1st Session, 1971.

——. *War-Related Civilian Problems in Indochina Part II: Laos and Cambodia.* Hearings, 92nd Congress, 1st Session, 1971.

——. *War-Related Civilian Problems in Indochina Part III: Vietnam.* Hearing, 92nd Congress, 1st Session, 1971.

——. *War Victims in Indochina.* Reports. 92nd Congress, 2nd Session, 1972.

——. *World Refugee and Humanitarian Problems.* Hearing, 92nd Congress, 1st Session, 1971.

U.S. Congress, *United States Statutes-at-Large.* Various dates.

OTHER GOVERNMENT AND INTERNATIONAL DOCUMENTS

California. *The Assimilation and Acculturation of Indochinese Children into American Culture.* Sacramento: California Department of Social Services, 1980.

——. *Indochinese Refugee Status Report.* Orange County: Human Services Agency, August 28, 1979.

——. *Indochinese Refugees.* Garden Grove: Department of Human Services, March 30, 1981.

——. *Orange County Refugee Resettlement Plan.* Orange County: County Administrative Office, February 2, 1982.

——. *Refugees: The Challenge of the 80s.* Hearings. Sacramento: California Department of Social Services, 1980.

———. *Refugees Receiving Cash Assistance: Characteristics Survey*. Sacramento: California Department of Social Services, 1982.

———. *Report on a Survey of Indochinese Refugee Assistance Payments Case Characteristics*. Los Angeles County: Department of Public Social Services, June 1980.

———. *Report on the Impact of Refugee Resettlement on Orange County*. Orange County: Human Relations Commission, January 1981.

Code of Federal Regulations, Title 3, Compilation, 1936–1938. Washington, D.C.: Government Printing Office, 1968.

Cuban-Haitian Task Force. *A Report of the Cuban-Haitian Task Force*. November 1, 1980. (Memo.)

Florida. Dade County, Florida, Task Force on Human Services for Haitian Aliens. *Final Report*. Miami, 1978.

———. *The Impact of Refugees and Entrants in Florida*. Tallahassee: Department of Health and Rehabilitative Services, February 1982.

Interagency Task Force for Indochina Refugees. *Final Report to Congress*. Washington, D.C.: Government Printing Office, December 15, 1975.

Intergovernmental Committee for Migration. "Bibliography on Undocumented Migrants or Migrants in an Irregular Situation," *International Migration*, 21 (1983).

International Refugee Organization. *The Facts about Refugees*. Geneva, Switzerland: IRO, 1959.

National Association of Counties. *Report of the NACO Task Force on Refugees, Aliens and Migrants*. Washington, D.C.: NACO, July 1981.

National Security Council. *Human Rights*. Presidential Review Memorandum/NSC 28. August 15, 1977.

———. *Refugee Policy and Processing from Indochina*. National Security Decision Directive No. 93. Washington, D.C.: The White House, May 13, 1983.

Organization of American States, Inter-American Commission on Human Rights. *Annual Report of the Inter-American Commission on Human Rights: 1981–1982*. Washington, D.C.: OAS, September 20, 1982.

———. *Annual Report of the Inter-American Commission on Human Rights: 1982–1983*. Washington, D.C.: OAS, September 27, 1983.

———. *Report on the Situation of Human Rights in Haiti*. Washington, D.C.: OAS, December 13, 1979.

———. *Report on the Situation of Human Rights in the Republic of Guatemala*. Washington, D.C.: OAS, October 13, 1981.

Thailand. Supreme Command. *Indochinese Displaced Persons in Thailand*. Bangkok: Joint Operations Center, Supreme Command, 1981–1985.

United Nations, *U.N. Convention Relating to the Status of Refugees*, 1951. No. 2545, 189 UNTS (UN Treaty Series) 137, Article 1A (1) July 28, 1951.

———. *United Nations Resolutions and Decisions Relating to the Office of the United Nations High Commissioner for Refugees*, 3rd ed. (Also Addendum) HCR/INF/48/Rev. 2. Geneva: UN, 1979.

United Nations, Economic and Social Council. "Situation of Human Rights in Guatemala, with note by the Secretary General." General Assembly A/38/485. November 4, 1983.

———. Commission on Human Rights. *Study of Human Rights and Mass Exoduses.* Report prepared by Sadruddin Aga Khan. New York: UNESCO, 1981.

United Nations, General Assembly. *Situation of Human Rights and Fundamental Freedoms in El Salvador.* A/37/611. New York: Economic and Social Council, November 22, 1982.

United Nations, Office of the High Commissioner for Refugees. Barber, Martin. *Resettlement of Indochinese in 1981–82.* UNHCR internal memorandum, April 22, 1981.

———. *Evaluation of Refugee Resettlement Needs: 1983–1984.* Geneva: UNHCR, 1984.

———. *Humanitarian Assistance to Kampucheans in Thailand in 1981.* Washington, D.C.: UNHCR, 1981.

———. *Report on the Regional Seminar on Protection of Refugees in Latin America.* Mexico City, August 20–24, 1979.

———. *Round Table of Asian Experts on Current Problems in the International Protection of Refugees and Displaced Persons.* International Institute of Humanitarian Law, University of the Philippines, Law Center. Manila, Philippines, April 14–18, 1980.

———. *UNHCR Assistance to Kampucheans in Thailand.* Washington, D.C.: UNHCR, November 1979.

———. *Workshop on Integration of Refugees from Indochina in Countries of Resettlement.* Geneva: UNHCR, October 30, 1980.

United Nations Treaty Series, Vol. 189.

U.S. Commission on Civil Rights. *Confronting Racial Isolation in Miami.* Washington, D.C.: Government Printing Office, 1982.

———. *The Tarnished Golden Door: Civil Rights Issues in Immigration.* Washington, D.C.: Government Printing Office, 1980.

U.S. Conference of Mayors. *Immigration and Refugee Policy.* Washington, D.C.: U.S. Conference of Mayors, June 1981.

U.S. Department of Commerce. Bureau of the Census. *Historical Statistics of U.S.: Colonial Times to 1910.* Washington, D.C.: U.S. Department of Commerce, 1975.

U.S. Department of Health and Human Services. *Office of Refugee Resettlement: Annual Report to Congress, 1981.* Washington, D.C.: ORR/Department of Health and Human Services, 1981.

———. *Refugee Resettlement in the United States: An Annotated Bibliography.* Washington, D.C.: U.S. Department of Health and Human Services, March 6, 1981.

———. *Refugee Resettlement Program.* Report to Congress. Washington, D.C.: Office of Refugee Resettlement, January 31, 1982.

———. *Refugee Resettlement Program: Report to Congress.* Washington, D.C.: U.S. Department of Health and Human Services, January 31, 1983.

U.S. Department of Justice, Immigration and Naturalization Service. *Asylum Adjudications: An Evolving Concept and Responsibility for the Immigration and Nationality Service.* Washington, D.C.: INS, June and December 1982.

——. *Asylum Applications for Fiscal Year 1982.* Washington, D.C.: Department of Justice, 1983.

——. Sureck, Joseph. Unclassified cablegram from INS, District Director, Hong Kong, to INS, Washington, D.C., April 7, 1981.

——. *Worldwide Guidelines for Overseas Refugee Processing—August 1983.* Washington, D.C.: INS, July 28, 1983.

U.S. Department of Justice, Office of the Attorney General. *Report of the President's Task Force on Immigration and Refugee Policy.* Washington, D.C., June 26, 1981.

U.S. Department of Justice, Office of Legal Counsel. *Memorandum: Re-interpretation of the Refugee Act of 1980.* Washington, 1981. Reprinted in U.S. Congress, House, Committee on the Judiciary, Subcommittee on Immigration, Refugees, and International Law, *U.S. Refugee Program: Oversight Hearings,* 91st Congress, 1st Session, 1981.

U.S. Department of State. *Action Memorandum: Report to Congress on Haiti.* June 30, 1982.

——. *American Foreign Policy, 1950–1955,* I and II. Washington, D.C.: Government Printing Office, 1957.

——. "Humanitarian Relief in Southeast Asia," *Current Policy,* 150 (March 24, 1980).

——. *Indochinese Refugees. GIST.* Washington, D.C., January 1980.

——. *Indochinese Refugees. GIST.* Washington, D.C., April 1983.

——. *Indochinese Resettlement in the United States.* Special Report No. 68. Washington, D.C.: Department of State, Bureau of Public Affairs, February 1980.

——. *Khmer Relief.* GIST. Washington, D.C.: Department of State, Bureau of Public Affairs, April 1980.

——. *Report to Congress on Haiti.* Action memorandum from Assistant Secretary Thomas Enders. Washington, D.C.: Department of State, June 30, 1982.

——. "Responsibility of Cuban Government for Increased International Tensions in the Hemisphere," *Department of State Bulletin,* 43, No. 1105 (August 29, 1960): 340–341.

——. "'Socialist Transformation' in South Vietnam." Cable from Ambassador Morton Abramowitz, Bangkok, August 1978.

——. *State Department Study Team on Haitian Returnees.* Memorandum. Washington, D.C.: Department of State, June 19, 1979.

——. *Vietnam's Refugee Machine.* Department of State statement distributed at July 1979 Geneva Conference. Washington, D.C.: Department of State, July 20, 1979.

——. "What to Do?" Cable from Ambassador Morton Abramowitz, Bangkok, November 26, 1979.

U.S. Department of State, Office of the U.S. Coordinator for Refugee Affairs. *A Conference on Ethical Issues and Moral Principles in U.S. Refugee Policy.* Washington, D.C.: Office of the U.S. Coordinator for Refugee Affairs and the Religious Advisory Committee, March 24–25, 1983.

———. *Country Reports on the World Refugee Situation.* Report to Congress. Washington, D.C.: Department of State, 1981.

———. *Country Reports on the World Refugee Situation.* Report to Congress. Washington, D.C.: Department of State, 1982.

———. *Country Reports on the World Refugee Situation.* Report to Congress. Washington, D.C.: Department of State, 1983.

———. *Country Reports on the World Refugee Situation.* Report to Congress. Washington, D.C.: Department of State, 1984.

———. *Country Reports on the World Refugee Situation.* Report to Congress. Washington, D.C.: Department of State, 1985.

———. *Issues in Refugee Resettlement: A Report from the Regional Conferences on the Domestic Resettlement of Refugees,* I. Washington, D.C.: Department of State, April 1981. (Mimeo.)

———. *Overview of the World Refugee Situation.* Washington, D.C.: Department of State, August 1982.

U.S. Displaced Persons Commission. *Semi-Annual Reports to the President and the Congress,* 1–6. Washington, D.C.: Government Printing Office, 1949, 1950, 1951, 1952.

———. *The DP Story: Memo to America.* Final report of the U.S. Displaced Persons Commission. Washington, D.C.: Government Printing Office, 1962.

U.S. General Accounting Office (GAO). *Assistance to Haiti: Barriers, Recent Program Changes and Future Options.* Washington, D.C.: GAO, February 22, 1982.

———. *Detention Policies Affecting Haitian Nationals.* Washington, D.C.: GAO, June 16, 1983.

———. *Domestic Resettlement of the Indochinese Refugees: Struggle for Self-Reliance.* Washington, D.C.: GAO, May 10, 1977.

———. *Evacuation and Temporary Care Afforded Indochinese Refugees: Operation New Life.* Washington, D.C.: GAO, June 1976.

———. *Greater Emphasis on Early Employment and Better Monitoring Needed in Indochinese Refugee Resettlement Program.* Washington, D.C.: GAO, March 1, 1983.

———. *The Indochinese Exodus: A Humanitarian Dilemma.* Washington, D.C.: GAO, April 24, 1979.

———. *Illegal Aliens: Estimating Their Impact on The United States.* Washington, D.C.: GAO, March 14, 1980.

———. *Indochinese Refugees: Protection, Care, and Processing Can Be Improved.* Washington, D.C.: GAO, August 19, 1980.

———. *International Assistance to Refugees in Africa Can be Improved.* Washington, D.C.: GAO, December 29, 1982.

———. *Number of Undocumented Aliens Residing in the United States Unknown.* Washington, D.C.: GAO, April 6, 1981.

———. *Problems and Options in Estimating the Size of the Illegal Alien Population.* Washington, D.C.: GAO, September 24, 1982.

———. *Prospects Dim for Effectively Enforcing Immigration Laws.* Washington, D.C.: GAO, November 5, 1980.

———. *Review of Preliminary Estimates of Evacuation Costs: Temporary Care, and Resettlement Costs of Vietnamese and Cambodian Refugees.* Washington, D.C.: GAO, May 1975.

———. *U.S. Assistance Provided for Resettling Soviet Refugees.* Washington, D.C.: GAO, June 20, 1977.

———. *U.S. Provides Safe Haven for Indochinese Refugees.* Washington, D.C.: GAO, June 1975.

U.S. Library of Congress, Congressional Research Service. *Cuban Exodus—1980, the Context.* Report prepared by Barry Sklar. August 25, 1980.

———. *El Salvador: U.S. Interests and Policy Options.* Issue Brief No. 80064, prepared by Mary Jeanne Reid Martz. August 1, 1980.

———. *Impediments to Economic and Social Change in Haiti.* Report prepared by R. Roberts. July 19, 1978.

———. *Nicaragua: Conditions and U.S. Interests.* Issue Brief No. 80013 prepared by Roslyn Roberts. October 1, 1980.

———. *Refugees in the United States: The Cuban Emigration Crisis.* Issue Brief No. 80063, prepared by Charlotte Moore. July 9, 1980.

———. *Refugees in the U.S.: Laws, Programs, and Proposals.* Issue Brief No. 77120, prepared by Catherine McHugh, 1978.

———. *The United States and International Human Rights Treaties.* Report No. 79-194F, prepared by Vita Bife and Dagnija Sterste-Perkins. September 6, 1979.

U.S. President. Executive Order No. 12324, "High Seas Interdiction of Illegal Aliens." *Federal Register* 46, No. 190, October 1, 1981, 48109-10.

———. Proclamation 4865, "High Seas Interdiction of Illegal Aliens." *Federal Register* No. 46, No. 190, October 1, 1981, 48107.

———. *Public Papers of the Presidents of the United States.* Washington, D.C.: Office of the *Federal Register*, National Archives and Record Service, 1963—Harry S. Truman, 1945-1953.

———. *Public Papers of the Presidents of the United States.* Washington, D.C.: Office of the *Federal Register*, National Archives and Record Service, 1958-1961—Dwight D. Eisenhower, 1953-1961.

———. *Public Papers of the Presidents of the United States.* Washington, D.C.: Office of the *Federal Register*, National Archives and Record Service, 1962-1964—John F. Kennedy, 1961-1963.

———. *Public Papers of the Presidents of the United States.* Washington, D.C.: Office of the *Federal Register*, National Archives and Record Service, 1964–1970—Lyndon B. Johnson, 1963–1969.

——. *Public Papers of the Presidents of the United States.* Washington, D.C.: Office of the *Federal Register*, National Archives and Record Service, 1970–1974—Richard M. Nixon, 1969–1973.

——. *Public Papers of the Presidents of the United States.* Washington, D.C.: Office of the *Federal Register*, National Archives and Record Service, 1974–1978—Gerald R. Ford, 1973–1977.

——. *Public Papers of the Presidents of the United States.* Washington, D.C.: Office of the *Federal Register*, National Archives and Record Service, 1979–1981—Jimmy Carter, 1977–1981.

——. *Public Papers of the Presidents of the United States.* Washington, D.C.: Office of the *Federal Register*, National Archives and Record Service, 1982–1984—Ronald S. Reagan, 1981–1983.

U.S. President's Commission on Immigration and Naturalization. *Whom We Shall Welcome: Report of the President's Commission.* Washington, D.C.: Government Printing Office, 1953.

U.S. Select Commission on Immigration and Refugee Policy. *U.S. Immigration Policy and the National Interest,* Final report and recommendations. Washington, D.C.: U.S. Government Printing Office, 1981.

——. *Staff Report with Appendices.* Washington, D.C.: U.S. Government Printing Office, 1981.

U.S. Vice President. *Vice President Mondale's Speech to U.N. Conference on Indochinese Refugees.* Geneva: Office of the Vice President, July 21, 1979.

Voorhees, Tracy S. *Report to the President of the United States on the Cuban Refugee Program* (January 18, 1961). Washington, D.C.: Government Printing Office, 1961. Reprinted in Carlos E. Cortes (ed.), *Cuban Refugee Programs* (New York: Arno Press, 1980).

World Bank. *Memorandum on the Haitian Economy.* May 13, 1981.

UNPUBLISHED MANUSCRIPTS

Browne, David Roger. "The History and Programming Policies of RIAS: Radio in the American Sector [of Berlin]." Ph.D. dissertation, Department of Speech and Theater, University of Michigan, 1961.

Palmieri, Victor. Introduction to unpublished manuscript on U.S. refugee policy, 1979–1980.

Rivera, Mario Antonio. "An Evaluative Analysis of the Carter Administration's Policy Toward the Mariel Influx of 1980." Ph.D. dissertation, Department of Government and International Studies, University of Notre Dame, December 1982.

Schienman, Ronald S. "The Office of the United Nations High Commissioner for Refugees and the Contemporary International System." Ph.D. dissertation, University of California at Santa Barbara, 1974.

Warren, George, Sr. "The Development of United States Participation in Intergovernmental Efforts to Resolve Refugee Problems." Memoir submitted to the Department of State. (1967?)

Index